SELECTED STORIES OF
KATHERINE MANSFIELD

Modernist Archives Series

Series Editors: Matthew Feldman (University of York, UK), Erik Tonning (University of Bergen, Norway) and David Tucker (Goldsmiths, University of London, UK)

Editorial Board: Chris Ackerley (University of Otago, New Zealand), Ronald Bush (University of Oxford, UK), Mark Byron (University of Sydney, Australia), Wayne K. Chapman (Clemson University, USA), Miranda Hickman (McGill University, Canada), Gregory Maertz (St John's University, USA), Alec Marsh (Muhlenberg College, USA), Steven Matthews (Oxford Brookes University, UK), Lois M. Overbeck (Emory University, USA), Dirk Van Hulle (University of Antwerp, Belgium).

From letters, journals, and notebooks to unpublished or out-of-print works, unfamiliar but important writings in translation and forgotten articles, Bloomsbury's Modernist Archives series makes available to researchers at all levels historical archival material that can reconfigure received views of Modernist literature and culture.

Annotated throughout and supported by extensive contextual essays by leading scholars, the Modernist Archives series is an essential resource for anyone with a serious interest in twentieth-century literature and culture.

Titles in Series

David Jones on Religion, Politics, and Culture
Edited by Thomas Berenato, Anne Price-Owen and Kathleen Henderson Staud

David Jones's *The Grail Mass* and Other Works
Edited by Thomas Goldpaugh and Jamie Callison

Ezra Pound and Globe Magazine: The Complete Correspondence
Edited by Michael T. Davis and Cameron McWhirter

Ezra Pound's and Olga Rudge's *The Blue Spill*: A Manuscript Critical Edition
Edited by Mark Byron and Sophia Barnes

Edith Ayrton Zangwill's *The Call*: A New Scholarly Edition
Edited by Stephanie Brown

James Joyce and Paul L. Léon: The Story of a Friendship Revisited
Edited by Alexis Léon, Anna Maria Léon and Luca Crispi

Man into Woman: A Comparative Scholarly Edition
Edited by Pamela Caughie and Sabine Meyer

The Fifth Notebook of Dylan Thomas
Edited by John Goodby and Adrian Osbourne

W. B. Yeats's Robartes-Aherne Writings
Wayne K. Chapman

Forthcoming Titles

The Correspondence of Ezra Pound and the Frobenius Institute, 1930–1959
Edited by Ronald Bush and Erik Tonning

SELECTED STORIES OF

KATHERINE MANSFIELD

A MANUSCRIPT CRITICAL EDITION

Edited by Todd Martin

BLOOMSBURY ACADEMIC

LONDON • NEW YORK • OXFORD • NEW DELHI • SYDNEY

BLOOMSBURY ACADEMIC
Bloomsbury Publishing Plc, 50 Bedford Square, London, WC1B 3DP, UK
Bloomsbury Publishing Inc, 1385 Broadway, New York, NY 10018, USA
Bloomsbury Publishing Ireland, 29 Earlsfort Terrace, Dublin 2, D02 AY28, Ireland

BLOOMSBURY, BLOOMSBURY ACADEMIC and the Diana logo are trademarks of Bloomsbury
Publishing Plc

First published in Great Britain 2023
Paperback edition published 2025

Cover image: Katherine Mansfield at her work table, Villa Isola, Menton, France.
Baker, Ida: Photographs of Katherine Mansfield. Ref: 1/2-011917-F.
Alexander Turnbull Library, Wellington, New Zealand.

A catalogue record for this book is available from the British Library.

A catalog record for this book is available from the Library of Congress.

Library of Congress Cataloging-in-Publication Data

Names: Mansfield, Katherine, 1888-1923, author. | Martin, W. Todd, editor.
Title: Selected stories of Katherine Mansfield : a manuscript critical
edition / edited by Todd Martin.
Description: London ; New York : Bloomsbury Academic, 2023. |
Includes bibliographical references and index.
Identifiers: LCCN 2022060169 | ISBN 9781350096653 (hardback) |
ISBN 9781350402447 (paperback) | ISBN 9781350096660 (epub) |
ISBN 9781350096677 (ebook)
Subjects: LCSH: Short stories, New Zealand. | Short stories–Women authors. |
New Zealand literature–20th century. | Mansfield, Katherine,
1888-1923–Criticism and interpretation.
Classification: LCC PR9639.3.M258 S45 2023 | DDC 823/.912–dc23/eng/20230210
LC record available at https://lccn.loc.gov/2022060169

ISBN: HB: 978-1-3500-9665-3
PB: 978-1-3504-0244-7
ePDF: 978-1-3500-9667-7
eBook: 978-1-3500-9666-0

Series: Modernist Archives

Typeset by RefineCatch Limited, Bungay, Suffolk

For product safety related questions contact productsafety@bloomsbury.com.

To find out more about our authors and books visit www.bloomsbury.com
and sign up for our newsletters.

*To Gerri Kimber, for her support and encouragement along
my Katherine Mansfield journey, and especially for her friendship.*

CONTENTS

ACKNOWLEDGMENTS

First and foremost, I would like to thank Brigitte, Meghan, and Elise for their love and support in all of my endeavors, and especially Elise who helped with some of the final editing of the manuscripts. I would also like to thank Annie Seboe and Thad Arnold, two of my students, who helped check the book proofs.

I must also sincerely thank the following for providing reference letters for various fellowship opportunities and for giving encouragement and insight at various stages of the project: Gerri Kimber, Claire Davison, Rishona Zimring, Matthew Feldman, Fiona Oliver, Sydney Janet Kaplan, and Naomi Milthorpe. Without them, I would not have had the wherewithal to explore the manuscripts.

I am indebted to the Newberry Library for awarding me the Lester J. Cappon Fellowship in Documentary Editing and to Huntington University for honoring me with the Edwina Patton Endowed Chair of Arts and Sciences as well Jack Barlow, Sr. Research and Artistic Creation Fund grant. The time and money that these afforded me were essential in both the initial exploration of the Katherine Mansfield manuscripts and the finalizing of the transcriptions.

I am also grateful to both the Newberry Library and the Alexander Turnbull Library for providing high quality images of many of the manuscripts and the photograph of Katherine Mansfield at her desk, the cover image; I would also like to thank Penguin Random House for permission to reprint "Six Years After" and "The Fly" as well as The Society of Authors as the Literary Representative of the Estate of Katherine Mansfield. A special thanks goes to Sarah Burton who helped walk me through the web of copyrights.

FIGURES

ABBREVIATIONS

Unless otherwise indicated, all references to Katherine Mansfield's works are to the editions listed below and abbreviated as follows. Letters, diary and notebook entries are quoted verbatim without the use of editorial "[*sic*]."

NB: Mansfield frequently uses style ellipses in both her personal writing and her short stories. Where these occur the stops are double-spaced thus: . . . To avoid any confusion, all *omission* ellipses are therefore placed in square brackets [. . .].

CW1 and CW2	*The Edinburgh Edition of the Collected Works of Katherine Mansfield*: Vols. 1 and 2—*The Collected Fiction*, ed. Gerri Kimber and Vincent O'Sullivan (Edinburgh: Edinburgh University Press, 2012).
CW3	*The Edinburgh Edition of the Collected Works of Katherine Mansfield*: Vol. 3—*The Poetry and Critical Writings*, ed. Gerri Kimber and Angela Smith (Edinburgh: Edinburgh University Press, 2014).
CW4	*The Edinburgh Edition of the Collected Works of Katherine Mansfield*: Vol. 4—*The Diaries of Katherine Mansfield, including Miscellaneous Works*, ed. Gerri Kimber and Claire Davison (Edinburgh: Edinburgh University Press, 2016).
Letters 1–5	*The Collected Letters of Katherine Mansfield*, 5 vols, ed. Vincent O'Sullivan and Margaret Scott (Oxford: Clarendon Press, 1984–2008).
Notebooks 1–2	*The Katherine Mansfield Notebooks*, 2 vols, ed Margaret Scott (Canterbury, NZ: Lincoln University Press, 1997).
Manuscripts	
JNPP-rough-NL	"Je ne parle pas français" [rough manuscript], Katherine Mansfield Papers, Newberry Library, (box 1, folder 27), 16 leaves.
JNPP-clean-NL	"Je ne parle pas français" [clean manuscript], Katherine Mansfield Papers, Newberry Library, (box 1, folder 26), 22 leaves.
JNPP-NB14-ATL	Notebook 14, "Mouse ["Je ne parle pas français"]," Writings and Personal Papers of Katherine Mansfield, Alexander Turnbull Library, (MS-Group-0038, qMS-1259), 40 pages.
Rev-NB4-NL	Notebook 4, "Revelations," Katherine Mansfield Papers, Newberry Library (box 2, folder 3), 1–11.

Stran-rough-NL   "The Stranger" [rough manuscript], Katherine Mansfield Papers, Newberry Library, (box 2, folder 22), 15 leaves.

Stran-clean-NL   "The Stranger" [clean manuscript], Katherine Mansfield Papers, Newberry Library, (box 2, folder 21), 18 leaves.

Pois-MS-NL   "Poison" [manuscript], Katherine Mansfield Papers, Newberry Library, (box 2, folder 8), 8 leaves.

Pois-TS-NL   "Poison" [typescript], Katherine Mansfield Papers, Newberry Library, (box 2, folder 9), 8 leaves.

DLC-MS-NL   "Non-Compounders [Daughters of the Late Colonel]," Katherine Mansfield Papers, Newberry Library, (box 1, folder 41), 32 leaves.

DLC-Frag-ATL   Fragment from "Daughters of the Late Colonel," Writings and Personal Papers of Katherine Mansfield, Alexander Turnbull Library, (MS-Papers-4000-38), 1 leaf.

MMD-MS-NL   "Mr and Mrs Dove," Katherine Mansfield Papers, Newberry Library, (box 1, folder 38), 14 pages.

MalaM-NB5-NL   Notebook 5, "Marriage à la Mode," Katherine Mansfield Papers, Newberry Library (box 2, folder 4), 2–12.

Voy-NB5-NL   Notebook 5, "The Voyage," Katherine Mansfield Papers, Newberry Library (box 2, folder 4), 14–25.

SYA-NB3-NL   Notebook 3, "Six Years After," Katherine Mansfield Papers, Newberry Library (box 2, folder 2), 1–5.

SYA-NB41-ATL   Notebook 41, "Six Years After," Writings and Personal Papers of Katherine Mansfield, Alexander Turnbull Library, (MS-Group-0038, qMS-1277), 4–8.

Fly-MS-NL   "The Fly [manuscript]," Katherine Mansfield Papers, Newberry Library, (box 1, folder 16), 6 leaves.

Fly-TS-NL   "The Fly [typescript]," Katherine Mansfield Papers, Newberry Library, (box 1, folder 17), 6 leaves.

A NOTE ON THE TRANSCRIPTIONS

Recreating a manuscript as a typescript creates a number of challenges, especially when an author's handwriting can become practically illegible in the heat of writing, as is the case with Katherine Mansfield. However, every attempt has been made to provide as complete and accurate a reflection of her words as well as the state of the manuscript as possible—such as when the hand becomes rushed or the ink changes. The transcriptions will reproduce the author's grammatical and spelling errors; however, Mansfield was notorious for consistently omitting apostrophes, failing to use questions marks when appropriate, etcetera, so the use of [*sic*] will be reserved for errors that are infrequent and isolated. Mansfield was also inconsistent with quotation marks (e.g., often opening but not closing them or the converse), her paragraph indentions are often slight, and her commas and periods are often indistinguishable, a problem exacerbated by her heavy use of the dash. In these instances, while every effort will be made to represent the manuscript as closely as possible, I will err toward consistency and clarity for the reader. Thus, when they have been inadvertently omitted, quotation marks may be added; when appropriate, regular indentions will be used to retain a sense of order; and when difficult to discern, punctuation will defer to standard usage.

Drawing on the transcription method set forth by Dirk Van Hulle in *Modern Manuscripts: The Extended Mind and Creative Undoing from Darwin to Beckett and Beyond*, I will represent passages from Mansfield's manuscripts by crossing out ~~deletions~~ and using superscript for ^{additions}. When a word or phrase is difficult to decipher, it will appear in **bold**. Because the works in this collection also appear in print, I will generally defer to the print version when words or phrases are difficult to discern in the manuscript but when it is evident that they coincide with the print version. However, if there is reasonable doubt, the word or phrase borrowed from the print version will be placed in **bold*** followed by an asterisk. Words which are indecipherable will otherwise be marked with three xxx (one x or two xx if the word is shorter).[1]

I have provided footnotes which, along with other details, compare the manuscripts with the final, published version of individual stories, using *The Edinburgh Edition of the Collected Works of Katherine Mansfield* which, for stories published in Mansfield's lifetime, "follow[s] the last printing which [Mansfield] corrected or approved."[2] *The Collected Works* will be referred to as the *Collected*, and sometimes more generically as the published or final versions. I have generally avoided making note of punctuation changes between the manuscript and published version because they can vary widely: the frequently used dash becomes an ellipsis, or a comma, or a period, while exclamation points and periods are often exchanged for one another. Still, such changes can affect the

---

[1] Dirk Van Hulle, *Modern Manuscripts: The Extended Mind and Creative Undoing from Darwin to Becket and Beyond* (London: Bloomsbury, 2014), x.
[2] Gerri Kimber and Vincent O'Sullivan, ed. *The Edinburgh Edition of the Collected Works of Katherine Mansfield*, vol. 1 (Edinburgh: Edinburgh University Press, 2012), xii.

meaning of a passage, and tracing these changes can provide further insight into the effects Mansfield was working toward.

Along with the *Collected*, I have also consulted the initial print publications of the stories when possible, which I will refer to using the title of the publication. Because variations between published versions—what Van Hulle terms "epigenesis"[3]—can further illuminate an author's revision process, I have made note of some of the more significant changes between these versions.

---

[3] Van Hulle, Modern Manuscripts, 214.

Introduction

Resurrecting Katherine Mansfield: The "Death of the Author" and the Possibilities of Genetic Criticism*

TODD MARTIN

The critical trend for literature just after Katherine Mansfield's death tended toward what is now known as "new criticism," a theoretical stance that emphasizes the work of art as self-contained; in other words, the text exists as a singular object, and artistic value lies only in the study of the object itself, not in any external cultural or biographical context surrounding the work. But it was W. K. Wimsatt Jr. and M. C. Beardsley's "The Intentional Fallacy" (1946) that sounded the death knell for the author.

While Wimsatt and Beardsley claim, perhaps rightly, that an author's intention should have no bearing on whether a work is deemed successful or not, they extend their argument beyond aesthetic judgment to interpretation. They contend that there is a "danger in confusing personal and poetic studies," suggesting that the critic should focus on the aesthetic and that evidence for a work's meaning and how it is achieved should be fully available to the reader, thus contained within the work itself.[1] For Wimsatt and Beardsley, "the poem is not the critic's own and not the author's. . . . The poem belongs to the public."[2] The final nail in the coffin for the author, however, came with Roland Barthes' essay, "The Death of the Author" (1967).

Wimsatt and Beardsley at least acknowledge the agency of the author, but argue that "to insist on the designing intellect [the author] as a *cause* of a poem is not to grant the design or intention as a *standard*."[3] Barthes, though, argues that not only should the work be considered apart from any authorial intent, but that it is only language that carries meaning: It is a "necessity to substitute language itself for the person who until then had been supposed to be its owner [. . .] it is language which speaks, not the author."[4] Later he suggests, "To give a text an Author is to impose a limit on that text, to furnish it with

* A version of this essay appeared in *The Turnbull Library Record*, 50 (2018): 43–55. It is republished with permission.

    Research for this project was completed through the funding of the Lester J. Cappon Fellowship for Documentary Editing, awarded by the Newberry Library, and through release time provided by Huntington University as part of the endowed Edwina Patton Chair. I would like to thank both organizations for their support.

[1] W. K. Wimsatt Jr. and M. C. Beardsley, "The Intentional Fallacy," *The Sewanee Review* 54, no. 3 (July–September 1946): 468–488 (477, 472–3).

[2] Ibid., 470.

[3] Ibid., 469.

[4] Roland Barthes, "The Death of the Author," in *Image, Music, Text*, trans. Stephen Heath (London: Fontana Press, 1977), 142–148 (143).

a final signified, to close the writing."[5] Barthes refuses such closure; instead, like Wimsatt and Beardsley, he defers to the reader.[6]

However, developing concurrently with the death of the author was genetic criticism, which offered an alternative textual approach, an approach traced back to Louis Hay, whose essay "Des manuscrits, pour quoi faire?" (1967) set the tone for this approach and whose role at the Institut des Textes et Manuscrits Modernes helped maintain its prominence in France. Rather than limiting a text to its published form, genetic critics explore authors' notes and drafts (*avant-textes*) used to develop the final version of a text. Unlike strict textual criticism, which focuses on developing authoritative versions of a work, genetic critics' interest lay in trying to understand the artistic process. Thus, they retained the aesthetic focus of Wimsatt and Beardsley and often followed suit in relegating authorial intention to the fringes. According to Jed Deppman, Daniel Ferrer, and Michael Groden, genetic criticism "remains deeply aware of the text's aesthetic dimensions. [. . .] It grows out of a structuralist and post-structuralist notion of 'text' as an infinite play of signs, but it accepts a teleological model of textuality and constantly confronts the question of authorship."[7] In other words, while post-structuralists view the text as constantly renewed through each individual reading, genetic criticism acknowledges the temporal development of the text through its various draft versions. The value of this, according to Pierre-Marc de Biasi, is that:

> The rough draft enables us to be present at the birth of the motivations, strategies, and metamorphoses of writing, which, more often than not, labors precisely at effacing its own tracks and at rendering its mechanisms untraceable, secret, or problematic in the completed form of the definitive text. The rough draft offers criticism an essential field in which to validate interpretations that the text often leaves in hypothetical state, and sometimes even in a state of simple conjecture.[8]

Manuscripts, then, have the potential not only to reveal the writing process of an individual author, but also to resuscitate the creative role of the author in a text.[9]

While one cannot really know the mind of the author—and perhaps an author doesn't fully know her own mind in the moment of creation—notes, manuscripts, and letters provide traces of intent. Insisting on the agency of the author of a work, Sally Bushell establishes some parameters for aligning the potential of genetic criticism with authorial intent, though she rightly stops short of attributing any finality to what one can know about an author's intentions. Her main point is that the preliminary works of a text reveal a process—the teleology noted above. Having materials showing a process, while it doesn't preclude the reader's experience of a text, certainly places a work within a temporal context so that, in contrast to the post-structuralist approach, the text does not exist simply in the act of reading.[10] Rejecting Wimsatt and Beardsley's contention that

---

[5] Ibid., 147.

[6] Ibid., 143.

[7] Jed Deppman, Daniel Ferrer, Michael Groden, Introduction, in *Genetic Criticism, Texts and Avant Textes*, ed. Jed Deppman, Daniel Ferrer, and Michael Groden (Philadelphia: University of Pennsylvania Press, 2004), 1–16 (2).

[8] Pierre-Marc de Biasi, "What is a Literary Draft? Toward a Functional Typology of Genetic Documentation," trans. Ingrid Wassenaar, *Yale French Studies* 89 (1996): 26–58 (29).

[9] For a discussion on how genetic criticism both denies the author and provides the only position of resistance to it, see Sally Bushell, "Textual Process and the Denial of Origins," *Textual Cultures: Texts, Contexts, Interpretation* 2, no. 2 (Autumn 2007): 100–117.

[10] For a full account of Bushell's response to post-structuralism (especially Roland Barthes' "death of the author"), see "Textual Process and the Denial of Origins."

even the act of revision reveals "only the very abstract, tautological, sense that he intended to write a better work and now has done it,"[11] Bushell draws from cognitive theory and speech act theory, arguing that to act on intention reveals it: "[T]here seems to be a distinction between a pre-planned and internally anticipated event and the more immediate putting of that aim or purpose into practice through action. The ulterior intention is thus more distanced from action than the immediate intention which either directly precedes, or somehow partakes of, the action."[12] In other words, while one may not be able to know what goes through another's mind, a semblance of that "ulterior intention" is revealed when someone acts on that intention. For the author, the act of intentionality is visibly preserved in the phrase or sentence struck through in a manuscript, or the word or punctuation substitution on the proof-sheet. Thus, according to Bushell, genetic criticism provides a point of overlap between textual criticism and literary criticism in which compositional material can be used "to clarify and pursue cruxes within the published text which are revealed, explained, or contradicted by knowledge of the shape, structure and development of the poem in the compositional process."[13]

The value of modern manuscript collections, like the Katherine Mansfield materials held at both the Turnbull Library and the Newberry Library, become evident in the potential of such an approach to an author's work. Margaret Scott and Vincent O'Sullivan have done an excellent service for Mansfield scholars in editing her letters and notebooks and making them more readily available. However, one of the oversights of the two volumes of notebooks that Scott edited is that she omitted drafts of Mansfield's works that had been published. Thus, unless one scours her footnotes, one may not realize that the notebooks include extant drafts of some of Mansfield's key stories. For example, the Newberry Library holds two distinct drafts of "Je ne parle pas français," one of which is a roughed-out draft and the other a cleaner, copied draft.[14] However, an even earlier draft of the story appears in Mansfield's Notebook 14, which the Turnbull Library has in its holdings.[15] Likewise, the Newberry has a draft of "The Garden Party,"[16] but another draft exists in the Turnbull's collection in Notebook 41.[17] While some British modernist writers like Virginia Woolf and James Joyce have had their manuscripts published in genetic versions or facsimile, only Vincent O'Sullivan's edited version of *The Aloe* printed alongside "Prelude" provides anything similar.[18] Thus, access to Mansfield's manuscripts is considerably limited, yet the potential of a genetic study of her writing process and the possibilities for illuminating some of her stories is significant.

The work of a genetic critic begins by chronologically arranging the available materials. While Mansfield has numerous notebooks, this is a relatively simple task because although the notebooks include many of Mansfield's false starts, most of her later stories appear to have been composed in full drafts. One gets a glimpse at Mansfield's process in her comment about the composition of "A Cup of Tea" (1922): "Wrote & finished <u>A Cup of Tea</u>. It took about 4–5 hours. [. . .] There is no feeling to be compared with the joy of

---

[11] Wimsatt and Beardsley, "The Intentional Fallacy," 470.
[12] Sally Bushell, "Intention Revisited: Towards an Anglo-American 'Genetic Criticism,'" *Text* 17 (2005): 55–91 (69).
[13] Bushell, "Intention Revisited," 86.
[14] See the Katherine Mansfield Papers, Newberry Library, (box 1, folders 27, 26).
[15] See Writings and Personal Papers of Katherine Mansfield, (MS-Group-38, qMS-1259).
[16] See the Katherine Mansfield Papers, Newberry Library, (box 1, folder 18).
[17] See Writings and Personal Papers of Katherine Mansfield, (MS-Group-38, qMS-1277).
[18] Vincent O'Sullivan, *"The Aloe" with "Prelude,"* ed. Vincent O'Sullivan (Wellington: Carcanet New Press, 1983).

having written and finished a story. I did not go to sleep but nothing mattered. There it was <u>new</u> and complete."[19] This is not to suggest that she wrote all of her stories quickly or even in one sitting, for one may have found crumpled pages of various drafts around her writing table. However, given that few draft notes exist beyond full drafts, despite her numerous notebooks, it at least appears that she wrote many of these in their entirety. Looking at the composition of the early drafts, one notes that her handwriting moves from relative legibility to almost indecipherable as the story unfolds. It appears, then, she formulated the stories in her head, working out the details, and then wrote them down in full, likely revising as she went and then again while reading back through the draft. Afterwards, she copied out a cleaner copy for a typist or, when able, typed them herself.

The changes made directly to a particular draft, as well as those occurring between drafts—including minute changes such as punctuation—are of particular interest to genetic critics. Such changes show the author making artistic choices, choices that not only affect the quality of the work but also the way readers respond to and understand a work. One difficulty in transcribing Mansfield, especially earlier drafts of her stories, is that what may indeed be quickly penned periods often look like dashes. But she frequently used the dash, so it is often difficult to determine how punctuation changes between an early draft and a cleaner draft. Yet changing a punctuation mark can make a significant difference in how one reads a sentence and the implications of the words forming that sentence.

Mansfield was very complacent about punctuation in her initial drafts, often omitting apostrophes and quotation marks, but in the revision process, she is more purposeful. However, at times, her various editors (often her husband John Middleton Murry) seem to make some choices in order to fit grammatical consistency. So, there are instances in the final, published drafts in which sentences are punctuated differently than they were in earlier versions, even the most finalized copies. It is hard to determine whether such changes were approved by Mansfield during the publication process, as we have no extant proofs of her works, so where punctuation becomes most significant is when Mansfield changes it herself, especially between the written draft and the typescript.

The significance of punctuation is revealed in Mansfield's "Poison" (1920), which is written from the perspective of an unnamed, possessive male lover. The narrator's possessiveness is precisely what drives his lover, Beatrice, away. Although it is never overtly stated, it is generally understood that Beatrice is waiting for a letter from another lover and presumably plans to leave the narrator. As the two spend a quiet afternoon lounging, Beatrice anticipates the coming of the postman, and seeds of doubt begin to form in the narrator's mind. Like many of Mansfield's stories, the emphasis in "Poison" is less on plot and more on the development of the psychological state of her characters. But while the narrator's jealousy is hard to miss, Mansfield's revisions accentuate the circumstances, showing that she is using her craft to create meaning throughout the story. For "Poison," we have both a fairly clean manuscript of the story and a typescript, most likely created from the manuscript version. It is probable that there was an earlier draft of the story, because the manuscript is so clean. However, because it is a cleaner draft, it is easier to distinguish between dashes and periods, allowing one to determine more accurately her conscious changes in punctuation between the manuscript and typescript versions.

---

[19] CW4, 402–3.

Among other things, Mansfield's punctuation adjustments reinforce Beatrice's desire to put off the narrator while continuing to string him along—seemingly until she has firmed things up with her other lover. In a letter to Murry, Mansfield indicates, "And when it [the letter] doesn't come even her *commonness* peeps out—the newspaper touch of such a woman. She can't disguise her chagrin. She gives herself away . . .,"[20] and this is reinforced through Mansfield's revisions. Even the simple addition of a comma can affect meaning. After Beatrice comments on the smell of food—"*Ça sent* [. . .] de la cuisine. . . ."[21]—the narrator reflects:

(Pois-MS-NL) I had noticed lately—we had been living in the South for two months—that when she wished to speak of food or the climate, or, playfully, of her love for me, she always dropped into French.[22]

(Pois-TS-NL) I had noticed lately—we had been living in the South for two months—that when she wished to speak of food, or the climate, or, playfully, of her love for me, she always dropped into French.[23]

Here one finds the addition of a comma after "food" in the typescript version of the story, and while it is unlikely Mansfield typed this version herself, she has made some hand-written corrections on it, suggesting that she approved of the change.[24] Of course, the change could have been made according to standard practice, but if we consider its effect, it makes more pronounced the equation of Beatrice's love of the narrator with the mundane topics of food and the weather. In the manuscript version, food and climate are paired together, distinguishing them from "her love for [him]," but inserting the comma after "food" in the typescript places each item on equal footing, diminishing the significance of her love for him.

In a similar instance, after Beatrice has reassured the narrator that she "wouldn't fly away," noting significantly that "I love this place" but stopping short of saying she loves the narrator,[25] the oblivious narrator effuses:

(Pois-MS-NL) This was such bliss—it was so extraordinary, so unprecedented to hear her talk like this that I had to try to laugh it off.
"Dont. You sound as if you were saying good-bye!"
"Oh, nonsense, nonsense. You mustn't say such dreadful things even in fun."[26]

(Pois-TS-NL) This was such bliss—it was so extra°rdinary, so unprecedented· to hear her talk like this that I had to try and laugh it off.
"Don't.ᴵ You sound as if you were saying good-byᵉ."
"Oh, nonseⁿse. You must'nyᵗ say such things even in fun.ᴵ"[27]

---

[20] *Letters* 4, 119. Emphasis in original.
[21] CW2, 256.
[22] Pois-MS-NL, leaf 1.
[23] Pois-TS-NL, leaf 1.
[24] While Mansfield had access to a typewriter in Hampstead during the summer of 1920, as suggested by her comment to Dorothy Brett—"My mornings are all spent *on* the typewriter"—it is unlikely she had access to one in Menton when she wrote "Poison," for in early November, just a few weeks before, she asks Murry to have one of her other stories typed for her. See *Letters* 4, 19, 98.
[25] CW2, 257.
[26] Pois-MS-NL, leaf 4.
[27] Pois-TS-NL, leaf 4.

Again, it seems as if Mansfield is adjusting the tone of the conversation. While the handwritten comma after "unprecedented" in the typescript appears to be stylistic, adhering to standard practice, it also emphasizes how unprecedented her comment is. The other changes in punctuation that follow, however, shift the emphasis to the narrator's protest, "Don't!" rather than his fear of her saying goodbye, perhaps implying a degree of confidence (or false bravado?) as he now holds her in his arms. He seems less worried that she will leave now and is trying to "laugh off" his initial fears, making it more playful than urgent. For Beatrice's part, her repetition of "nonsense" echoes her earlier protest of "No! No!" responding to his concern that she would fly away, but her protest comes across as disingenuous. Mansfield's choice to omit "dreadful" from Beatrice's playful objection suggests that Mansfield is deemphasizing the extent of her protest, for the tone reveals that her heart isn't really in it.

There are also word replacements that appear to suggest a similar distancing. Just before the exchange above, the narrator reveals that

> (Pois-MS-NL) And when she lay on her back, the pearls slipped under her chin and murmured: "I'm thirsty, darling. <u>Donne-moi un orange!</u>"[28]

> (Pois-TS-NL) And when she lay on her back, the pearls slipped under her chin and *sighed*: "I'm thirsty, *dearest*. <u>Donne-moi un orange.</u>"[29]

The final print version adds "with" before "the pearls" as well as a comma after "chin," making this more clearly a nonrestrictive clause, allowing more clarity for the compound verb—"she lay . . . and sighed"—thus clarifying the grammar of the sentence, but these changes are not evident in the earlier drafts.[30] A more pronounced change between the manuscript and the typescript, though, is the substitution of "dearest" for "darling." According to the *Oxford English Dictionary*, "darling" is often used as an "endearing address" and refers to "a person who is very dear to another; the object of a person's love; one dearly loved."[31] "Dearest," on the other hand, though the *Oxford English Dictionary* notes that in its noun form it is synonymous with "darling," in its earlier sense as an adjective meant "'esteemed, valued' rather than 'loved.'"[32] Therefore, "darling" seems to be more intimate, while "dearest" has broader connotations and could be indicative of a mocking affection, one used to incite another to do one's bidding, suggesting manipulation. That Mansfield changes "murmured" in the manuscript to "sighed" in the typescript reinforces the manipulative factor, as the latter could be a contrived appeal.

The narrator responds to this appeal by noting to the reader that he would dive into the jaws of a crocodile to retrieve an orange for her, suggesting how far he is willing to go to please Beatrice. His love is both possessive and naïve, as Mansfield indicates in her letter to Murry:

> He [the narrator] of course laughs at it now, and laughs at her. Take what he says about her "sense of order" & the crocodile. But he also regrets the self who dead privately would have been young enough to have actually wanted to *Marry* such a woman. [. . .]

---

[28] Pois-MS-NL, leaf 3.
[29] Pois-TS-NL, leaf 3. Emphasis added.
[30] CW2, 257.
[31] "Darling" noun, *Oxford English Dictionary*, entry A1, http://www.oed.com.elibrary.huntington.edu, 15 May 2017.
[32] "Dear," *Oxford English Dictionary*, entries B, A2, http://www.oed.com.elibrary.huntington.edu, 15 May 2017.

And the story is told by a man who gives himself away & hides his traces at the same moment.[33]

If we accept what Mansfield states, the narrator realizes in retrospect how overzealous he was in his passion, and perhaps even how foolish he was to be taken in by Beatrice's manipulations. If such were Mansfield's intentions, then her revisions reveal how she used punctuation and word choice to affect the tone in her story as a means of reinforcing both the maneuvering of Beatrice and the naïveté of the narrator, though his possessive nature makes him appear more sinister than perhaps Mansfield had hoped, suggesting that on some level she was right in supposing, "I haven't brought it off in 'Poison'. It wanted a light, light hand."[34]

Mansfield's drafts of "The Stranger" (1920) are different from "Poison," for rather than a fairly clean manuscript and a typescript, we have a rather rough draft manuscript and a cleaner manuscript that reflects some of the in-text changes noted on the rough draft, most likely copied for either a typist or to send directly to a publisher.[35] Whatever the case, the progression of the story's writing seems obvious from the respective drafts. Like "Poison," the story focuses on the mental state of a male narrator who becomes jealous of his wife, but the scenario is very different. The protagonist, John Hammond, has been anxiously waiting for his wife Janey's steam liner to dock, anticipating a romantic reunion. Wanting her all to himself, he even keeps her from reading the letters their children have sent along. But once they are finally alone, Janey shares the experience of having had another passenger—a man—die in her arms. Hammond, rather than comforting his wife, sees the stranger as an interloper (the original title of the story)[36] who has shared an intimacy with his wife that he will never know.

Many of the revisions in this story are tied to Mansfield's artistic sensibility. In several passages she omits details that appear not only extraneous but also, in their exclusion, help to create more mystery around the death of the stranger, thus creating more tension in the story. Early in the first draft, for example, Mansfield has a false start in which Hammond begins to consider that Janey may be hiding something from him. However, she opts to omit this more direct suspicion, leaving him to merely wonder about Janey's desire to speak directly with the ship's doctor.

(Stran-rough-NL) She could have sent a note from the hotel even—if the affair had been urgent. Urgent! Did it—could it mean that she'd been ill on the voyage—that she was keeping something from him? That was it. ~~He~~ Hammond seized his hat. He was going off to find that fellow + to get the truth out of him at all costs. He thought he'd noticed just something—she was just a touch too calm—too steady. She was keeping something from him.[37]

(Stran-clean-NL) She could have sent a note from the hotel, even, if the affair had been urgent. Urgent? Did it—could it mean that she'd been ill on the voyage, ~~that~~ she was keeping something from him? That was it! He seized his hat. He was going off

---

[33] *Letters* 4, 119.

[34] Ibid.

[35] A note at the top of the rougher draft indicates, "Rough copy. Much corrected copy posted to Jack 9.x.1920" (Stran-rough-NL, leaf 1).

[36] Ibid. The original title, "The Interloper," is struck through and replaced with "Stranger."

[37] Stran-rough-NL, leaf 7.

to find that fellow and to wring the truth out of him at all costs. He thought he'd noticed just something. She was just a touch too calm—too steady. From the very first moment . . .[38]

Initially in the passage, Hammond is concerned that perhaps Janey had been ill and is keeping it from him, and Mansfield's punctuation reveals his conclusion by placing an exclamation point after "That was it!" which wasn't in the initial draft. Likewise, she minimizes the urgency by omitting the original exclamation point after "Urgent," making it a question which indicates concern, instead. Noting a difference in Janey—that she was "a touch too calm—too steady"—Hammond sees her as more empowered but does not appear to consider this a positive change. In the first draft, he reiterates his sense that Janey is hiding something from him, which although it refers directly to his concern about her illness, also has the effect of raising greater suspicion in the reader's mind about what she might be hiding. In this sense, it anticipates the revelation at the end of the story heavy-handedly. In the second draft, however, Mansfield omits the second reiteration, "She was keeping something from him." She adds instead the more ambiguous "From the very first moment. . . ." This suggests that Hammond is still suspicious of something, but it emphasizes how Janey is acting differently. In this way, Mansfield deflects attention from the fact that Janey has some secret, but still has the reader (and Hammond) wondering what has evoked this change in her.

A more pronounced instance is when Mansfield, in the second draft, omits some of the stranger's backstory, ensuring that he remains obscure and therefore forcing both Hammond and the reader to infer Janey's relation with him.

(Stran-rough-NL) He was one of the 1st class passengers. Quite young. I saw he was very ill when he came on board, ~~but nobody else seemed to realise it. He never ought to been~~ [sic] ~~allowed to travel. And we got to know each other don't you know and I think he realized I had guessed about him—about how ill he was. How sorry I was for him. Then~~ in ~~He~~ He fell **awfully** ~~ill in the tropics. There wasn't a nurse or one creature on board to help the doctor so I . . . offered to, said Janey—And after that—off and on— until it culminated in~~ Then he seemed to be so much better until until [sic] yesterday—He had a very severe attack in the afternoon—excitement, nervousness about arriving I think and after that he never really recovered.[39]
[see Figure 17]

(Stran-clean-NL) "He was one of the first class passengers. I saw he was very ill when he came on board. But he seemed to be so much better until yesterday. He had a severe attack in the afternoon—excitement—nervousness I think, about arriving. And after that he never recovered."[40]

Initially, Mansfield notes not only the stranger's illness and how Janey came to tend to him, but also that they "got to know each other," suggesting a friendly relationship. The factual details about the stranger's illness and that it worsened in the tropics and that Janey acted as a surrogate nurse seem immaterial, having little effect on the story one way or another. In fact, because they are unnecessary details, omitting them strengthens the

---

[38] Stran-clean-NL, leaf 9.
[39] Stran-rough-NL, leaves 13–14.
[40] Stran-clean-NL, leaf 17.

story. Mansfield even omits that the stranger was "quite young" in the second draft. Excluding these specifics about their relationship leaves it ambiguous and serves to feed Hammond's suspicion, strengthening his jealousy.

The effectiveness of "The Stranger" lies in the reader's ability to see into Hammond's thoughts—perhaps empathizing with his situation even if his jealousy is off-putting. Tracing the revisions that Mansfield makes in the various drafts of the story reveals her choice to eliminate details from the backstory that she envisioned in order to create a stronger work of fiction. Some of the information that she eliminates is simply unnecessary, but much of the elimination also allows her to create tension in a story that relies on the psychology of its protagonist.

By studying the process of a text's becoming, especially the "material traces of the writing act," one can "attempt to reconstruct the intellectual, linguistic and cultural processes that were involved in the genesis of a work of art."[41] These "material traces" reveal artistic choices, reinforcing the author's role in the creation of a story and suggesting at least a degree of intentionality. Though many genetic critics prefer to focus on the dynamics of writing rather than the intentions of the author,[42] studying draft materials such as the Mansfield holdings at both the Turnbull Library and the Newberry Library have the potential to not only reinforce certain interpretations of her work, but also to expand our understanding of her writing process and even to provide new insights into some of her key works. Such is the purpose of this book, which gathers together manuscript transcriptions of several of Katherine Mansfield's most well-known stories alongside numerous facsimiles as well as critical engagements with these manuscripts by some of the top Mansfield scholars. The transcriptions provide scholars a degree of access to a selection of Mansfield's manuscripts that has previously only been available to those able to travel either to the Newberry Library in Chicago, USA, or to the Alexander Turnbull Library in Wellington, NZ. Of course, nothing quite substitutes for the physicality of the archive, the touch and smell of original documents. But the hope is that, aside from saving the reader from having to pour over Mansfield's often illegible writing, that these transcriptions can provide a greater understanding of Mansfield's work and process. The critical essays offer examples of how these transcriptions can be employed toward that understanding, illuminating the value of working with manuscripts in general, but also shedding light on how Mansfield's art works by showing the artist at work.

Claire Davison begins the critical section with her chapter, "'With a strong accent on the less': Tracing Voices in the Textual Genetics of 'Je ne parle pas français,'" in which she explores how Mansfield's own self-silencing through the process of revision reveals how she both represses and flaunts the voices of the text, creating various forms of voice and "'countervoice'" (238). Beginning with biographical context for the story, Davison turns to how Mansfield manipulates language—introducing the French language into parts of the drafts and suppressing it in others—to signal foreignness even as the story invites intimacy, in much the same way that Raoul Duquette takes us into his confidence only to withdraw. After discussing the associative and auditory implications of language, Davison elaborates on the "sonic and dramatic depth" of the story by exploring how Mansfield

---

[41] Marion Schmid, *Process of Literary Creation: Flaubert and Proust* (Oxford: Legenda, European Humanities Research Centre, 1998), 8.
[42] Deppman, Ferrer and Groden, Introduction, 8.

integrates musical, cinematographic, and theatrical references in "Je ne parle pas français" and its drafts to reveal the artifice of the self and other. Davison reveals that, despite the limitations of genetic criticism, if one listens intently enough one can discover resonant meaning.

In "The Journey from 'Non-Compounders' to 'The Daughters of the Late Colonel,'" Gerri Kimber discusses the genesis, publication, and reception of another of Mansfield's most celebrated stories; she addresses key themes and techniques Mansfield employs in "Daughters of the Late Colonel" before turning to the manuscripts to reveal how Mansfield's edits reinforce these. Kimber notes Mansfield's use of affectation, especially with respect to Nurse Andrews; her experimentation with genre, finding traces of the gothic; and her use of sun imagery. Drawing on Mansfield's letters and journals, Kimber provides a comprehensive overview of the biographical elements of the story and offers a reading of key themes and techniques that belie overly simplistic readings of the story, suggesting that the sisters have a greater degree of agency and recognize their sacrifice, noting particularly the sun and moon imagery. Kimber also argues that the story, more than a simple tragedy, integrates elements of the comic, and that the narrative techniques that she uses—comparable to those in "Prelude"—reveal Mansfield at her modernist best.

In the third chapter of this section, Janet Wilson analyzes three sea journeys and the changes incurred to demonstrate how Mansfield "demarcate[s] transitions in states of being" (269). Wilson reveals in "'All at Sea': Sea Journeys in 'The Stranger,' 'The Voyage,' and 'Six Years After,'" how Mansfield uses the sea voyage to distort ordinary reality in order to explore the psychological changes in her protagonists, particularly those experiencing death and bereavement. Each of the stories have biographical ties, and "The Stranger" and "Six Years After" have a particular connection to Mansfield's father, Harold Beauchamp. These stories, according to Wilson, reveal a gendered response to death and grief in which the women subvert more masculine responses by finding more affective responses to tragedy in which they draw on memory and subjective associations. Wilson concludes that the genesis of these stories expose Mansfield's own attempt to "work[] creatively through the overwhelming shock of her brother's [Leslie Heron Beauchamp's] tragic death" and to find "artistic ways to approach and come to terms with her own mortality" (283).

Jenny McDonnell focuses her attention on two of Mansfield's "popular" stories, stories that appeared in the "middlebrow" magazine, *The Sphere*. However, as she argues in "'A Wholesale Hanging': Katherine Mansfield's *Sphere Stories*," these stories do not follow traditionally popular narratives; she explains that the ambiguities of the stories' endings are reflected in the textual instabilities of the manuscripts. Specifically, both stories feature two romantically involved couples without fulfilling the expectations of a traditional marriage plot, primarily by refusing to provide closure in her endings. The relationships are left in a state of flux. Similarly, each story undergoes transformations between the drafts, their initial publication in *The Sphere*, and their inclusion in the *Edinburgh Edition of the Collected Fiction of Katherine Mansfield*, making them "'protean, existing in multiple and equally authorized forms' simultaneously, in ways that mirror George Bornstein's materialist reading of modernism" (296).

In the final critical essay, "'What was it?': The *avant-texte* and the 'grinding feeling of wretchedness' in Katherine Mansfield's 'The Fly,'" I argue against previous readings of the story which understand the ending as the boss's return to the status quo. These readings tie the boss's assertion of power by ordering Macy to fetch more blotting paper to a willful and *successful* forgetting of his son's death. I propose, however, that the two-staged structure of the story and evidence from the story's manuscript suggest that the boss's attempt to dissociate himself from his wretchedness by re-immersing himself in his work is unsuccessful. The wretched feeling that his work has been built on a lie, no matter how much he tries to assert otherwise, cannot be so easily quelled.

Selected Stories

A Note on the Manuscripts of "Je ne parle pas français"

Originally published by the Heron Press, a publishing venture of Katherine Mansfield and John Middleton Murry, the story was later included in Mansfield's second collection of short stories, *Bliss and Other Stories* (1920), albeit in bowdlerized form, as Claire Davison discusses in her essay in this collection.

In a letter to Murry dated February 3 and 4, 1918, Mansfield mentions writing the story and preparing a copy of the story for him: "My work excites me so tremendously that I almost feel *insane* at night and I have been at it with hardly a break all day. A great deal is copied and carefully addressed to you, in case any misfortune should happen to me. Cheerful!"[1] The copy she mentions is the clean manuscript transcribed below (JNPP-clean-NL), now held at the Newberry Library.

The earlier drafts present an interesting conundrum. Part of an early draft appears in Notebook 14, held at the Alexander Turnbull Library (JNPP-NB14-ATL), and another part is written on loose leaves of paper, held at the Newberry Library (JNPP-rough-NL). However, aside from a short section of overlap, the two documents together create a full draft of the story despite the fact that Notebook 14, which contains the middle of the story, appears to have been written before the rough Newberry manuscript. That Notebook 14 preceded the Newberry manuscript is evident because in the overlapping section the Newberry manuscript incorporates edits made in the notebook. Interestingly, the clean copy Mansfield made for Murry corresponds with Notebook 14 where the rough Newberry manuscript leaves off, suggesting that there is not another, intermediary draft. However, while I have compiled and transcribed these two documents to align chronologically with the narrative of the story, it is possible that what I have identified as the verso leaves of the Newberry manuscript may actually have been written first, making it concurrent with the writing of Notebook 14, while the recto pages—which coincide with the beginning of the story—may be a clean, recopying of this earlier draft whose earlier pages no longer exist.

Following the narrative of the story, though, the first part of "Je ne parle pas français" is written on the recto of the leaves of the rough manuscript held by the Newberry Library, while the versos of these leaves include later sections of the story. After leaf sixteen recto, the story continues chronologically on page two of Notebook 14, with some overlap with leaves fifteen and sixteen. Page twenty-nine of Notebook 14 includes a circled "x" which is replicated on leaf sixteen verso of the Newberry manuscript followed by "continued from same sign in buff notebook." The cover of Notebook 14 is buff. The story continues—working backwards—on the verso leaves of the sixteen pages of the rough manuscript; it then picks back up on page thirty of Notebook 14, continuing to the end of the notebook and then on the verso pages, in reverse order.

---

[1] *Letters* 2, 55. Emphasis in original.

I do not know why I have such a fancy for this little café. Its dirty, and its sad—sad! It isn't as if it had anything to distinguish it from a hundred others—it hasnt; or as if the same strange "types" came ~~in~~ here every day whom one could watch from ones corner and ~~get to~~ recognise and more or less (with a strong accent on the <u>less</u>) get the hang of. [N.P.] But[2] pray don't think those brackets are a confession of my humility before the mystery of the human soul. Not at all; I don't believe in the human soul. I never have. I believe that people are like portmanteaux—packed with certain things, started off, thrown about, tossed about,[3] dumped down, lost and found, half emptied suddenly or squeezed fuller than ever until finally the Ultimate Porter swings them on to the Ultimate Train and away they rattle . . .[N.P.] Not but what portmanteaux can be very fascinating. Oh but very! I see myself standing in front of them, don't you know, like a customs official. [new line] "Have you anything to declare? Any wines, spirits, cigars, perfumes, silks?" And the moment of hesitation just before I chalk that squiggle as to whether I am going to be fooled,[4] and then the other moment of hesitation—just after, as to whether I have been [fooled,] are perhaps the [two] most thrilling instants in life. Yes, they are to me.

But before I started that rather far fetched and not frightfully original digression what I meant to

say quite simply was that there are no "portmanteaux" to be examined here because the clientèle of the café, ladies and gentlemen, does not sit down. No, it stands at the counter, and it consists of a handful of workmen who come up from the river, all powdered over with white flour, or lime, or something, and a few soldiers ~~who~~ bring[ing] with them thin dark girls with silver rings in their ears and baskets over their arms.

Madame is thin and dark, too, with white cheeks and white hands. In certain lights she looks quite transparent, shining out of her black shawl with an extraordinary effect. When she is not serving she sits on a stool with her face turned, always, to the window— ~~h~~Her dark-ringed[5] eyes search among and follow after the people passing, but not as if she were looking for anybody.[6] ~~No, p~~Perhaps fifteen years ago she was, but now the ~~expression~~ [pose that] has become a habit from ~~from~~ [sic] [You can tell from] her [air of] fatigue and hopeless ~~air~~ [ness][7] she must have given "them" up for the last ten years at least.

And then there is the waiter. Not pathetic—decidedly not comic. Never making one of those perfectly insignificant remarks which amaze you so as coming from "a waiter" (as though the poor wretch were a sort of cross between a coffee pot and a [wine] bottle and ~~wasn't~~ not expected to hold as[8] much as a drop of anything else.) He is grey, flatfooted

---

[2] In the margin next to "But" are the initials "NP," meaning "New Paragraph." This editorial mark, as well as "NL," or "New Line," appear throughout the manuscript and are reproduced accordingly.

[3] "Tossed about" becomes "tossed away" in subsequent versions.

[4] The phrase "as to whether I am going to be fooled" is circled and an arrow directs its placement before "just before I chalk that squiggle," which is as it appears in the clean manuscript.

[5] It appears that a hyphen follows "ringed," connecting it with eyes, but it has been stricken out.

[6] "Anybody" becomes "somebody" in subsequent versions.

[7] "Ness" is superimposed on "air," changing the original "hopeless air" to "hopelessness."

[8] "As" becomes "so" in subsequent versions.

and withered with long brittle nails that set your ~~teeth~~ nerves on edge when~~ile~~ he scrapes up your ~~tip~~ 2 sous ~~off the table, and bad teeth~~. When he is smearing[9] over the table or flicking at a dead fly or two he stands with one hand on the back of a chair, in his far too long

[JNPP-rough-NL, leaf 3 recto][10]

apron and over his other arm the three cornered dip of dirty napkin, ~~as though he were~~ waiting to be photographed in connection with some wretched murder: <u>Interior of</u> ~~c~~Café ~~w~~Where ~~b~~Body ~~w~~Was ~~f~~Found. ~~He couldn't be more perfect . . .~~ Youve seen him countless times.

Do you believe that every place has its hour of the day when it really does "come alive"? ~~No,~~ thats not exactly what I mean—Its more like this. There does seem to be a moment that you realise that quite by accident you have happened to come[11] on to the right stage at exactly the moment you were expected—Everything's arranged for you—waiting for you—Now was the ~~time~~ hour and you are there[12]—Ah ~~m~~Master of the situation. You fill with important breath and at the same time you smile, secretly, meaningly,[13] because ~~l~~Life seems to be opposed to granting you these ~~moments~~ entrances, seems indeed to be engaged in snatching them from you + making them impossible—in <u>Keeping you</u> ~~down~~ in the wings in fact in fact [sic] until it is too late[14] . . . ~~and~~ ~~j~~Just for once youve beaten the old hag! ~~But~~

The first time I ever came in here I enjoyed one of those moments.[15] Thats why I keep coming back I suppose—**revisiting*** the scene of my triumph—or the scene of the crime where I had the old bitch by the throat for ~~a moment~~ once + did what I pleased.[16] N.L. Query Why am I so bitter ~~about~~ against Life? And why do I see her as a rag picker on the american cinema—~~and her hair in a horsetail~~ shuffling along wrapped ~~up~~ in a **filthy*** shawl with her old claws crooked over a stick. ~~Affection or as xxx say mind.~~ I am ~~perhaps~~ N.L. Answer the direct result of the cinema most likely[17] acting upon a weak mind—)

[JNPP-rough-NL, leaf 4 recto]

Anyhow the "short winter afternoon was drawing to a close" as they say and I was drifting along either going home or not going home when I found myself in here, walking over to this seat in the corner. I hung[18] up my english overcoat + grey felt hat ~~with the black band~~ on that same peg behind me + after I had allowed the waiter time for at least 20 photographers to snap their fill of him I ordered a coffee ~~in a glass~~. N.L. He ~~shuffled off~~ poured me out a glass of the familiar purplish stuff with a green wandering light playing ~~in~~ over it + shuffled off: and I sat pressing my fingers against the glass because it was **bitterly*** cold outside. N.L. Suddenly I realised that I was apart from myself. I was smiling.[19]

---

[9] The clean draft reads, "When he is not smearing" (JNPP-clean-NL, leaf 2), the negative making more sense.

[10] This page is not numbered, but follows chronologically.

[11] This is revised to "you happen to have come" in subsequent versions.

[12] Revised versions of the story omit "Now was the hour and you are there."

[13] "Slyly" replaces "meaningly" in subsequent versions.

[14] While "until it is too late" is clearly marked to follow "in fact" here, later versions invert the phrases.

[15] Mansfield circles the first part of this sentence, "The first time I ever came in here," and an arrow indicates that it should be placed after "I enjoyed one of these moments," a change that is retained in subsequent versions.

[16] Revised versions add "with her" after "what I pleased."

[17] "Most likely" is omitted in later versions.

[18] Mansfield retraced the "un" of "hung," making these letters more legible.

[19] This is revised to: "suddenly I realized that quite apart from myself, I was smiling" (JNPP-clean-NL, leaf 4).

Slowly I raised my head + saw myself in the mirror opposite. Yes, there I sat leaning over the table, smiling my deep sly smile, the glass of coffee with its vague plume of steam before me + ~~beside it~~ ~~on the~~ ring of white saucer with 2 pieces of sugar. [N.L.] I opened my eyes very wide—There I had been for all eternity—as it were and ~~here~~ now at last was my moment for coming to life . . . [N.P.] It was very quiet in the café—outside, one could just see through the dusk that it had begun to snow. One could just see the shapes of horses and carts + people soft and white, moving through the feathery air. The waiter disappeared + reappeared with [an] armful of straw. He strewed it ~~on~~ over the floor from the door to the counter—and round about the stove with humble, almost **adoring*** gestures ~~of his hands~~. One would not have ~~seemed~~ been[20] surprised ~~to see~~ if the door had open~~ed~~ + the Virgin Mary had come in riding upon **an***

[JNPP-rough-NL, leaf 5 recto]

ass her meek hands folded over her big belly.

Thats rather nice don't you think? That ~~little~~ bit about the Virgin? It comes ~~off~~ from the pen so gently[21] it has such a "dying fall." [N.L.] I thought so at the time and decided to make a note of it. One never knows when a little tag like that may come in useful to round off a paragraph. [N.L.] So taking care to move as little as possible because the "spell" was still unbroken (you know that?) I reached over to the next table for a writing ~~album~~ pad—[N.P.] No paper or envelopes, of course. Only a tiny morsel of pink blotting paper, ~~so~~ incredibly limp so soft[22]—almost moist. ~~It felt~~ ~~it was~~ like like [sic] the tongue of a little dead kitten— which Ive never felt: [NL] I sat but always, underneath in this sense of expectation mind you ~~stroking the little dead tongue~~ + rolling the little kittens[23] tongue round my fingers and rolling the soft phrase round my mind while my eyes took in ~~all~~ the names and dirty jokes + drawings of bottles—+ hearts ~~+ le xxx xxx petit chocolat qualiteé—that xxx of~~ rings and cups that wouldn't sit in the saucers ~~that were~~ **scattered*** over the blotting pad[24]—[N.L.] They are always the same, you know, ~~the same girls name,~~ the girls all have the same names, the cups never ~~fit~~ sit in the saucers, all the hearts are ~~always~~ stuck + tied up with ribbons.

But then quite suddenly at the bottom of the page, written in green ink I ~~read~~ fell on to that silly[25] stupid, stale little phrase "~~I dont spik Engleesh~~ [sic]." je ne parle pas francais There! It had come the moment—the "geste" + though I was so ready—it caught me—+ ~~bowled~~ tumbled me over—I was simply overwhelmed . . . [N.L.] And the physical feeling was so curious—so "particular." It was as if all of me except for my head + my arms—all of me that was under the table had simply dissolved[,] melted—**turned*** into water.

---

[20] "Been" is written over what appears to be "seem" or "seemed."
[21] The "g" and "n" have been retraced.
[22] Later revisions invert "limp" and "soft."
[23] Subsequent versions add the modifier, "dead," reading: "little dead kitten's tongue."
[24] Revisions in later versions change "names" to "girls' names," omit "hearts" from the list of drawings, and change "blotting pad" to "writing pad."
[25] "Silly" is omitted in later versions.

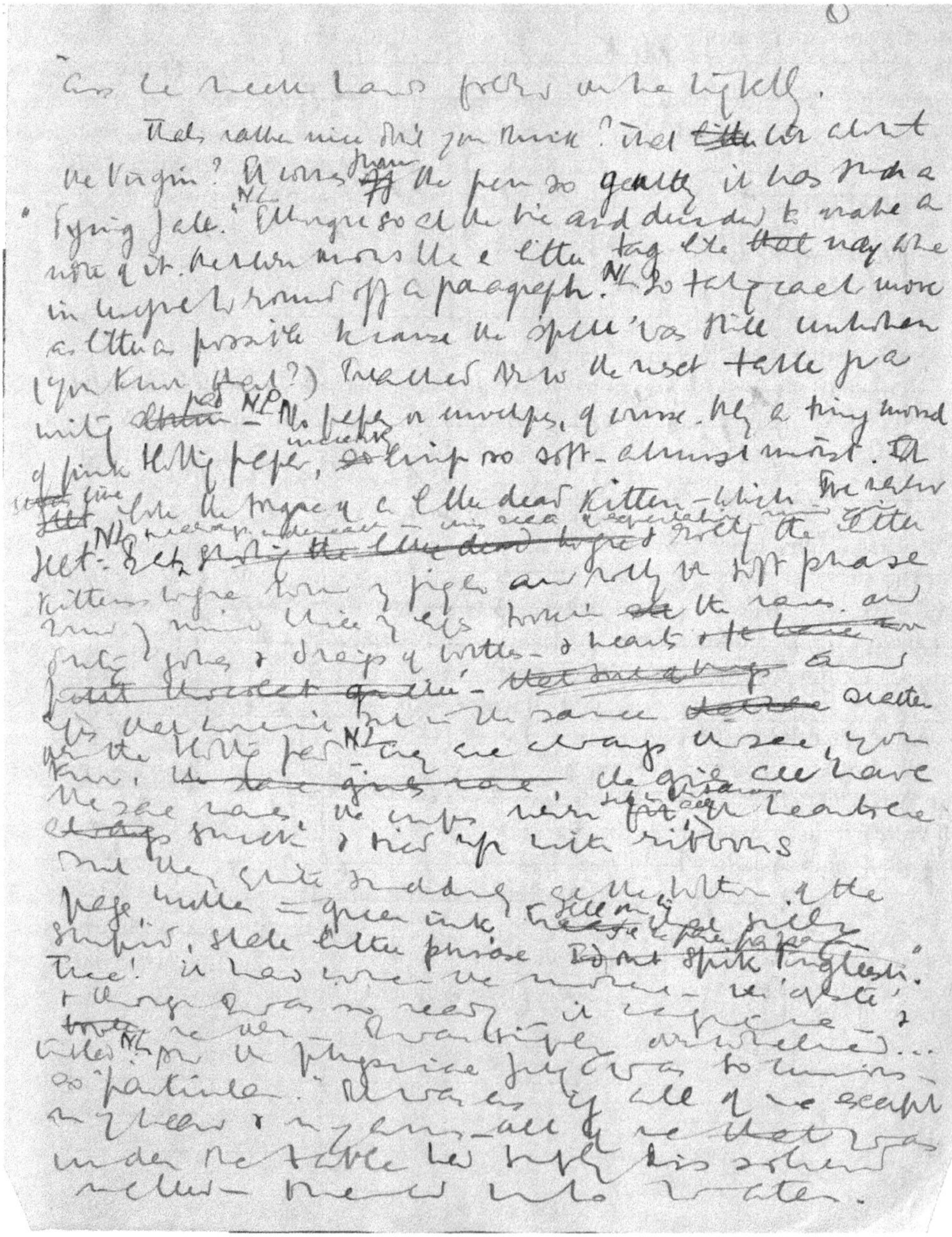

FIGURE 1: Leaf 5, "Je ne parle pas français" [rough manuscript], Katherine Mansfield Papers, Newberry Library, (box 1, folder 27), 16 leaves. Image courtesy of the Newberry Library.

[JNPP-rough-NL, leaf 6 recto]

Just my head remained ~~with~~ ~~two~~ ~~round eyes~~ + two of arm **sticks*** ~~leaning~~ pressing on the table[26]—But ah! the agony of that moment, the sheer release of agony how can I describe it![27] I didn't think of anything—didn't even cry out to myself—just for one second I was not—— I was agony agony agony + [NL.] then it passed—and the very second after I was thinking. "Good God! am I capable of feeling as strongly as that. But I was absolutely unconscious. I was over come—I was swept off my feet. I hadn't a phrase to meet it with—I didn't even try—in the **dimmest*** way to put it down." [NL] And up I puffed + puffed—**blowing off*** finally with "after all I must ~~have a~~ [be] first ~~class~~ [rate] ~~mind~~. No second rate ~~person~~ [mind] could have experienced such an intensity—of **feeling***—so <u>purely</u>—

The waiter has touched a spill at the red stove and lighted a bubble of gas under a spreading shade. Its no use looking **out of*** [the] window—Madame—its quite dark [now]. Your white hands hover over your dark shawl—like two birds that have come home to roost.[28] ~~You~~ [They are restless, restless.] You tuck them finally under your warm little armpits. [Fais Dodo mes petits.[29] NL.] Now the waiter has ~~taken~~ [seized] a long pole xx and clashed the curtains together with it[30]—"All gone" as the children say—[NP31] And besides Ive no patience with people who can[']t let go of things—who will follow after and cry out—When a things gone its gone—its over and done with.

[JNPP-rough-NL, leaf 7 recto]

Let it go then—Ignore it—and comfort yourself if you want **comforting*** with the thought that you never <u>do</u> recover the same thing that you ~~lost~~[lose].[32] It's always a new thing. The minute[33] it leaves your ~~hand~~ its a changed—Why thats even true of a hat you chase after. Its never quite the same hat again—and I dont mean superficially—I mean "profound speaking."[34] [N.P.] I have made it a rule of my life never to regret and never to look back ~~after~~ ~~what has gone—For~~ regret is ~~the most~~ [an] appalling waste of energy and no one who ~~wou~~[intends][35] to be an ~~artist~~ [writer] can afford to indulge in it. You **never** get it into shape,[36] you cant build on it. It's a huge swamp[37] ~~thats~~ [and] only good for wallowing in—~~and~~ ‡Looking back of course is ~~just as~~ [equally] fatal ~~for~~ [to] Art ~~as to its~~—its **keeping*** yourself poor—and Art can[']t [and wont stand poverty.] ~~go hungry~~—

---

[26] It appears that Mansfield originally had "two arm sticks"; there is an editorial mark indicating that "sticks" be placed before "of arms," and "of" is further left in the margin, so was likely added later to create the phrase "two sticks of arms."

[27] Subsequent versions omit "the sheer release of agony."

[28] Revised versions have this as an independent clause: "They are like two birds that have come home to roost."

[29] This addition does not make it into subsequent versions.

[30] Later versions revert to "taken" rather than "seized," and "with it" is omitted.

[31] "NP" is circled.

[32] "Lose" is superimposed on "lost."

[33] "Minute" becomes "moment" in later versions.

[34] The clean manuscript reorders the last few sentences, reading: "Why, that's even true of a hat you chase after, and I dont mean superficially—I mean, 'profoundly' speaking . . ." (JNPP-clean-NL, leaf 7).

[35] "Intends" is written over what appears to be the beginning of "would."

[36] "Never" becomes "can't" in later versions.

[37] Subsequent versions omit "a huge swamp," retaining only: "its only good for wallowing in" (JNPP-clean-NL, leaf 7).

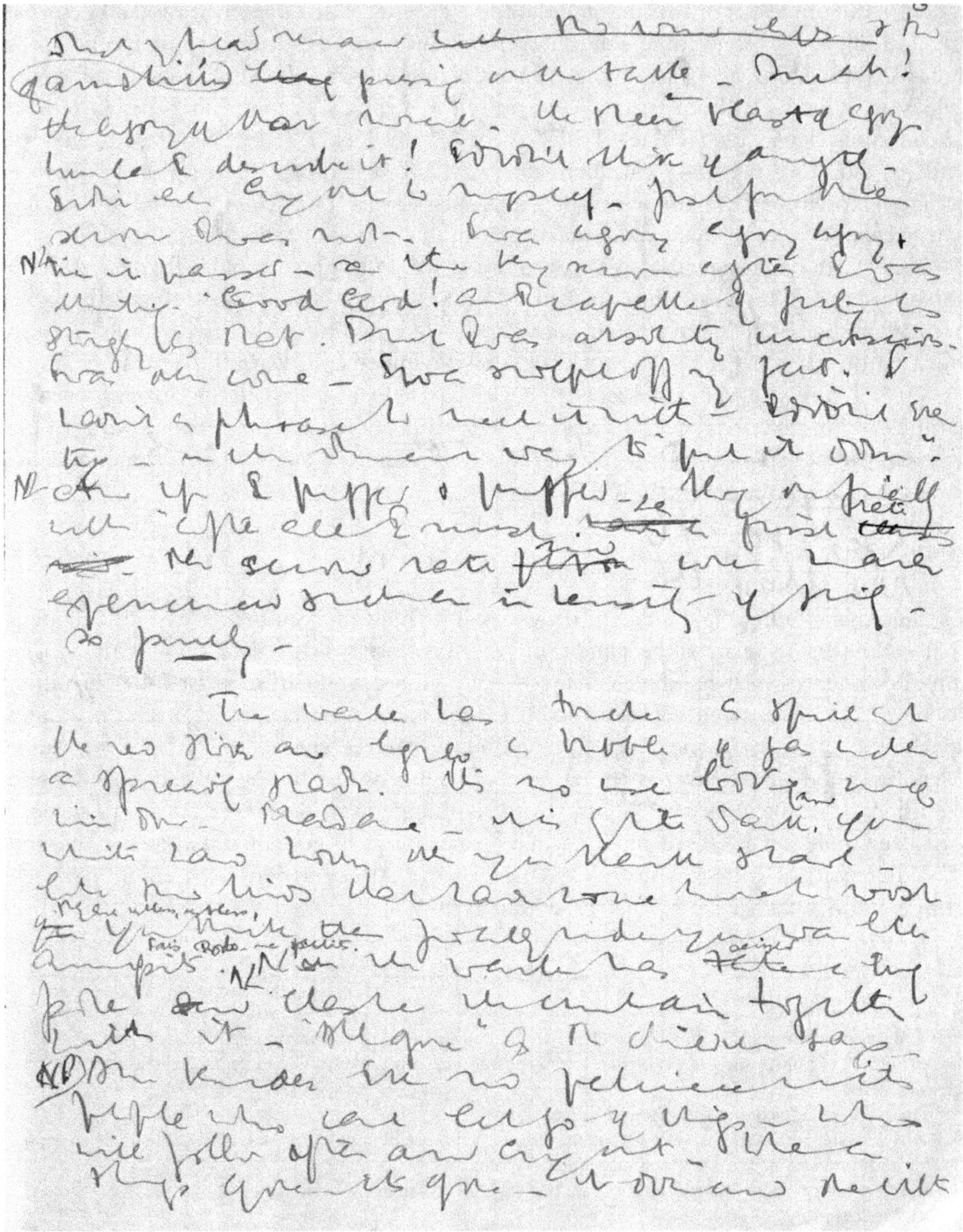

FIGURE 2: Leaf 6 recto, "Je ne parle pas français" [rough manuscript], Katherine Mansfield Papers, Newberry Library, (box 1, folder 27), 16 leaves. Image courtesy of the Newberry Library.

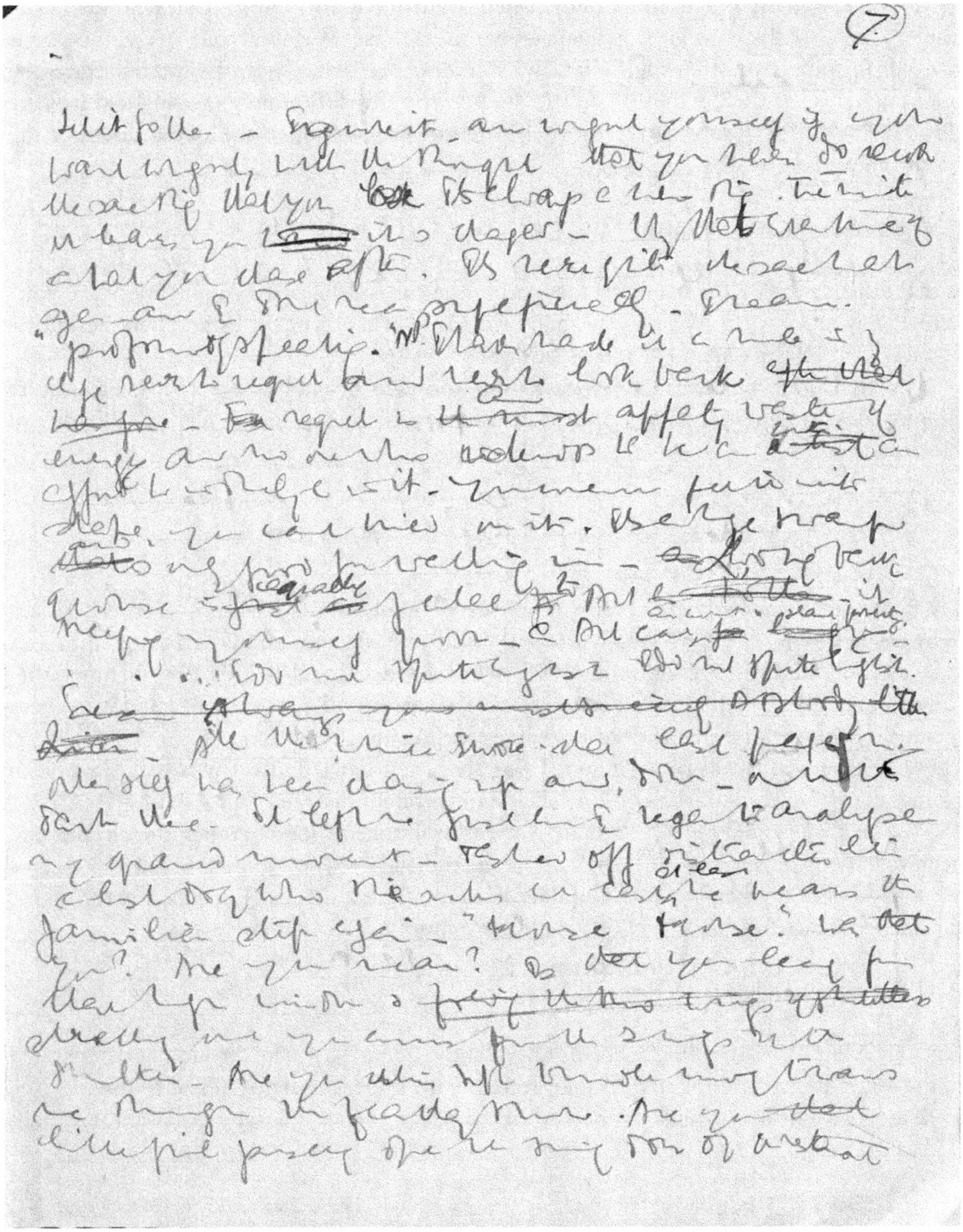

FIGURE 3: Leaf 7 recto, "Je ne parle pas français" [rough manuscript], Katherine Mansfield Papers, Newberry Library, (box 1, folder 27), 16 leaves. Image courtesy of the Newberry Library.

I do not spik [*sic*] English. I do not spik English.[38]

~~I mean always~~ **you must xxx** ~~anybody little Liar.~~ All the while I wrote that last page[39] my other self has been chasing up and down—**out in the*** dark there. It left me just as I began to analyse my grand moment—dashed off distracted like a lost dog who tha'nks at last ᵃᵗ ˡᵃˢᵗ he hears the familiar step again—"Mouse Mouse. Was that you? Are you near? Is that you leaning from that high window + ~~freeing the two wings of shutters~~ stretching out your arms for the 2 wings of shutter[40]—Are you this soft bundle moving towards me through the feathery snow. Are you that little girl pressing open the swing doors of the restaurant

[JNPP-rough-NL, leaf 8 recto]

Is that your dark shadow leaning[41] forward in the cab—Where are you—Where are you? Which way must I turn. Which way shall I run? And every moment I stand here hesitating you are further away again—Mouse! Mouse!"

Now the poor dog ~~was~~ ʰᵃˢ ᶜᵒᵐᵉ back into the cafe his tail between his legs—quite exhausted. It was a false alarm. She['s] nowhere to be seen. Lie down then—Lie down! Lie down!

My name is Raoul Duquette. I am twenty six years old and a Parisian—a true Parisian. ~~Why my family is~~ ᴬᵇᵒᵘᵗ ᵐʸ ᶠᵃᵐⁱˡʸ—really doesn[']t matter. I have no family + I dont want any. I never think about my childhood ᴵ ʰᵃᵛᵉ ᶠᵒʳᵍᵒᵗᵗᵉⁿ ⁱᵗ—In fact there[']s only one memory that stands out at all ~~xxx~~—that is rather interesting, ~~singly~~ because it seems to me now so very ~~much the **sort** of thing that should have happened to me~~. ˢⁱᵍⁿⁱᶠⁱᶜᵃⁿᵗ ᶠʳᵒᵐ ᵗʰᵉ ˡⁱᵗᵉʳᵃʳʸ ᵖᵒⁱⁿᵗ ᵃˢ ʳᵉᵍᵃʳᵈˢ **ᵐʸˢᵉˡᶠ*** ᵒᶠ ᵛⁱᵉʷ42—~~That I will~~ It was this. [When] I was about ten our laundress was ⁱˢ an ~~old~~ african woman, very big, very dark—with a check handkerchief over her frizzy hair—ᵂʰᵉⁿ ˢʰᵉ ᶜᵃᵐᵉ ᵗᵒ ᵒᵘʳ ʰᵒᵘˢᵉ She always ~~paid me~~ ᵗᵒᵒᵏ particular ~~attention~~ notice of me ᵃⁿᵈ ~~A~~after the clothes had been taken out of her basket ~~+ she had been paid~~ she ~~used to~~ ʷᵒᵘˡᵈ lift me up ⁱⁿᵗᵒ ⁱᵗ + give me a rock—while I held tight to the handles + screamed for joy + fright. I was tiny for my age—+ pale—with a lovely little half open mouth. I feel sure of that.

[JNPP-rough-NL, leaf 9 recto]

One day while I was standing at the door watching her go she turned round and beckoned to me—nodding + smiling in a strange **secret*** way. I never thought of not following. She took me into a little outhouse at the end of the passage + set[43] down her basket + caught

---

[38] This is changed to "<u>Je ne parle pas français. Je ne parle pas français</u>" in the clean manuscript)JNPP-clean-NL, leaf 7).

[39] There is a dark, indecipherable mark following "page."

[40] The clean manuscript simply reads "the wings of the shutters," omitting "2" (JNPP-clean-NL, leaf 7).

[41] "Leaning" becomes "bending" in subsequent versions.

[42] "As regards myself" is squeezed into the margin and is used in the clean manuscript: "That <u>is</u> rather interesting because it seems to me now so very significant as regards myself from the literary point of view" (JNPP-clean-NL, leaves 8–9).

[43] "Set" becomes "put" in the clean manuscript.

me up in her arms + began kissing me—Oh such kisses[44]—especially those kisses inside my ears that nearly deafened me! And then with a soft growl she tore open her xxx bodice + put me to her—~~to~~

When she set me down again she took out of her pocket a little round fried cake covered with sugar + I reeled along the passage back to our door. [N.P.] As this performance was repeated once a week + its no wonder I remember it so vividly. ~~When~~ ~~Also~~ Besides from that very first afternoon my childhood was to put it prettily kissed away——I became very languid, very caressing, ~~and~~ greedy beyond measure. ~~And with it~~ so quicke[ened] so sharpened—I seemed to understand everybody + to be able to do what I liked with everybody—~~Truth was~~ I suppose I was ~~constantly more or less~~ in a state of [more or less constant] physical excitement + that [was what] appealed ~~to them~~[45] for Parisians of ~~our~~ classe[46] [sic] are more than half—Oh* well enough of that! And enough of my childhood. Bury it under a laundry basket instead of a shower of roses and <u>passon</u> **oultre***.

I date myself from the moment that I became the tenant of ~~the~~ [a][47] small bachelor flat

[JNPP-rough-NL, leaf 10 recto]

on the fifth floor [of] a tall not too shabby house, in a street that might or might <u>not</u> be decreet—very useful that!

There I emerged, came up into the light—put out my two horns, with a study and a bedroom + a kitchen on my back. And real furniture planted in the rooms—a wardrobe with a long glass, a big bed covered with a yellow puffed up quilt—a bed table with a marble top—~~and a washing stand xxx~~ a xxx slip ~~cover~~[48] sprinkled ~~xxx~~ with little apples.[49] In my **study***—writing table[50] with drawers—writing chair with leather cushions ~~arm chair~~ books xxx armchair—side table with paper knife + lamp on it—and some nude studies in **red checks**[51]—on the walls—I didn't use the kitchen except to throw old newspapers into.—— –

Ah I can see myself that first evening after the furniture men had left and I'd managed to shut out my atrocious old concierge—walking about on tiptoe—arranging—+ standing in front of the long glass—with my hands in my pockets + saying to that radiant vision: I am a young man with his own ~~appartement~~ [flat]. I write for 2 newspapers. I am going in for literature.[52] I am starting a career. [The book] ~~I~~ intend to bring out a ~~book that~~ will simply <u>stagger</u> the critics.[53] I am going to write about things that have never been touched before. I am going to make a name for myself as a writer about the under world.[54] But not as others have[55]

---

44 Subsequent versions read: "Ah, those kisses!"
45 A small check mark is written above where this has been crossed out, suggesting it is to be retained, as it is in subsequent versions.
46 Later versions omit "of our classe."
47 "A" is written over "the."
48 The clean manuscript has "toilet set."
49 Subsequent versions add "In the bedroom" before "a wardrobe [. . .]." The "slip cover" becomes a "toilet set."
50 "Writing table" becomes "English writing table" in later versions.
51 "Red checks" is omitted in subsequent versions.
52 Later versions add "serious" (i.e. "serious literature").
53 This becomes: "The book that I shall bring out [. . .]" in later versions.
54 "Under world" becomes "submerged world" in later versions.
55 There is a presumably stray mark through the "e" of "have."

[JNPP-rough-NL, leaf 11 recto]

done before me. Oh no—~~write~~ very naively—with a sort of tender humour and <u>from the inside</u> as though it were all quite simple—quite natural—I see my way perfectly—Nobody has ever done it as I shall because ~~nobody has ever~~ none* of the others have lived my experiences— Im rich—Im rich –

All the same I had no more money than I have now—It's extraordinary how one can live without money—I have quantities of good clothes, silk under clothes—2 evening suits a **smoking** [jacket]—four pairs of patent leather boots with light uppers all sorts of little things—like powder boxes—a manicure set, perfumes—very good soap—and nothing is paid for.[56] If I ~~do really need~~ really find myself in need of cash[57]—well theres always an african laundress + an outhouse—+ I am very frank + bon enfant about the **plenty**[58] **of sugar*** on the little fried cake afterwards————[59]

And here Id like to put something on record. Not ~~with~~ from any **strutting*** conceit but ~~just~~ rather with a mild sense of wonder—Ive never yet made the first advances to any woman—And it isn't as though Ive only known one class of woman—not by any means. But from little prostitutes and kept women and elderly widows and shop girls and wives of respectable men and even advanced modern literary ladies at the most select little dinners + soirees (Ive been there) Ive **invariably*** met with **not only*** the same readiness[60]— with the same positive invitations. It ~~even~~ surprised me ~~sometimes~~ at first. I used to look across the table + think "Is that

[JNPP-rough-NL, leaf 12 recto]

very serious very distinguished young lady talking Ravel[61] with the gentlemen with the beard[62] really pressing my foot under the table—And I was never quite certain until I had pressed hers————Curious—isnt it! Why should I be **able to*** have any woman I want. I don't look at all like a Maidens Dream. [N.L.] I am little + light with an olive skin black eyes with long lashes black silky hair cut short, even[63] square teeth that **show*** when I smile. My hands are supple and small—a woman in a bread shop once said to me you have hands are [sic] making fine little pastries—— and I confess without my clothes I am **rather charming***. Plump almost like a girl with smooth shoulders + I wear a **thin*** gold chain bracelet above my right elbow. [N.P.] But wait! how strange it is[64] I should have written that as unconsciously about my body + so on—It's the result of my "bad life" my "submerged life." I am like a little woman in [a] café who has to introduce herself with a handful of

---

[56] Subsequent versions omit "smoking [jacket]" and add "gloves" before "powder boxes."
[57] Later versions add "right-down" (i.e. "right-down cash").
[58] This word has been written over and is illegible for the most part.
[59] A blot at the end of this line suggests Mansfield may have begun the next sentence on this line, but thought better of it.
[60] The clean version reads: "Ive met invariably with not merely the same readiness" (JNPP-clean-NL, leaf 12).
[61] The clean manuscript replaces "Ravel" (Maurice Ravel), a French composer associated with impressionism and widely known in the 1920s and 1930s, with a French variation of the English author, Rudyard Kipling (i.e. "le Kipling") (JNPP-clean-NL, leaf 12). The latter is retained in the published version.
[62] Later versions add "brown" (i.e. "brown beard").
[63] "Even" becomes "tiny" in later versions.
[64] Subsequent versions read: "Isn't it strange [. . .]."

photographs—"me in my chemise coming out of an eggshell"—"me upside [down] in a swing with a frilly behind like a cauliflower"—you know the things . . . . . .

If you think what Ive written is merely superficial + impudent + cheap you're wrong. Ill admit **it does*** read so but then it is not "all." If it were how **could*** I have experienced what I did when I read that stale little phrase written in green ink in the writing pad? That proves theres more in me + that I really am important. **Doesn't*** it?

[JNPP-rough-NL, leaf 13 recto]

Anything a fraction less than that moment of anguish I might have put on. But no that <u>was</u> real.

"Waiter! A whisky!"

I hate whisky. Every time I take it into my mouth [my] stomach rises against it and the stuff they keep here is sure to be particularly vile.

Ive ordered it because I ~~was~~ ᵃᵐ going to write about an englishman. We french we parisians are incredibly old fashioned and superficial still in some ways.[65] I wonder I did not ask at the same time for a pair of tweed knickerbockers, a pipe, some long teeth + a set of ginger whiskers.

Thanks mon vieux. You havent **got*** perhaps a set of ginger whiskers?

"No Monsieur he answers, ˢᵃᵈˡʸ ʷᵉ ᵈᵒⁿ'ᵗ ˢᵉˡˡ ᵃᵐᵉʳⁱᶜᵃⁿ ᵈʳⁱⁿᵏˢ ~~without the least surprise~~, + having smeared a corner of the table he goes back to have another couple of dozen taken by artificial light.

Ugh! the smell of it! and the sickly sensation when ones throat contracts!

"Its bad stuff to get drunk on" says Dick Harmon, **turning*** his little glass in his fingers + smiling his slow dreaming smile, ~~while~~ ˢᵒ he gets drunk on it slowly + dreamily + at a certain moment begins to sing very low very low ~~something~~ **about a man ~~xxx xxx + xx friend in every xxx xxx~~ about a man who*** walked up and down trying to find some place where he could get some dinner. Ah! **how*** I loved that song + how I loved the way he sang it slowly slowly, in a dark soft voice.

---

[65] Later versions omit "we Parisians" and change "superficial" to "out of date."

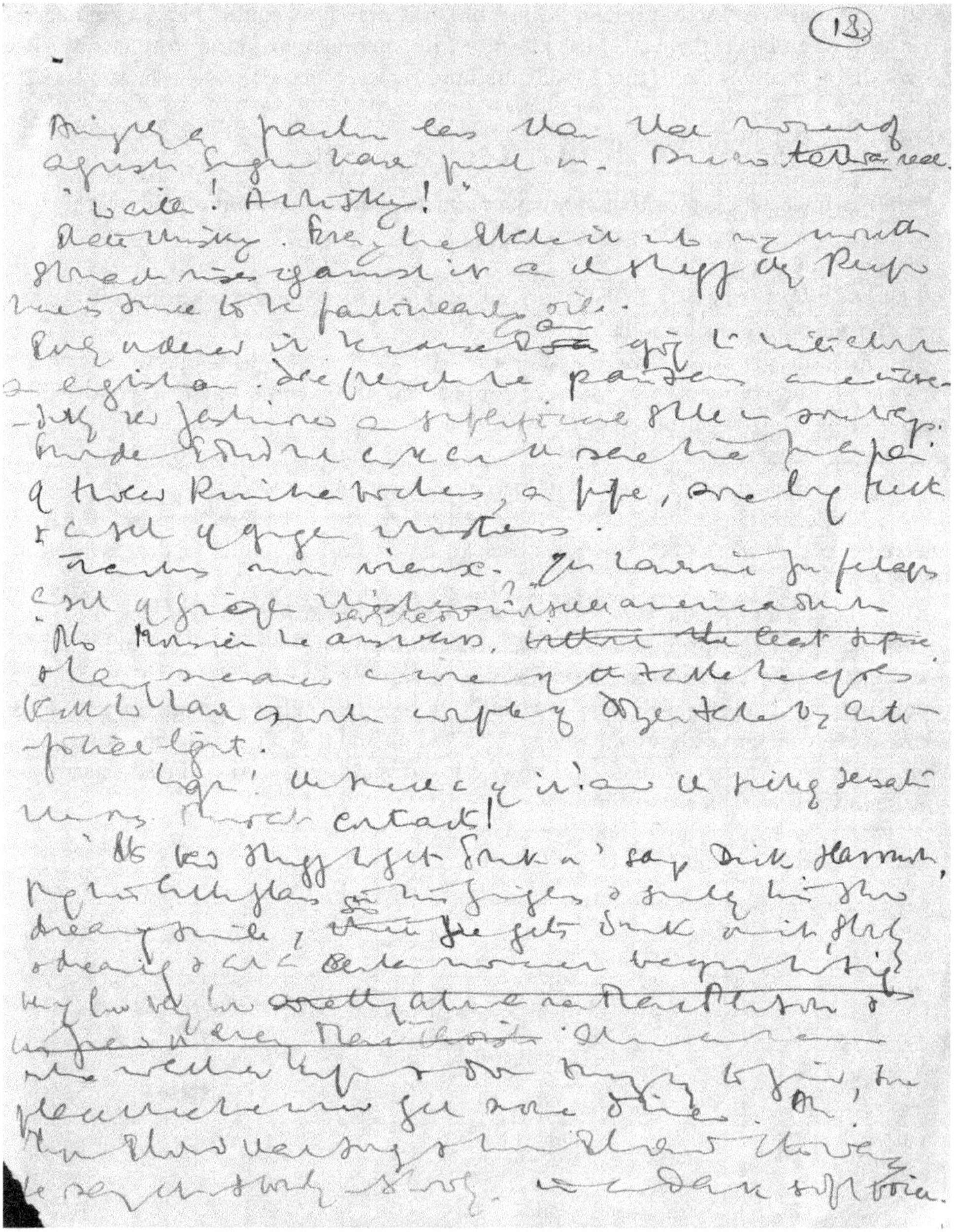

FIGURE 4: Leaf 13 recto, "Je ne parle pas français" [rough manuscript], Katherine Mansfield Papers, Newberry Library, (box 1, folder 27), 16 leaves. Image courtesy of the Newberry Library.

[JNPP-rough-NL, leaf 14 recto]

There was a man
Walked up + down
To get a dinner in the town—town—[66]
It seemed to hold in its gravity + muffled measure all those tall grey **buildings***—those
fogs, those endless streets those sharp[67] shadows of policemen that mean England—And
then the subject. The ~~poor~~ ᴸᵉᵃⁿ starved creature walking up + down—with every house
barred against him because he has <u>no</u> home—how extraordinary english that is! I
remember **it ended*** ~~when~~ʷʰᵉʳᵉ⁶⁸ he did at last find a place—+ ordered a xxx cake of fish
but when he asked for bread the waiter said[69] contemptuously in a low voice we don't
serve bread with a "fish ball." What more do you want! How profound these songs are—
there is the whole pysology [*sic*] in a people—+ ~~w~~how unfrench how unfrench!

Once more Deeck![70] Once more! ~~How~~ I would ~~beg xxx~~ ᵖˡᵉᵃᵈ, **clasping*** my hands +
making ~~my~~ a pretty mouth **at him*** . . . He was perfectly content to sing it for ever——

There again: Even with Deeck[71] it was he who made the first advances. I met him ~~first~~
at an evening given by the editor of a new review. It was a very select, very fashionable
affair! One or two of the older men were there and the ladies were all extremely comme
il faut. They sat on cubist sofas in full evening dress + ~~we handed~~ ᵃˡˡᵒʷᵉᵈ ᵘˢ ᵗᵒ ʰᵃⁿᵈ them
thimbles* of

[JNPP-rough-NL, leaf 15 recto]

cherry brandy + ᵗᵒ talk~~ed about~~ ᵗᵒ them[72] ᵃᵇᵒᵘᵗ ᵗʰᵉⁱʳ poetry ~~to them~~—for as far as I can
remember—they were all poetesses.

It was impossible not to notice Deeck[73] ~~for~~ ⁱⁿ ~~xxx~~ ~~he was~~ ~~besides being~~ ᴴᵉ ʷᵃˢ the only
Englishman present and instead of circulating gracefully round the room as we all did he
stayed in one place, leaning against the wall his hands in his pockets—that dreamy **half
smile on*** his lips—— ~~talking~~ + ʳᵉᵖˡʸⁱⁿᵍ in excellent french in his low soft voice to anybody
who spoke to him.

---

[66] The repetition of "town" is omitted in subsequent versions.
[67] The "sh" and "p" of "sharp" are superimposed over another word, perhaps "dark."
[68] The letters "ere" are superimposed over the last part of "when."
[69] "Said" becomes "cried" in later versions.
[70] The clean manuscript uses "Dick," but "Deeck" is recovered in the published version.
[71] Subsequent versions simply use "Dick."
[72] As it is written, the word could be either "their" or "them." Given the changes in the structure of sentence, it
seems evident that it was initially intended to be "their" but afterwards "them" in the second iteration.
[73] "Deeck" becomes "Dick" in later versions.

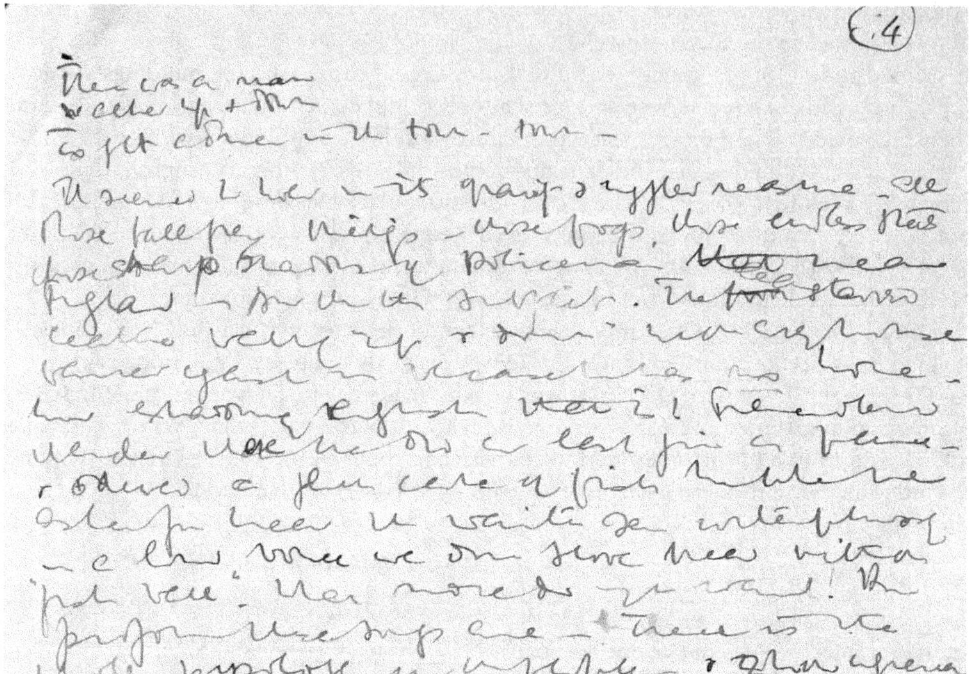

FIGURE 5: Leaf 14 recto, "Je ne parle pas français" [rough manuscript], Katherine Mansfield Papers, Newberry Library, (box 1, folder 27), 16 leaves. Image courtesy of the Newberry Library.

[JNPP-NB14-ATL, page 2 recto][74]

Who is he?

An Englishman ^from London a writer—and hes making a special study of modern french literature—

That was enough for me—+ we had not talked for **more than** a few moments when he suddenly xxx his head and looking at ^My little book False Coins had just been published.75

I was a young serious writer **extremely interested** in modern english literature, but I really hadn't flung my line before he said—giving himself a soft shake as though he **came up** out of water for the bait. But wont you come and see me at my hotel—Come about **five*** oclock + we can talk xxx ~~xxx~~ ^before ^we go **out to dine** ~~sometime~~ ^afternoon

Enchanted—I was so deeply deeply flattered that I had to leave him then and there + ~~preen myself before~~ **somebody** + rush off + preen myself + preen myself before the cubist sofas———

What a catch. An englishman a writer reserved serious making a special study of french literature.76

[JNPP-NB14-ATL, page 3 recto][77]

That same night False Coins with a carefully **cordial*** inscription was posted off + a day or two later we did dine together and spent the evening talking.

Talking but not only of literature—I discovered to my **amazement**, that it wasnt* necessary to ^keep to that tendency of the modern english novel its need of a new form + the reason why our young **men*** appeared to be just missing it and ~~so on—little by little, xxx my way~~ now and again as if ~~xxx~~ by accident **I threw in*** a card that seemed to have nothing to do with the game just to see how hed take it—**But*** each time he ~~swept~~ ^gathered it ~~up~~ into his hand—with his **dreamy***

[JNPP-NB14-ATL, page 4 recto]

look and smile.[78] Perhaps he murmured thats very curious but as though it were not curious at all.

That calm acceptance went to my head at last. It fascinated me.[79] It led me on and on until I ~~simply~~ threw every card I possessed at him—+ sat back + watched him arrange them in his hand. ^"Very curious + interesting."

By this time we were both **fairly*** drunk + he began to sing for the first time his song about the man who walked up + down—I leaned back quite breathless at the

---

[74] Notebook 14 is written in pencil and picks up "Je ne parle pas" when Raoul meets Dick at the party, leaf 15 (of 16) of JNPP-rough-NL, thus the overlap. Because the edits of Notebook 14 appear to have been incorporated into the JNPP-rough-NL, suggesting it was written first, I have opted to place its transcription on the left.

[75] Mansfield has written this on the opposing page, even with this section. This is where it appears in the published version.

[76] An "X" is written at the bottom of the page, and on the facing page a second "X" is written flush with the final lines of this page, where Mansfield adds this passage, a version of which also appears in the published version.

[77] The facing page includes pencil sketches of what appear to be tulips, two wine glasses, a cup and a tea pot.

[78] "Look and smile" is written with a much duller pencil, and it overlays an illegible phrase.

[79] Much of this sentence is superimposed over a previous sentence, using the same dulled pencil. It is difficult to decipher what it is written over, though it appears that Mansfield is—for the most part—merely recopying what was already written, but in a neater hand.

[JNPP-rough-NL, leaf 15 recto, cont'd]

"Who is he?"

An Englishman—from London. A writer. And he is making a special study of modern french literature."

That was enough for me. My little book "False Coins" had just been published.

I was a young serious writer making[80] a special study of modern english literature—

But I really hadn't flung my line before he said ~~x~~ **giving*** him self [*sic*] a soft shake **coming right out*** of the water for the bait, as it were: –

"**Wont*** you come and see me at my hotel—Come about five oclock + we can **have*** a talk before we go out to dinner."

"Enchanted!"

I was so deeply deeply flattered that I had to leave him then + there to rush off + preen and preen myself before the cubist sofas. N.L. What had a catch! An englishman, reserved, serious making a special study of french literature[81] . . . That same night "False Coins" with a carefully cordial **inscription*** was posted off and a day or two later we did dine together + spent the evening talking.

Talking—but not only of literature. I discovered to my relief that it wasnt necessary to

[JNPP-rough-NL, leaf 16 recto]

keep to the tendency of the modern novel, the need of a new form + the reason why our young men appear to be just missing it and so on[82]—Now and then, as if by accident I threw in a card that seemed to have nothing to do with the game just to see how he would take it. But each time he gathered it into his hand with his dreamy look + smile unchanged. **Perhaps*** he murmured: "That's very curious" but not as though it were curious at all—— –

That calm acceptance went to my head at last. It fascinated me. It led me on and on until I threw every card I possessed at him + sat back and watched him arranged them in his hand.

"Very curious + interesting."

By that time we were both **fairly*** drunk and he began to sing his song, very low, very low, about the man who walked up + down seeking his dinner.

But I was quite **breathless at the**

---

[80] Subsequent versions add "who was" (i.e. "who was making a special study").

[81] The clean manuscript adds "modern" (i.e. "modern French literature"); however, the published version omits it.

[82] Subsequent versions omit "and so on."

[JNPP-NB14-ATL, page 5 recto]

the thought of what Id done. ~~For the first time~~ I had shown somebody <u>both sides</u> of my life—I had told him everything as sincerely and truthfully[83] as I could—I['d] **been at immense*** pains to explain things about my submerged life which really were disgusting and never could possibly see the literary light of day. On the whole I had made myself out far worse than I was—more boastful more cynical and calculating + there sat the ~~first~~ man I ~~xxx xxx~~ had[84] **confided*** in, singing to himself and

[JNPP-NB14-ATL, page 6 recto]

smiling*. It moved me so **immensely** that real tears came into my eyes—I saw them in the glass, glittering in my long silky lashes—so ~~pretty~~ charming—_____

~~The delight of that first evening xxx became xxx xxx~~. After that[85] I took ~~him~~ Dick about with me ~~xxx~~everywhere[86] + he came to my ~~appartment~~ flat and sat in the armchair, **very*** indolent playing with the paper knife. I cant think why his

---

[83] "Tru" is retraced over the original word.
[84] "Had" is written in large letters over two words that are illegible.
[85] The opposing page has "after that" written even with this paragraph with a line indicating it should be added at this point.
[86] "Every" of "everywhere" is superimposed onto another, illegible word.

[JNPP-rough-NL, leaf 16 recto cont'd]

thought of what* I had done—I had shown somebody <u>both sides</u> of my life. **Told him*** everything as sincerely + as truthfully as I could. ~~Explained~~ Taken immense pains to explain things about my submerged life which really were disgusting + never could possibly see the literary light of day. **On*** the whole I had made myself out far worse than I was, more boastful, more cynical, more calculating. And there sat the first[87] man I had confided in singing to himself and smiling. It moved me so that real tears came into my eyes. I saw them in the glass, glittering on my long, silky lashes so pretty[88] . . . .

After that ~~Dick~~ I took Dick about with me everywhere—+ he came to my flat + sat in the armchair, very indolent, playing with the paper knife. [NL] I cannot think why his

---

[87] "First" is omitted in later versions.
[88] Subsequent versions use "silk lashes" rather than "silky," and "pretty" becomes "charming," reflecting an edit made in Notebook 14.

[JNPP-NB14-ATL, page 6 recto, cont'd]

indolence and **dreaminess*** always gave me the impression that he had been to sea—

[JNPP-NB14-ATL, page 7 recto]

and all his leisurely slow ways seemed to be allowing for the movement of the ship. Somehow[89] this impression was so strong that often when we were together and he got up + left the little **woman*** just when she didn't expect him to get up + leave her but quite the contrary—I used to explain[90] "he has to go back to his ~~ship~~ ᵇᵃᵇʸ baby [*sic*]! He cant help it."[91] And I believed it far more than she did.

[JNPP-NB14-ATL, page 8 recto]

All[92] the while we were together Dick never went with a woman. I sometimes wondered whether he wasn't completely innocent. Why didn't I ask him. But I didn't ask him anything about himself ever.[93]

Only[94] late one night he took out his pocket book and a photograph dropped out of it. I picked it up + ~~looked~~ ᵍˡᵃⁿᶜᵉᵈ[95] at it before I gave it to him.

It was of a woman. Not[96] quite young, dark handsome **wild*** looking but so ~~filled~~ ᶠᵘˡˡ[97] in every line of her xxx a haggard ~~xxxx~~ pride ˣˣˣ ˣˣˣ[98]

[JNPP-NB14-ATL, page 9 recto]

that if ᵉᵛᵉⁿ if [*sic*] Dicks hand[99] had not stretched out so quick I would not have looked longer—Out of my sight you little **perfumed*** foxterrier of a frenchman said she. (In my very worst moments my nose reminds me of a foxterriers) That's my mother said Dick putting up the pocketbook. Ah, ha! She is beautiful—but if he had not been Dick I should have been tempted to cross myself just for fun—

X ᵀʰⁱˢ ʷᵃˢ ʰᵒʷ ʷᵉ ᵖᵃʳᵗᵉᵈ[100] ~~Thxx xxx just xxx xxx~~ as we stood outside his hotel one night waiting for the concierge to release the catch of the

---

[89] "Somehow" is omitted in later versions.

[90] "I used to explain" becomes "I would explain" in later versions.

[91] Subsequent versions invert these two clauses: "'He can't help it, Baby. He has to go back to his ship'" (CW2, 120–121).

[92] Mansfield retraces "All."

[93] This last sentence becomes: "Because I never did ask him anything about himself" (JNPP-clean-NL, leaf 18).

[94] "Only" becomes "but" in later versions.

[95] The change is written in ink, while the rest is in pencil.

[96] "Not" is retraced in ink.

[97] "Full" is in ink, as is the strikethrough of "filled."

[98] The last addition is written below the final line of the page in ink.

[99] "Dick's hand" becomes simply "Dick" (i.e. "if Dick had not stretched [. . .]").

[100] An "X" is written at the beginning of this line. Likewise, on the opposing page, Mansfield has written "X This was how we parted," indicating that it was to be inserted here.

[JNPP-NB14-ATL, page 10 recto]

outer door he said looking up at the sky ~~he said I say~~[101] I hope it will be fine tomorrow. I am leaving for England in the morning.

Youre not serious

Perfectly—I have to get back. Ive ~~got~~[102] some work to do that I cant manage here—

But have you made all your preparations?

Preparations? ~~He whispered and~~ almost grinned I've none to make—

But ~~don't you xxx~~ ~~through a plan even~~ enfin Dick England is not on the other side of the Boulevard.

But it is not much further off said he ~~xxx xxx xxx~~ ˣˣˣ Its only a few hours, you know.

[JNPP-NB14-ATL, page 11 recto]

The door cracked open. Ah I wish Id known at the beginning of the evening—I felt hurt. I felt like a **woman must*** feel when the man takes out his watch and remembers an appointment that cannot possibly concern her except ~~so far as it is xxx~~ that its claim is the stronger. Why didnt you tell me—He put out his hand—+ stood lightly swaying on the doorstep[103] as though the whole hotel were his ship + the anchor was ~~just taken up~~ weighed104—I forgot. Truly I did. But you [sic] write wont you—**Good night*** old **man.**[105] ~~After~~ Ill be over again one of these days.

[JNPP-NB14-ATL, page 12 recto]

And then I stood on the shore alone[106] more like a foxterrier than ever — —[107]

But after all—it was you who whistled to me—you who asked **me to come***—what a spectacle Ive cut wagging my tail + leaping around you only to be left like this while the boat sails off in this[108] slow **dreamy*** way—

Curse these english! No, ~~that is~~ ˣˣˣ too insolent altogether. Who does he imagine I am?[109] ~~to xxx off like that.~~[110] A little paid guide to the night pleasures of Paris?

[JNPP-NB14-ATL, page 13 recto]

No Monsieur I am a young man,[111] very serious and extremely interested in Modern English literature and I have been insulted insulted—

---

[101] The deletion is in ink.

[102] The deletion is in ink.

[103] "Doorstep" becomes "step" in later versions.

[104] The cross out is in ink, as is the added "weighed."

[105] Later versions read "old chap" instead of "old man."

[106] "Alone" is superimposed on another word, possibly also "alone."

[107] A short piece of clear tape is centered vertically near the top of the page, though there does not appear to be a tear.

[108] "This" becomes "its" in later versions.

[109] The question mark is in ink. Later versions read: "Who do you imagine I am?"

[110] The double strike-through is in ink.

[111] "Man" is changed to "writer" in subsequent versions.

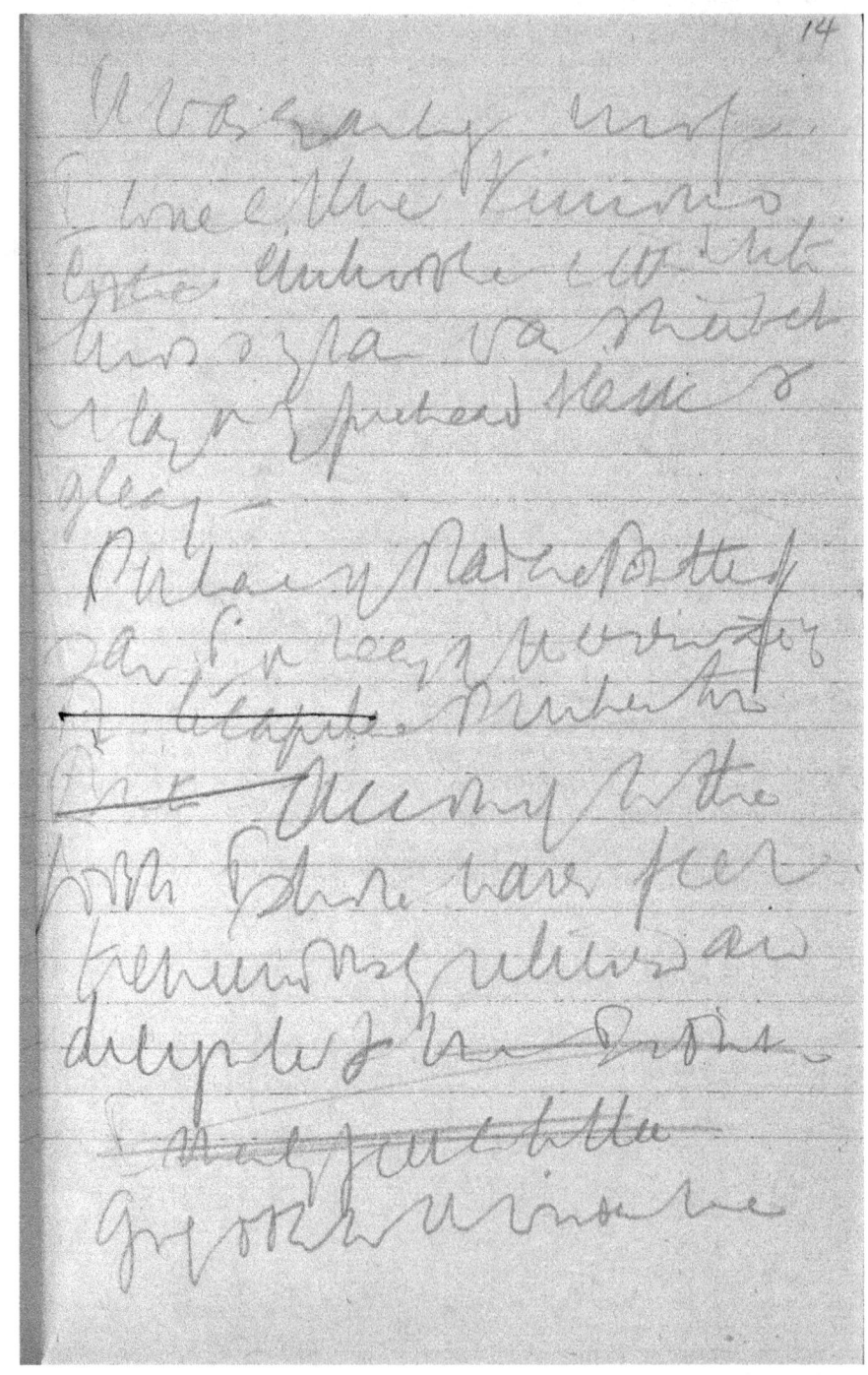

FIGURE 6: Page 14 recto, Notebook 14, "Mouse ["Je ne parle pas français"]," Writings and Personal Papers of Katherine Mansfield, Alexander Turnbull Library, (MS-Group-0038, qMS-1259), 40 pages. Image courtesy of the Alexander Turnbull Library.

Two days later came a long charming letter from him written in French that was just a shade too French—but saying how ~~much~~[112] he missed me and how he counted on our friendship[113] **xx on keeping in touch*** ~~and~~ and[114] [*sic*]—I read it standing in front of the ~~long mirror in~~ the unpaid for wardrobe ^{mirror.}[115]

[JNPP-NB14-ATL, page 14 recto]

It was early morning. I wore a blue Kimono ~~covered~~ embroidered with white birds + my hair was still wet. It lay on my forehead black + gleaming—
    Portrait of Madame Butterfly said I on hearing of the arrival of ~~Mr le capitain~~ ^{ce cher}[116] Pinkerton.
    ~~But~~ According to the books I should have felt tremendously relieved and delighted + ~~but I didn't—I mainly felt a little~~ Going **over to the window he***

[JNPP-NB14-ATL, page 15 recto]

drew the curtains + looked out on to the ~~little~~ ^{Paris} trees just **breaking*** into green.[117] Dick! Dick! My English friend.
    But ~~he~~ [I] didn't. ~~He~~ [I] merely felt a little sick[118]—~~After~~ ^{Having*}[119] been ^{as it were} for my[120] first ride in an aeroplane ~~he~~ [I] didn't want to go up ~~so high~~ again just now—~~The~~ **passion** ~~was~~
    That passed and months after in the winter ~~he~~ ^{Dick}[121] **wrote that*** he was coming back to Paris **to*** stay indefinitely. Would I take

[JNPP-NB14-ATL, page 16 recto][122]

rooms for him? He was bringing a woman friend.[123] Of course I would. Away the little foxterrier ran.[124] It happened most usefully too, for ~~at the little~~ I owed too much money at the ~~little~~ hotel where I took my meals + two english people **requiring*** 2 rooms for an indefinite period was an excellent ~~little~~ sum on account.
    Perhaps I did rather

---

[112] The strike out is in ink.
[113] Subsequent versions read: "[. . .] saying how much he missed me and counted on our friendship [. . .]."
[114] The first "and" is struck through in ink.
[115] The strike out is in ink, and a line after "wardrobe" directs one to "mirror" written below it, also in ink.
[116] "Ce cher" is written in ink on the opposing page, even with this line.
[117] The clean manuscript changes "drew the curtains" to "drew apart the curtains" and revises "looked out on to the Paris trees" to "looked out at the Paris trees" (JNPP-clean-NL, leaf 20).
[118] The "I" is written in ink over "he" in both instances.
[119] While it isn't clear, it appears that "Having" has been written over "After."
[120] "My" is written in ink over what appears to be "his."
[121] "Dick" is superimposed over what looks to be "he."
[122] On the opposing page, Mansfield has sketched four flowers of various types.
[123] Subsequent versions add "with him" at the end of the sentence.
[124] "Ran" becomes "flew" in later versions.

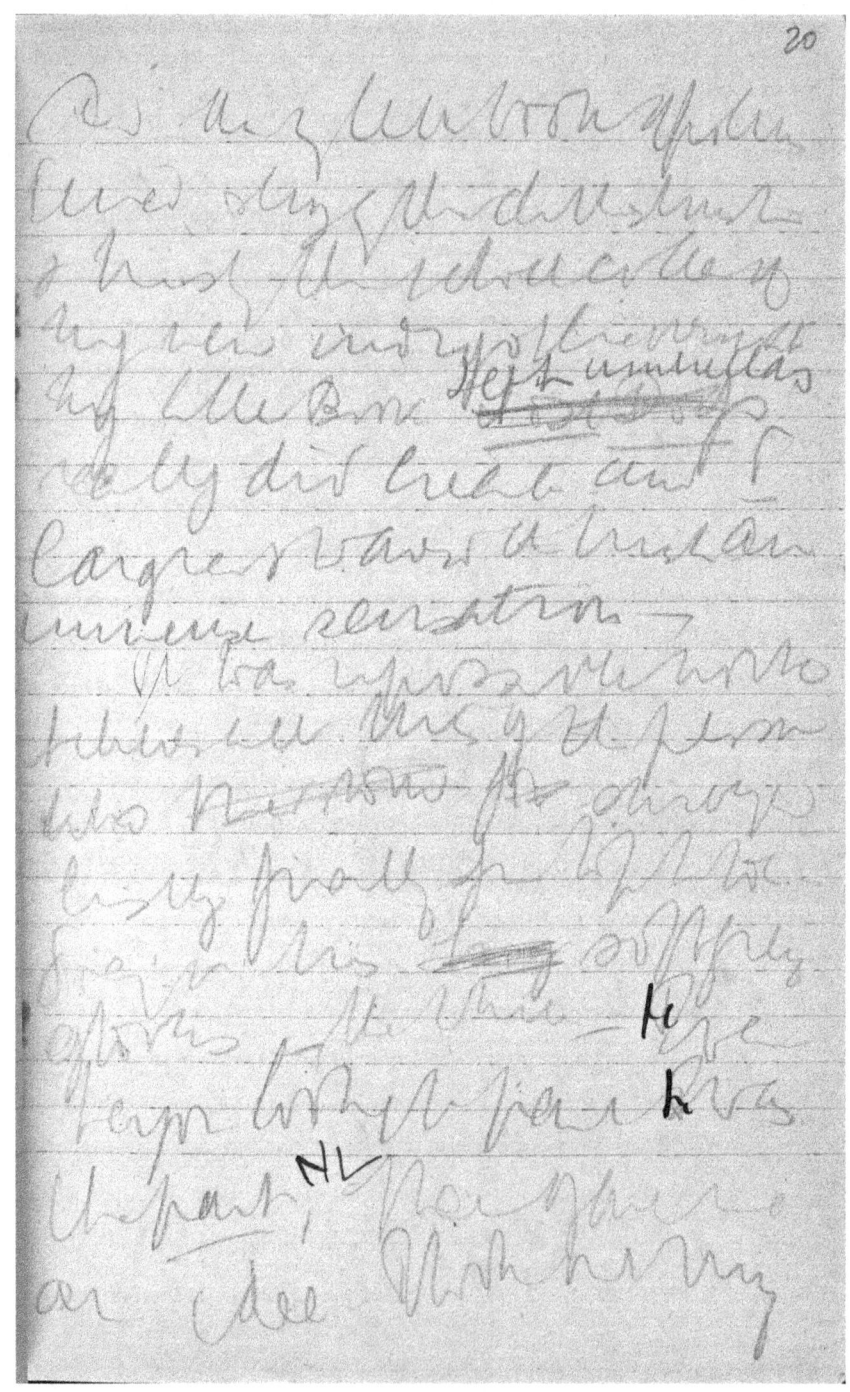

FIGURE 7: Page 20 recto, Notebook 14, "Mouse ["Je ne parle pas français"]," Writings and Personal Papers of Katherine Mansfield, Alexander Turnbull Library, (MS-Group-0038, qMS-1259), 40 pages. Image courtesy of the Alexander Turnbull Library.

[JNPP-NB14-ATL, page 17 recto][125]

wonder as I stood in the larger of the **two**[126] rooms saying ["]admirable["] to Madame. What the woman friend would be like—but only vaguely. Either she would be very **severe**, flat back + front with a nose that never kissed a powder puff or she would be tall, fair, dressed in mignonette,[127] name Daisy + smelling of rather **sweetish*** lavender water—

You see by this time, according to my rule of never looking

[JNPP-NB14-ATL, page 18 recto]

~~xxx~~ back128—Id almost forgotten Dick.[129]

=== | ===

I even got the tune of his song about the unfortunate man a little bit wrong when I tried to hum it![130]

[JNPP-NB14-ATL, page 19 recto]

Chapter II.

~~After all~~ I very nearly did not turn up at the station after all. I had arranged to and ~~in~~ had in131 fact ~~had~~ dressed with particular care for the occasion. **For*** I **intended*** to take a new line with Dick this time.NL.132 No more confidences + tears on eyelashes—~~No, I was~~ No thank you.

"Since you left Paris["] said I **knotting*** my black **silver*** spotted tie in the (also unpaid for) mirror over the mantlepiece. I have been very successful you know. I have 2 more books in preparation + then I have written a serial story "Wrong Doors" which is just on the point of being published + **will bring me in a good bit of money**.[133]

[JNPP-NB14-ATL, page 20 recto]

And then my little book **of poems*** I cried **seizing*** the clothes brush + brushing the velvet collar of my new indigo-blue overcoat. My little Book [sic] ~~Lost Dogs~~ Left Umbrellas really did create [–] and I laughed + waved the brush [–] an immense sensation—

It was impossible **not to believe*** all[134] this of the person who ~~turned round for~~ **surveyed*** himself finally from top to toe **drawing*** on his ~~xxx~~ **soft grey*** gloves—the

---

[125] The opposing page has what appear to be two tulips, one flowering and the other a bud, with a circled "X" between. There is a short phrase I'm unable to decipher.

[126] "Two" is omitted in the clean manuscript, but it is reinserted in the published version.

[127] Later versions add "green" (i.e. "mignonette green").

[128] "Back" is written over an illegible word.

[129] A line is drawn from the end of this line to the next section. A thick vertical line with several horizontal lines is drawn between the two sections.

[130] Following this is a heavily marked asterisk within a diamond shape. This also marks the end of the clean version of the manuscript.

[131] "Had" is written over what appears to be "in," and the added "in" is on the opposite page, adjacent. All of the corrections are in ink, including the strike through of the following "had."

[132] "NL" is in ink.

[133] The published version reads: "[. . .] on the point of publication and will bring me in a lot of money" (CW2, 122–123).

[134] "All" is omitted in the published version.

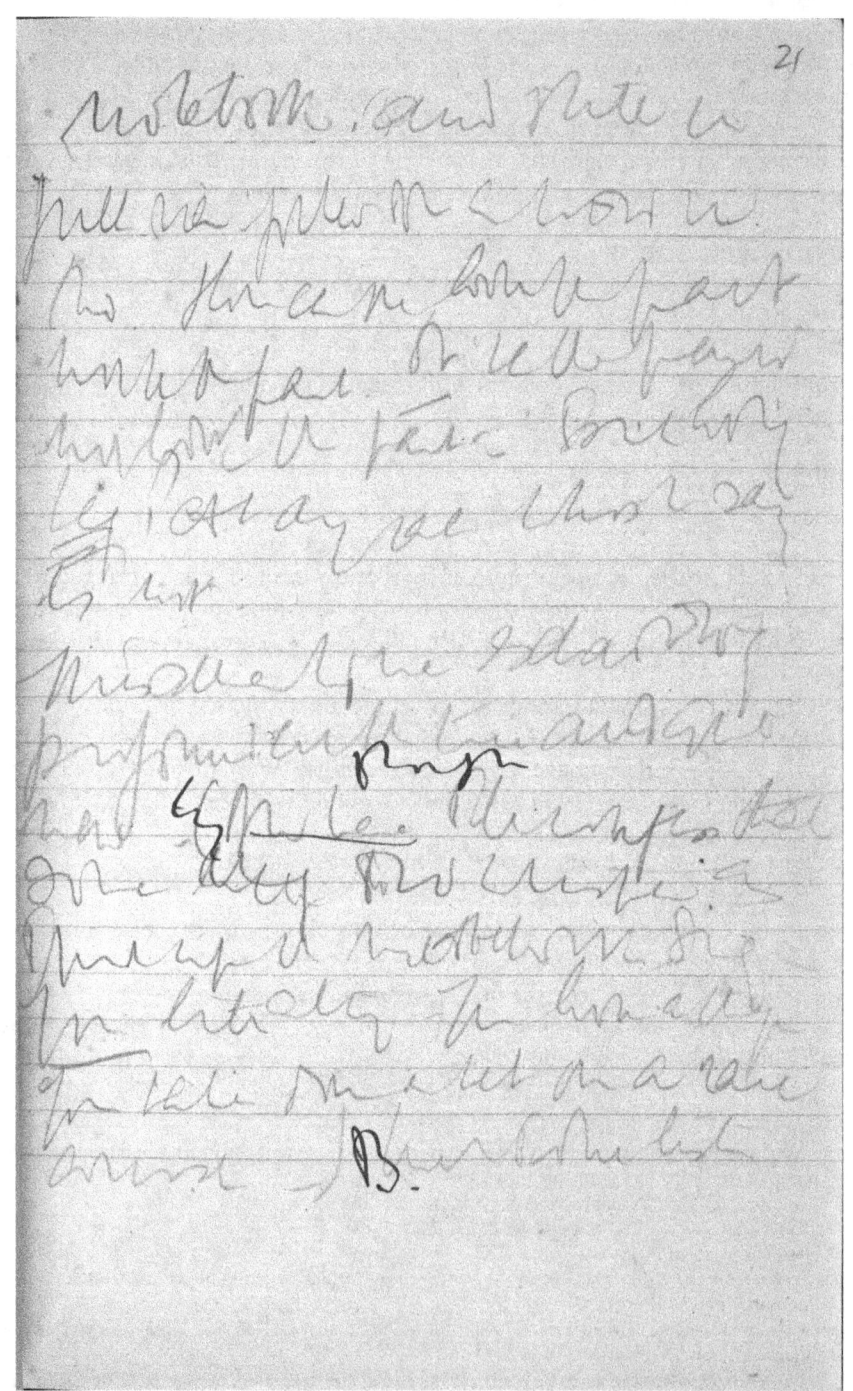

FIGURE 8: Page 21 recto, Notebook 14, "Mouse ["Je ne parle pas français"]," Writings and Personal Papers of Katherine Mansfield, Alexander Turnbull Library, (MS-Group-0038, qMS-1259), 40 pages. Image courtesy of the Alexander Turnbull Library.

while—~~Ive~~ ^{he} **begun** looking the part ~~I~~ ^{he} was the <u>part</u>,^{135 NL} that gave me an idea. I took out my

[JNPP-NB14-ATL, page 21 recto]

notebook and still in full view **jotted down a note or two***. How can one look the part + not be the part. Or be the part + not look the part.¹³⁶ Isnt **looking*** <u>being</u>?¹³⁷ At any rate who is to say its not.

This **seemed to me extraordinarily*** profound at the time and quite new. (~~But here~~ ^{though} I confess that some ~~xxx~~ ^{thing*138} did whisper as¹³⁹ I put up the **notebook*** saying¹⁴⁰ <u>You literary—You look as though **you've*** taken down a bet on a race course</u> –) ~~b~~But I didnt listen.¹⁴¹

[JNPP-NB14-ATL, page 22 recto]

I ~~went out~~ ^{went out142} **shutting the door*** ~~xxx~~ ^{of the} ~~flat~~ ^{flat143} with a ~~light~~ ^{soft} quick pull so as not to warn the concierge of my departure + ~~running~~ ran¹⁴⁴ down the stairs light as a rabbit for the same reason.

But ah! the old spider! She was too quick for me. She let me run down the last little ladder of the web and then she pounced—

One moment—one little moment **Monsieur*** she **whispered*** odiously confidential. Come in come in—+ she **beckoned*** with a dripping soup ladle.

[JNPP-NB14-ATL, page 23 recto]

I went to the door but that wasnt good enough. Xxx right inside and the door shut—before she would speak.

There are two ways of managing your concierge if you havent any money—One is—take [the] high hand—make her your enemy—bluster refuse to discuss anything + the other is to keep in with her—butter her up to the two knots of the ^{black} handkerchiefs ~~tied over her ears~~ ^{tying up her} ~~head~~ ^{jaws145}—pretend to confide in her—+ rely upon her to arrange with the gas man for you¹⁴⁶ + put off the landlord.

---

¹³⁵ The *Collected* omits "the while" and changes the sentence structure to "He was looking the part; he was the part" (CW2, 123). The inserted "he" in both textual revisions is in ink, superimposed over "I"; following this line Mansfield as written "NL," also in ink.

¹³⁶ "+ not look the part" becomes "and not look it" in the *Collected*.

¹³⁷ At this point, the published version adds: "Or being—looking?" (CW2, 123).

¹³⁸ Both "though" and "thing" are added in ink. "Though" becomes "but" in the *Collected*.

¹³⁹ The *Collected* adds "smiling" here: "[. . .] something did whisper as, smiling, I put up the notebook" (CW2, 123).

¹⁴⁰ "Saying" is omitted in the *Collected*.

¹⁴¹ The capital "B" is superimposed in ink over the original "b."

¹⁴² "Went out" is retraced in a duller pencil.

¹⁴³ "Flat" is retraced.

¹⁴⁴ "Ran" is written in ink.

¹⁴⁵ This addition is written in pencil on the opposing page, aligned with this section. "Head" is crossed out and "jaws" added in ink.

¹⁴⁶ "For you" is omitted in the *Collected*.

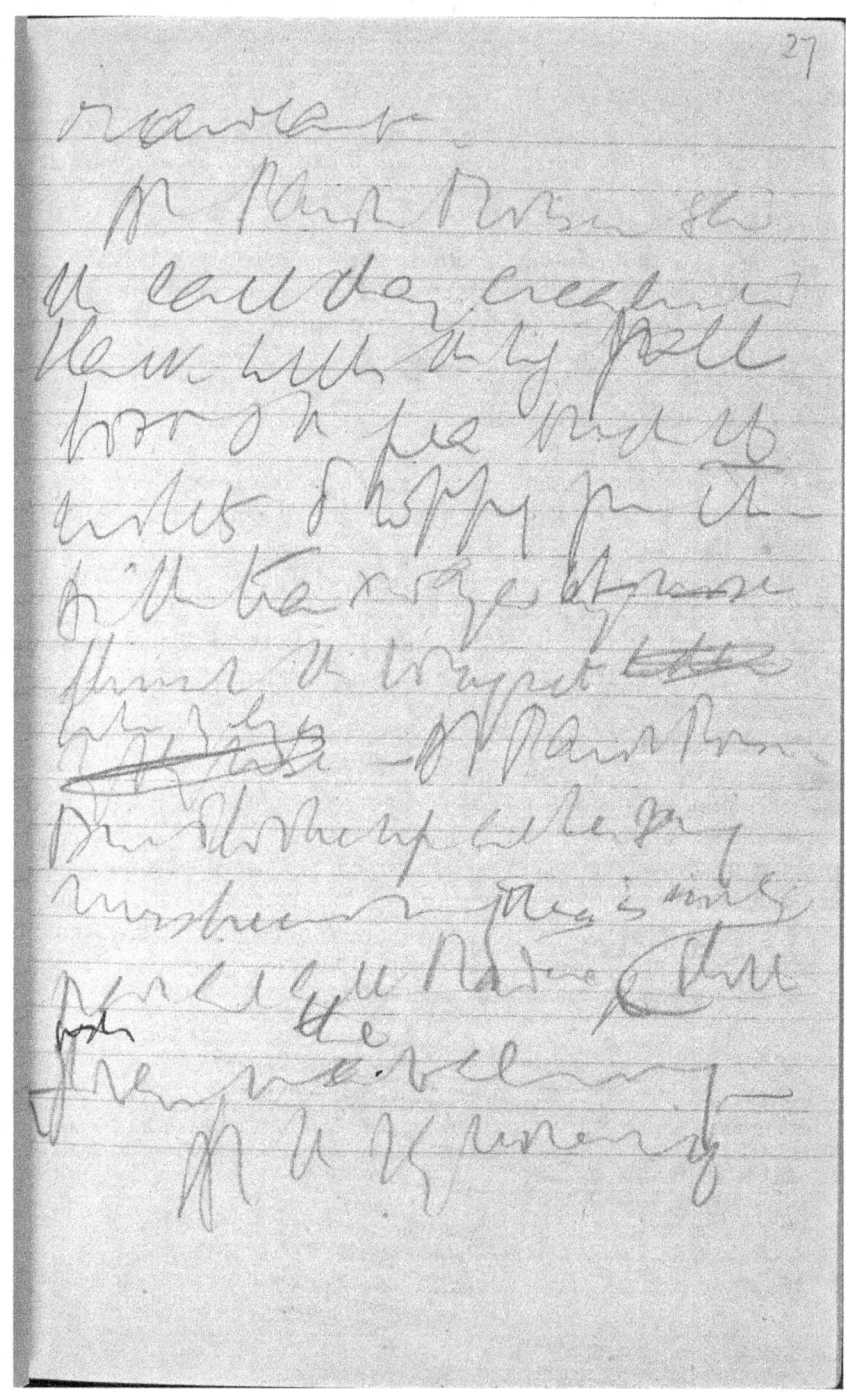

FIGURE 9: Page 27 recto, Notebook 14, "Mouse ["Je ne parle pas français"]," Writings and Personal Papers of Katherine Mansfield, Alexander Turnbull Library, (MS-Group-0038, qMS-1259), 40 pages. Image courtesy of the Alexander Turnbull Library.

[JNPP-NB14-ATL, page 24 recto]

I had tried the second **with her,**[147] but both are equally detestable and unsuccessful.

At any rate whichever one you are trying ~~at the time~~[148] is the worse[,] is the impossible one—It was the landlord this time. Imitation of the landlord by the concierge threatening to toss me out. Imitation of the concierge by the concierge ~~studying~~ ᵗᵃᵐⁱⁿᵍ* the wild bull. **Imitation of the*** landlord **rampant*** again

[JNPP-NB14-ATL, page 25 recto]

breathing in the concierge's face (I was the concierge) No it was too nauseous—And all the while the black pot on the gas ring bubbling away—stewing out the hearts + livers of every tenant in the place—

Ah I cried **staring*** at the clock on the mantlepiece + then seeing[149] that it didnt go—striking my forehead ~~at the same time~~ as though the ~~xxx~~ ⁱᵈᵉᵃ[150] had nothing to do with it—

[JNPP-NB14-ATL, page 26 recto]

Madame I shall be late.[151] I have a very important appointment with the director of my newspaper at 9.30 tonight. Perhaps tomorrow I shall be able to give you—

Out! Out! And down the metro and squeezed into a full carriage. The more the ~~merrier~~ ᵇᵉᵗᵗᵉʳ! ~~Everyone was xxx xxx xxx xxx xxx xxx more between me and~~* ~~the concierge~~ ᴱᵛᵉʳʸ/ᵇᵒᵈʸ ⁱˢ ᵒⁿᵉ ᵇᵒˡˢᵗᵉʳ ᵗʰᵉ ᵐᵒʳᵉ ᵇᵉᵗʷᵉᵉⁿ ᵐᵉ + ᵗʰᵉ ᶜᵒⁿᶜⁱᵉʳᵍᵉ.[152]—I was

[JNPP-NB14-ATL, page 27 recto]

radiant*.

Ah **Pardon Monsieur said the tall charming*** creature in black with the big full bosom + a **great*** bunch of violets dropping from it—As the train swayed ~~my nose~~ ⁱᵗ[153] thrust the bouquet ~~under my very nose~~ ⁱⁿᵗᵒ ᵐʸ ᵉʸᵉˢ[154]—Ah Pardon Monsieur—But I looked up at her **saying**[155] mischievously ["]there is **nothing*** xxx at all Madame, I love[156] ᵐᵒʳᵉ ᵗʰᵃⁿ[157] flowers ˣˣˣ[158] on ~~a~~ ᵗʰᵉ balcony—["]

At **the very moment of***

---

[147] The *Collected* leaves out "with her."

[148] The deletion is in ink.

[149] The *Collected* replaces "seeing" with "realizing."

[150] "Idea" is written in ink over the previous word.

[151] "I shall be late" is left out of the *Collected*.

[152] Mansfield has written this addition in ink on the opposing page.

[153] "It" is written over "my."

[154] The published version reads: "[. . .] right into my eyes" (CW2, 124).

[155] "Saying" becomes "smiling" in the final version.

[156] A line indicates that this section is to be moved, following "nothing."

[157] "More than" is written on the opposing page, aligned with this section. The placement here follows the *Collected*.

[158] This is written in ink.

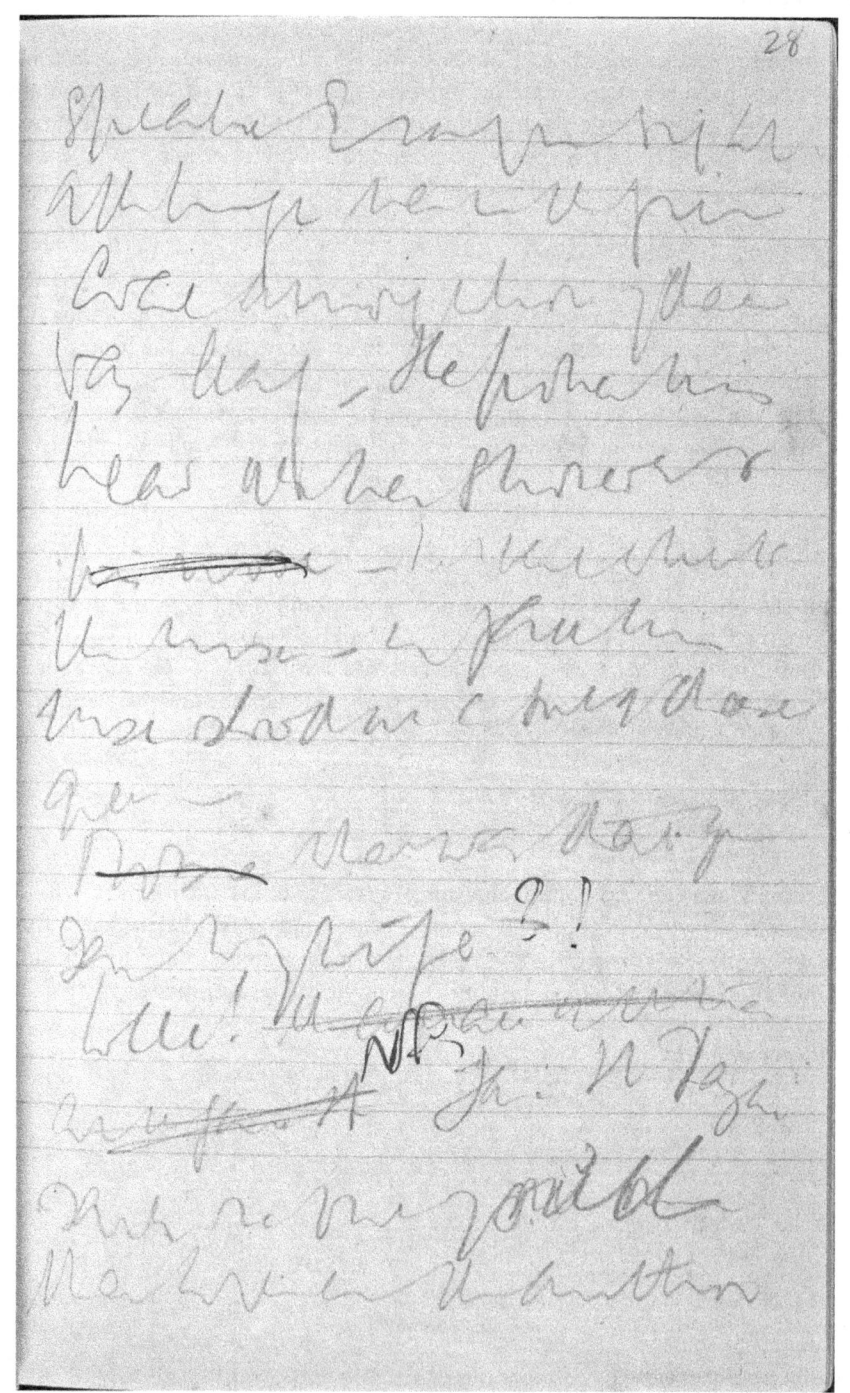

FIGURE 10: Page 28 recto, Notebook 14, "Mouse ["Je ne parle pas français"]," Writings and Personal Papers of Katherine Mansfield, Alexander Turnbull Library, (MS-Group-0038, qMS-1259), 40 pages. Image courtesy of the Alexander Turnbull Library.

[JNPP-NB14-ATL, page 28 recto]

speaking I caught sight of the huge man in the fur coat among[159] whom my **charmer*** was leaning—He poked his head over her shoulder + ~~his nose~~[160]—he went white to the nose—in fact his nose stood out a **sort*** of cheese green—

~~Monsieur~~ what was that you said to my wife—?![161]

Well! ~~It appeared we were at a face off~~. N.P. Gare St Lazare saved me but ~~you own~~ you'll [own][162] that even as the author

[JNPP-NB14-ATL, page 29 recto][163]

of False Coins, Wrong Doors + Left Umbrellas (+ 2 in preparation) it wasnt too easy to go on my triumphant way.

164

[JNPP-rough-NL, leaf 16 verso]

(continued from same sign in **buff** note book)[165]

~~You **may** have many lives like trains coming in as you wait at a station.~~

At length after countless trains had steamed into my mind, emptied[166] + countless Dick Harmons had come rolling softly[167] towards me the real train came—~~t~~The ˣˣˣ little **knot*** of us, waiting at the barrier moved up close **craned forward*** + **broke into*** ~~little~~ cries + as though we were some kind of many headed beast[168] and Paris behind us was[169] nothing but a great trap we had set to catch these sleepy innocents. ~~Yet they came—~~ NL. Into* the trap they walked + were snatched + taken off to be devoured. Where was my prey?

Good God! My smile + my lifted hand fell together—**For one*** terrible moment I thought this was ~~Dicks mother~~ the woman of the photograph. Dicks **mother walking towards*** me, in Dicks hat and coat.[170] In the effort ~~he made to~~ (and you saw what an effort it was to smile) his lips **curled*** in just xxx xxx way + he made for me, haggard

---

[159] "Among" is replaced with "against" in the *Collected*.

[160] The strike-through is in ink.

[161] The deletion and final two punctuation marks are in ink.

[162] "You'll" is written over "you own."

[163] The verso of page twenty-eight has a seemingly unrelated passage about insects running away or towards one. See Scott, *Notebooks* 2, 145.

[164] A circled "X" directs one to JNPP-rough-NL, leaf 16 verso. Following this is a brief passage dated 7 February, quoted in Scott, *Notebooks* 2, 145. Below that is another short passage that is not included in Scott: "xxx + Murry / The xxx of the flies in the air the green sea + the **fishes** in xxxxx."

[165] A circled "x" is the sign indicated, and the like sign appears on page 29 of Notebook 14, which is a tan color (i.e. "buff"). The story is continued on the verso of the pages of the rough manuscript, in reverse order.

[166] "Emptied" is omitted in the published version.

[167] The final version eliminates "softly."

[168] "Beast" becomes "monster" in the published version.

[169] Something illegible is written over "was."

[170] The published version inverts "hat and coat."

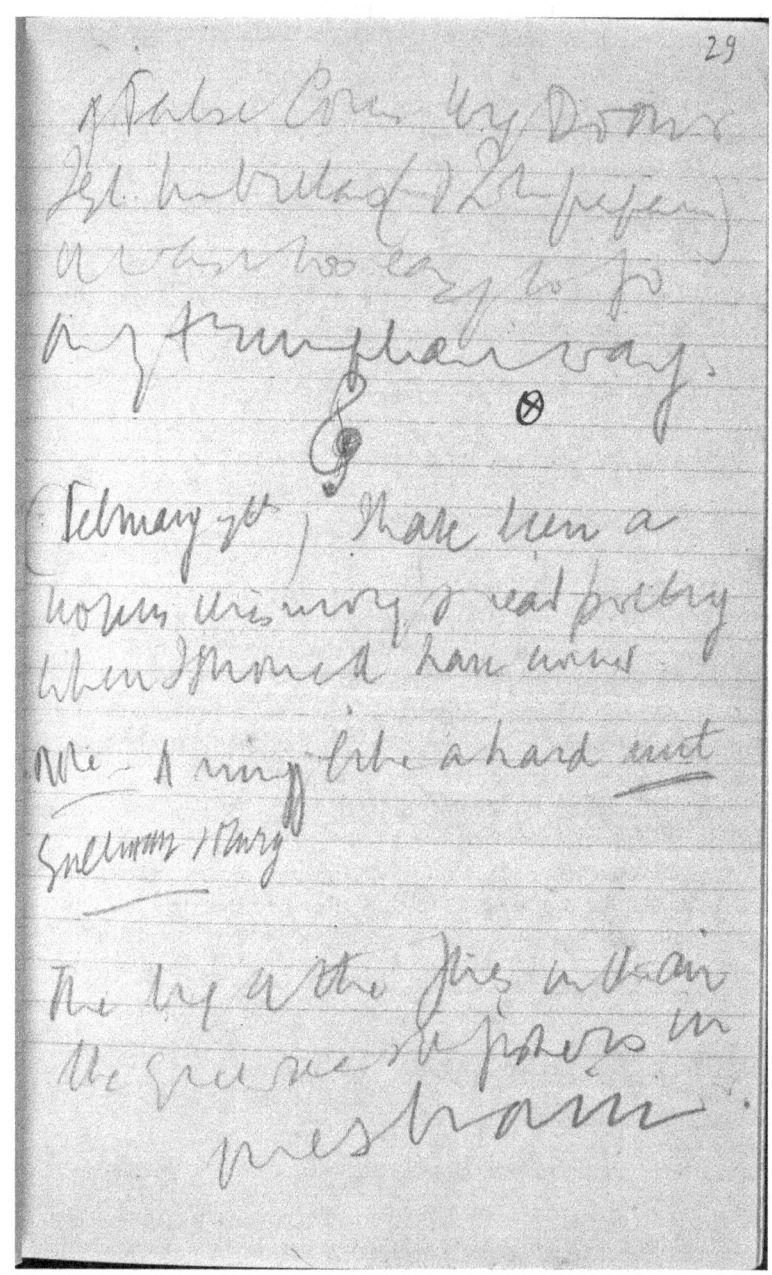

FIGURE 11: Page 29 recto, Notebook 14, "Mouse ["Je ne parle pas français"]," Writings and Personal Papers of Katherine Mansfield, Alexander Turnbull Library, (MS-Group-0038, qMS-1259), 40 pages. Image courtesy of the Alexander Turnbull Library.

+wild + proud. What had happened?[171] What **on earth**[172] could have changed him like this? Should I mention it? I waited for him + was even conscious of **venturing*** a fox terrier wag or two—to see if he could possibly respond in

[JNPP-rough-NL, leaf 15 verso]

in [*sic*] the way I said—

"Good Evening Dick. How are you old chap? Alright?"

~~Thanks~~ "Alright! Alright!" He almost gasped. "Youve got the rooms?"

Twenty times* Good! God! I saw it all. Light broke on the dark water ^{and my sailor hadn't been drowned.} + I almost turned a somersault with amusement.

It was nervous^{ness of course}. It was embarrassment. It was the famous english seriousness. Ah[173] what fun I was going to have! I could have **hugged*** him.

"Yes ~~of course~~ Ive got the rooms ^{I said nearly shouted}. But where is xxx Madame –

"Shes been looking after the luggage.["] He panted. ["]Here she comes now –["]

Not this baby walking beside the old porter as though he were her nurse + had just lifted her out of her ugly perambulator while **he*** ~~wheeled~~ ^{trundled} it—^{boxes on it!174} [*sic*]

And she's not Madame said Dick. ^{drawling suddenly.175}

At that moment she caught sight **of him** + **hailed*** with her minute muff.

She broke away from her old[176] nurse + ran ~~to Dick~~ ^{up} + said **something*** very quick, in English, but he replied in French.

Oh alright[177] Ill manage. But before he **turned*** to the porter he indicated me with a vague wave ~~of the hand~~ + muttered something. We were introduced. She **held out*** her hand

[JNPP-rough-NL, leaf 14 verso]

in that strange boyish way english women do—+ standing very straight in front of me with her chin raised—+ **obviously**[178] making [–] she too—the effort of her life to control her preposterous **excitement*** she said—~~almost~~ **wringing*** my hand—I'm sure she did not know it was mine! Je ne parle pas français—

"But I'm sure you do!" I answered, so tender **so reassuring***—I might have been a dentist about to pull[179] her first little milk tooth—

"Of course she does" Dick **swerved*** back to us. "Here cant we get a cab or a taxi or something. We don't want to stay in this cursed station **all night*** Do we?" ^{NL} This was so **rude*** that it took me a minute[180] to recover + he must have noticed for he flung his arm

---

¹⁷¹ In the right-hand margin, there is a small drawing of what looks like a shirt.

¹⁷² The final version eliminates "on earth."

¹⁷³ "Ah" is left out of the final version.

¹⁷⁴ "Boxes on it" is in a darker ink. The published version reads: "[. . .] while he trundled the boxes on it" (CW2, 125).

¹⁷⁵ "Drawling suddenly" is in a darker ink, following the period. A small circle or "O" appears in the righthand margin.

¹⁷⁶ "Old" is omitted in the final version.

¹⁷⁷ "Alright" becomes "very well" in the published version.

¹⁷⁸ The final version omits "obviously."

¹⁷⁹ "Pull" becomes "draw" in the final version.

¹⁸⁰ "Minute" becomes "moment" in the published version.

across[181] my shoulder **in the old*** way—saying—~~O~~Ah forgive me, old chap. But weve had a xxx journey and loathsome **hideous*** journey[182]—~~haven't we~~ weve taken years + years coming **haven't*** we—to her

But she did not answer ~~she bent~~ ^{bent} her ~~head~~ ^{head} + began stroking her grey muff. ~~She waited beside xxx constantly stroking her grey muff~~ hand all the while—[183]

Good Heavens! thought I.[184] Have I been wrong? Is this simply a case of frenzied impatience on their part—Are they merely in need of a bed as we say? Have they been suffering agonies on the journey? Sitting perhaps

[JNPP-rough-NL, leaf 13 verso]

very close and warm under the same traveling rug—+ so on and so on while the driver strapped on the boxes—That done:

"Look here Dick. I go home by metro. Here is the address of your hotel. Everything is arranged. Come + see me as soon as you can."

Upon my life. I thought he was going to faint. He was **white*** to [the] lips—

"But youre **coming*** back with us he ~~said~~ ^{cried}—I thought it was all settled. Of course youre **coming*** youre not going to leave us!

No. I gave it up—it was too difficult, too english for me.

Certainly certainly. **Delighted***—I only thought perhaps! You <u>must</u> come said Dick to the foxterrier[185] + again he made that **big*** awkward turn towards her—

"Get in Mouse."

And Mouse crept[186] into the black hole ~~stroking it~~ + sat in the corner stroking Mouse II + not saying a word.

Away we jolted and rattled like 3 little dice that Life had decided to have a fling with. I had insisted on taking the flap seat facing them because I would not have missed

[JNPP-rough-NL, leaf 12 verso]

for anything those occasional flashing glimpses I had as we broke through the white circles of lamplight.

^{NP} They revealed Dick, sitting far back in his corner his coat collar **turned*** up his hands thrust deep in his pockets and his broad dark hat shading him as if it were part of him—**a sort*** of wing that he hid under—~~It~~ ^{they} showed her sitting up very straight—her **lovely little face*** more like a **drawing*** than a ^{real} face: ~~It~~ ^{every line} was so ~~sharp cut + severe so~~ full of meaning[187] and so sharp cut against the ~~surrounding~~ ^{swimming} dark.

---

[181] "Across" is replaced with "round" in the published version.
[182] The published version simply reads: "But we've had such a loathsome, hideous journey" (CW2, 125).
[183] The final version reads: "[. . .] she walked beside us stroking her grey muff all the way" (CW2, 125).
[184] The published version omits this exclamatory phrase.
[185] The final version adds "little" (i.e. "little fox-terrier").
[186] The published version substitutes "got" for "crept."
[187] "Full of meaning" is circled, and a line indicates it is to be placed after "every line was so [. . .]."

NP For Mouse was beautiful: she was exquisite and so fragile so fine[188] that each time ~~you~~
I looked at her ~~as~~ it was as if for the first time—**How can I describe** that? She came upon you with the same kind of shock that you feel when you have been drinking tea [out] of a thin innocent cup + suddenly at the bottom you see a tiny creature, half butterfly half woman, **bowing*** to you with her hands in her sleeves.

Not that ~~she was in the least~~ looked in the least Japanese or Chinese ~~looking~~ or as if ~~she would dream for one moment of~~ looked as though there were the least chance of her bowing to you with her hands almost in her sleeves . .[189]

As far as I could see[190] she ~~was~~ had dark hair and grey[191] or blue or black eyes. Her long lashes, + the two little feathers traced above ~~these rather heavy eyelids~~ were most important ~~if you know what I mean~~ **but but**—~~so was her mouth—so was her chin~~—she **wore*** a long dark cloak—just[192] as one sees in

[JNPP-rough-NL, leaf 11 verso]

old* fashioned pictures **paper** of englishwomen ~~visiting France~~ abroad—Where her arms came out of it ~~it was old fur xxx~~ there was grey fur—~~there was~~ fur round her neck too + ~~she~~ her close fitting cap was ~~of the same~~ furry. **Carrying out the*** mouse idea—I decided—

Ah it was intriguing! intriguing![193] Their excitement ~~xxx to come~~ came nearer + nearer to me ~~while~~ while I ran out to meet it—waded in it walked and[194]—flung myself far out of my depth—until ~~at*~~ last I was ~~as*~~ hard put it to [sic] ~~control~~ keep ~~myself~~ in **control as*** they.xxx But what I wanted to do was to behave in the most extraordinary fashion way like a clown—to[195] start **singing*** with large extravagant gestures to point out [the] window + cry ~~you~~ "We were now passing Ladies + Gentlemen one of the **sights*** for which notre Paris is justly famous—to ~~have suddenly~~ jumped suddenly[196] **out*** of the taxi while it was going—climbed over the roof + dived in by the other door;[197] to ~~lean half~~ hang out of the window + ~~begin looking~~ search[198] for the **hotel*** through the long end of a broken telescope—which was also a peculiarly ear splitting trumpet!

I watched myself do all this, you understand + even manage to applaud in a **particularly**[199] private way by patting[200] my gloved hands gently together while I said to Mouse

And ~~this is~~[201] this ~~your~~ your first visit to Paris?

---

188 The final version reads: "so fragile and fine."
189 This short paragraph is absent in the published version. The corrections are in lighter ink, and a tighter hand.
190 "See" becomes "make out" in the final version.
191 The published version leaves out "grey."
192 "Such" replaces "just" in the published version.
193 The published version reads: "Ah, but how intriguing it was—how intriguing!" (CW2, 126).
194 This becomes "bathed in it" in the final version.
195 Mansfield has written something over "to."
196 "Suddenly" is not retained in the final version.
197 While Mansfield has revised "jumped" to "jump," "climbed" and "dived" remain in the past tense.
198 The published version changes "search" to "look."
199 "Particularly" is omitted in the final version.
200 "Patting" becomes "putting" in the final version.
201 There is a check mark under "is," suggesting it is to be retained.

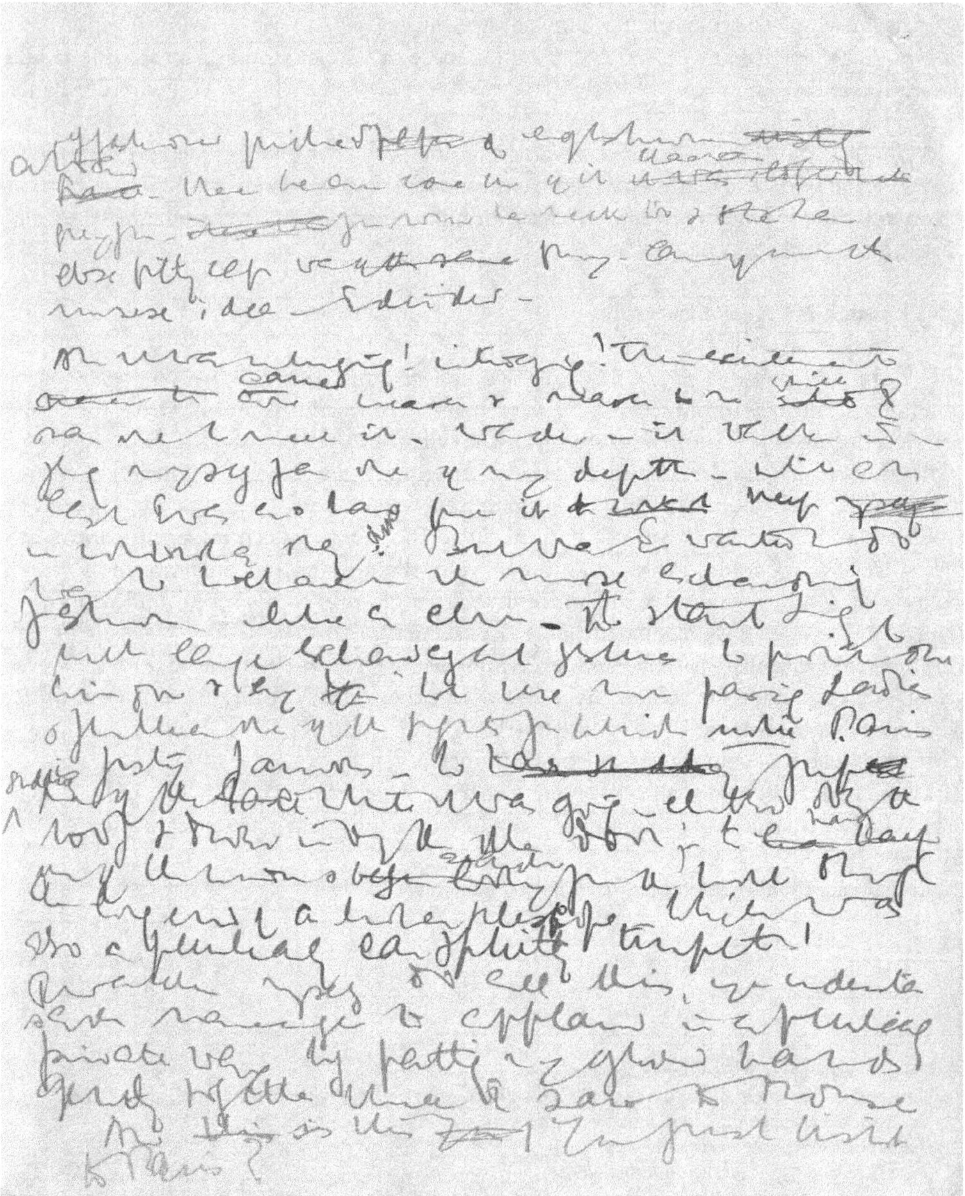

FIGURE 12: Leaf 11 verso, "Je ne parle pas français" [rough manuscript], Katherine Mansfield Papers, Newberry Library, (box 1, folder 27), 16 leaves. Image courtesy of the Newberry Library.

[JNPP-rough-NL, leaf 10 verso]

"Yes, Ive not been here before."

"Ah! then you have a great deal to see!"

And I was just going to touch lightly upon the objects of interest + the museums when we wrenched to a stop—

$$\clef{treble}$$

Do you know—its very absurd—but as I pushed open the door for them + followed ~~them~~ up the stairs to the ~~bure~~au ~~office~~ on the landing ~~that~~ I felt somehow that this hotel was mine [N.L.]—There was a vase of flowers on the **window sill*** of the **bureau*** + I even went so far as to rearrange a bud or two + stand off to ~~see~~ [note] the effect while the manageress welcomed them—And when she **turned*** to me + handed me the keys [—] the garcon was hauling up the boxes [—] + said M Duquette will show you your rooms. I had a longing to ~~touch~~ [tap] Dick on the arm with a key + say very confidentially ["]Look here old chap— As a friend of **mine*** I[']ll be only too glad[202] to make a slight reduction."———

Up + up we climbed—round + round—past an occasional pair of boots (why is it one seldom sees[203] an attractive pair of boots outside a door) higher + higher.

I am afraid they are a little high up—I murmured idiotically. But I chose them because———

[JNPP-rough-NL, leaf 9 verso]

They so obviously did not care why I chose them that I went no further.

They accepted everything. They did not expect anything to be different. This was just part of what they were ~~living~~ [going] through—**thats*** how I **analyzed*** it.

"Arrived at last—" ~~and~~ I ran from one side of the passage to the other **turning*** on the lights—explaining—

"This[204] one—I thought for you Dick—the other is larger + has a little dressing room in the alcove—My **proprietary*** eye noted the clean towels + covers[,] the bed linens **embroidered*** in red cotton—I thought them charming rooms[205]—sloping, full of angles just the sort of rooms one would expect to find if one hadn't been in Paris before—Dick dashed his hat down on the bed—["]**oughtn't*** I to help that chap with the boxes["]—he asked of nobody—

Yes you might replied Mouse. Theyre dreadfully heavy + she turned to me with that first glimmer of a smile. Books you know! Oh he darted such a strange look at her before he ~~dashed~~ [rushed] out—and he not only helped;—he must have torn the box off the garcon's ~~box~~[ack] for he ~~came~~ [staggered] back carrying one—dumped it down—+ fetched in the other.

["]That's yours Dick["] said she

---

[202] The published version changes "glad" to "willing."

[203] The final version reads: "why is it one never sees [. . .]" (CW2, 127).

[204] "This" is superimposed over something illegible.

[205] "Rather" is added in the final version (i.e. "rather charming rooms").

[JNPP-rough-NL, leaf 8 verso]

["]Well you **don't mind*** it **staying**^{nding206} over here[207] for the present do you[?]" he asked breathing hard[208] the box must have been **incredibly** heavy. He ~~took~~ ^{pulled} out a ^{xxx} handful of money. I suppose I ought to pay this chap ~~he said~~—^{N.L.} **The garcon standing by seemed to think*** so too.

And will you require anything further—Monsieur?

No, no, said Dick impatiently.

But ^{at that} Mouse stepped forward. She said too deliberately not looking at Dick—~~in~~ ^{with} her **quaint*** clipped english accent "yes Id like some tea. Tea for three –["] + suddenly she raised her muff as though her hands were clasped inside it and she was telling the ~~waiter~~ pale sweaty garcon **that** by that action that she was at the end of her resources, that she **cried out*** to him to save her life—her life—Tea—<u>immediately</u>.[209]

This seemed to me so amazingly "in the picture" so exactly the ~~right~~ gesture and cry that one would imagine[210] (another[211] I couldn't have imagined it) to be wrung from[212] an englishwoman faced with a great crisis that I was almost tempted to hold up my hand and protest—

[JNPP-rough-NL, leaf 7 verso]

No ~~really~~! ^{No!} Enough. I was quite set to leave off there at the word tea—<u>To be continued tomorrow.</u>[213] For really—really—you have fed your greediest contributor so full that he will burst if heas[214] to swallow another word!

It even pulled Dick up. Like someone who has been unconscious for a long long time he **turned*** slowly to Mouse + slowly looked at her with his tired haggard eyes—and murmured with the echo of his old dreamy voice.

"Yes yes[215] thats a good idea["]—And then ["]you must be **tired*** Mouse. Sit down –"

^{NP}She sat in a chair with lace tabs on the arms[;] he leaned against the bed and I established myself on a ~~little~~ straight-back chair, crossed my legs + brushed ~~an~~ ^{some} imaginary ~~speck~~ ^{dust} off the knees of my trousers (the Parisian ~~always at my~~ ^{at his} ease)

---

[206] While it appears that Mansfield intends to revise the word, there is no deletion indicated.

[207] "Over here" becomes "here" in the published version.

[208] The published version adds "breathless" before "breathing hard."

[209] The published version reads: "[. . .] that she cried out to him to save her with 'Tea. Immediately!'" (CW2, 128).

[210] The final version uses "expect" in lieu of "imagine."

[211] "Another" is replaced by "though" in the published version.

[212] "Wrung from" becomes "wrung out of" in the final version.

[213] The published version repeats "Enough." What follows is changed to: "Let us leave off there. At the word—tea" (CW2, 128).

[214] It looks as if "as" overlays the "e" of "he" to create "has," but this eliminates the subject.

[215] The final version does not repeat "yes."

There came a tiny pause—Then he said **wont*** you take off your coat Mouse?
No Ill keep it on—Im cold. Xxx you.[216]
No thanks not just now.
Were they going to ask me? Or should I hold up my hand + call out in a baby voice—
its my **turn*** to [be] asked.
No, I shouldn't. They didn't ask me. The pause became a silence a real silence. Come!
My parisian

[JNPP-rough-NL, leaf 6 verso]

foxterrier. Amuse these ~~poor~~ ˢᵃᵈ english. Its no wonder ~~they are a nation xxx so for xxx~~
_{theyre such a nation for} dogs. But after all why should I. Its not my job as they would say. ᴺᴸ Never
the less I made a vivacious little bound at Mouse.
What a pity it is you didn't arrive by day-light. There is such a charming view from
these two windows. You know the hotel is on a corner—+ each window looks down an
immensely long straight street.
"Yes["] said she.
Not that that sounds very charming—I laughed. But there[']s so much animation—so
many absurd little boys on bicycles + people hanging out of windows—and Oh well youll
see for yourself in the morning. **Very amusing*** very **animated***.
"Oh yes" said she.
If the pale sweaty garcon had <u>not</u> appeared[217] at that moment carrying the tea tray ^{high}
xxx xxx high as ~~though~~ ⁱᶠ the cups were cannon balls + he were[218] a heavy weight ~~lifter~~[219]
^{champion} in **its xxx halls**—[220]
He managed to lower it on to a round table.
Bring the table over here said Mouse. The waiter seemed to be the only person she

[JNPP-rough-NL, leaf 5 verso]

cared to talk to![221] She took her hands out of her muff, drew off her ~~xx~~gloves + **flung
back*** the old fashioned cape—
Do you take milk + sugar?
No milk thank you + no sugar—I went over for mine like a little gentleman—she
poured out another cup. That's for Dick—
And the faithful foxterrier carried it across to him—+ laid it at his feet as it [were][222]
"Oh* thanks["] said Dick—And then I went back to my chair ~~again~~ + she sank back in
hers—But Dick was off again—he stared at the cup of tea **wildly*** for a moment,[223] glanced
round him—**put it down on the*** bed table caught up his hat + **stammered*** at full
gallup—

---

[216] This line is omitted in the published version.
[217] "Come in" replaces "appeared" in the final version.
[218] The published version omits "were" here.
[219] A check is written under "lifter," suggesting it is to be retained, as it is in the published version, replacing the added "champion."
[220] The published version changes "in the music halls" to "on the cinema."
[221] The final version has "cared to speak to."
[222] The published version reads "as it were," but "were" is not evident in this version of the manuscript.
[223] In the published version, "wildly" is placed after "stared."

["]Oh by the way do you mind **posting*** a leter [*sic*] for me? I want to get a letter off by tonight[']s post. I must[.] Its very urgent." Feeling his eyes on her he flung[224]—its to my mother—But I wont be long.[225] Ive got everything I want. But it must go off tonight. You don't mind? It wont take me any time—— ——[226]

^{Of course Ill post it. Delighted!} Wont you drink your tea first suggested Mouse.[227]

NP . . . Tea? Tea? Yes of course—Tea. A cup of tea

[JNPP-rough-NL, leaf 4 verso]

on the **mantlepiece**.[228] In his racing dream he flashed the brightest most charming smile at his little hostess—

"No thanks—not just now."

And still hoping it wouldn't be **inconvenient**[229] to me he went out of the room + shut[230] the door + we heard him cross the passage.

I scalded myself with mine in my **hurry*** to take my cup back to the table + say as I stood there—

"You mustnt forgive me if I am impertinent. If Im too frank—But Dick hasn't tried to disguise it—Has he—Is There ⁱˢ something the matter. Can I help?

~~Ah that's strange. I almost expected we should have heard~~ sSoft music—+ Mouse ~~stood xxx xxx~~ ᵍᵉᵗˢ up walkedˢ the stage for a moment or so—before she returns to her chair + pours me out oh such a ~~cup~~ ᵇʳⁱᵐᵐⁱⁿᵍ* ~~so brimming so full~~ ˢᵘᶜʰ ᵃ ᵇᵘʳⁿⁱⁿᵍ* ᶜᵘᵖ then the tears came into the friends eyes while he sipped while he drained it to the bitter dregs.[231]

I had **time*** to think[232] all that before she replied. First she looked into the tea pot, filled it with hot water ~~+ poured~~

[JNPP-rough-NL, leaf 3 verso]

~~me out a second cup.~~ ⁺ ˢᵗⁱʳʳᵉᵈ ⁱᵗ ᵍᵉⁿᵗˡʸ + stirred it xxx233

"Yes there is something the matter. No Im afraid you cant help thank you." And again I got that glimmer of a smile. "Im awfully sorry. It must be very horrid for you!"

---

[224] While the published version has "Feeling her eyes on him," which makes more sense, this version of the manuscript reverses the pronouns.

[225] The final version reads: "To me: 'I won't be long [. . .]'" (CW2, 129).

[226] The published version reads: "'It . . . it won't take any time'" (CW2, 129).

[227] "Softly" is added in the final version (i.e. "suggested Mouse softly").

[228] "Mantlepiece" becomes "bed-table" in the final version, making it consistent with the earlier passage when Dick sets the cup down (JNPP-rough-NL, leaf 5 verso).

[229] The final version changes "inconvenient" to "any trouble."

[230] "Shut" becomes "closed" in the published version.

[231] "Sipped" and "drained" are in the present tense in the published version.

[232] The final version changes "to think" to "to do."

[233] The published version reads: "and stirred it with a spoon" (CW2, 130).

Horrid*! Indeed! Ah why couldn[']t I tell her that it was months + months since Id been so entertained!

"But you are suffering," I ventured softly as though that was what I couldn't <u>bear</u> to <u>see</u>.

She didn't deny it. She nodded + bit her under lip + I thought I saw her chin tremble.

And there is really nothing I can do? more softly still. She shook her head, pushed back the table + jumped up. Oh it will be alright. She **breathed*** walked over to the dressing table + standing with her back turned[234] to me—["]It will be alright. It cant go on like this."

But of course of course it cant![235] I agreed, wondering if[236] it would look heartless if I lit a cigarette. I had a sudden longing to smoke.

In some ~~mysterious~~ way she saw my hand move to my breast pocket half draw out a cigarette case + put it back again for the **next thing*** she said was ["]matches in the candlestick. I saw them.["] + I heard from her voice she was crying.

237

Ah thank you yes yes. Ive found them. I lighted my cigarette + walked

[JNPP-rough-NL, leaf 2 verso]

up + down smoking. It was ~~very~~ ˢᵒ quiet—it might have been 2 oclock in the morning. It was so quiet that you heard the boards creak + pop as one does in a house in the country. I smoked a whole cigarette ˢᵗᵃᵇᵇᵉᵈ + ~~then~~ xxx xxx end into my ᵉᵐᵖᵗʸ ~~tea cup~~ ˢᵃᵘᶜᵉʳ[238] before Mouse **turned*** round + came back to the table.

Isnt Dick being rather a long time? ~~she said~~. You are very tired. I expect you want to go to bed. I said kindly. (And pray don't mind me if you do, said my mind)

But isnt he being a long time? she insisted.

I shrugged. He is rather. Then I saw that she looked at me **strangely***—she was listening. Hes been gone ages! she said + she went with little light steps to the door opened it ~~crossed the passage~~ and across the passage[239] + into his room—

I waited—I listened to[o] now. I couldnt have **borne*** to miss a word.

She had left the door open. I stole across the room + looked after her. Dick[']s door was open too—**but*** there wasnt a word to miss.

You know I had a mad idea that they were kissing in that quiet room—a long comfortable kiss. ᴼⁿᵉ ᵒᶠ ᵗʰᵒˢᵉ ᵏⁱˢˢᵉˢ ᵗʰᵃᵗ ⁿᵒᵗ ᵒⁿˡʸ ᵖᵘᵗˢ ᵍʳⁱᵉᶠ ᵗᵒ ᵇᵉᵈ, ᵇᵘᵗ ⁿᵘʳˢᵉˢ ⁱᵗ ᵃⁿᵈ ʷᵃʳᵐˢ ⁱᵗ ᵃⁿᵈ ᵗᵘᶜᵏˢ ⁱᵗ ᵘᵖ ᵃⁿᵈ ᵏᵉᵉᵖˢ ⁱᵗ ᶠᵃˢᵗ ᵉⁿᶠᵒˡᵈᵉᵈ ᵘⁿᵗⁱˡ ⁱᵗ ⁱˢ ˢˡᵉᵉᵖⁱⁿᵍ ˢᵒᵘⁿᵈ—ᴬʰ! ʰᵒʷ ᵍᵒᵒᵈ ᵗʰᵃᵗ ⁱˢ![240] Ah how good it is.[241]

---

[234] "Turned" is left out in the published version.
[235] The final version does not repeat "of course."
[236] "If" becomes "whether" in the final version.
[237] This treble clef is squeezed in between the two lines, suggesting it was added later—which is reiterated by the fact that the ink is darker.
[238] "Stabbed" and "saucer" are written in pencil.
[239] The published version reverts to the deleted phrase "crossed the passage" in lieu of "and across the passage."
[240] An "X" in pencil is written beside "comfortable kiss," which is circled lightly in pencil. The image of the "comfortable kiss" that makes up this addition is from JNPP-rough-NL, leaf 1 verso, signaled by an asterisk.
[241] The repetition here is omitted in the final version.

It was over at last. I heard some one move—+ tiptoed away—~~Mouse came back~~ It was Mouse[242]

[JNPP-rough-NL, leaf 1 verso][243]

*One of those kisses that not only puts grief to bed, but nurses it and warms it and tucks it up and keeps it fast enfolded until it is sleeping sound—Ah! how good that is![244]

She came back; she felt her way back into the room carrying the letter for me, but it wasnt in an envelope; it was just a single sheet of paper—+ she held it by the **corner*** ~~that wasn't dry yet~~ as if it was still wet. Her head was bent so low so ~~hidden in~~ tucked into her furry collar that I hadnt a notion—until she let the paper fall—And almost <u>fell</u> herself on to the floor by the side of the bed—leaned her cheek against it flung out her hands as though the last of her poor little weapons was gone and ~~she yielded yielded to the heavy drowning~~ tears Now* ~~she~~ let herself be carried away, washed **away out into*** the deep ~~wavy~~ waving water.[245]

Flash! went my mind. Dick has shot himself and then a succession

[JNPP-NB14-ATL, page 30 recto][246]

~~xxx xxx~~[247] flashes while I **rushed*** in saw the body[,] head unharmed[,] small blue hole over temple[,] ~~roused hotel~~ roused hotel[,] arranged for funeral[,] attended funeral ~~in black mourning coat~~ closed cab, black[248] mourning coat.[249]

She wept so strangely! With her eyes shut[,] with her face quite calm except for her quivering eyelids. The tears **pearled down*** her white cheeks +[250]

[JNPP-NB14-ATL, page 31 recto]

she let them fall.

I stooped down + picked up the paper + would you **believe*** it![251] My parisian sense of <u>comme il faut</u> ~~was so strong that~~ I murmured <u>pardon</u> before I read it[252]—

---

[242] This is written very lightly in pencil.

[243] This page is written in pencil with a few corrections in ink.

[244] As noted above, the asterisk signals that this is an elaboration of the "comfortable kiss" on JNPP-rough-NL, leaf 2 verso, next to which Mansfield has written an "X."

[245] The published version omits "away" after "washed" and "waving" before "water," reading: "[. . .] now she let herself be carried away, washed out into the deep water" (CW2, 131).

[246] Page thirty of Notebook 14 picks up where the JNPP-rough-NL, leaf 1 verso, leaves off.

[247] The strike-through is in ink.

[248] "Black" becomes "new" in the final version.

[249] Two slanted lines are drawn between the end of this sentence and the following sentence, which is indented on the following line.

[250] A rough circle on page thirty-six recto of Notebook 14 signals that this passage about Mouse crying is to be moved to that spot, which is how it appears in the published version.

[251] An arrow, in ink, is drawn under "believe" and appears to indicate the following page; it may be the indication to move the passage about Mouse's tears forward, to page 36 recto of Notebook 14.

[252] The opposing page includes a potential revision related to Raoul's "sense of <u>comme il faut</u>": The initial passage is in pencil while the edits are in ink:

"~~such a part of me that~~ (so ingrained is mine Even at this critical moment"

Mouse[253]—my little mouse. It's no good[,] its impossible—I cant see it through. O I do love you[,] I do love you Mouse, but ~~shes~~ I cant **hurt*** her. People have been **hurting*** her all her life—I simply dare not give

[JNPP-NB14-ATL, page 32 recto]

her this final blow. You see though she[']s stronger than both of us shes so frail and so proud. It would kill her kill her Mouse—and ^{Oh God} I cant kill my mother—Not even for you—for us.[254] You do see that—don't you?

It all seemed so possible when ~~you~~ ^{we255} talked and planned but the very moment the train started it was all over. I felt her drag me back to her—calling—I can hear her now as I write—and

[JNPP-NB14-ATL, page 33 recto]

shes alone and she doesnt know—A man would have to be a devil to tell her—+ Im not a devil Mouse. She mustn't know—I must go back to her now this instant before it is too late[256]—Oh Mouse somewhere—somewhere in you—dont you agree? Its all so unspeakably awful that I don't know whether I want go or not—Do I or is ~~she~~ ^{Mother} just dragging me—Oh I don't know—my head is too tired.

[JNPP-NB14-ATL, page 34 recto]

Mouse Mouse what will you do? But I cant think of that either—I dare not—Id break down + I must not break down. All Ive got to do is just to tell you this and go. I couldn't have gone without telling you—you would have been frightened—And you must not be frightened. You wont will you. I cant bear—but no more of that.

And don't write—I should never have the courage

[JNPP-NB14-ATL, page 35 recto]

to open your letters[257] and the sight of your tiny[258] spidery handwriting—

Forgive me. Dont love me any more—Yes—love me love me—

Dick[259]

What do you think of that? ~~Was~~^{Wasnt260} that a rare find? My relief at his not having shot himself was mixed with a wonderful sense of elation—I was even—more than even with

---

[253] Dick's letter to Mouse begins here.

[254] The published version reads: "Not even for us" (CW2, 131).

[255] "We" is superimposed over "you."

[256] The final version eliminates this sentence.

[257] The published version changes the wording to: "I should not have the courage to answer your letters" (CW2, 132).

[258] Mansfield has re-traced the "ti" of "tiny" a few times. "Tiny" is omitted in the published version.

[259] Mansfield draws a horizontal line separating the letter from the section that follows.

[260] "Wasnt" is written over "was," retaining the original "w."

[JNPP-NB14-ATL, page 36 recto]

my thats very curious + interesting englishman.

She wept so strangely! With her eyes shut[,] with her face quite calm except for her quivering eyelids. The tears **pearled down*** her white cheeks
+261

But feeling my glance on her she opened her eyes + saw me[262] holding the letter—

Youve read it—Her voice was ~~quite~~ calm [too263] but it wasn't her voice any more—it was like **the*** voice you **might imagine coming*** out of a tiny cold sea shell ~~left~~ swept high + dry at last by the **salty*** tide.[264]

[Notebook 14, page 37 recto]

I nodded, quite overcome you understand and laid the letter down.

["]Its incredible—incredible["] I whispered.

At that she got up from the floor[,] walked over to the washstand[,] dipped her handkerchief into the jug + ~~dabbed~~ sponged[265] her eyes—saying oh no its not <u>incredible</u> at all.

[JNPP-NB14-ATL, page 38 recto]

And still pressing the wet ball ~~of handkerchief~~ to her eyes she came back to me to her chair with the lace tabs + sank into it—["]I **knew*** it xx all along of course!["] ~~It was in that~~ said the cold salty little voice[266]—["]From the very moment that we started—I felt it all through me but I ~~didnt~~[267] still went on—~~I~~ hoping["][268]—she[269] took the handkerchief **down*** + gave me this final **glimmer*** ["]one so stupidly does you know.["]

[JNPP-NB14-ATL, page 39 recto]

Yes—one does –[270]

But what will you do? Youll go back? Youll see him?

That made her sit right up + <u>stare</u> across at me ~~frowning~~—What an extraordinary idea she said—more coldly than ever—Of course I shall not dream of seeing him—As to going back ~~she xxx that xxx xxx~~ thats quite out of the question—I cant go back.

---

[261] A rough circle is drawn before "But," a signal to bring this short passage from pages 30–31 recto of Notebook 14 forward, which is how it appears in the published version.
[262] Mansfield retraces "me."
[263] The strike-through is in ink, as is the addition of "too," which does not make it into the final version.
[264] The change of "left" in favor of "swept" as well as the omission of the "y" of "salty" is in ink.
[265] This change is in ink.
[266] All of the adjustments to this point are in ink; "the" is superimposed onto "that."
[267] In this instance, the omission is in pencil.
[268] Mansfield began writing "I" but then reworked the vertical line to create the "h."
[269] The final version adds "and here" (i.e. "and here she took [. . .]").
[270] The published version reads "As one does" and adds on the following line, "Silence" (CW2, 132).

[JNPP-NB14-ATL, page 40 recto][271]

But?

Its impossible—For one thing all my friends think Im married—
I put out my hand—Ah my poor little friend—
But she shrank ~~back into the armchair~~ away (False move)
Of course there was one question at the back of [my] mind all this time—I dared it[272]
Have you any money?
Yes ~~she said~~—Ive got[273] £20—here—+ she laid her hand on her breast.

[JNPP-NB14-ATL, page 40 verso][274]

I bowed—It was a great [deal] more than Id expected—And what ~~will you do~~are your plans?
Yes Ill own that my question was the **most*** idiotic, clumsy one I could have put[275]—
She xxx had been so tame—so confiding—Letting me at any rate spiritually speaking hold
her tiny quivering body in one hand + stroke her furry head—but now Id thrown her
away! Oh I could have kicked myself.

[JNPP-NB14-ATL, page 39 verso][276]

I ~~wont*~~ do anything have no plans ~~she said~~ but its very late. You must go—Now—please—and
she stood up[277] ——
How could I get her back? I **wanted*** her back. I swear I wasnt acting ~~now~~ then—
Do feel Im your friend—I cried—youll let me come tomorrow? Early? Youll let me
look after you a little—Take care of you a little?[278]—Youll use me just as you think fit.

[JNPP-NB14-ATL, page 38 verso]

I succeeded. She came out of her little hole timid but she came out –
"Youre very kind—Yes, do come tomorrow—~~and~~ thankful you [sic][279]—I shall be
glad—~~xx~~ it makes things rather difficult because["] + again ~~she gave~~ I clasped her boyish hand
[– "] Je ne parle pas francais.["][280]

Not until I was half way down the boulevard

---

271 This is the last page of Notebook 14; at this point, Mansfield begins writing on the verso pages, working
backwards. All of the edits on this page are in ink.
272 "Dared" is replaced by "hated" in the published version.
273 "I've got" becomes "have" in the final version.
274 The edits on this page are all in ink.
275 In the published version, "Yes I'll own" becomes "Yes, I know" and "the most idiotic, clumsy one" is changed
to "the most clumsy, the most idiotic one" (CW2, 133).
276 The edits on this page are all in ink.
277 "She stood up" is partially circled in ink with a line leading up to just before "I wont do," which is how it
appears in the final version.
278 The initial "a little" is written over "after"; the second is written over "of you," but I've arranged them as they
appear in the published version.
279 This phrase is omitted in the final version.
280 The excision of "she gave" in favor of "I clasped" is in ink.

[JNPP-NB14-ATL, page 37 verso]

did it come over me the full force of it—

Why they were suffering? those 2, really suffering. I have seen two people **suffer*** as I suppose I ever shall again—And ["]goodnight my little cat[" I] said impudently to the fattish old prostitute picking her way home through the slush. I didnt give her time to reply.

[JNPP-NB14-ATL, page 36 verso]

Of course you know what to expect—you anticipate fully what I'm going to write—It wouldnt be <u>me</u> otherwise—I never went near the place again—

Yes I still owe that considerable amount for lunches and dinners but thats beside the mark, its vulgar to mention it –

[JNPP-NB14-ATL, page 35 verso]

in the same breath with ~~xxx~~ the[281] fact that I never saw Mouse again.

~~Of course~~ naturally I intended to.

~~Of course~~ naturally I started out[282]—got to the door—wrote [and] tore up letters—did all these things—but I simply couldnt make the final effort.[283]

Even now I dont fully understand why ~~I didnt~~. Of course I knew I couldn't have kept it

[JNPP-NB14-ATL, page 34 verso]

up—that had a great deal to do with it. But you would have thought that putting[284] [it] at its lowest[,] curiosity couldn't have kept my foxterrier nose away—

<u>Je ne parle pas francais</u> that was her swan song for me—

But how she makes me break my rule! Oh youve seen for yourself but I could give you

[JNPP-NB14-ATL, page 33 verso]

countless examples—

Evenings when I sit in some gloomy cafés[285] + ~~some~~ an automatic piano starts[286] a mouse tune (there are dozens of **tunes*** that evoke her[287]) And I begin to **dream*** of things like a little tiny[288] house on the edge of the sea somewhere, far—far away—and a girl outside in a frock rather like red Indian women wear hailing a light dark haired[289] boy who comes up bare foot—from the beach[290]—What have you got—A fish

---

[281] "The" is written over an illegible word.
[282] The published version omits the second "naturally," reading: "Naturally, I intended to. Started out [. . .]" (CW2, 133).
[283] The adjustments are in ink.
[284] This is in ink.
[285] While "gloomy" is in pencil, the addition of "some" is in ink; however, Mansfield does not make "cafés" singular to coincide with the change. The following edit of "some" to "an" is also in ink.
[286] "Playing" is added in the final version (i.e. "and automatic piano starts playing").
[287] The final version adds "just" (i.e. "that evoke just her").
[288] "Tiny" is omitted in the published version.
[289] An arrow indicates the insertion in ink.
[290] The published version reads: "[. . .] hailing a light, bare-foot boy who runs up from the beach" (CW2, 134).

[JNPP-NB14-ATL, page 32 verso]

+ I smile + give[291] it to her—the same girl the same boy—different costumes—sitting at an open window +[292] **eating*** fruit + leaning out and laughing—All the wild strawberries are for you Mouse all. I wont touch them![293]

~~This~~ A wet night. ~~Xxx see xxx~~ They are going home together under an umbrella—+ They stop~~ping~~ on the doorstep[294]

[JNPP-NB14-ATL, page 31 verso]

to press their wet cheeks together + to laugh[295]—and so on and so on until some dirty old gallant comes up to my table + sits opposite and begins to grimace and yapp [sic]. Until I hear myself say—"But Ive got the little girl for you mon vieux—so little—so little[296]—and a **virgin***.["] I kiss ~~my lips~~ the tips of my fingers—["]a virgin["] and lay them on my **heart***.

[JNPP-NB14-ATL, page 30 verso][297]

[JNPP-NB14-ATL, page 29 verso]

I give you the word of honour of a gentleman[,] a writer, serious young + extremely interested in modern english literature.[298]

I must go—I must go—I reach down my hat + coat—Waiter![299]

Madame knows me—"You havent dined yet" she said.[300]

No, not yet Madame—

[JNPP-NB14-ATL, page 28 verso][301]

[JNPP-NB14-ATL, page 27 verso]

I['d] rather like to dine with her—Even to sleep with her afterwards—would she be pale like that all over——

But no. She[']d have large moles—They go with that kind of skin and I cant bear them. They remind me, somehow, disgustingly of mushrooms.[302]"JE NE PARLE PAS FRANÇAIS"
63"JE NE PARLE PAS FRANÇAIS"   63

---

[291] Mansfield retraces "smile" and "give" more boldly.

[292] This is marked out in ink.

[293] The second "all" is omitted in the final version, and "them" becomes "one."

[294] The omission of "This" is in pencil, but the other corrections are in ink. "Doorstep" becomes "door" in the final version.

[295] "And to laugh" is eliminated in the published version.

[296] The second "little" becomes "tiny" in the final version.

[297] The few lines on this page seem to be potential revisions related to page 31 recto of Notebook 14. See note 252.

[298] Mansfield has drawn a double horizontal line; underneath is a wavy line moving down, vertically.

[299] "Hat and coat" are inverted and "Waiter" is omitted in the final version.

[300] The published version substitutes "she smiles" for "she said."

[301] The passage written on this page seems to be unrelated to the story. See note 163.

[302] Mansfield has drawn a succession of horizontal lines at the bottom of the page, signaling the end of the story.

"Je ne parle pas Français" [*sic*]
by
Katherine Mansfield
= =

Chapter I.

I do not know why I have such a fancy for this little café. It's dirty, and it's sad—sad![1] It isn't as if[2] it had anything to distinguish it from a hundred others—it hasnt; or as if the same strange "types" came here every day whom one could watch from one's corner and recognise and more or less (with a strong accent on the <u>less</u>) get the hang of.

But pray dont think[3] those brackets are a confession of my humility before the mystery of the human soul. Not at all; I don't believe in the human soul. I never have. I believe that people are like portmanteaux—packed with certain things, started off, thrown about, tossed away, dumped down, lost and found, half emptied suddenly, or squeezed fatter than ever until finally the Ultimate Porter swings them onto the Ultimate Train and away they rattle . . .

Not but what portmanteaux can be very fascinating. Oh, but very! I see myself standing in front of them, don't you know, like a customs official.

"Have you anything to declare? Any wines, spirits, cigars, perfumes, silks?"

And the moment of hesitation as to whether I am going to be fooled, just before I chalk that squiggle, and then the other moment of hesitation, just after, as to whether I have been, are perhaps the two most thrilling instants in life. Yes, they are, to me.

But before I started that rather far fetched and not frightfully original digression what I meant to say quite simply was that there are no portmanteaux to be examined here because the clientèle of the café, ladies and gentlemen, does not sit down. No, it stands at the counter, and it consists of a handful of workmen who come up from the river, all powdered over with white flour, or lime, or something, and a few soldiers, bringing with them thin, dark girls with silver rings in their ears and market baskets over their arms.

Madame is thin and dark too, with white cheeks and white hands. In certain lights she looks quite transparent, shining out of her black shawl with an extraordinary effect. When she is not serving she sits on a stool with her face turned, always, to the window. Her dark-ringed eyes search among and follow after the people passing, but not as if she were looking for somebody. Perhaps fifteen years ago, she was; but now the pose has become a habit. You can tell from her air of fatigue and hopelessness that she must have given them up for the last ten years, at least.

And then there is the waiter. Not pathetic—decidedly not comic. Never making one of those perfectly insignificant remarks which amaze you so as coming from a waiter, (as though the poor wretch were a sort of cross between a coffee pot and a wine bottle and not expected to hold so much as a drop of anything else.) He is grey, flat-footed and

---

[1] The print version reads: "It's dirty and sad, sad" (CW2, 112).

[2] The verb structure is slightly changed in the published version: "It's not as if [. . .]" (CW2, 112).

[3] "Think" becomes "imagine" in the print version.

withered, with long brittle nails that set your nerves on edge while he scrapes up your two sous. When he is not smearing over the

[JNPP-clean-NL, leaf 3]

tables or flicking at a dead fly or two, he stands with one hand on the back of a chair, in his far too long apron, and over his other arm the three cornered dip of dirty napkin, waiting to be photographed in connection with some wretched murder. <u>Interior of Café Where Body Was Found</u>. You've seen him countless times . . .[4]

Do you believe that every place has its hour of the day when it really does come alive? Thats not exactly what I mean. Its more like this. There does seem to be a moment when you realise, that, quite by accident, you happen to have come on to the right stage at exactly the moment you were expected. Everything is arranged for you—waiting for you. Ah, mMaster[5] of the situation! You fill with important breath! And at the same time you smile, secretly, slyly, because Life seems to be opposed to granting you these entrances, seems indeed, to be engaged in snatching them from you and making them impossible—keeping you "in the wings" until it is too late, in fact . . . Just for once you've beaten the old hag!

I enjoyed one of these moments the first time I ever came in here. That's why I keep coming back, I suppose. Revisiting the scene of my triumph, or the scene of the crime where I had the old bitch by the throat for once and did what I pleased with her.

Query: Why am I so bitter against Life. And why do I see her as a rag picker on the American cinema

[JNPP-clean-NL, leaf 4]

shuffling along, wrapped in a filthy shawl, with her old claws crooked over a stick?

Answer: The direct result of the American cinema acting upon a weak mind.

Anyhow, "the short winter afternoon was drawing to a close" as they say, and I was drifting along, either going home or not going home when I found myself in here, walking over to this seat in the corner. I hung up my english [*sic*] overcoat and grey felt hat on that same peg behind me and after I had allowed the waiter time for at least twenty photographers to snap their fill of him, I ordered a coffee.

He poured me out a glass of the familiar purplish stuff with a green wandering light playing over it, and shuffled off: and I sat pressing my fingers against the glass because it was bitterly cold outside.

Suddenly I realised that quite apart from myself, I was smiling. Slowly I raised my head and saw myself in the mirror opposite. Yes, there I sat, leaning on the table, smiling my deep, sly smile, the glass of coffee with its vague plume of steam before me and beside it the ring of white saucer with two pieces of sugar.

I opened my eyes very wide. There I had been for all eternity, as it were, and now at last was my moment for coming to life . . .[6]

It was very quiet in the café. Outside, one could just see through the dusk that it had begun

---

[4] This becomes "You've seen him hundreds of times" in the published version.
[5] A capital "M" is written over a lowercase "m."
[6] The print version reads: "[. . .] and now at last I was coming to life. . . ." (CW2, 114).

[JNPP-clean-NL, leaf 5]

to snow. One could just see the shapes of horses and carts and people, soft and white, moving through the feathery air. The waiter disappeared and reappeared with an armful of straw. He strewed it over the floor from the door to the counter and round about the stove, with humble, almost adoring gestures. One would not have been surprised if the door had opened and the Virgin Mary had come in, riding upon an ass, her meek hands folded over her big belly . . .

That's rather nice—don't you think? That bit about the Virgin? It comes from the pen so gently; it has such a "dying fall."

I thought so at the time and decided to make a note of it. One never knows when a little tag like that may come in useful to round off a paragraph.

So taking care to move as little as possible, because the "spell" was still unbroken (you know that?) I reached over to the next table for a writing pad.

No paper or envelopes, of course. Only a morsel of pink blotting paper, incredibly soft and limp and almost moist, like the tongue of a little dead kitten—which I've never felt.

I sat (but always, underneath, in this state of expectation) rolling the little dead kitten's tongue round my finger, and rolling the soft phrase round my mind while my eyes took in the girls' names and dirty jokes and drawings of bottles and cups that wouldn't sit in the saucers, scattered over the writing pad.

[JNPP-clean-NL, leaf 6]

They are always the same, you know. The girls all[7] have the same names, the cups never sit in the saucers, all the hearts are stuck and tied up with ribbons!

But then, quite suddenly, at the bottom of the page, written in green ink I <u>fell</u> on to that stupid, stale little phrase: <u>je ne parle pas français</u>.

There! It had come—the moment—the "geste"! And although I was so ready, it caught me, it tumbled me over, I was simply overwhelmed . . . And the physical feeling was so curious, so particular. It was as if all of me except my head and my arms, all of me that was under the table, had simply dissolved, melted, turned into water. Just my head remained and two sticks of arms pressing on to the table.

But Ah! the agony of that moment. How can I describe it! I didn't think of anything; I didn't even cry out to myself. Just for one second[8] I was not. I was Agony, Agony, Agony!

Then it passed, and the very second after I was thinking:—"Good God! am I capable of feeling as strongly as that? But I was absolutely unconscious. I was overcome. I was swept off my feet. I hadn't a phrase to meet it with.[9] I didn't even try, in the dimmest way, to 'put it down'!"

And up I puffed and puffed, blowing off finally with:—"After all, I must be 'first rate.' No second rate mind could have experienced such an intensity of feeling—so . . . 'purely.'"

The waiter has touched a spill at the

---

[7] The print version replaces "all" with "always."

[8] "Second" becomes "moment" in the published version.

[9] The published version rearranges these sentences, bringing this sentence in front of "I was overcome!" (CW2, 115).

[JNPP-clean-NL, leaf 7]

red stove and lighted a bubble of gas under a spreading shade. It is no use looking out of window [*sic*], Madame, it is quite dark now. Your white hands hover over your dark shawl. They are like[10] two birds that have come home to roost. They are restless, restless. You tuck them, finally, under your warm little armpits.

Now the waiter has taken a long pole and clashed the curtains together. "All gone," as children say.

And besides Ive no patience with people who can[']t let go of things, who will follow after and cry out. When a thing's gone—its gone—its over and done with. Let it go, then! Ignore it, and comfort yourself, if you want comforting, with the thought that you never do recover the same thing that you lose. Its always a new thing. The moment it leaves you, its changed. Why, that's even true of a hat you chase after, and I dont mean superficially—I mean, "profoundly" speaking . . .

I have made it a rule of my life never to regret and never to look back. Regret is an appaling [*sic*] waste of energy and no one who intends to be a writer can afford to indulge in it. You can't get it into shape; you can't build on it; its only good for wallowing in. Looking back, of course is equally fatal to Art. Its keeping yourself poor. Art cant and wont stand poverty . . .

Je ne parle pas français. Je ne parle pas francais [*sic*]. All the while I wrote that last page my other self has been chasing up and down, out in the dark there.

[JNPP-clean-NL, leaf 8]

It left me just as[11] I began to analyse my grand moment—dashed off, distracted, like a lost dog who thinks at last, at last, he hears the familiar step again.

"Mouse! Mouse! Was that you?[12] Are you near? Is that you leaning from the high window and stretching out your arms for the wings of the shutters? Are you this soft bundle moving towards me through the feathery snow? Are you that little girl pressing open[13] the swing doors of the restaurant? Is that your dark shadow bending forward in the cab? Where are you? Where are you? Which way must I turn? Which way shall I run! And every moment I stand here hesitating you are further away again! Mouse! Mouse!"

Now the poor dog has come back into the café, his tail between his legs, quite exhausted.

"It was—a false—alarm. She's nowhere—to be seen!"

"Lie down, then! Lie down! Lie down!"

My name is Raoul Duquette. I am twenty-six years old and a parisian—a true parisian. About my family—it really doesn't matter. I have no family; I don't want any. I never think about my childhood—Ive forgotten it.

---

[10] "Like" is written over another, indecipherable word.
[11] "When" replaces "as" in the print version.
[12] Instead of "Was that you?" the published version reads: "Where are you?"
[13] "That" is changed to "this," and "Pressing open" becomes "pressing through" in the final version.

In fact there's only one memory that stands out at all. That <u>is</u> rather interesting because it seems to me now so very significant as regards myself

[JNPP-clean-NL, leaf 9]

from the literary point of view. It is this.

When I was about ten, our laundress was an african woman, very big, very dark, with a check handkerchief over her frizzy hair. When she came to our house she always took particular notice of me, and after the clothes had been taken out of her[14] basket she would lift me up into it and give me a rock while I held tight to the handles and screamed for joy and fright.

I was tiny for my age, and pale, with a lovely little half open mouth—I feel sure of that.

One day when I was standing at the door watching her go she turned round and beckoned to me, nodding and smiling in a strange secret way. I never thought of not following. She took me into a little outhouse at the end of the passage, put down her basket,[15] caught me up in her arms and began kissing me. Ah, those kisses! Especially those kisses inside my ears that nearly deafened me!

And then with a soft growl she tore open her bodice and put me to her.

When she set me down again[16] she took from her pocket a little round fried cake covered with sugar and I reeled along the passage back to our door.

As this performance was repeated once a week its no wonder I remember it so vividly. Besides, from that very first afternoon, my childhood was, to put it prettily, "kissed away." I became very languid, very caressing and greedy beyond

[JNPP-clean-NL, leaf 10]

measure. And so quickened, so sharpened—I seemed to understand everybody and to be able to do what I liked with everybody.

I suppose I was in a state of more or less constant physical excitement and that was what appealed to them. For all parisians are more than half—Oh, well, enough of that. And enough of my childhood, too. Bury it under a laundry basket instead of a shower of roses and <u>passons oultre</u>.

I date myself from the moment that I became the tenant of a small bachelor flat on the fifth floor of a tall, not too shabby house, in a street that might or might not be discreet. Very useful, that!

There I emerged, came up into the light and put out my two horns with a study and a bedroom and a kitchen on my back. And real furniture planted in the rooms! In the bedroom a wardrobe with a long glass, a big bed covered with a yellow puffed-up quilt, a

---

[14] "Her" becomes "the" in the published version.
[15] The print version omits the phrase, "put down her basket."
[16] "Again" is omitted in the published version.

bed table with a marble top and a toilet set sprinkled with little[17] apples. In my study—english writing table with drawers, writing chair with leather cushions, books, armchair, side table with paper knife and lamp on it, and some nude studies on the walls. I didn't use the kitchen except to throw old newspaper[18] into.

Ah, I can see myself that first evening, after the furniture men had left and I'd

[JNPP-clean-NL, leaf 11]

managed to shut out[19] my atrocious old concierge—walking about on tip toe, arranging, and standing in front of the long glass with my hands in my pockets and saying to that radiant vision:—"I am a young man who has his own flat. I write for two newspapers. I am going in for serious literature. I am starting a career. The book that I shall bring out will simply <u>stagger</u> the critics. I am going to write about things that have never been touched before. I am going to make a name for myself as a writer about the submerged world. But not as others have done before me. Oh, no. Very naïvely, with a sort of tender humour and from the inside—as though it were all quite simple—quite natural. I see my way perfectly. Nobody has ever done it as I shall do it because none of the others have <u>lived</u> my experiences. I'm rich—I'm rich!"

All the same I had no more money than I have now. Its extraordinary how one can live without money . . . I have quantities of good clothes, silk underwear, two evening suits, four pairs of patent leather boots with light uppers, all sorts of little things, like gloves and powder boxes and a manicure set, perfumes, very good soap—and nothing is paid for! If I really find myself in need of right-down cash well—there's always an african laundress and an outhouse and I am very frank and <u>bon enfant</u> about about [sic] plenty of sugar on the little fried cake, afterwards . . .

[JNPP-clean-NL, leaf 12]

And here Id like to put something on record. Not from any strutting conceit but rather with a mild sense of wonder. I've never yet made the first advances to any woman. And it isn't as though I've only known one class of woman[20]—not by any means. But from little prostitutes and kept women and elderly widows and shop girls and wives of respectable men and even advanced modern literary ladies at the **most*** select dinners and soirées (Ive been there) Ive met invariably with not merely[21] the same readiness, but with the same positive invitation.

It surprised me at first. I used to look across the table and think:—"Is that very serious,[22] very distinguished young lady discussing 'le Kipling' with the gentleman with the brown beard really pressing my foot?" And I was never quite certain until I had pressed hers . . .

Curious—isn't it! Why should I be able to have any woman I want? I don't look at all like a "maiden's dream."

---

[17] "Little" becomes "tiny" in the final version.
[18] In the published version, "newspapers" becomes simply "papers."
[19] The print version changes "to shut out" to "to get rid of."
[20] The published version omits the "And" as well as inverting "only known."
[21] "Merely" becomes "only" in the print version.
[22] The final version eliminates "very serious."

I am little and light with an olive skin, black eyes with long lashes, black silky hair cut short, tiny square teeth that show when I smile. My hands are supple and small. A woman in a bread shop once said to me:—"You have hands for making fine little pastries" . . . I confess, without my clothes I am rather charming. Plump, almost like a girl, with smooth shoulders and I wear a thin gold chain bracelet above my right elbow.

But wait! Isn't it strange I should

[JNPP-clean-NL, leaf 13]

have written that so unconsciously[23] about my body and so on. Its the result of my "bad life," my "submerged life." I am like a little woman in a café who has to introduce herself with a handful of photographs . . . "Me, in my chemise, coming out of an eggshell . . . Me, upside down, in a swing, with a frilly behind like a cauliflower" . . . You know the things.

If you think that[24] what Ive written is merely superficial and impudent and cheap you're wrong. I'll admit it does read[25] so but then its not "all." If it were how could I have experienced what I did when I read that stale little phrase, written in green ink, in the writing pad? That proves there's more in me and that I really am important—doesn't it? Anything a fraction less than that moment of anguish I might have put on. But no! That was real.

"Waiter! A whisky!"

I hate whisky. Every time I take it into my mouth my stomach rises against it, and the stuff they keep here is sure to be particularly vile.

I only ordered it because I am going to write about an englishman. We french are incredibly old-fashioned and out of date still in some ways. I wonder I didn't ask him at the same time for a pair of tweed knickerbockers, a pipe, some long teeth and a set of ginger whiskers.

"Thanks, <u>mon vieux</u>. You haven't got perhaps a

[JNPP-clean-NL, leaf 14]

set of ginger whiskers?"

"No, Monsieur," he answers, sadly. "We dont sell american drinks."

And having smeared a corner of the table he goes back to have another couple of dozen taken by artificial light.

Ugh! the smell of it! And the sickly sensation when one's throat contracts.

"Its bad stuff to get drunk on," says Dick Harmon, turning his little glass in his fingers and smiling his slow, dreaming smile. So he gets drunk on it slowly and dreamily and at a

---

[23] "All" is added before "that," and "so unconsciously" is omitted in the published version.
[24] The print version eliminates "that."
[25] "Sound" replaces "read" in the final version.

certain moment begins to sing, very low, very low, about a man who walked up and down trying to find a place where he could get some dinner.[26]

Ah! how I loved that song, and how I loved the way he sang it, slowly, slowly, in a dark, soft voice.

> There was a man
> Walked up and down
> To get a dinner in the town!

It seemed to hold, in its gravity and muffled measure, all those tall grey buildings, those fogs, those endless streets, those sharp shadows of policemen that mean England.

And then—the subject. The lean, starved creature walking up and down with every house barred against him because he has no "home." How extraordinarily english that is! . . I remember it it [*sic*] ended where he did at last "find a place" and ordered a little cake of fish but when he asked for

[JNPP-clean-NL, leaf 15]

bread the waiter cried contemptuously, in a loud voice:—"We dont serve bread with one fish ball."

What more do you want! How profound these songs are. There is the whole psychology of a people—and how un-french—how un-french!

"Once more, Dick.[27] Once more!" I would plead, clasping my hands and making a pretty mouth at him. He was perfectly content to sing it for ever . . .

There again! Even with Dick—it was he who made the first advances.

I met him at an evening party given by the editor of a new review. It was a very select, very fashionable affair. One or two of the older men were there and the ladies were all[28] extremely <u>comme il faut</u>. They sat on cubist sofas in full evening dress and allowed us to hand them thimbles of cherry brandy and to talk to them about their poetry. For, as far as I can remember they were all poetesses.

It was impossible not to notice Dick. He was the only englishman present, and instead of circulating gracefully round the room as we all did he stayed in one place leaning against the wall, his hands in his pockets, that dreamy half smile on his lips, and replying in excellent french in his low soft voice to anybody who spoke to him.

"Who is he?"

"An englishman. From London. A writer. And he is making a special study of modern french literature."

---

[26] The published version uses the historical present tense instead, when discussing the plot of the song.
[27] The published version emphasises Raoul's accent, stretching out the pronunciation of "Dick" to "Deeck."
[28] "All" is omitted in the print version.

[JNPP-clean-NL, leaf 16]

That was enough for me. My little book—"False Coins"—had just been published.

I was a young, serious writer who was making a special study of modern english literature. But I really hadn't flung my line,[29] before he said, giving himself a soft shake, coming right out of the water for the bait, as it were: –

"Wont you come and see me at my hotel? Come about five oclock and we can have a talk before we go out to dinner."

"Enchanted!"

I was so deeply, deeply flattered that I had to leave him then and there, to rush off and preen and preen myself before the cubist sofas.[30]

What a catch! An englishman, reserved, serious, making a special study of modern french literature . . . That same night "False Coins"[31] with a carefully cordial inscription was posted off and a day or two later we did dine together and spent the evening talking.

Talking—but not only of literature. I discovered to my relief that it wasn't necessary to keep to the tendency of the modern novel, the need for a new form, or the reason why our young men appeared to be just missing it. Now and again, as if by accident, I threw in a card that seemed to have nothing to do with the game, just to see how he'd take it. But each time he gathered it into his hand[32] with his dreamy look and smile unchanged. Perhaps he murmured: –

[JNPP-clean-NL, leaf 17]

"That's very curious!" but not as though it were curious at all.

That calm acceptance went to my head at last. It fascinated me. It led me on and on until I threw every card I possessed at him and sat back and watched him arrange them in his hand.[33]

"Very curious and interesting" . . .

By that time we were both fairly drunk and he began to sing his song, very low, very low,[34] about the man who walked up and down, seeking his dinner.

But I was quite breathless at the thought of what I had done. I had shown somebody both sides of my life. Told him everything as sincerely and truthfully as I could. Taken immense pains to explain things about my "submerged" life which really were disgusting and never could possibly see the literary light of day.[35] On the whole I had made myself out far worse than I was—more boastful, more cynical, more calculating.

---

[29] The final version reads: "But I really had not time to fling my line before [. . .]" (CW2, 119).

[30] "To rush off" is eliminated in the published version.

[31] The print version reads: "a copy of *False Coins*" (CW2, 120).

[32] "Hand" is plural in the final version.

[33] In the published version, "until" becomes "till" and "I possessed" is changed to "that I possessed."

[34] This becomes "very soft, very low" in the print version.

[35] The final version reworks this to "the light of literary day."

And there sat the man I had confided in, singing to himself and smiling . . . It moved me so that real tears came into my eyes. I saw them in the glass,[36] glittering on my long silk lashes—so charming!

After that I took Dick about with me everywhere, and he came to my flat, and sat in the armchair, very indolent, playing with the paper knife. I cannot think why his indolence and dreaminess always gave me the impression that[37] he had been to sea, and all his leisurely, slow ways seemed to be allowing for the movement of the ship. This impression was

[JNPP-clean-NL, leaf 18]

so strong that often when we were together and he got up and left a little woman just when she didn't expect him to get up and leave her, but quite the contrary, I would explain:—"He cant help it, baby. He has to go back to his boat."[38] And I believed it far more than she did . . .

All the while we were together Dick never went with a woman. I sometimes wondered whether he wasn't completely innocent. Why didn't I ask him? Because I never did ask him anything about himself. But late one night he took out his pocket book and a photograph dropped out of it. I picked it up and glanced at it before I gave it to him. It was of a woman. Not quite young. Dark, handsome, wild looking, but but [sic] so full in every line of a kind of haggard pride that even if Dick had not stretched out so quickly I wouldn't have looked longer.

"Out of my sight—you little perfumed fox terrier of a frenchman!" said she.

(In my very worst moments my nose reminds me of a fox terrier's)

"That is my mother," said Dick, putting up his pocketbook.

"Ah-ha! She is beautiful."[39]

But if he had not been Dick I should have been tempted to cross myself, just for fun.

This is how we parted. As we stood outside his hotel one night waiting for the concierge to release the catch of the outer door, he said, looking up at the sky:—"I hope it will be fine tomorrow. I am

---

[36] "In the glass" is omitted in the published version.
[37] "That" is eliminated in the final version.
[38] "Boat" becomes "ship" in the published version.
[39] This line of dialogue is omitted in the print version.

[JNPP-clean-NL, leaf 19]

leaving for England in the morning."

"You're not serious."

"Perfectly. I have to get back. Ive some work to do that I cant manage here."

"But—but have you made all your preparations?"

"Preparations?" He almost grinned. "Ive none to make."

"But—enfin, Dick, England is not the other side of the Bouldevard!"

"It isn't much further off," said he. "Only a few hours, you know."

The door cracked open.

"Ah, I wish I'd known at the beginning of the evening!" I felt hurt. I felt as a woman must feel when a man takes out his watch and remembers an appointment that cannot possibly concern her, except that its claim is the stronger. "Why didn't you tell me?"

He put out his hand, and stood lightly swaying on the step as though the whole hotel were his ship, and the anchor weighed.

"I forgot. Truly I did. But you'll write won't you? Good night, old chap. Ill be over again one of these days."

And then I stood on the shore alone, more like a little fox terrier than ever.

"But after all it <u>was</u> you who whistled to me, you who asked me to come! What a spectacle I've cut wagging my tail and leaping round you ~~while Ive~~ only to be left like this while the boat sails off in its slow, dreamy way! Curse these english! No, this is too insolent altogether! Who do you

[JNPP-clean-NL, leaf 20]

imagine I am? A little paid guide to the night pleasures of Paris? . . No, Monsieur. I am a young writer, very serious, and extremely interested in modern english literature! And I have been insulted—insulted!"

Two days later[40] came a long charming letter from him, written in french that was just a shade too french, but saying how he missed me and counted on our friendship, on keeping in touch. I read it standing in front of the (unpaid for) wardrobe mirror. It was early morning. I wore a blue kimono embroidered with white birds and my hair was still wet; it lay on my forehead, black and gleaming.[41]

"Portrait of Madame Butterfly," said I, "upon hearing of the arrival of <u>ce cher</u> Pinkerton." . . .

According to the books I should have felt tremendously[42] relieved and delighted .. [sic] "Going over to the window he drew apart the curtains and looked out at the Paris trees, just breaking into green.[43] Dick, Dick! My english friend!"

---

[40] The published version changes "later" to "after."

[41] "Black and gleaming" becomes "wet and gleaming" in the final version.

[42] In the print version, "tremendously" becomes "immensely."

[43] The final version adds "buds": "[. . .] breaking into buds and green" (CW2, 122).

But I didn't.[44] I merely felt a little sick. Having been, as it were,[45] for my first ride in an aeroplane I didn't want to go up again, just now.

That passed and months after, in the winter, Dick wrote that he was coming back to Paris to stay indefinitely. Would I take rooms for him? He was bringing a woman friend with him.

[JNPP-clean-NL, leaf 21]

Of course I would. Away the little foxterrier flew. It happened most usefully, too, for I owed too[46] much money at the hotel where I took my meals, and two english people, requiring two rooms[47] for an indefinite time was an excellent sum on[48] account.

Perhaps I did rather wonder, as I stood in the larger of the rooms saying "admirable" to Madame, what the woman friend would be like—but only vaguely.[49]

Either she would be very severe, flat back and front, with a nose that never kissed a powder puff,[50] or she would be tall, fair, dressed in mignonette green, name—Daisy, and smelling of rather sweetish lavender water.

You see by this time, according to my rule of not looking back, I had almost forgotten Dick. I even got the tune of his song about the unfortunate man a little bit wrong when I tried to hum it . . .

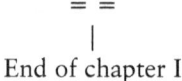

End of chapter I

[JNPP-clean-NL, leaf 21 verso]

Read explanatory letter[51]

---

[44] "But" is eliminated in the final version.

[45] The published version eliminates "as it were."

[46] "Too" is omitted in the print version.

[47] The published version reads: "[. . .] two English people requiring rooms [. . .]" (CW2, 122).

[48] It appears that Mansfield originally had "of" but struck out the lower part of the "f" and added the "n" to make "on."

[49] The syntax is clarified in the print version: "Perhaps I did rather wonder, as I stood in the larger of the two rooms with Madame, saying 'Admirable,' what the woman friend would be like [. . .]" (CW2, 122).

[50] This phrase is omitted in the final version.

[51] This appears very lightly in pencil and is circled, most likely by an editor.

This manuscript is the property of:—[52]
John Middleton Murry
47 Redcliffe Road
Fulham S.W. 10.
London
England
A reward will be paid to any person
delivering it to him at the above
address.

---

[52] This note is written in ink at the bottom right of the page, evidently intended to be included with the clean copy of the manuscript to be sent for publication. Two lines are drawn on the left-hand side of the note.

A Note on the Manuscript of "Revelations"

While Margaret Scott typically did not transcribe Mansfield's manuscripts in *The Katherine Mansfield Notebooks*, simply noting their placement in the notebooks with a footnote, she does include a transcription of "Revelations" from Notebook 4.[1] However, in her transcription, she does not include any of Mansfield's edits in the draft, choosing rather to omit any sections which Mansfield crossed through. For a study of the manuscripts, this is a significant oversight, especially as this draft, more than any other, reveals Mansfield editing out direct dramatization in favor of free indirect discourse. This is particularly apparent in the revisions made between pages 4 recto and 4 verso.

As this is probably the original draft of the story, suggested by the fact that it is heavily edited, it is likely there was a now lost intermediate version; Mansfield at the very least would have made a clean copy to send to the *Athenaeum*, where it was first published in June 1920. This is reinforced by the fact that there are significant differences between this draft and the published version. The most significant of these differences can be found between pages 5 recto and 5 verso as compared to the *Collected*, which is based on the version published in *Bliss and Other Stories* (1920). It would be worth exploring any shifts between the version published in the *Athenaeum* and that published in *Bliss*, which I have not done.

---

[1] See Notebooks 2, 211–215.

This is the first draft of
Revelations in "Bliss"[3]

But this morning she'd been awakened by one great slam of the front door. Bang![4] The flat shook. What is it![5] She jerked up in bed, clutching the eider down—and she felt as if that "bang!" her heart beat.[6] Then she heard voices in the passage, the clatter of crockery.[7] Marie knocked—come in ᵉⁿᵗʳᵉ—she cried faintly[8]—and as the door opened—with a sharp tearing, flip rip out flew the blind and the curtain, stiffening, flapping, jerking—the tassel of the blind knocked knocked **against*** the window—Ah—voila, said Marie, setting down the **tea + running*** to the window then ˢʰᵉ cried in that ᵃ high sharp voice as though she were trying to make herself xxxx **in a ship at sea.**[9] ["]C'est le vent, madame, c'est un vent insupportable!"

Up flew the blind, the window pane jerked upward—[10]a whitey grayish light filled the room. Monica caught a glimpse of a huge pale sky with a cloud like a torn shirt dragging across, before she hid her eyes with her sleeve—

Marie the curtains—Quick draw the curtains.[11] and in her exuberance Marie clashed them across

forgetting in one dreadful moment xx of three years.

Monica fell back into the bed. No, no tea—impossible. My valium tablets **are** in the little gold box on the dressing table + then go—She almost broke down on the last word. She shut her eyes + she felt big tears ready to fall. But if Maria would **take** over a little cup of tea instead of water sugge xxx Marie. At last she understood. Monica was **past speech** she heard Marie pour out the tea.[12]

Ring-ing a ting Ring Ring Ring a ting ping—It was the telephone—At that she **grew quite calm***. There are always these moments in life when the limits of suffering are reached and **we become** heroes and heroines. Monica sat up in bed + sipped her tea! Go and see who it is Marie.[13]

It is Mr said M. He wishes to know if Madame will lunch with him at 130 at **Princes***.[14]

---

[2] The top righthand corner has a circled 3, indicating a page number; however, quite a few pages prior to this page have been torn out, so the first few paragraphs of the story are missing.

[3] This is not in Mansfield's hand. The inside front cover of the notebook includes the same reference detail in the same hand. "KMM I:V:1920" is written neatly in the center by Mansfield. There are a few scribbled phrases: one is illegible and the other is simply "xxx's friend."

[4] The *Collected* changes the exclamation point to a period.

[5] The exclamation point becomes a question mark in the *Collected*.

[6] The dash before "her heart beat" becomes a semi-colon in the *Collected*.

[7] The *Collected* does not include the phrase, "the clatter of crockery."

[8] Monica's response does not appear in the *Collected*.

[9] Many of the dashes are changed to different punctuation in the *Collected*. It also has "tray" instead of "tea" and omits the phrase: "ˢʰᵉ cried in that ᵃ high sharp voice as though she were trying to make herself xxxx in a ship at sea."

[10] The *Collected* reads: "Up rolled the blind; the window went up with a jerk" (CW2, 213).

[11] The *Collected* omits "draw."

[12] Except for the first sentence, the rest of this paragraph is omitted from the *Collected*.

[13] In the *Collected*, this section is pared down to: "'Ring-ting-a-ping-ping, ring-ting-a-ping-ping.' It was the telephone. The limit of her suffering was reached; she grew quite calm. 'Go and see, Marie'" (CW2, 214).

[14] The tag line is omitted in the *Collected* and the last sentence truncated.

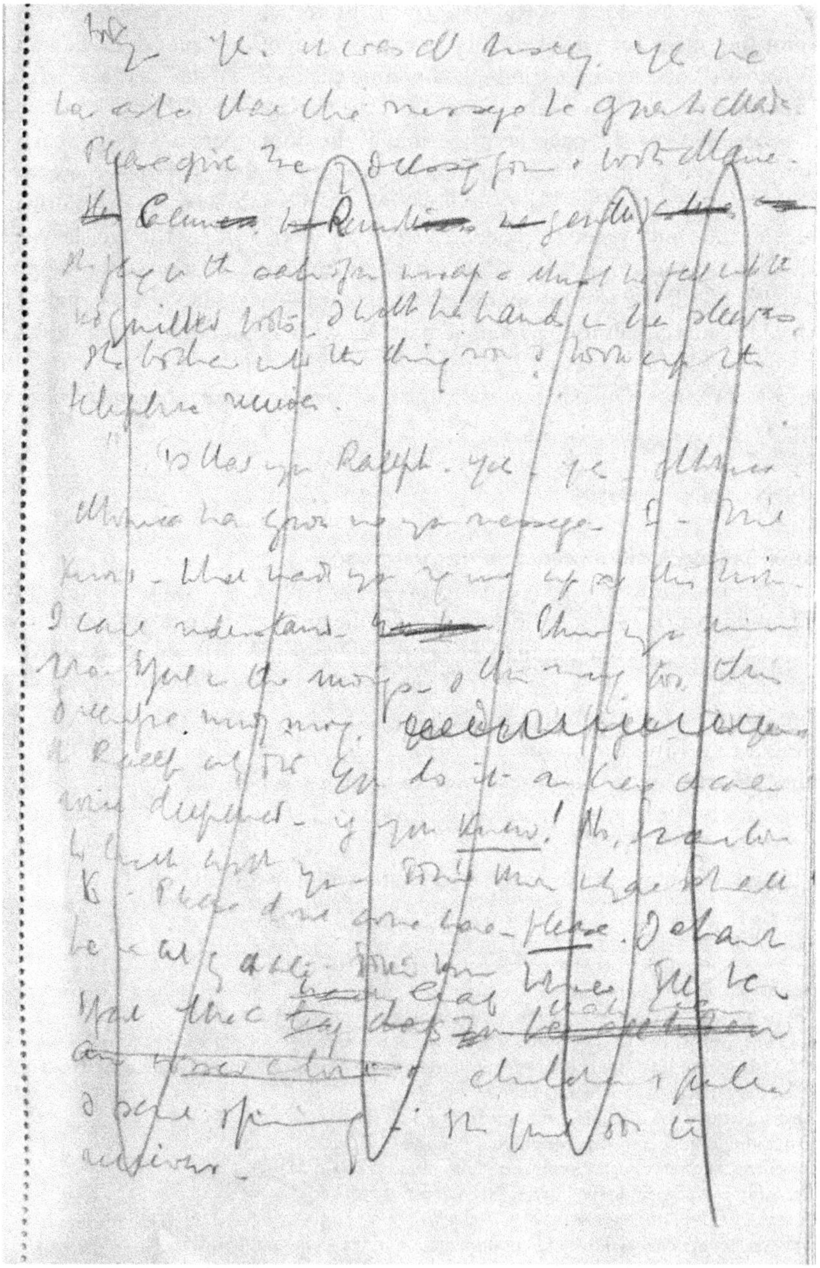

FIGURE 13: Page 2 recto, Notebook 4, "Revelations," Katherine Mansfield Papers, Newberry Library (box 2, folder 3), 1–11. Image courtesy of the Newberry Library.

[Rev-NB4-NL, page 4 recto][15]

today. Yes, it was Mr **himself**. Yes he has asked that the message be given to Madam.[16] ~~Please give me my~~ **dressing** gown + boots ~~Marie. Her Ccalmness her Rrxxxness her~~ ~~gentle~~ **gesture** ~~xxx she flung on the satin + fur wrap + thrust her feet into the red quilted~~ ~~boots + with her hands in her sleeves, she~~ **withdrew** ~~into the dining room + took up the~~ ~~telephone receiver.~~

 ~~"Is that you Ralph. Yes, yes, Monica. Monica~~[17] ~~has given me your message—I—don't~~ ~~know—what had you ring me up at this~~ **hour** ~~—I can't understand—you know. I~~ **know** ~~you xxxxx xxx + xxx in the mornings—+ this morning too, this dreadful windy morning.~~ ~~You didn't~~ ~~forget—did you~~ ~~then Ralph why did you do it and here the calm voice~~ ~~deepened—if you~~ ~~knew~~! ~~No, I xxxxx to lunch with you—I don't know what I shall do—~~ ~~Please don't come here—~~ ~~please~~. ~~I shant be in at any xxxxx. I don't know where Ill be—I~~ ~~feel like a leaf thats xxx been all~~ **broken** ~~xxxxx leaf that's been~~ ~~and tossed about +~~ ~~clutched +~~ ~~pulled + sent xxxxx—she put down the receiver.~~[18]

[Rev-NB4-NL, page 4 verso]

Instead of replying she put the tea cup down + asked Marie in a small wondering voice what time it was.[19] It was half past nine. She lay still + half closed her xxxxx.[20] Tell Monsieur I cannot come—and as Marie waited—that's all said she gently.[21]

 But as the door shut the strange bedfellow who had slipped in, **unsettled** with Marie's message, suddenly gripped her, close close, violent, half strangling her—xxxxx xxxxx why.[22]

 How dared he.[23] How dared Ralph do such a thing when **he** knew how agonizing her nerves were in the morning—[24]Hadn't she explained implored + even—though lightly of course—she couldnt say such a thing directly given him to understand that was the unforgivable thing![25] ~~As xxxxx xxxxx~~

[Rev-NB4-NL, page 5 recto]

~~a windy frightful xxxxx~~—Did he think it was just a fad of hers—a little feminine folly to be laughed at + tossed aside—[26]And only last night he had said: ["]You know I know you

---

[15] This page has wavy, vertical lines scribbled from top to bottom, suggesting the entire contents was to be omitted.

[16] The *Collected* adds "immediately" after "to be given to Madame."

[17] It seems that Mansfield has confused the names here. It should probably be Marie.

[18] Rather than having Monica speak directly to Ralph as in this passage, the following page shows Mansfield shift to free indirect discourse to convey Monica's feelings about Ralph's calling.

[19] The *Collected* replaces "she put" with "Monica put."

[20] The *Collected* has "eyes" where this unknown word appears, but the word Mansfield has written looks more like "voice." The manuscript repeats "Half past nine" (stricken out) between these two lines; there is no indication where it might be intended to go.

[21] The *Collected* simply reads: "'Tell Monsieur I cannot come,' she said gently" (CW2, 214).

[22] The *Collected* instead reads: "But as the door shut, anger—anger suddenly gripped her close, close, violent, half strangling her" (CW2, 214).

[23] The period becomes a question mark in the *Collected*.

[24] This dash is changed to an exclamation point in the *Collected*.

[25] The *Collected* has: "Hadn't she explained and described and even—though lightly, of course; she couldn't say such a thing directly—given him to understand that this was the one unforgivable thing" (CW2, 214).

[26] The first dash becomes a comma in the published version, while the second dash becomes a question mark.

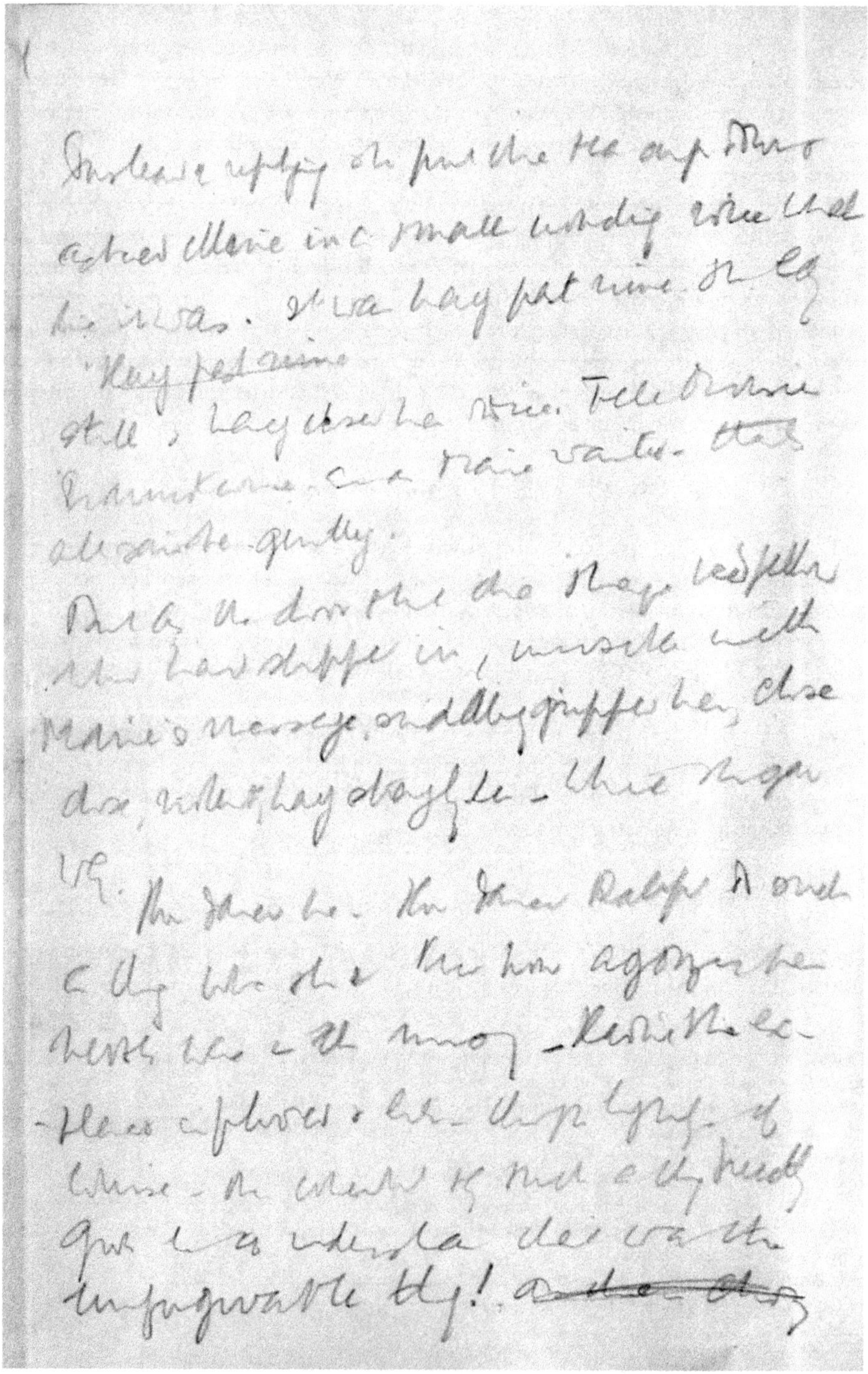

FIGURE 14: Page 2 verso, Notebook 4, "Revelations," Katherine Mansfield Papers, Newberry Library (box 2, folder 3), 1–11. Image courtesy of the Newberry Library.

much better than you **know** me—though of course you won't believe it. And I know myself better than you know me—You see women do have a way of flying off at awfully brilliant tangent and men, dull, story, half alive men go plodding on. Collecting impression after impression, testing then verifying them. Yes laugh + laugh. I know the way your lip lifts and your **eye** ~~shine~~ lights. And he leaned across the table as if intoxicated. I adore you—youre ^more^ beautiful than all the xxx xxx of the world." I dont care who sees that. I love you—let them look. xxx xxx Id like to be on a mountain top with you + all the search lights of the earth **might play** upon us![27]

Heavens! Monica almost

[Rev-NB4-NL, page 5 verso]

clutched her head—How incredible men were! Was it possible she really loved him? How could she love a person who talked like that—What had she been doing all these months—ever since that dinner party when he had seen her home + asked her if he might come + see her afterward. I want to come + see again your slow Arabian smile. Oh what nonsense. What utter nonsense! And she remembered how at the time a strange deep thrill unlike anything she ever had felt before had made her almost faint ----- But now.[28]

Coal coal coal
and
Old iron old iron old iron[29]
sounded from below—it was all over—Understand her?[30] He had

[Rev-NB4-NL, page 6 recto]

understood nothing, that ringing her up on a windy morning was immensely **immensely** [*sic*] significant.[31] <u>And</u> it was the End. Xxxx, her strange bed fellow slipped away—she felt empty and cold—when Marie came in later to take her to her bath she said: Mr replied he would be in the vestibule at half past one if Madame changed her mind—

---

[27] This paragraph undergoes considerable revision, based on the published version which reads:

Why only last night she had said: "Ah, but you must take me seriously, too." And he had replied: "My darling, you'll not believe me, but I know you infinitely better than you know yourself. Every delicate thought and feeling I bow to, I treasure. Yes, laugh! I love the way your lip lifts"—and he had leaned across the table—"I don't care who sees that I adore all of you. I'd be with you on a mountain-top and have all the searchlights of the world play upon us" (CW2, 214).

[28] This paragraph is revised significantly. The *Collected* reads:

"Heavens!" Monica almost clutched her head. Was it possible he had really said that? How incredible men were! And she had loved him—how could she have loved a man who talked like that. What had she been doing ever since that dinner party months ago, when he had seen her home and asked if he might come and "see again that slow Arabian smile?" Oh, what nonsense—what utter nonsense—and yet she remembered at the time a strange deep thrill unlike anything she had ever felt before (CW2, 214).

[29] These calls from below are punctuated with exclamation points in the *Collected*, and they appear within the same paragraph.

[30] The published version replaces the dashes with periods.

[31] The final version places a period after "understood nothing" and eliminates the second "immensely."

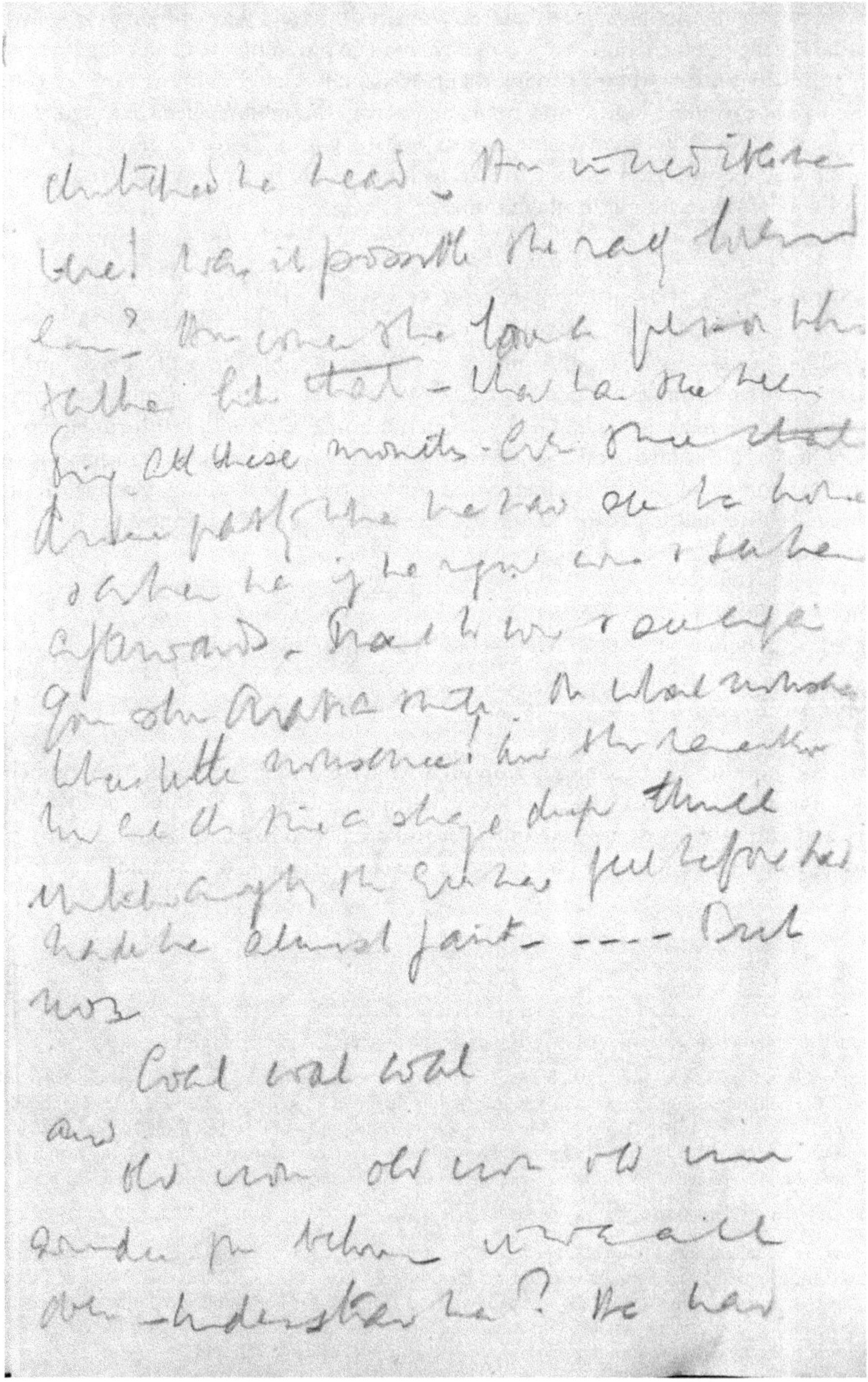

FIGURE 15: Page 3 verso, Notebook 4, "Revelations," Katherine Mansfield Papers, Newberry Library (box 2, folder 3), 1–11. Image courtesy of the Newberry Library.

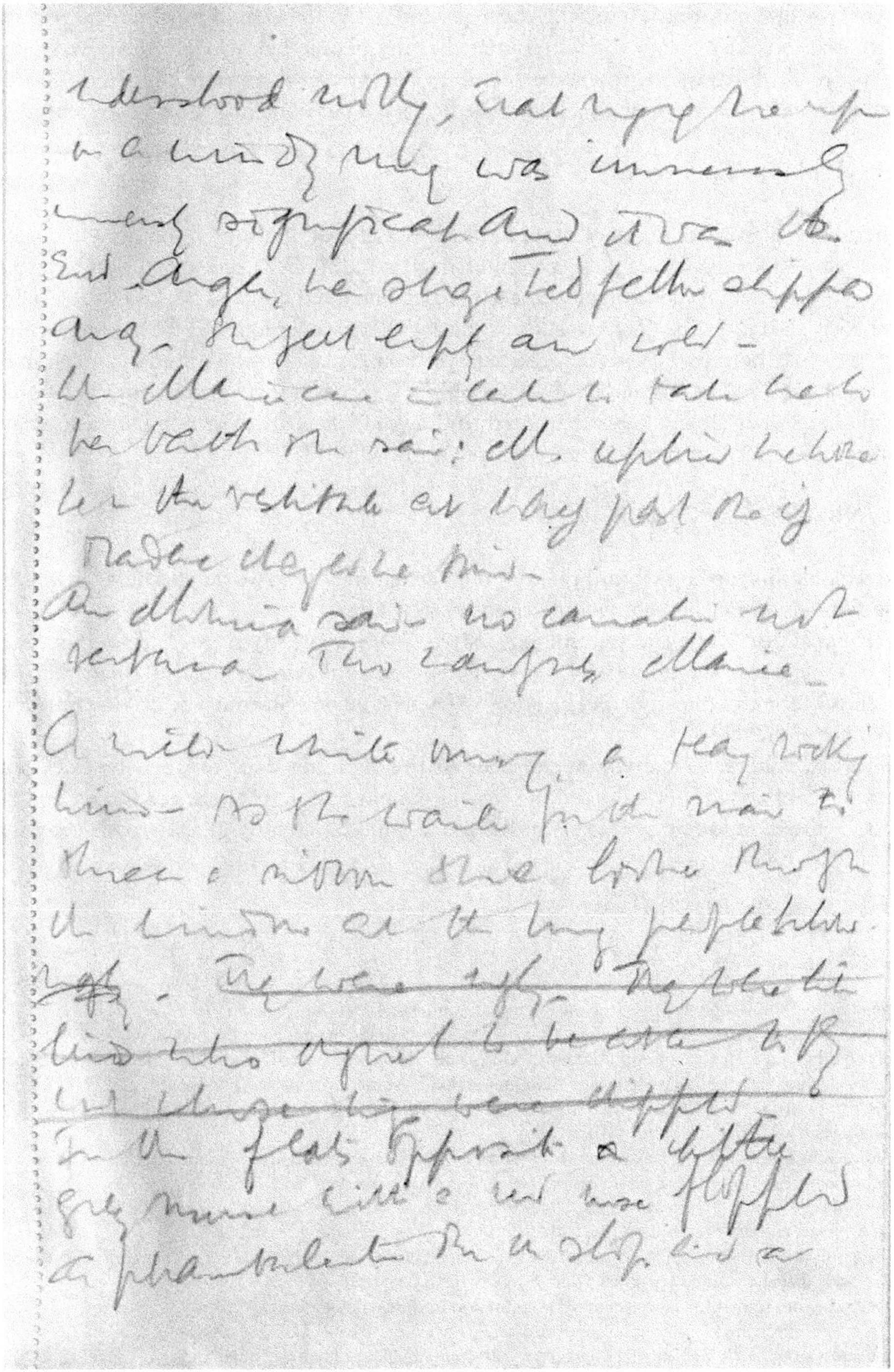

FIGURE 16: Page 4 recto, Notebook 4, "Revelations," Katherine Mansfield Papers, Newberry Library (box 2, folder 3), 1–11. Image courtesy of the Newberry Library.

And Monica said no **carnation*** not **verbena***. Two handfuls, Marie—[32]

A wild white **morning***, a tearing rocking wind[33]—As she waited for the maid to xxx **a mirror she** looked through the window at the tiny people below. ~~Ugly. They were ugly. They were like birds who ought to be able to fly but whose wings were clipped.~~ In the flats opposite a little grey nurse with a **bent nose** flopped a perambulator down the steps and a

[Rev-NB4-NL, page 6 verso]

woman ~~with a great~~ let a xxxxx tapped the ~~glass~~ xxx xxx wind + waved her—her—xxx to the baby—~~I xxx~~! Monica almost **found herself** nodding her head, too. I don't xxx xxx any[34]—+ sat down **to her mirror***. She was pale. The maid combed back her dark hair—combed it all back + her face was like a mask. There was a ~~line of blue under~~ ~~each eye~~ shadow under her eyes—her lips were dark red—her eyes **very** pink.[35] As she stared at herself in the blueish shadowy glass, she suddenly felt—oh the strangest **most*** tremendous excitement **filling*** her slowly slowly—+ she wanted to fling out her arms to ~~xxx~~ to laugh, to scatter everything—to cry Im free Im free—Im free as the wind![36]

[Rev-NB4-NL, page 7 recto]

And now all this ~~rattling~~ vibrating—trembling, **exciting**, flying world was hers—it was her Kingdom—No, no, she belonged to nobody—but Life—[37]

That will do, **Marie** she stammered—My hat. My coat. My bag—And then get me a taxi.[38] Where was she going? Oh, anywhere—She could not stand this silent flat, ~~pale~~ noiseless Marie this ghostly quiet <u>interior</u>—She must be out. She must be driving quickly—anywhere anywhere—[39]

The taxi is here, Madame—~~At the door~~ As the big outer door of the flat xxxxx open the wild wind caught her—floated her across the pavement.[40] Where to? Oh where. She got in ~~+ the man looking~~ ~~cross~~ ~~slammed the~~ + smiled radiantly at the cross sleepy man she said[41]—**Take me**—

---

[32] This line and the last half of the previous paragraph undergo significant revision: Would he understand that? She could almost have laughed. "You rang me up when the person who understood me simply couldn't have." It was the end. And when Marie said: "Monsieur replied he would be in the vestibule in case Madame changed her mind," Monica said: "No, not verbena, Marie. Carnations. Two handfuls" (CW2, 214).

[33] The section from this point to where Monica sits at her mirror, just before "She was pale," is not included in the final version.

[34] Mansfield has drawn a line separating this section from what follows, perhaps indicating that what precedes should be omitted, as it is in the final version. See note 32.

[35] The *Collected* reads: "The maid combed back her hair—combed it all back—and her face was like a mask, with pointed eyelids and dark red lips" (CW2, 214).

[36] The published version adjusts to more standard punctuation; otherwise, the main change is that the final version adds that she wanted "to shock Marie" by crying out.

[37] The dashes are traded for more standard punctuation in the final version.

[38] "Then" becomes "now" in the published version.

[39] The most notable change in this passage is that "feminine" is added to "quiet <u>interior</u>," making it "quiet feminine interior." Otherwise, the *Collected* exchanges more standard punctuation for the dashes.

[40] The beginning of this sentence reads "As she pressed open the big outer doors of the flats [. . .]" in the published version.

[41] The final version describes the taxi driver as "the cross, cold-looking driver."

[Rev-NB4-NL, page 7 verso]

And then gave him the name of her hair dresser.[42] What would she have done without her hairdresser.[43] Whenever Monica had nowhere else to go to +or nothing to do she drove there.[44] She might just as well have her hair waved + by the time it was done she would have thought out a plan. **Then just** xxxxx xxx xx came flying past the windows. One fell on to her lap. A happy xxxxx! As she saw herself as a lovely little girl with bobbing curls trying to catch xxxxx the school xxxxx xxxx. I love xxxxx—I love xxxxx she said **lying** back in the cab.[45] The sleepy driver drove at a tremendous pace—Weaving in and out of the traffic and she let herself be tossed from side to side[46]—She wished he could

[Rev-NB4-NL, page 8 recto]

go faster and faster! **Oh*** to be free of Princes at 1.30, of being the eat kitten in the **basket hidden** swans down basket—of being an Arabian and a **grave***, delighted child and a strange wild little creature and . . . .[47] Never again she cried aloud, clenching her small hands. The xxxxx But **the cab stopped***. The **driver*** was standing holding the door open for her.[48]

∧   ∧   ∧   ∧

Here was the xxxx **warm glittering*** shop Mr She hairdresser's shop was warm + glittering.[49] It smelled of soap and burnt paper and wallflower brilliantine. And there was Madame **behind*** the counter like a pain du jour round, white xxx fat[50]—her like xxxx a p her head like a powder puff rolling on a black satin pincushion. Monica always

Yes Madame—xx xxx

had the feeling that they loved her in this shop + understood her—the real her—far better than many of her friends did. She did not know why.[51] She was

[Rev-NB4-NL, page 8 verso]

herself here—She + Madame had often talked - - - quite strangely together + George who did her hair—young, dark slender George She was really fond of.[52]

But today—how curious! Madame hardly greeted her. Her face was whiter than ever but **rims*** of bright red showed round her blue bead eyes + even xxxthe rings on her tiny fingers did not flash.[53] They were cold—dead, like chips of glass.[54] When she had her back

---

[42] The *Collected* reads: "she told him to take her to her hairdresser's" (CW2, 215).
[43] A line points to this addition at the top of the page.
[44] "Or" is superimposed on a + sign, changing "and" to "or." The published version also adds "on earth," to make "nothing on earth to do."
[45] The passage from "Then just" to this point is omitted in the published version.
[46] The "sleepy driver" becomes the "cross, cold driver" in the final version, which also omits "weaving in and out of traffic."
[47] The published version adds "tiny" in front of "kitten" and changes the dash to a comma.
[48] The final version combines the last two sentences. On the line below this section, Mansfield has added what appear to be four small arrows pointing up and separating it from what follows.
[49] "Hairdresser's" is superimposed on another, illegible word.
[50] "White and fat" are inverted in the published version.
[51] This sentence is omitted in the *Collected*.
[52] The final version reads: "She was her real self here, and she and Madame had often talked—quite strangely—together. Then there was George who did her hair, young, dark, slender George. She was really fond of him" (CW2, 215).
[53] The published version has "pudgy fingers" rather than "tiny fingers."
[54] The dash is replaced by a comma in the final version.

to Monica—+ ~~whispered~~ ^{called*} over the wall telephone Georges—there was a note in her voice that had never been there before—But **Monica*** would not believe it no—She refused to—It was just **her*** imagination[55] +

[Rev-NB4-NL, page 9 recto]

She sniffed **greedily*** the warm scented air—+ passed **behind*** the curtain **into*** the small cubicle.[56]

~~She~~ Her hat + jacket were off + **hanging*** on a peg + still Georges did not come— This was the first time he had ever not been there to hold the chair for her—to take her hat to **hang*** up her ~~xxx~~ bag—**dangling*** it in ~~its~~his[57] fingers as though it were something he'd never seen before—something faery. And how quiet the shop was.[58] There was nobody else there no **sound*** from Madame.[59] ~~The~~ **window** ~~of the cubicle even looked~~ **as** ~~if xxx Monica~~ **Every time** wind blew the old house seemed to shake—the wind **hooted***— the portraits of Ladies of the Pompadour period looked down and smiled, cunning + sly.[60] Monica wished she hadnt come. Oh what a mistake to have come. Fatal! Fatal![61]

[Rev-NB4-NL, page 9 verso]

If George did not **come*** that **next*** moment she would go away.[62] She took off the white Kimono—She didnt want to look at herself any more. When she opened a big pot of cream on the glass shelf her fingers trembled. There was a tugging feeling at her heart as though her happiness her **marvelous*** happiness were trying to get free.[63] Oh, Ill go. Ill not stay. She took down her hat. But just at that moment there was a **movement** from out- side + ~~the light~~ steps sounded + looking in the mirror she saw Georges [*sic*] **bowing*** in the doorway—How strangely he smiled. It was the mirror, of course.[64]

[Rev-NB4-NL, page 10 recto]

She turned round—quickly his lips curled back in a sort of grin + —wasn't he unshaved? He looked almost green in the face![65] Very sorry to **have*** kept you waiting he said, sliding, gliding forward.[66]

---

[55] The *Collected* omits "she had her back to Monica" and changes the dashes to more standard punctuation.

[56] The published version changes the dash to a comma and adds "velvet" (i.e. "velvet curtain").

[57] Mansfield has written "his" over what appears to have originally been "its."

[58] The published version reproduces these sentences with only minor adjustments to punctuation and syntax.

[59] The *Collected* omits "There was nobody else there," reading: "There was not a sound even from Madame" (CW2, 216).

[60] The final version of the first part of this sentence reads: "Only the wind blew, shaking the old house" (CW2, 216), and the dashes become more standard punctuation.

[61] The exclamation points become periods in the final version.

[62] The published version adds "Where was George?" before this sentence, and replaces "George" with "he" and "come" with "appear."

[63] The published version places "her marvellous happiness" between dashes.

[64] The final version omits "there was a movement from out-side" and changes the dash to a period. It also changes "strangely" to "queerly" and ends this sentence with an exclamation point.

[65] The *Collected* reads: "She turned round quickly. His lips curled back in a sort of grin and—wasn't he unshaved?—he looked almost green in the face" (CW2, 216).

[66] "He said" becomes "he mumbled" in the published version.

Oh no, she wasn't going to stay. Im afraid she said.[67] But he had lighted the gas + laid the tongs across, + was **handing her** the Kimono.[68]

It's a wind he said—Monica **submitted***[69]. She smelt his fresh young fingers **pinning***[70] the jacket under her chin—

Yes there is a wind, said she, sinking back into the chair—and silence fell.

George took out the pins

[Rev-NB4-NL, page 10 verso]

in ~~the~~ his[71] expert way—her hair tumbled back but he didn't hold it as he usually did—as tho to feel **how*** fine + soft + heavy it was. He didnt say it was in a lovely condition—he let it fall—and taking a brush out of a drawer he coughed faintly + said—"Yes it's a pretty strong one. I should say it was."[72]

~~T~~She had no reply to make. The brush fell on her hair. Oh oh how mournful—how mournful.[73] It fell quick + light ~~parting—dividing—+ xxx~~ it fell like leaves, + then it fell more heavy, **tugging** tugging like the xxx at her heart.[74]

[Rev-NB4-NL, page 11 recto]

Thats enough, said she shaking herself free.[75]

Did I do it too much, said ~~he~~ George + he crouched over the tongs.[76] Im **sorry***—There came the smell of burnt paper—the smell she loved—+ he swung swung swung the hot tongs round in his hand—[77]

"I shouldn't be surprised when it rained"[78]—**and** he was just taking up the first piece of her hair when she stopped him—[79]

She looked at him. She saw herself looking at him in the white kimono like a nun looks.[80] ~~at a~~[81] "Is there something the matter. Has something happened."[82] But Georges gave a queer half shrug + grimace.[83] Oh no Madame. Just a little occurrence—

---

[67] "She said" becomes "she began" in the final version.

[68] The published version changes "handing her" to "holding out."

[69] While the word here clearly begins as "submitted"; however, the ending appears misspelled: "submitete."

[70] The word is illegible. It appears she may have begun writing "attaching" and then written "pinning" over it, but neither is clearly evident.

[71] "His" is written over what appears to be "the."

[72] In the final version, the dashes are changed to more standard punctuation. The *Collected* changes "he coughed faintly and said" to "he coughed faintly, cleared his throat and said dully" (CW2, 216).

[73] In the final version, commas are added after the two "ohs" and the sentence ends with an exclamation point.

[74] The *Collected* reads: "It fell quick and light, it fell like leaves; and then it fell heavy, tugging like the tugging at her heart" (CW2, 216).

[75] "Said she" becomes "she cried" in the final version.

[76] The published version makes this into two sentences and substitutes "asked George" for "said George."

[77] The final version eliminates the repetition of "swung" and adds "staring before him."

[78] The final version changes "when" to "if."

[79] The *Collected* reads: "He took up a piece of her hair, when—she couldn't bear it any longer—she stopped him" (CW2, 216).

[80] The published version joins the two sentences with a semicolon and omits "looks" (i.e. "like a nun").

[81] The period after "looks" was most likely added after, as "at a" seems to have been intended as a continuation of the simile.

[82] The final period becomes a question mark in the final version.

[83] "Queer" is eliminated in the published version.

[Rev-NB4-NL, page 11 verso]

√ √ √ √

~~+ he took up the piece of hair again.~~

~~Just the front—only the front. Just a wave or two here + then a xxx she said.~~ √√√[84]

Oh, she wasn't deceived.[85] That was it! Something had happened![86] ~~It wasn't her xxx to~~ The silence—really—the silence seemed to come drifting through the air like flakes of snow. It was cold in the little cubicle—all cold and **glitering*** [*sic*].[87] The nickel taps the jets—the sprays looked somehow almost malignant.[88] The wind rattled the window pane—a piece of iron banged—+ the young man went on changing the tongs crouching over her.[89] Oh, how terrifying Life is—how dreadful—[90] It

[Rev-NB4-NL, page 12 recto]

is the loneliness which is so appalling. We whirl along like leaves—+ nobody knows, nobody cares where we fall—in what dark river we float away.[91]

The tugging feeling seemed to rise into her throat. It ached ached. She wanted to cry.[92]

"That will do," she ~~said~~ ᵂʰⁱˢᵖᵉʳᵉᵈ give me the pins. And as he stood beside her with the pins in his hand, leaning forward, so submissive, so silent, she nearly dropped her arms + sobbed.[93] She couldn't bear it.[94] Like a wooden man, the gay young George still slided [*sic*] glided, handed her her hat + **veil*** her coat—taking the note + **brought*** back her change.[95] She stuffed it away—Where was she going to now.[96]

[Rev-NB4-NL, page 12 verso]

George took a brush. There is a white powder on your coat, he murmured—He brushed it **away***—+ then suddenly he raised himself—and looking at Monica—he gave a strange wave with the brush + said: The truth is Madame, since you are an old customer—my

---

[84] The four check marks at the top of the page seem to indicate that the section that was stricken out is to be retained. However, only "+ he took up the piece of hair again" is part of the published version. The three check marks at the end perhaps signaling this section should indeed be eliminated.

[85] The final version includes "But" at the beginning of this sentence.

[86] The exclamation point becomes a period in the published version.

[87] The second and third dashes are changed to commas in the final version, and "She shivered" is added between the two sentences.

[88] The dash is omitted and "and" is added to create a list in the final version.

[89] "Window pane" becomes "window-frame" in the published version, and the dashes are changed to a semicolon and comma respectively.

[90] The *Collected* reads: "Oh, how terrifying Life was, thought Monica. How dreadful" (CW2, 217).

[91] In the published version, the two dashes become commas, and the comma after "nobody knows" is changed to a dash.

[92] In the *Collected*, a comma is placed after the first "ached" and the period changed to a semicolon. "Wanted" is revised as "longed."

[93] The phrase "with the pins in his hand, leaning forward" is omitted in the final version, as is the "and" at the beginning of the sentence.

[94] "Any more" is added to the end of this sentence in the published version.

[95] The *Collected* reads: "Like a wooden man the gay young George still slid, glided, handed her her hat and veil, took the note, and brought back the change" (CW2, 217).

[96] Rather than "She stuffed it away," the published version reads: "She stuffed it into her bag." The period of the last sentence becomes a question mark.

little daughter died dis[97] morning. A first child—+ then his white face crumpled like paper and he turned his back on her + began brushing the kimono—[98]

~~How old Monica xx felt the tears flow on under her veil~~—The tears ran over Monica's cheek—How old? she whispered[99]

[Rev-NB4-NL, page 13 recto]

Then as a xxx came from xxx—she ran out of the shop, into the taxi.[100]

The driver looking furious swung off his seat + slammed the door again—Where to?[101]

"Princes!" she sobbed.

And all the way there she saw nothing but a tiny tiny wax doll with a feather of hair—lying meek, its little hands + feet crossed—[102]

And then just before she came to Princes she saw a flower shop full of white flowers. Oh what a thought. What a perfect thought.[103] Lilies-of-the-valley and white pansies + double white violets sent to **him at the**[104]

[Rev-NB4-NL, page 13 verso]

From an unknown friend. From one who understands—~~xxx To a Dear~~ For a ^{little girl} hair dressers shop.[105] She tapped against the window, but the driver did not hear, and , any way, they were at Princes already—[106]

---

[97] While "dis" could be "this" given Mansfield's handwriting, the beginning letter of the word is very much like the "d" of "died" just before. Earlier in the story, Mansfield writes "Georges," suggesting a foreign spelling, and if the current word is in fact "dis," it may signal an attempt to reflect a foreign accent which is abandoned in the published version.

[98] Except for the dash after "A first child," which is retained, the others are changed to more standard punctuation in the final version. "Cotton" is also added to describe the kimono.

[99] These last two sentences are changed to simply: "'Oh, oh,' Monica began to cry" (CW2, 217).

[100] The first part of this sentence is omitted in the published version.

[101] The final version adds commas surrounding "looking furious," and the dash becomes a period.

[102] The second "tiny" is omitted in the published version, and "gold" is added before "hair" (i.e. "feather of gold hair"). The dashes become a comma and a period, respectively.

[103] These two sentences become simply "Oh, what a perfect thought" in the *Collected*.

[104] "And a white velvet ribbon" is added after "white violets," and the rest of the sentence is abandoned in the published version.

[105] A line is drawn beginning under "shop" and pointing toward the inserted "little girl" between the two lines. In the published version, the line reads: "For a little girl," omitting "hair dressers shop." An ellipsis follows each phrase.

[106] After the final line, written in ink rather than pencil (but stricken out in pencil by a wavy line), is the following: "You know we've got you, she hissed. And he nodded his **quiet** xxx in queer approval.

This pen simply must **not** get **crossed**—thereby the way we showed xxx it xxx xxx xx by sharing it with those who need it less."

Then, at a different angle, this phrase appears: "The Peer cometh Kingsway."

The right hand margin has three 3-dimensional boxes drawn in ink, two of which appear to be open.

A Note on the Manuscripts of "The Stranger"

The Newberry Library has two manuscript versions of "The Stranger," which was originally titled "The Interloper." The cleaner version (Stran-clean-NL), possibly that which Mansfield copied from the rougher draft (Stran-rough-NL), likely to submit for publication in the *London Mercury*, where it appeared in January 1921, a speculation supported by the fact that Mansfield has added her return address on the verso of the final page of this clean manuscript. The rougher version, which includes some significant edits, may be the original draft, but it is difficult to say for sure as the story is fully intact. If it is the original draft, it suggests that the writing of the story followed a similar genesis as "A Cup of Tea," which Mansfield indicates that she wrote in a single sitting.[1]

As with many of her drafts, Mansfield widely employs the dash, and this comes up in her correspondence with Murry. Of the dash, she writes:

> About the punctuation in The Stranger. [. . .] No, my dash isn't quite a feminine dash (certainly when I was young it was). But it was intentional in that story. I was trying to do away with the three dots. They have been so abused by female & male writers that I fight shy of them—*much* tho' I need them. [. . .] Ill try however to remember *commas*.[2]

Dashes are heavily used even in the published versions, confirming her intentionality in their use in the story; in the published versions of other stories, dashes are often replaced by commas or periods.

---

[1] See CW4, 402–3.
[2] *Letters* 4, 118–119. Emphasis in original.

Rough copy. Much corrected copy posted to Jack 9.XI.1920[3]

The ~~Interloper~~ Stranger
By
Katherine Mansfield

It seemed to the little crowd on the wharf that she was never going to move again. There she lay, immense, motionless on the grey crinkled water, a loop of smoke above her, an immense flock of gulls screaming and diving after the galley droppings at the stern. You could just see little couples parading, little flies walking up and down the dish on the grey crinkled tablecloth. Other flies clustered and swarmed at the **edge***. Now there was a gleam of white on the lower deck—the cook's apron or the stewardess perhaps. Now a tiny black spider raced up the ladder on the ~~deck~~ bridge.

In the front of the crowd a strong looking middle aged man dressed very well very snugly in a grey overcoat grey silk scarf—thick gloves—a dark felt hat marched up + down **twirling*** his folded umbrella. He seemed to lead the little crowd on the wharf—+ at the same time[4] to keep them together.[5] He was something between the sheep dog and the shepherd. What a fool—what a fool he had been not to bring any glasses.[6]

There wasn't a pair of glasses among the whole lot of them.

"Curious thing, Mr. Scott that none of us thought of glasses. We might have been able to stir 'em up a bit. We might have managed a little signaling. Dont Hesitate to Land. Natives Harmless. Or A Welcome Awaits You. All is Forgiven. What? Eh?"

Mr. Hammond's quick, eager glance, so nervous and yet so friendly and confiding, took in everybody on the wharf, roped in, even, those old chaps lounging against the gangways. They knew, every man-Jack of them, that Mrs. Hammond was on that boat, and he was so tremendously excited that[7] it never entered his head not to believe that this marvelous fact meant something to them, too. They were his friends; he shared it with him [sic].[8] For They were as decent a crowd of people he decided . . .[9] Those old chaps over by the gangways, too—fine, solid old chaps. What chests—by Jove. And he squared his own, plunged his thick gloved hands into his pockets, rocked from heel to toe.

"Yes, my wife's been in Europe for the last ten months."

---

[3] This is written in pencil at the top of the page.

[4] This addition is written under the passage with an arrow at the beginning of the phrase indicating this is to be added at this point. Another line from the end of the phrase seems to be a false start, leading to a different point in the passage.

[5] "He seemed to lead [. . .]" is changed to "He seemed to be the leader [. . .]" in the clean manuscript.

[6] This entire paragraph is squeezed into white space between what precedes and follows it, suggesting that it was added later.

[7] "That" is omitted in the clean draft.

[8] This sentence is omitted in the clean manuscript, and Mansfield adds: "It warmed his heart toward them" (Stran-clean-NL, leaf 2).

[9] The clean draft places "he decided" after "They were": "They were, he decided, as decent a crowd of people" (Stran-clean-NL, leaf 2).

[Stran-clean-NL, leaf 1]

The Stranger
By
Katherine Mansfield

– –

– –

|

It seemed to the little crowd on the wharf that she was never going to move again. There she lay, immense, motionless on the grey crinkled water, a loop of smoke above her, an immense flock of gulls screaming and diving after the galley droppings at the stern. You could just see little couples parading—little flies walking up and down the dish on the grey crinkled table cloth. Other flies clustered and swarmed at the edge. Now there was a gleam of white on the lower deck, the cook's apron or the stewardess, perhaps. Now a tiny black spider raced up the latter on to the bridge.

In the front of the crowd a strong-looking, middle aged man dressed very well, very snugly in a grey overcoat, grey silk scarf, thick gloves and dark felt hat marched up and down twirling his folded umbrella. He seemed to be the leader of the little crowd on the wharf[10] and at the same time to keep them together. He was something between the sheep dog and the shepherd.

But what a fool—what a fool he had been not to bring any glasses. There wasn't a pair of glasses among the whole lot of them.

"Curious thing, Mr Scott, that none of us thought of glasses. We might have been able to stir 'em up a bit. We might have managed a little signalling. <u>Dont Hesitate to Land. Natives Harmless</u>. Or: <u>A Welcome Awaits You. All is forgiven</u>. What? Eh?"

Mr. Hammond's quick, eager glance, so nervous yet so

[Stran-clean-NL, leaf 2]

friendly and confiding, took in everybody on the wharf, roped in, even those old chaps lounging against the gangways. They knew, every man-jack of them, that Mrs Hammond was on that boat, and he was tremendously excited it never entered his head not to believe that this marvellous fact meant something to them, too. It warmed his heart towards them. They were, he decided, as decent a crowd of people . . . Those old chaps over by the gangsways, [*sic*] too—fine, solid old chaps. What chests!—by Jove! And he squared his own, plunged his thick-gloved hands into his pockets, rocked from heel to toe.

"Yes, my wife's been in Europe for the last ten months.

---

[10] The "h" of "wharf" appears to be written over another, illegible letter.

On a visit to our eldest girl, who was married last year. Yes, yes, yes." The shrewd grey eyes narrowed again and searched anxiously, quickly,

[Stran-rough-NL leaf 2]

the motionless liner. Again his overcoat was unbuttoned. Out came the thin, butter-yellow watch ^{again} and for the twentyeth, fiftyeth [sic] hundredth time he made the calculation.

Let me see, now. It was two fifteen when the doctor's launch went off. Two-fifteen! It is now exactly twenty-eight minutes past four. That is to say the doc's been gone two hours and thirteen minutes.[11] Wheeo-oh! He gave a queer little half whistle and snapped the watch to again. "But I think we should have been told if there was anything, up, don't you—Gaven?"[12]

"Oh, yes Mr. Hammond. I don't think there's anything to worry about," said Mr. Gaven, knocking out his pipe against his shoe heel.[13] At the same time . . ."

"Quite so, quite so!" cried Mr Hammond. "Dashed annoying." He paced quickly up and down and came back to his stand between Mr and Mrs Scott and Mr Gavin [sic].[14] "Its getting quite dark too,"[15] and he waved his folded umbrella as though the dusk, at least, might have had the decentcy[16] to keep off for a bit. But the dusk came slowly, spreading like a slow stain over the water.[17]

Little Jean Scott dragged at her mother's hand.

"I wan' my tea, mammy" she wailed.

"I expect you do," said Mr Hammond. I expect all these ladies want their tea. And his kind, flushed almost pitiful glance roped them all in again. He wondered whether Janey was having a final cup of tea in the saloon out there. He hoped so; he thought not. It would be just like her not to leave the deck. In that case perhaps the deck steward would bring her a cup. If he'd been there—he'd have got it for her, somehow. And for a moment he was on deck, standing over her, watching her little hand fold round the cup in the way she had, while she drank the only cup of tea to be got on board. But now he was I [sic] back here, and

[Stran-rough-NL, leaf 3]

the Lord only knew when that curséd Captain would stop hanging about in the stream. He took another turn up and down, up and down. He walked as far as the cabstand to make sure his driver hadn't disappeared, back he swerved again to the little flock huddled in the shelter of the banana crates.

---

[11] In the clean version, Mansfield repeats "Two hours and thirteen minutes!"
[12] The clean manuscript formalizes this address to "Mr Gaven."
[13] The clean draft reads: "against the heal of his shoe."
[14] This misspelling is retained in the clean manuscript.
[15] The comma is placed over a dash.
[16] The "c" looks to have been written over a "t."
[17] With this sentence and following, the ink is darker.

On a visit to our eldest girl who was married last year. I brought her up here, as far as Auckland myself. So I thought Id better come and fetch her back. Yes, yes, yes." The shrewd, grey eyes narrowed again and searched anxiously, quickly, the motionless liner. Again his overcoat was unbuttoned, out came the thin, butter-yellow watch again and for the twentieth, fiftieth, hundredth time he made the calculation.

"Let me see, now.[18] It was two-fifteen when the doctor's launch ~~cast~~ went[19] off. Two-fifteen. It is now exactly twenty-eight minutes past four. That is to say the doctor's been gone two hours and thirteen minutes. Two hours and thirteen minutes! Whee-ooh!" He gave a queer little half-whistle and snapped his watch to again. "But I think we should have been told if there was anything up—dont you, Mr Gaven?"

"Oh, yes Mr Hammond. I don't think theres anything to worry about" said Mr Gaven, knocking out his pipe against the heel of his shoe.[20] "At the same time . . ."

"Quite so. Quite so!" cried Mr Hammond. "Dashed annoying." He paced quickly up and down and came back again to his stand between Mr and Mrs Scott and Mr Gavin [*sic*]. "Its getting quite dark, too," and he waved his folded umbrella

[Stran-clean-NL, leaf 3]

as though the dusk, at least, might have had the decency to keep off for a bit. But the dusk came slowly, spreading like a slow stain over the water.

Little Jean Scott dragged at her mother's hand.

"I wan' my tea, mammy," she wailed.

"I expect you do," said Mr Hammond. "I expect all these ladies want their tea." And his kind, flushed almost pitiful glance roped them all in again. He wondered whether Janey was having a final cup of tea in the saloon out there. He hoped so; he thought not. It would be just like her not to leave the deck. In that case perhaps the deck steward would bring her up a cup. If he'd been there he'd have got it for her, somehow. And for a moment he was on deck, standing over her, watching her little hand fold round the cup ~~while she drank~~ in the way she[21] had~~x~~[22] while she drank the only cup of tea to be got on board . . . But now he was back here, and the Lord only knew when that cursed Captain would stop hanging about in the stream. He took another turn, up and down, up and down. He walked as far as the cab stand to make sure his driver hadn't disappeared; back he swerved again to the little flock huddled in the shelter of the banana crates.

---

[18] From this point on, the ink is darker, suggesting Mansfield has changed pens.
[19] "Went" is written over another word, perhaps "cast."
[20] The published version adds repetition to Mr. Gaven's response: "'I don't think there's anything to—anything to worry about,' said Mr. Gaven [. . .]" (CW2, 241).
[21] The addition here is present in the earlier draft, suggesting that Mansfield unintentionally omitted the phrase while copying the draft, only to reinsert it.
[22] There is an additional letter or punctuation mark which is stricken out, but it is not clear what it was.

~~and~~ Little Jean Scott was still wanting her tea. Poor little beggar! He wished he had a bit of chocolate on him.

"Here, Jean," he said, "like to be lifted up?" And easily, ~~lightly~~ gently he swung the little girl on to a high barrel. ~~It was astonishing him~~ t The moment of holding her + steadying her relieved him wonderfully*, lightened his heart.

"Hold on" he said to little Jean, but it was really he who clung to her.[23] But suddenly little Jean caught him by the ear and gave a loud scream. Lo-ok! Mr. Hammond. ~~Its~~ Shes moving. ~~Its~~ She's moving. Look—~~its~~ she's coming in."

"By Jove, so she was—At last. She was slowly slowly turning round. A bell sounded far over the water and a great spout of steam gushed into the air The gulls rose; they whirled away like bits of white paper. Whether that deep throbbing was her engine or his heart Hammond couldn't say. He had to nerve himself to bear it whatever it was. And at that moment old Captain Johnston[24] the harbour master came striding down the wharf with a leather portfolio under his arm.

"Dont bother about Jean" said Mr. Scott. "I'll hold her."[25]

He was just in time. Mr. Hammond had forgotten about Jean. He sprang away to greet Captain Johnson.[26]

"Well, Captain," the eager nervous voice rang out again, "youve taken pity on us at last."

"Its no good blaming me" Mr. Hammond, [sic] wheezed old Captain Johnson starring at the liner. "You got Mrs. Hammond on board, havent yer?"[27]

"Yes yes," said Hammond, + he kept by the Harbour Master's side. "Mrs Hammond's there. Hul -lo! We shan't be long now."

~~Cutting through the dark water came~~ t The big liner came cutting ~~great white shavings~~ sharp through the dark water and great white shavings fell to either side.[28]

[Stran-rough-NL, leaf 4]

~~They were out there~~
~~There they were. He~~ Hammond + the Harbour master ~~just in~~ kept front of the rest + ~~watch~~ ~~Where~~ As She came ~~was coming~~ nearer + nearer—her telephone ringing the thrum of her screw filling the air.[29] Hammond took off his hat—he raked the deck—they were crammed with passengers—he waved his hat.

---

[23] The revised version omits "but it was really he who clung to her" and adds "keeping an arm round her." It goes on to elaborate on the exchange between Hammond and Jean's parents. See Stran-rough-NL, leaf 3 and 4.

[24] The published version has "Captain Johnson," as it appears below, but here it is "Johnston."

[25] The clean manuscript reads "Jean'll be all right" in place of "Dont bother about Jean."

[26] "Old" is added to "Captain Johnson" in the clean copy.

[27] "Havent yer" becomes "aint yer" in the clean manuscript.

[28] In Mansfield's revision, she brings the image of the ringing phone from below (Stran-rough-NL, leaf 4) and adds it here. The clean copy reads: "With her telephone ring-ringing, the ~~sound~~ thrum of her screw filling the air the big liner bore down on them, cutting sharp through the dark water so that big white shavings curled ~~on~~ to either side" (Stran-clean-NL, leaf 4).

[29] As indicated in note 28, this sentence is moved.

Little Jean Scott was still wanting her tea. Poor little beggar! He wished he had a bit of chocolate on him.

"Here, Jean," he said. "Like a lift up?" And easily, gently he swung the little girl on to a high barrel.[30] The moment of holding her, steadying her, relieved him wonderfully, lightened his heart.

"Hold on," he said, keeping an arm round her.

"Oh don't worry about Jean,[2] Mr Hammond," said Mrs Scott.

"That's all right, Mrs Scott. No trouble. It's a pleasure. Jean's a little pal of mine, aren't you, Jean?"

"Yes, Mr Hammond" said Jean, and she ran her finger down the

[Stran-clean-NL, leaf 4]

dent of his felt hat.

But suddenly she caught him by the ear and gave a loud scream.

"Lo-ok, Mr Hammond! She's moving she's moving![31] Look, She's coming in!"

By Jove! So she was. At last. She was slowly, slowly turning round. A bell sounded far over the water and a great spout of steam gushed into the air. The gulls rose; they fluttered away like bits of white paper. And whether that deep throbbing was her engines or his heart Mr Hammond couldn't say. He had to nerve himself to bear it, whatever it was. At that moment old Captain Johnson the harbour-master, came striding down the wharf, a leather portfolio under his arm.

"Jean'll be all right," said Mr Scott. "I'll hold her."

He was just in time. Mr Hammond had forgotten about Jean. He sprang away to greet old Captain Johnson.

"Well, Captain," the eager nervous voice rang out again, "you've taken pity on us at last."

"Its no good blaming me," Mr Hammond, [*sic*] wheezed old Captain Johnson, staring at the liner. "You got Mrs Hammond on board—aint yer?"

"Yes, yes," said Hammond, and he kept by the harbour-master's side "Mrs Hammond's there. Hul-lo! We shant be long now."

With her telephone ring-ringing, the ~~sound~~ [thrum] of her screw filling the air the big liner bore down on them, cutting sharp through the dark water so that big white shavings curled ~~on~~ [to32] either side.

Hammond and the harbour-master kept in front of the rest. Hammond took off his hat; he raked the decks—they were crammed with passengers—he waved his hat

---

[30] The published version has "higher barrel" in lieu of "high barrel."
[31] "She's moving" is not repeated in the published version.
[32] "To" is written over "on."

He ~~gave~~ ^{bawled} a loud strange Hul -lo ^{across the water} + then turned round + burst out laughing*—+ said—something—nothing to old Captain Johnson.

"Seen her," said the Harbour master.

"No, not yet. Steady wait—a bit—And suddenly between those ~~those~~ ^{two} clumsy* idiots—get out of the way there—he ~~waved~~ ^{signed* with} his umbrella—he saw a hand raised—a white glove shaking a handkerchief. Another moment—+ thank God thank God—there she was—there was Janey—there was Mrs Hammond yes yes yes standing by the rail + smiling + nodding + waving the handkerchief.

"Well thats first class. First class. Well well well." He positively stamped. He drew out his cigar case. Like lightning ~~he~~ ^{and} offered it to Captain Johnston [*sic*].[33] Have a cigar captain—theyre pretty good. Have a couple. Here—+ he pressed all the cigars in the case on ~~Captain Johnston~~ [*sic*] ^{the Harbour master}. Ive got a hundred up at the hotel.[34]

"Thenks ^{Mr. Hammond}" ~~said~~ ^{wheezed} old Captain Johnson.

Hammond stuffed* the cigar box box [*sic*] back. His hands were shaking. But hed got ~~the xxx on~~ himself ^{under} again.[35] He was able to face Janey—there she was—leaning on the rail—talking to some woman + at the same time—ready for him.[36] It struck him as the gulf of water grew ~~narrower~~ ^{closed} [*sic*] how small she ~~was~~ ^{looked on that huge ship.} His heart was wrung with such a spasm of tenderness[37] that he would have cried out—How little she ~~was~~ ^{looked} to have gone[38] all that way + back by herself. Just like her, though. ^{Just like Janey.} She had the courage of—+ now the crew ~~had~~ parted the passengers they had lowered the rails for the gangway –[39]

[Stran-rough-NL, leaf 5]

The voices on shore—the voices on board[40], flew to greet each other –

All well?

All well.

How's mother.

Much better.

^{Hullo Jean!}

^{Hullo Aun' Emily}41

Had a good voyage

Splendid!

Shant be long now.

Not long now.

The engines stopped. Slowly she ~~swung~~ ^{edged} to the wharf side. "Make way there—make way make way" and the wharf[42] hands brought the heavy gangway along at a ^{sweeping} run.

Hammond signed to Janey to stay where she was. The old Harbour master stepped forward he followed—As to Ladies first or any rot like like [*sic*] that it never entered his head—

---

[33] The clean version reads: "Like lightening he drew out his cigar case and offered it to old Captain Johnson" (Stran-clean-NL, leaf 5).

[34] "'Ive got a hundred up at the hotel'" becomes "'Ive a couple boxes up at the hotel'" in the clean manuscript.

[35] This is revised as: "but he'd got hold of himself again."

[36] The clean manuscript adds "watching him" between "at the same time" and "ready for him."

[37] "Of tenderness" is not retained in the revised manuscript.

[38] "Gone" becomes "come" in the clean manuscript.

[39] The revised version reads: "And now the crew had come forward and parted the passengers" (Stran-clean-NL, leaf 5).

[40] The "o" is written over an "a."

[41] These two lines are added in the white space beside the rest of the dialogue, with a line pointing after "Much better."

[42] The "h" is written over an "a."

and bawled a loud strange "hul-lo" across the

[Stran-clean-NL, leaf 5]

water and then turned round and ~~with a~~ burst out laughing and said—something—nothing—to old Captain Johnson.

"Seen her?" asked the harbour-master.‡

"No, not yet. Steady—wait—a bit." And suddenly, between two great clumsy idiots—get out of the way there! he signed with his umbrella—he saw a hand raised, a white glove shaking a handkerchief. Another moment and—thank God—thank God—there she was. There was Janey. There was Mrs Hammond. Yes, yes, yes—standing by the rail and smiling and nodding and waving her handkerchief.

"Well, that's fist class. First class! Well—well—well!" He positively stamped. Like lightening he drew out his cigar case and offered it to old Captain Johnson. "Have a cigar, Captain. They're pretty good. Have a couple. Here –" and he pressed all the cigars in the case on the harbour-master. "Ive a couple of boxes up at the hotel."

"Thenks, Mr Hammond," wheezed old Captain Johnson.

Hammond stuffed the cigar case back. His hands were shaking, but he'd got hold of himself again. He was able to face Janey. There she was, leaning on the rail, talking to some woman, and at the same time, watching him, ready for him. It struck him, as the gulf of water closed, how small she looked on that huge ship. His heart was wrung with such a spasm that he would have cried out. How little she looked to have come all that way and back by herself. Just like her, though. Just like Janey. She had the courage of a—And now the crew had come forward and parted the passengers, they had lowered the rails for the gangways.

[Stran-clean-NL, leaf 6]

The voices on shore and the voices on board, flew to greet each other.

"All well?"

"All well!"

"How's mother?"

"Much better."

"Hullo Jean!"

"Hil-lo, Aun' Emily!"

"Had a good voyage?"

"Splendid!"

"Shan't be long now!"

"Not long now."

The engines stopped. Slowly she edged to the wharf side.

"Make way there—make way—make way!" And the wharf hands brought the heavy gangways along at a sweeping run.

Hammond signed to Janey to stay where she was. The old harbour-master stepped forward; he followed. As to "Ladies First" or any rot like that it never entered his head.

After you Captain cried Hammond genially + **treading*** on the old mans heels he strode up the gangway—on to the deck ^{in a bee-line to Jane [sic]}—and clasped, Janey ^{was} in his arms.[43]

"Well well well, yes yes." here were we at last [*sic*]. He stammered. It was all he could say—And Janey emerged—+ the her [*sic*] cool little voice. The only voice in the world for him said to well darling have you been waiting long.

No, ~~xx~~ not long—or at any rate it didn't matter. It was over now.

But the point was—he had a cab waiting at the end of the wharf—was she ready to go off? Was her luggage ready. In that case———They could cut off sharp with her cabin luggage + let the rest go hang until tomorrow. He bent over her and she looked up with her familiar half-smile—she was just the same—not a day changed—just as hed always known her—+ she laid her little hand on his sleeve

"How are the children –" she asked[44]

Hang the children![45]

Perfectly well. Never better in their lives

Havent they sent me letters.

Yes yes—of course. Ive left them at the hotel for you to digest later on.[46]

[Stran-rough-NL, leaf 6]

We cant go quite so fast, she said—Ive got people to say goodby [*sic*] to—+ then theres the Captain—~~though~~ as his face fell she gave his arm a small understanding squeeze. If the Captain comes off the Bridge I want you to thank him for having looked after ~~me~~ ^{your wife} so beautifully.

Well, he'd got her. If she wanted another ten minutes .. As he gave way she was surrounded. The whole first class seemed to want to say goodbye to her + to ~~her + to her alone~~ Janey.[47]

Goodbye <u>dear</u> Mrs. Hammond. And ~~if ever~~ ^{next time} you're in Sydney Ill <u>expect</u> you . . . .

Darling Mrs. Hammond. You wont forget to write to me—will you.

Well Mrs. Hammond what we should have done without you[48]———

It was as plain as a pike staff that she was by far the most popular woman on board. And she took it all—just as usual—absolutely composed—just her little self—just Janey all over—standing there with her veil thrown back—~~He~~ ^{Hammond} never noticed what ~~she~~ ^{his wife} had on from years end to year **in it**—she looked just the same to him whatever it was—

[43] The clean manuscripts reads: "and Janey was clasped in his arms" (Stran-clean-NL, leaf 6).
[44] Mansfield adds "John" after "'How are the children'" in the revised manuscript.
[45] This is written in the margin to the left of the rest of the dialogue.
[46] The whole exchange is squeezed in at the bottom of the page.
[47] The clean manuscript merely reads, "[. . .] to say 'goodbye' to Janey."
[48] The revised version reads, "'what this boat would have done without you!'" (Stran-rough-NL, leaf 7).

"After you, Captain," he cried genially. And treading on the old man's heels he strode up the gangway on to the deck in a bee-line to Janey and Janey was clasped in his arms.

"Well—well—well. Yes, yes. Here we are at last," he stammered.

It was all he could say. And Janey emerged and her cool little voice—the only voice in the world for him said: "Well, darling. Have you been waiting long?"

No, not long. Or at any rate it didn't matter. It was over now. But the point was—he had a cab waiting at the end of the wharf. Was she ready to go off? Was her luggage ready? In that case—

[Stran-clean-NL, leaf 7]

they would cut off sharp with her cabin luggage and let the rest go hang until tomorrow. He bent over her and she looked up with her familiar half-smile. She was just the same. Not a day changed. Just as he'd always known her. She laid her small hand on his sleeve.

"How are the children, John," she asked.

(Hang the children!) "Perfectly well. Never better in their lives."

"Haven't they sent me letters?"

"Yes, yes. Of course. I've left them at the hotel for you to digest later on."

"We can't go quite so fast," said she. "I've got people to say good-bye to—and then there's the Captain"—as his face fell she gave his arm a small understanding squeeze—"If the Captain comes off the bridge I want you to thank him for having looked after your wife so beautifully." Well, he'd got her. If she wanted another ten minutes . . . As he gave way she was surrounded. The whole first class seemed to want to say "goodbye" to Janey.

"Goodbye, <u>dear</u> Mrs. Hammond. And next time you're in Sydney I'll <u>expect</u> you."

"Darling Mrs Hammond. You wont forget to write to me—will you?"

"Well, Mrs Hammond—what this boat would have done without you!"[49]

It was as plain as a pike staff that she was by far the most popular woman on board. And she took it all—just as usual. Asolutely [sic] composed. Just her little self—just Janey all over—standing there with her veil thrown back. Hammond never noticed what his wife had on. It was all the same to him whatever she wore.

---

[49] The published version changes "done without you" to "been without you."

but ^today he did notice ~~today~~ that she wore a black suit with white frills, **trimmings*** he supposed they were at the neck and sleeves.⁵⁰ All this while Janey handed him round. ~~Love~~ "John dear"—and then I must introduce you too [*sic*]. Finally they did escape + she led the way to her stateroom. To follow Janey down the passage that she knew so well— that was so strange to him, to part the green curtain after her + to step into the cabin that had been hers gave him an exquisite happiness. But confound it—the stewardess was there on the floor—strapping up the rugs.

"Thats the last Mrs Hammond" ~~she said~~ ^said the stewardess rising pulling down her cuffs.⁵¹ He was introduced again. And ~~at the same moment~~ ^then Janey + the steward⁵² disappeared into the passage. ^He heard whispering ~~went on~~. She was getting the tipping business over.⁵³ He

[Stran-rough-NL, leaf 7]

sat down on the red plush sofa⁵⁴ ^took his hat off. There were the rugs shed taken with her—they looked good as new—all her luggage looked ~~as~~ fresh ~~and~~ perfect. The labels were written in her beautiful little clear hand.⁵⁵

"Mrs John Hammond." He gave a long sigh of content + leaned back crossing ~~xxx class passenger.~~ ^his arms. The strain was over. He felt he could have sat there forever sighing his relief—the relief at being rid of that horrible tug—pull grip on his heart. The danger was over. That was the feeling. They were out of the water.⁵⁶ They were on dry land again. But at that moment Janeys head came around the curtain.⁵⁷

"Darling do you mind? I just want to go + say goodbye to the doctor."

He started up "Ill come with you."

"No—no," she said—"don't bother. Id rather not. Ill just be a minute." And before he could answer she was gone—He had half a **mind to*** rush⁵⁸ after her but instead he sat down again.

"Would she really not be long. What was the time now." Out came the watch. ^He stared at nothing.⁵⁹

---

⁵⁰ Mansfield reworks the sentence structure and adds Hammond's self-questioning: "Hammond never noticed what his wife had on. It was all the same to him whatever she wore. But today he did notice that she wore a black 'costume'—didn't they call it?—with white frills, trimmings he supposed they were, at the neck and sleeves" (Stran-clean-NL, leaf 7).

⁵¹ This addition is in a darker ink, suggesting it was added later.

⁵² This is "stewardess" in the published version, maintaining consistency.

⁵³ The clean manuscript adds "he supposed" at the end of this sentence.

⁵⁴ This becomes "striped sofa" in the revised manuscript.

⁵⁵ The revised version adds "Mrs John Hammond" at the end of this sentence, echoed by the sentence that follows.

⁵⁶ This sentence is omitted in the clean manuscript.

⁵⁷ "Curtain" becomes "corner" in the clean draft. This long addition is fitted between lines, so the elaboration on Hammond's state of mind was added after the paragraph was initially concluded.

⁵⁸ "Rush" becomes "run" in the revised version.

⁵⁹ While the insertion is above "watch," an arrow indicates the addition should come after "doctor" below; however, Mansfield decided to leave it here in the published version.

But today he did notice that she wore a black "costume"—didn't they call it?—with white frills, trimmings he supposed they were, at the neck and sleeves. All

[Stran-clean-NL, leaf 8]

this while Janey handed him round.

"John, dear!" And then: "I want to introduce you to . . ."

Finally they did escape and she led the way to her stateroom. To follow Janey down the passage that she knew so well—that was so strange to him; to part the green curtain after her and to step into the cabin that had been hers gave him exquisite happiness. But—confound it!—the stewardess was there on the floor, strapping up the rugs.

"That's the last, Mrs Hammond," said the stewardess, rising and pulling down her cuffs.

He was introduced again, and then Janey and the stewardess disappeared in to [*sic*] the passage. He heard whispering. She was getting the tipping business over, he supposed. He sat down on the striped sofa and took his hat off. There were the rugs she had taken with her; they looked good as new. All her luggage looked fresh, perfect. The labels were written in her beautiful little clear hand—Mrs John Hammond.

"Mrs John Hammond!" He gave a long sigh of content and leaned back, crossing his arms. The strain was over. He felt he could have sat there for ever sighing his relief—the relief at being rid of that horrible tug—pull—grip on his heart. The danger was over. That was the feeling. They were on dry land again.

But at that moment Janeys head came round the corner.

"Darling—do you mind? I just want to go and say 'goodbye' to the doctor."

[Stran-clean-NL, leaf 9]

Hammond started up. "Ill come with you."

"No—no," she said. "Don't bother. I'd rather not. I'll not be a minute."

And before he could answer she was gone. He had half a mind to run after her, but, instead, he sat down again.

Would she really not be long? What was the time now? Out came the watch; he stared at nothing.

This indeed was "queer" ~~xxx a frightful~~ But that was rather queer of Janey wasn't it? Why hadn't she told the stewardess to say goodbye for her.[60] Why did she have to go chasing after the ship's doctor. She could have sent a note from the hotel even—if the affair had been urgent. Urgent! Did it—could it mean that she'd been ill on the voyage—that she was keeping something from him? That was it.

~~He~~ Hammond[61] seized his hat. He was going off to find that fellow + to get[62] the truth out of him at all costs. He thought hed noticed just something—she was just a touch too calm— too steady. She was keeping something from him.[63]

The curtains rang Janey was back—he jumped to his feet.

"Janey—have you been ill on this voyage?"[64]

"Ill?" Her airy little voice mocked him. She stepped over the rugs, came up close[,] **laid** her hand on his breast[65] + looked up at him—Darling she said don't frighten me. Of course I havent. Whatever makes you think I have. Do I look ill. but he didn't see her. He only felt she was looking at him + that there was no need to worry about anything. She was here to look after things. ~~No~~ it was all right. Everything was.

She was speaking the[66]

[Stran-rough-NL, leaf 8]

truth.[67] The gentle pressure of her hand was so calming that he put his hand over hers to ~~hold~~ keep[68] it there. And she said.

"Stand still. I want to look at you. I haven't seen you yet. You've had your beard beautifully trimmed—and you look younger I think—and decidedly thinner. Bachelor life agrees with you."

Agrees with me. He groaned for love + caught her close again. And again as always he had the feeling he was holding something that never was quite his—his—something too delicate too precious that would fly away ~~when~~ if he let it go.[69]

"For Gods sake lets get off to the hotel so that we can be by ourselves." And he rang for someone or other to look sharp with this luggage.[70]

---

[60] The clean manuscript omits "This indeed was 'queer'" and the "But" before the following sentence. The verb form is adjusted in the next sentence: "Why couldn't she have told the stewardess to say 'goodbye' for her" (Stran-clean-NL, leaf 9).
[61] Mansfield reverts back to "He" in the revised version.
[62] "Get the truth out of him" becomes "wring the truth out of him" in the clean manuscript.
[63] The revised version omits this final sentence, adding the more ambiguous: "From the very first moment . . ." (Stran-clean-NL, leaf 9).
[64] The clean manuscript adds: "'You have!'"
[65] "xxx her hand on his breast" becomes "touched his breast."
[66] These additions are in a tighter hand and darker ink.
[67] This last sentence is eliminated in the clean version.
[68] The clean manuscript reverts back to "hold."
[69] The revised version reads: "once he let go" (Stran-clean-NL, leaf 10).
[70] The clean draft reads: "And he rang the bell hard for someone to look sharp ~~after~~ with this luggage" (Stran-clean-NL, leaf 10). Underneath, Mansfield has drawn a straight line, separating this section from the next. The ink in the following section is slightly darker.

That was rather queer of Janey—wasn't it? Why couldn't she have told the stewardess to say "goodbye" for her. Why did she have to go chasing after the ship's doctor? She could have sent a note from the hotel, even, if the affair had been urgent. Urgent? Did it—could it mean that she'd been ill on the voyage, ~~that~~ she was keeping something from him? That was it! He seized his hat. He was going off to find that fellow and to wring the truth out of him at all costs. He thought he'd noticed just something. She was just a touch too calm—too steady. From the very first moment . . .

The curtains rang. Janey was back. He jumped to his feet.

"Janey—have you been ill on this voyage? You have!"

"Ill?" Her airy little voice mocked him. She stepped over the rugs, came up close, touched his breast and looked up at him.

"Darling," she said, "dont frighten me. Of course I haven't. Whatever makes you think I have? Do I look ill?"

But Hammond didn't see her. He only felt that she was looking at him and that there was no need to worry about anything. She was here to look after things. It was all right. Everything was.

The gentle pressure of her hand was so calming that he put his

[Stran-clean-NL, leaf 10]

over hers to hold it there. And she said:

"Stand still. I want to look at you. I haven't seen you yet. You've had your beard beautifully trimmed and you look—younger. I think—and decidedly thinner! Bachelor life agrees with you."

"Agrees with me!" He groaned for love and caught her close again. And again—as always—he had the feeling he was holding something that never was quite his—his. Something too delicate, too precious—that would fly away once he let[71] go.

"For God's sake lets get off to the hotel so that we can be by ourselves!" And he rang the bell hard for someone to look sharp ~~after~~ with this luggage.[72]

---

[71] There are some strikeouts over the final letter of "let."

[72] The published version has "the luggage."

Walking down the wharf together she took his arm. He had her on his arm again. And the difference it made to get into the cab after Janey—to throw the red and yellow striped blanket around them both—to say to the driver—you might be as sharp as you can because neither of them had had any tea[73]—No more going without his tea or pouring out his own. She was back. He **turned to her*** squeezed her hand + said very gently + half teasingly—in the voice that only she knew was his voice,[74] "Glad to be home again dearie?" She smiled; she didn't even bother* to answer ~~and the town lights~~ but gently she drew his hand away as they came to the lighted streets.

"We^ve got the best room at the hotel, he said. I wouldnt be put off with another + ^asked the chambermaid to put in a bit of a fire in case you feel chilly. Shes a nice attentive girl. I thought now we were here we wouldn't bother to go home tomorrow but spend a day looking around and leave the morning after. Does that suit you? Theres no hurry is there; the children will have you soon enough.[75]

[Stran-rough-NL, leaf 9][76]

I thought . . . days sight seeing might make a nice break in your journey—eh, Janey?"

"Have you taken the tickets for the day after, dear?"[77] she asked.

~~Yes~~. ^I should think I have. He unbuttoned his overcoat + took out his large, ~~shabby~~ pocket book.[78] I reserved a first class carriage to Napier—~~he said~~,[79] showing her the registration slip.[80] There it is Mr and Mrs John Hammond ~~2 seats. I thought~~ we might as well do ourselves comfortably. And we didnt[81] want people butting in—do we? But if you'd like to stop her a bit longer.

Oh no Oh no[82] said Janey quickly—not for the world the day after tomorrow then. And the children—

But they had reached the hotel. The manager was standing at the broad, brilliantly lighted porch: he came over[83] to greet them. A porter ran from the hall for their boxes.

---

[73] This becomes "to tell the driver to hurry because neither of them had had any tea" in the clean manuscript (Stran-clean-NL, leaf 10).

[74] The clean manuscript omits "half" before "teasingly" and "in the voice that only she knew was his voice" becomes "in the 'special' voice he had for her" (Stran-clean-NL, leaf 10).

[75] The last two words are written under this last clause.

[76] At this point in the manuscript, Mansfield stops numbering the pages.

[77] The clean version removes "dear."

[78] "Large" becomes "bulging" in the clean version. "Book" is written over another word.

[79] Mansfield has placed a check mark above this omission, suggesting it should be retained; however, it is not included in the published version.

[80] The clean copy adds "'Here we are'" before this sentence (Stran-clean-NL, leaf 11).

[81] "Didnt" becomes "don't" in the clean draft.

[82] "Oh no" appears only once in the revised version.

[83] "Over" becomes "down" in the clean draft.

Walking down the wharf together she took his arm. He had her on his arm again. And the difference it made to get into the cab after Janey—to throw the red and yellow striped blanket round them both—to tell the driver to hurry because neither of them had had any tea. No more going without his tea ~~any more~~ or pouring out his own. She was back. ~~Sh~~He[84] turned to her, squeezed her hand and said gently, teasingly, in the "special" voice he had for her: "Glad to be home again, dearie?" She ^smiled. She^ didn't even bother to answer, but gently she drew his hand away as they came to the lighted streets.

"We've got the best room in the hotel," he said. "I wouldn't be put off with another. And I told[85] the chambermaid to put in a bit of

[Stran-clean-NL, leaf 11]

~~of~~ a fire in case you felt chilly. She's a nice, attentive girl. And I thought now we were here we wouldn't bother to go home tomorrow, but spend the day looking round and leave the morning after. Does that suit you? There's no hurry—is there? The children will have you soon enough . . ." I thought—a day's sight-seeing might make a nice break in your journey—eh, Janey?"

"Have you taken the tickets for the day after?" she asked.

"I should think I have!" He unbuttoned his overcoat and took out his bulging pocket book. "Here we are. I reserved a first class carriage to Napier"—showing her the registration slip[86]—"There it is. 'Mr <u>and</u> Mrs John Hammond.' I thought we might as well do ourselves comfortably—and we don't want other people butting in—do we? But if you'd like to stop here a bit longer—?"

"Oh no," said Janey quickly. "Not for the world. The day after tomorrow, then. And the children –"

But they had reached the hotel. The manager was standing in the broad, brilliantly lighted porch; he came down to greet them. A porter ran from the hall for their boxes.

---

[84] The "H" is written over "Sh" in "She."
[85] "Told" becomes "asked" in the published version, which follows the initial draft of the story.
[86] This last phrase is not retained in the published version.

"Well Mr Arnold. Heres Mrs Hammond at last." + ~~Mr Hammond's voice sounded as though she had~~. The manager led them through the hall ^{himself} + pressed the elevator bell ~~himself~~. There were men sitting at the small hall tables having a drink before diner—but Hammond looked neither to the right nor the left. He was not going to risk interruption.[87] They could think what they pleased. If they didn't understand the greater fools they—+ he stept [*sic*] out of the lift—unlocked the door their room + shepherded Janey in. The door shut. Now at last they were alone together. He turned up the light. The curtains were drawn the fire blazed—he flung ~~off~~ his hat on the huge bed + went towards ~~Janey~~—her—but again they were interrupted.[88] This time it was the porter with the luggage . . He made two journeys of it; leaving the door open in between taking his time, whistling through his teeth in the corridor. Hammond paced up + down the room, **tearing*** off his gloves: tearing off his scarf—Finally he flung his overcoat on to

[Stran-rough-NL, leaf 10]

the bed ^{side}—At last! The fool was gone. The door clicked—he caught Janey to him.[89]
~~That fool thank God,~~ sSaid Hammond—I feel Ill never have you to myself again. These cursed people! Janey—and he bent his flushed eager gaze upon her—lets have diner up here. **If*** we go down to that restaurant well be interrupted + then theres the confounded music (the music hed praised so highly, applauded so loudly last night!) We shant be able to hear each other speak. Lets have something up here in front of the fire. ~~and~~ Just you and me.[90] Its too late for tea. Ill ~~go down and~~ order a little supper—Shall I—How does the idea strike you—
    "Do, darling, said Janey. Go now[91] + while youre away—the childrens letters—
    Oh later on will do said Hammond.
    But then wed get it over said Janey + Id **just*** have time to unpack a little[92]—But I needn't go down said **Hammond***—Ill just ring + order what we want ˣˣˣ ˣˣˣ.[93] You don't want to send me away do you?
    Janey[94] shook her head + smiled—But you're thinking of something else said Hammond.

---

[87] This section about the men in the hallway is revised in the clean manuscript: "Hammond knew there were business pals of his sitting at the little hall tables having a drink before dinner. But he wasn't going to risk interruption; he looked neither to the right nor the left" (Stran-clean-NL, leaves 11–12).
[88] The clean manuscript adds "would you believe it!" after "but" (Stran-clean-NL, leaf 12).
[89] The clean draft omits "he caught Janey to him" but adds: "Now they <u>were</u> alone" (Stran-clean-NL, leaf 12).
[90] Mansfield omits this sentence in the clean version.
[91] The clean version eliminates "Go now."
[92] The clean version omits "to unpack a little," adding instead a dash, leaving this open-ended.
[93] The clean manuscript reads: "'Oh, I needn't go down,' explained Hammond. 'I'll just ring and give the order . . .'" (Stran-clean-NL, leaf 13).
[94] Written just above this is "Ja," perhaps a false start.

"Well, Mr Arnold, here's Mrs Hammond at last."

The manager led them through the hall himself and pressed the elevator bell. Hammond knew there were business pals of his sitting at the little hall tables having a drink before dinner. But he wasn't going to risk interruption; he looked neither to the right nor the

[Stran-clean-NL, leaf 12]

left. They could think what they pleased. If they didn't understand the more fools they— and he stepped out of the lift, unlocked the door of their room and shepherded Janey in. The door shut. Now at last they were alone together. He turned up the light. The curtains were drawn; the fire blazed. He flung his hat on to the huge bed and went toward her.

But—would you believe it!—again they were interrupted. This time it was the porter with the luggage. He made two journeys of it, leaving the door open in between, taking his time, whistling through his teeth in the corridor. Hammond paced up and down the room, tearing off his gloves, tearing off his scarf. Finally he flung his overcoat on to the bed side.

At last that fool was gone. The door clicked. Now they _were_ alone. Said Hammond "I feel Ill never have you to myself again. These cursed people! Janey –" and he bent his flushed, eager gaze upon her—"let's have dinner up here. If we go down to the restaurant we'll be interrupted and then there's the confounded music" (the music he'd praised so highly, applauded so loudly last night!) "We shant be able to hear each other xxx speak. Let's have something up here in front of the fire. Its too late for tea. I'll order a little supper—shall I? How does the idea strike you?"

"Do, darling," said Janey, "and while you're away—the children's letters . . ."

"Oh, later on will do!" said Hammond.

[Stran-clean-NL, leaf 13]

"But then we'd get it over," said Janey. "And Id just have time to –"

"Oh, I needn't go down," explained Hammond. "I'll just ring and give the order . . . You don't want to send me away—do you?"

Janey shook her head and smiled.

"But you're thinking of something else.

You're worrying about something," said Hammond. "What is it? Come and sit here—come and sit on my knew before the fire."

"I'll just unpin my hat," said Janey, and she went over to the dressing table. "A-Ah!" She gave a little cry.

"What is it?"

Nothing darling. Ive just found the childrens letters that's all right—They will keep[95]— She turned to him clasping them. She tucked them in her frilled blouse. She cried quickly gaily how typical the dressing table is of you.

[Stran-rough-NL, leaf 11]

Why Whats the matter with it said Hammond—

If I saw that dressing table floating in Eternity I should say John,[96] laughed Janey— staring at the big bottle of hair tonic, the wicker bottle of eau de cologne—two hair brushes and a dozen new collars tied with pink tape. Is this <u>all</u> your luggage.

Oh Hang my luggage said Hammond—but all the same he liked Janey to laugh at him[97]— Lets talk—lets get down to things. Tell me and as Janey perched on his knee he leaned back + drew her into the deep ugly chair—tell me youre really glad to be back, Janey—

Yes, darling Im glad she said. But just as when he embraced her he felt she would fly away so Hammond never knew never knew [*sic*] for dead certain that she was as glad as he was. How could he know! Would he ever know—would he always have this craving— this pang like hunger to somehow make Janey so much a part of him that there wasn't any of her to escape. ~~It wasn't of course—that he doubted~~ He wanted to blot out everybody— everything—~~to~~ He wished hed switched off the light. That might ~~xxx~~ ^have^ her nearer [*sic*]—And now those letters ^from the children^ rustled in her blouse—he could have chucked them into the fire –

"Janey" he whispered.

"Yes dear?" She lay on his breast—but so lightly—so remotely—their breathing rose + fell together.

"Janey –"

What is it.

"Turn to me –" ^he whispered^ He shut his eyes[98]—A slow deep flush flowed into his forehead. Kiss me Janey—You kiss me

~~And he felt her come nearer—he felt her~~

[Stran-rough-NL, leaf 12]

And it seemed to him there was a tiny pause ~~he~~ but* long enough for him to suffer torture before her ~~mouth~~ lips touched his, firmly, lightly. Kissing him as she always kissed him as though it ^the kiss^—it—how could he describe it—confirmed what they were saying— sealed the compact. But that wasn't what he wanted! That wasn't at all what he thirsted for! ~~Which rendered him.~~ He felt suddenly horribly tired.

~~Then~~ If you knew he said ~~not~~ opening his eyes—what its been like—waiting today. I thought ~~you~~ ^the boat^ never would come in—the doctors launch was gone 2 hours + a half. ~~What kept you so long.~~

---

[95] Mansfield adds "They will keep" in the revision (Stran-clean-NL, leaf 13).
[96] This becomes simply, "'If it were floating in Eternity [. . .]'" (Stran-clean-NL, leaf 13).
[97] The clean version deletes the "Oh" and the verb form becomes passive: "he liked being laughed at by Janey" (Stran-clean-NL, leaf 13).
[98] The clean manuscript omits "He shut his eyes."

You're worrying about something," said Hammond. "What is it? Come and sit here—come and sit on my knew before the fire."

"I'll just unpin my hat," said Janey, and she went over to the dressing table. "A-Ah!" She gave a little cry.

"What is it?"

"Nothing darling. Ive just found the children's letters. That's all right. They will keep. No hurry now." She turned to him, clasping them. She tucked them into her frilled blouse. She cried quickly, gayly: "Oh how typical this dressing table is of you!"

"Why—what's the matter with it," said Hammond.

"If it were floating in Eternity I should say 'John,' laughed Janey, staring at the big bottle of hair tonic, the wicker bottle of <u>eau de cologne</u>, the two hair brushes and a dozen new collars tied with pink tape. "Is this all your luggage."

"Hang my luggage," said Hammond, but all the same he liked being laughed at by Janey. "Let's talk. Lets get down to

[Stran-clean-NL, leaf 14]

things. Tell me"—and as Janey perched on his knees he leaned back and drew her into the deep, ugly chair. "Tell me you're really glad to be back, Janey."

"Yes, darling. I am glad," she said.

But just as when he embraced her he felt she would fly away so Hammond never knew—never knew for dead certain that she was as glad as he was. How could he know! Would he ever know? Would he always have this craving—this pang like ~~hunger~~ hunger to somehow[99] make Janey so much part of him that there wasn't any of her to escape. He wanted to blot out every | body[100]—every thing. He wished now he'd turned off the light. That might have brought her nearer. And now those letters from the children rustled in her blouse. He could have chucked them into the fire.

"Janey," he whispered.

"Yes, dear?" She lay on his breast, but so lightly, so remotely. Their breathing rose and fell together.

"Janey!"

"What is it?"

"Turn to me," he whispered. A slow, deep flush flowed into his forehead. "Kiss me, Janey. You kiss me."

It seemed to him there was a tiny pause—but long enough

[Stran-clean-NL, leaf 15]

for him to suffer torture before her lips touched his, firmly, lightly, kissing them as she always kissed him—as though the kiss—how could he describe it?—confirmed what they were saying, signed the contract . . . But that wasn't what he wanted. That wasn't at all what he thirsted for. He felt suddenly, horribly tired.

"If you knew," he said, opening his eyes, "what its been like—waiting, today. I thought the boat never would come in. There we were—hanging about. What kept you so long?"

---

[99] The published version inverts "to somehow," avoiding the split infinitive: "[. . .] this pang like hunger, somehow, to make Janey so much part of him [. . .]" (CW2, 247).

[100] Mansfield draws a line separating "every" from "body."

There we were, hanging about that wharf I felt **inclined** to **charter** a boat + get rowed out.[101]

She made no answer. She was looking away from him at the fire. The ~~coal~~ flames **hurried hurried**** over the coals, flickered fell.

Not asleep are you—said Hammond. And he jumped her up + down.

No—she said—and then Dont do that dear. No I was thinking. As a matter of fact— she said, one of the passengers died last night—a man. That's what held us up. We brought him in: he wasn't buried at **sea***.[102] ~~Thats what xxx~~ So of course the ~~ships~~ shore doctor + our doctor[103]—

What was it asked Hammond ^uneasily^. He hated to hear of death—He hated this to have happened in some queer way—It was as though he + Janey had met a funeral on their way to the Hotel –[104]

Oh it wasnt anything in the least infectious said Janey. She was speaking scarcely above her breath. It was <u>heart</u>. A pause. Poor fellow, she said. Quite young. And she watched the fire flicker and fall. He died in my arms said Janey—

The blow was so terrific[105] that Hammond thought he'd faint.

[Stran-rough-NL, leaf 13]

He couldn't move—he couldn't breathe—He felt all his strength flowing flowing [*sic*] into the big dark chair + the big dark chair held him fast—~~made him~~ gripped him forced[106] him to bear it.

What he said dully—Whats that you say.

"The end was quite peaceful" said the ~~little~~ small voice—he just, and he saw her ^lift her gentle^ hand ~~gentle~~ ~~lift~~ breathed his life away at the end. And her hand fell.

Who—else—was there—Hammond managed to ask.

Nobody –[107]

Ah my God what was she saying! What was she—doing to him? This would kill him— And all the while she spoke –

I saw the change coming + Id just sent[108] the steward for the doctor but the doctor was too late. He couldn't have done anything—anyway—

But why you why you—moaned Hammond –

At that Janey turned quickly—quickly searched his face –

"You <u>dont</u> mind do you" she asked[109]—you dont. Its nothing to do with you and me –

Somehow* or other he managed to shake some sort of smile at her. Somehow or other he stammered—No, go on go on I want you to tell me –

But John –[110]

---

[101] The clean version eliminates the references to the doctor's launch and chartering a boat and adds: "'What kept you so long?'" (Stran-clean-NL, leaf 15).

[102] "Sea" seems to be superimposed over another word. The clean draft adds "I mean" at the beginning of this sentence.

[103] This becomes: "[. . .] the ship's doctor and the shore doctor" (Stran-clean-NL, leaf 15).

[104] Mansfield revises the structure of this sentence: "It was, in some queer way, as though he and Janey had met a funeral [. . .]" (Stran-clean-NL, leaf 15).

[105] "Terrific" becomes "sudden" in the clean manuscript.

[106] Mansfield retraces the first part of this word.

[107] The clean version adds: "'I was alone with him'" (Stran-clean-NL, leaf 16).

[108] This becomes "'I sent'" in the clean version.

[109] The clean manuscript adds "John": "'You don't <u>mind</u>, John, do you?'" (Stran-clean-NL, leaf 16).

[110] "Darling" is added after "John" in the clean draft.

She made no answer. She was looking away from him at the fire. The flames hurried—hurried over the coals—flickered—fell.

"Not asleep—are you?" said Hammond. And he jumped her up and down.

"No," she said. And then: "Dont do that, dear. No, I was thinking. As a matter of fact," she said, "one of the passengers died last night—a man. That's what held us up. We brought him in. I mean he wasn't buried at sea. So, of course, the ship's doctor and the shore doctor –"

"What was it?" asked Hammond uneasily. He hated to hear of death. He hated this to have happened. It was, in some queer way, as though he and Janey had met a funeral on their way to the hotel.

[Stran-clean-NL, leaf 16]

"Oh, it wasn't anything in the least infectious," said Janey. She was speaking scarcely above her breath. "It was _heart_." A pause. "Poor fellow!" she said, "Quite young." And she watched the fire flicker and fall. "He died in my arms," said Janey.

The blow was so sudden that Hammond thought he would faint. He couldn't move; he couldn't breathe. He felt all his strength flowing—flowing into the big dark chair, and the big dark chair held him fast, gripped him, forced him to bear it.

"What?" he said, dully. "Whats that you say?"

"The end was quite peaceful," said the small voice. "He just –" and Hammond saw her lift her gentle hand—"breathed his life away at the end"—and her hand fell.

"Who—else was there?" Hammond managed to ask.

"Nobody. I was alone with him."

Ah, my God. What was she saying! What was she doing to him. This would kill him! And all the while she spoke.

"I saw the change coming and I sent the steward for the doctor but the doctor was too late. He couldn't have done anything, anyway."

"But—why you—why you –" moaned Hammond.

At that Janey turned quickly—quickly searched his face.

"You don't _mind_, John, do you?" she asked. "You dont . . . Its nothing to do with you and me."

[Stran-clean-NL, leaf 17]

Somehow or other he managed to shake some sort of smile at her. Somehow or other he stammered: "No—go on, go on. I want you to tell me . . ."

"But John, darling –"

Tell me, Janey —[111]

Theres nothing to tell she said wondering. He was one of the 1st class passengers. Quite young.[112] I saw he was very ill when he came on

[Stran-rough-NL, leaf 14]

board, ~~but nobody else seemed to realise it. He never ought to been~~ [sic] ~~allowed to travel. And we got to know each other don't you know~~ ~~and I think he realized I had guessed about him—about how ill he was.~~[113] ~~How sorry I was for him.~~ ~~Then~~ in ~~He fell awfully~~ ill in the tropics. There wasn't a nurse or one creature on board to help the doctor so I . . . offered to, said Janey ~~And after that—off and on—until it culminated in~~[114] Then he seemed to be so much better until[115] until [sic] yesterday—He had a very severe attack in the afternoon—excitement, nervousness about arriving I think and after that he never really recovered.[116]

But why didnt the stewardess—

Oh my dear ~~she was hopeless~~ the stewardess! said Janey—And besides that what he would have felt! ~~He~~ You see [sic] might have wanted to leave a message to—[117]

Didn't he, muttered Hammond, Didnt he—say anything.

"No darling not a word." She said softly. He droned mostly for home said she.[118] He was far ~~too~~ weak + He was too weak to move even a finger ~~even~~.[119]

At that Hammonds ~~desolation was complete.~~ xxx xxx felt as though his heart ~~came~~ stopped beating. Janey ceased speaking but her xx words seemed to float to hover—to ~~settle slowly—fall~~ settle in his heart covering his [sic]120

[see Figure 17]

---

[111] This line is indented further than the previous line.

[112] "Quite young" is omitted in the clean version.

[113] While Mansfield has drawn several diagonal lines through this whole section, indicating it is to be omitted, "and I think he realized I had guessed about him—about how ill he was" is stricken out separately.

[114] "And after that—off and on——until it culminated" is stricken out separately.

[115] "To be" is added to the clause after the initial addition.

[116] The revised version changes the sentence structure slightly: "[. . .] excitement—nervousness I think, about arriving" (Stran-clean-NL, leaf 17).

[117] The clean manuscript reads: "'What would he have felt. And besides—he might have wanted to leave a message—to—a'" (Stran-clean-NL, leaf 17).

[118] Because the additions "He droned . . ." and "She said softly" are placed one above and one below the preceding statement, respectively, it is difficult to know which Mansfield intended to place first. However, "She said softly" is in a darker ink as are some of the other revisions of this section, suggesting it was added later.

[119] The revised version has Janey shake her head and omits the part about the young man's "dron[ing] for home": "She shook her head, softly. 'All the time I was with him he was too weak . . . He was too weak even to move a finger . . .'" (Stran-clean-NL, leaf 17).

[120] "Settle" is inserted later. The clean version omits the sentence about Hammond's heart and develops the imagery: "Janey was silent. But her words—so light—so soft—so chill seemed to hover in the air to rain into his breast—like snow" (Stran-clean-NL, leaf 17).

"Tell me, Janey."

"There's nothing to tell," she said, wondering. "He was one of the first class passengers. I saw he was very ill when he came on board. But he seemed to be so much better until yesterday. He had a severe attack in the afternoon—excitement—nervousness I think, about arriving. And after that he never recovered."

"But why didn't the stewardess –"

"Oh, my dear—the stewardess!" said Janey. "What would he have felt. And besides— he might have wanted to leave a message—to –"

"Didn't he?" muttered Hammond. "Didn't he say anything?"

"No, darling, not a word." She shook her head, softly. "All the time I was with him he was too weak . . . He was too weak even to move a finger . . ."

Janey was silent. But her words—so light—so soft—so chill seemed to hover in the air to rain into his breast—like snow.

The fire had gone red—now it fell in with a sharp sound + the room was ~~darker~~ colder. Then even crept up his arms.121 The room was huge, immense, ~~terrible~~ + glittering—it was122 his whole world—There was the great blind bed—with his coat flung across it—like some horrible headless man **kneeling*** there123—There was the luggage ready to be carried away again—anywhere—tossed into a train^s—on to a boat^s. ~~The light jerked xxx on the white gloves~~124

"He was too weak—too weak to move a finger." And yet—and yet he died in Janeys arms—Ah, my God125

[Stran-rough-NL, leaf 15]

She who'd never once never in all these years126

~~What had she done. Janey had taken him—held him~~—clasped him—~~Ah, my God he couldn't think about it—he couldn't face it—he couldn't stand it. She whod never even Janey had taken that other.~~ No, no he must ~~never~~ think of it again madness ~~lay~~ in thinking about it. ~~His whole life **ever be ruined.** Everything changed—Had **been haunted**~~

No, he wouldnt face it he couldnt stand it. It was too much to bear.

And now Janey touched his tie with her fingers. She pinched the edges together.

Youre not—sorry I told you John darling. It hasn't spoilt our evening—our being alone together —127

But at that he had to hide his ~~face~~—he put his face in her bosom + her arms ~~went round him~~ folded round him –128

Spoilt ~~our~~ their evening—spoilt ~~our~~ their being together—~~They would~~ Didnt she know never be alone together again [sic]!129

3.XI.1920
Isola Bella130 [see Figure 18]

---

121 This becomes: "Cold crept up his arm" (Stran-clean-NL, leaf 17).
122 "Was" becomes "filled" in the clean version.
123 Instead of "kneeling there," the clean version uses "saying his prayers" (Stran-clean-NL, leaf 18).
124 After the major deletion at the top of the page, most of the corrections are in a darker ink.
125 The clean manuscript eliminates one "and yet" and "Ah, my God" (Stran-clean-NL, leaf 18).
126 This becomes: "She—who'd never—never once in all these years—never on one single, solitary occasion . . ." (Stran-clean-NL, leaf 18).
127 The clean version adds "'It hasn't made you sad?'" before this sentence (Stran-clean-NL, leaf 18).
128 The clean version has him clasp her, instead: "his arms enfolded her" (Stran-clean-NL, leaf 18).
129 The clean manuscript reads: "Spoilt their evening! Spoilt their being alone together! They would never be alone together again" (Stran-clean-NL, leaf 18).
130 Isola Bella is circled.

The fire had gone red. Now it fell in with a sharp sound and the room was colder. Cold crept up his arm. The room was

[Stran-clean-NL, leaf 18]

huge, immense, glittering. It filled his whole world. There was the great, blind bed—with his coat flung across it like some headless man saying his prayers. There was the luggage—ready to be carried away again—anywhere—tossed into trains, carted on to boats.

. . . "He was too weak. He was too weak to move a finger." And yet he died in Janey's arms. She—who'd never—never once in all these years—never ~~in~~ [on][131] one single, solitary occasion . . .

No, he mustn't think of it. Madness lay in thinking of it. No, he wouldn't face it. He couldn't stand it. It was too much to bear!

And now Janey touched his tie with her fingers. She pinched the edges of the tie, together.

"You're not—sorry I told you, John, darling? It hasn't made you sad? It hasn't spoilt our evening—our being alone together?"

But at that he had to hide his face. He put his face into her bosom and his arms enfolded her.

Spoilt their evening! Spoilt their being alone together! They would never be alone together again.

— —
— —

[132]

[November: 1920]

[Stran-clean-NL, leaf 18 verso]

Please return to:

Katherine Mansfield
c/o The Athenaeum
10 Adelphi Terrace
W.C.I[133]
London

---

[131] "On" appears to be written over "in."
[132] The treble clef Mansfield has drawn is large and the interior filled in with ink.
[133] This is WC1, the postal code for the Bloomsbury area of London, but Mansfield has used the Roman numeral "I."

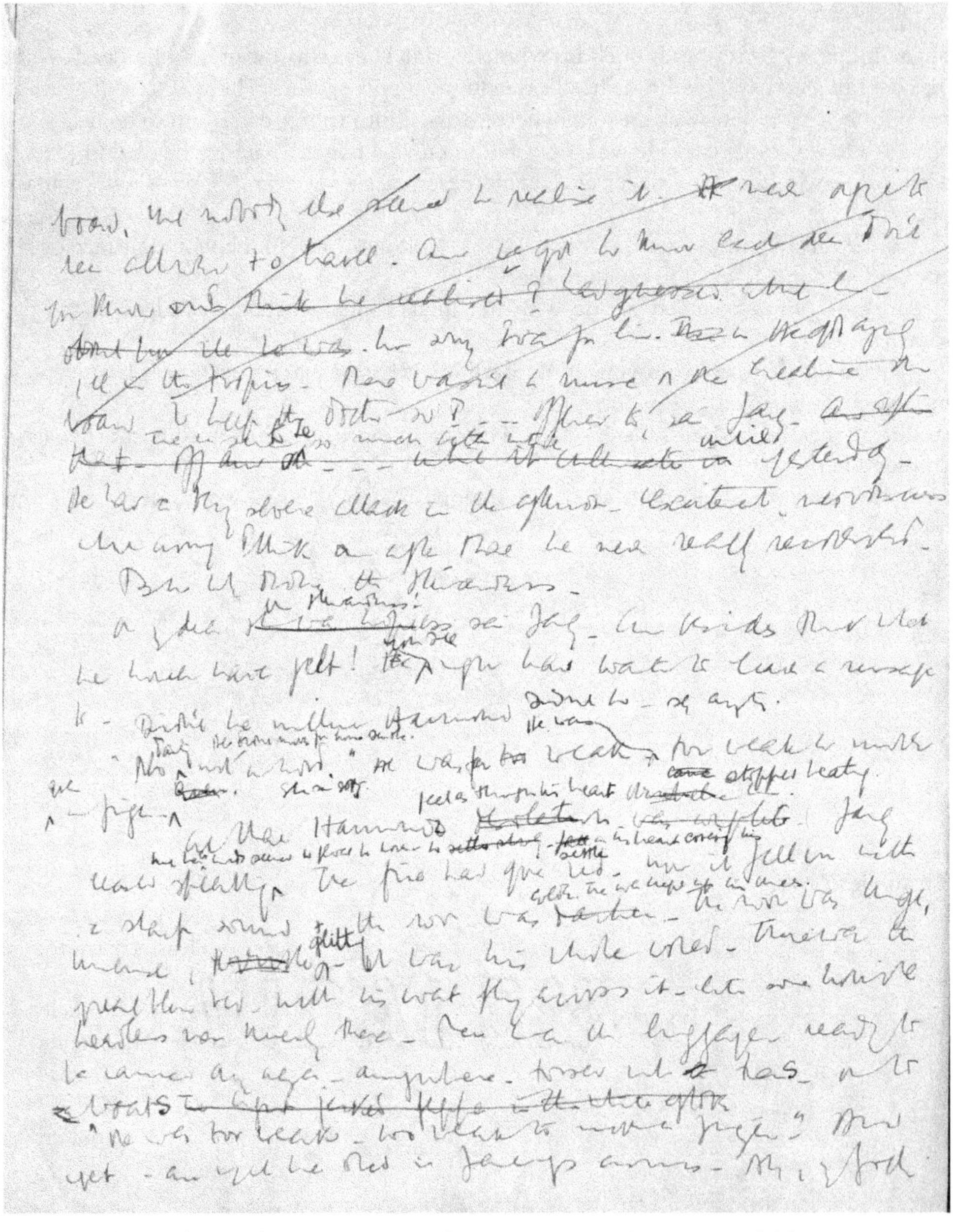

FIGURE 17: Leaf 14, "The Stranger" [rough manuscript], Katherine Mansfield Papers, Newberry Library, (box 2, folder 22), 15 leaves. Image courtesy of the Newberry Library.

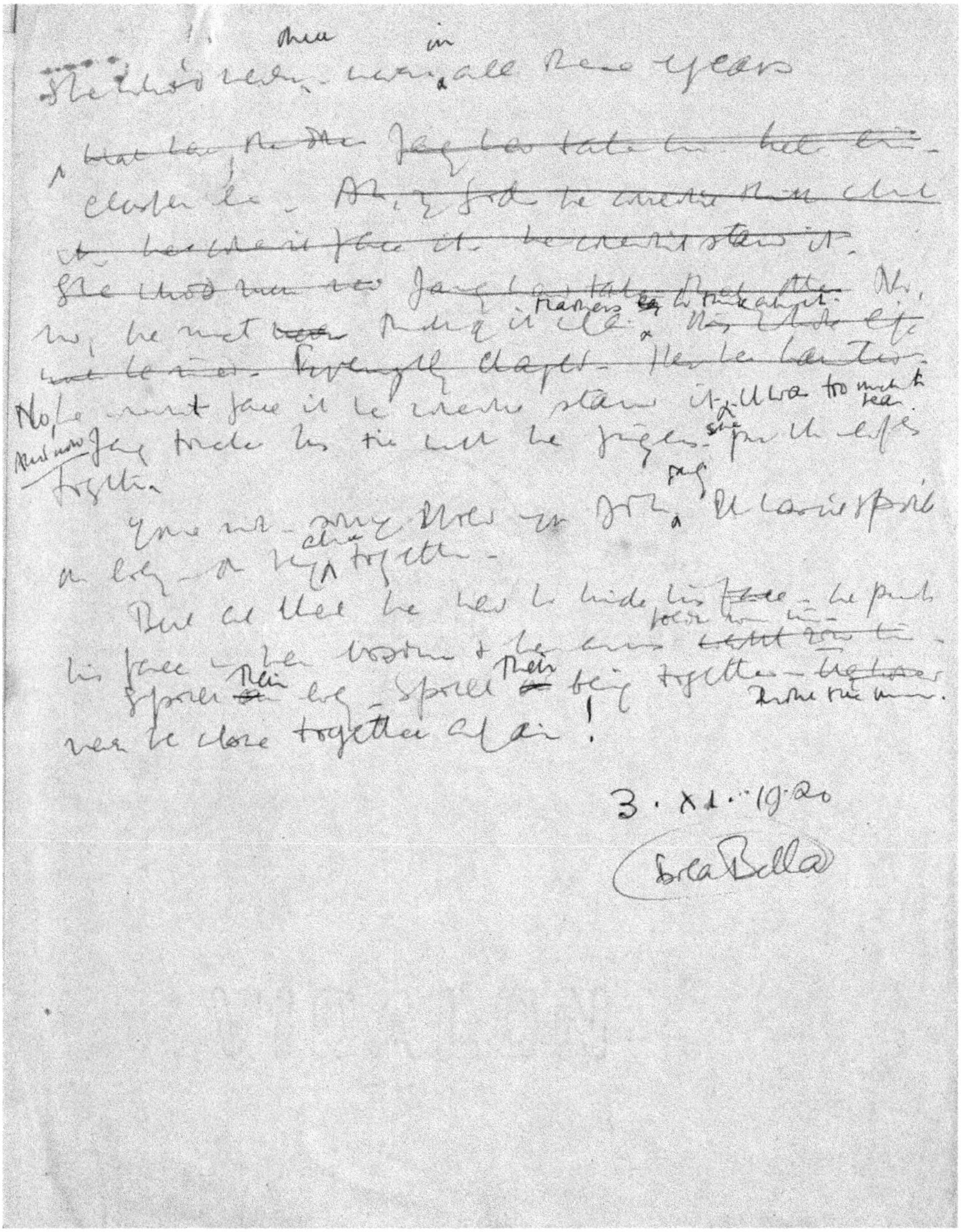

FIGURE 18: Leaf 15, "The Stranger" [rough manuscript], Katherine Mansfield Papers, Newberry Library, (box 2, folder 22), 15 leaves. Image courtesy of the Newberry Library.

A Note on the Manuscript and Typescript of "Poison"

"Poison" was not published in Mansfield's lifetime but was part of the second posthumous collection of stories, *Something Childish and Other Stories* (1924), that John Middleton Murry compiled from the papers Mansfield bequeathed to him. The source of this published version is the typescript held in the Newberry Library, so unless indicated otherwise, any references to the typescript should be presumed to be identical in the published version, as republished in the *Collected*. Mansfield has made numerous handwritten changes on the typescript, but most of these are simple, editorial corrections.

Besides the typescript, the Newberry Library also holds a manuscript version of the story. However, compared to the others transcribed here, the manuscript of "Poison" is very clean, which suggests that an earlier draft of the story existed at one time. It is likely that this version was copied by Mansfield for the typist who would have been charged with preparing the document to be sent to publishers. That this is the case is reinforced by the fact that Mansfield signs the manuscript, which she typically only did when she was sending a story to an editor or to Murry to forward to an editor.

While Mansfield had a typewriter in Hampstead during the summer of 1920, as suggested by her comment to Dorothy Brett—"My mornings are all spent *on* the typewriter"—it is unlikely she had access to one in Menton when she wrote "Poison," for in early November, just a few weeks before, she asks Murry to have one of her other stories typed for her.[1]

---

[1] *Letters* 4, 19, 98. The typewriter is part of the Alexander Turnbull Library as part of its Katherine Mansfield collection (Curios-018-1-010).

Poison.

The post was very late. When we came back from our walk **before**[2] lunch it still had not arrived.

"<u>Pas encore</u>, Madame,"[3] sang Annette, scurrying back to her cooking.

We ~~xxx~~ carried our parcels into the dining room.[4] The table was laid. As always, the sight of the table laid for two—for two people only—and yet so finished, so perfect[5] there was no possible room for a third, gave me a queer, quick thrill as though I'd been struck by that silver lightning that quivered over the white cloth, the brilliant glasses, the shallow bowl of freezias.[6]

"Blow the old postman! Whatever can have happened to him!"[7] said Beatrice. ["]Put those things down, dearest."[8]

"Where would you like them . . ."[9]

She raised her head; she smiled her sweet, teasing smile.

"Anywhere—Silly!"

But I knew only too well that there was no such place for her[10] and I would have stood holding the squat liqueur[11] bottle and the sweets for months—for years—rather than risk giving another tiny shock to her exquisite sense of order.[12]

"Here—Ill take them." She plumped them on to the table[13] with her long gloves and a basket of figs. "The Luncheon Table. A Short Story by—by—" She[14] took my arms. "Let's go on to the terrace—" and I feel her shiver. "<u>Ca sent</u>," she said, faintly, "<u>de la cuisine</u>."[15]

I had noticed lately—we had been living in the South[16] for two months—that when she wished to speak of food[17] or the climate, or, playfully, of her love for me, she always dropped into French.[18]

We perched on the balustrade under the awning.

---

[2] While the manuscript appears to read "before," the typescript has "after."

[3] The *Collected* places the underlined portion along with "Madame" in italics.

[4] The typescript uses "dining-room."

[5] A comma is added after "perfect" in the typescript.

[6] The spelling of "freezias" is changed to "freesias" in the *Collected*.

[7] The exclamation point is changed to a period in the typescript and then to a question mark in the *Collected*.

[8] On the typescript, "Put those things down, dearest" appears on a separate line, and Mansfield has drawn a line to clarify that it should be a part of Beatrice's dialogue.

[9] The *Collected* adds a question mark at the end of this line.

[10] The *Collected* adds a comma here, which is not in the typescript.

[11] At the bottom of the manuscript page, Mansfield has jotted the word "liqueur" several times, as if she was trying to determine its proper spelling; the typescript misspells it as "liquer," but it is corrected with a handwritten "u."

[12] The typescript exchanges commas for the dashes.

[13] The typescript adds "down," reading: "She plumped them down on the table . . . ." (Pois-TS-NL, leaf 1).

[14] The typescript removes the capital "s" in "She," but the *Collected* restores it.

[15] The *Collected* omits the comma after "she said" and adds an ellipsis after "*de la cuisine*."

[16] The *Collected* changes "South" to "south."

[17] The typescript adds a comma after "food."

[18] Interestingly, Mansfield has drawn parentheses in ink around this whole passage in the typescript, as if to designate it for omission or perhaps to be moved. However, there is no indication as to why she has done so, and all editions retain the passage in its original placement.

[Pois-MS-NL, leaf 2]

Beatrice leaned over gazing down—down to the white road with its guard of lifted cactus spears.[19] The beauty of her ear, just her ear, the marvel of it was so great that I could have turned from regarding it to all that sweep of glittering sea below and stammered: "You know—her ears![20] She has ears that are simply the most . . ."

She was dressed in white[21] with pearls round her throat and lilies-of-the-valley tucked in[22] her belt. On the third finger of her left hand she wore one pearl ring—no wedding ring.

"Why should I, *mon ami*? Why should we pretend? Who could possibly care?" And of course I agreed, although dead privately,[23] in the depths of my heart, I would have given my soul to have stood beside her in a large, yes, a large fashionable church[24] crammed with people, with old reverend clergymen, with The Voice that Breathed o'er Eden,[25] with palms and the smell of scent, knowing there was a red carpet and confetti outside and,[26] somewhere, a wedding cake and champagne and a satin shoe to throw at[27] the carriage—if I could have slipped our wedding ring on her finger.

Not because I cared for such horrible shows but because I felt it might possibly perhaps lessen this ghastly feeling of absolute freedom—her absolute freedom, of course.[28]

Oh, God! What torture happiness was—what anguish! I looked up at the villa, at the windows of our room hidden so mysteriously behind the green straw blinds. Was it possible that she ever came moving through the green light and smiling that secret smile, that languid, brilliant

[Pois-MS-NL, leaf 3]

smile that was just for me? She put one arm round my neck; the other hand softly, terribly, brushed back my hair.

"Who are you?" Who was she! She was—woman.[29]

. . . On the first warm evening in spring[30] when lights shine like pearls through the lilac air and voices murmured in the fresh-flowering gardens it was she who sang in the tall house with the tulle curtains.[31] As one drove in the moon-light through the foreign city hers was the shadow that fell across the quivering gold of the shutters. When the lamp

---

[19] The *Collected* omits "lifted" from the phrase "guard of lifted cactus spears."

[20] The typescript underlines "ear," but this emphasis is not retained in the *Collected*.

[21] The *Collected* adds a comma after "white."

[22] "In" becomes "into" in the typescript.

[23] The typescript changes "although" to "though" and omits "dead" in "dead privately."

[24] A comma is inserted after "fashionable church" in the typescript.

[25] On the typescript, Mansfield has handwritten quotation marks around the song title; it is italicized in the *Collected*.

[26] A comma is inserted after "outside" and the one after "and" is omitted in the typescript.

[27] "At" is changed to "after" in the typescript.

[28] The *Collected* places a comma after "horrible shows" and emphasizes "her" with italics in "her absolute freedom."

[29] It is difficult to say whether the "w" of "woman" is capitalized in the manuscript; however, it is clear that Mansfield chose that it should be. The typescript shows that the "w" was originally lower-case, but a handwritten capital "W" is superimposed over the lower-case "w."

[30] The typescript capitalizes the "s" of "spring," and the *Collected* adds a comma after "spring."

[31] The typescript adds a comma after gardens, and while it omits "who" in "she who sang," it is restored in the published version.

was lighted, in the new-born stillness her steps passed your door. And she looked out into the autumn twilight, pale in her furs, as the automobile swept by.[32]

In fact—to put it shortly—I was twenty-four at the ~~xxxx~~^time . . .[33] And when she lay on her back, the pearls slipped under her chin and murmured:[34] "I'm thirsty, darling.[35] Donne-moi un orange!"[36] I would gladly, willingly, have dived for an orange into the jaws of a crocodile—if crocodiles ate oranges.

"Had I two little feathery wings
And were like a feathery bird"[37]
sang Beatrice.

I seized her hand. "You wouldn't fly away?"

"Not far," said she. "Not further than the bottom of the road."[38]

"Why on earth there?"

She quoted: "He cometh ~~not~~^not, she said."[39]

"Who? The silly old postman? But youre not expecting a letter?"[40]

"Not.[41] But its maddening all the same. Ah!" suddenly she laughed and leaned against me. "There he is—look!—like a blue beetle."[42]

And we pressed our cheeks together and looked at the blue beetle beginning to climb.[43]

[Pois-MS-NL, leaf 4]

"Dearest!"[44] breathed Beatrice. And the word seemed to linger in the air, to throb in the air like the note of a violin."

"What is it?"

"I dont know," she laughed softly. "A wave of—a wave of affection."[45]

I put my arm round her. "Then you wouldn't fly away?"

And she said rapidly and softly: "No, no.[46] Not for worlds. Not really. I love this place. I have loved being here.[47] I could stay here for years, I believe.[48] Ive never been so happy as I have these last two months, and you've been so perfect to me, dearest, in every way."

---

[32] The typescript replaces the final period with an ellipsis.

[33] The typescript replaces the dashes with commas and the ellipsis with a period.

[34] This sentence undergoes a few changes in each iteration. The typescript replaces "Murmured" with "sighed," while the *Collected* adds "with" to the phrase "with the pearls slipped under her chin" and separates it with commas. It also omits the colon, leaving no punctuation.

[35] "Darling" is replaced with "dearest" in the typescript.

[36] The exclamation point is replaced with a period in the typescript and a comma in the *Collected*.

[37] The *Collected* adds an ellipsis at the end of this line.

[38] The typescript places a period after "Not far" and omits "said she."

[39] The *Collected* adds an ellipsis at the end of the quotation.

[40] The question mark becomes a period in the typescript.

[41] The *Collected* changes the period to a comma.

[42] The typescript capitalizes "Suddenly" and omits the exclanation point after "look."

[43] The typescript replaces "looked at" with "watched."

[44] The exclamation point becomes a comma in the typescript.

[45] The typescript changes the end punctuation to a comma and adds "I suppose" at the end: "A wave of—a wave of affection, I suppose" (Pois-TS-NL, leaf 4).

[46] The periods after each "no" are changed to exclamation points in the typescript.

[47] "I have" becomes "I've" in the typescript.

[48] The period after "I believe" is omitted in the typescript but reinstated in the *Collected*. The omission of the period opens up the sentence for a variety of interpretations, and that there are numerous hand-written corrections on the typescript, but nothing here, suggests Mansfield may have approved of its omission.

This was such bliss—it was so extraordinary, so unprecedented to hear her talk like this that I had to try to laugh it off.[49]

"Dont. You sound as if you were saying good-bye!"[50]

"Oh, nonsense, nonsense. You mustn't say such dreadful things even in fun."[51] She slid her little hand under my white jacket and clutched my shoulder.

"Youve been happy—haven't you?"

"Happy! Happy![52] Oh, God!—if you knew what I feel at this moment.[53] Happy! My wonder! My Queen!"[54]

And I dropped off the balustrade and embraced her, lifting her up, and while I held her lifted I pressed my face in her breast and muttered:[55] "You are mine?"[56] And for the very first time in all the desperate months I'd known her even counting the last month of—surely—Heaven, I believed her absolutely when she answered:[57] "Yes, I am yours."[58]

The creak of the gate and the postman's steps on the

[Pois-MS-NL, leaf 5]

gravel drew us apart. I was dizzy for the moment. I simply stood there smiling, I felt, rather stupidly.[59]

Beatrice walked quickly over to the cane chairs.[60]

"You go—go for the letters," said she[.]

I—well I almost reeled away.[61] But I was too late. Annette came running. "Pas de lettres!" she sang.[62]

My reckless smile in reply as she handed me the paper must have surprised her. I was wild with joy. I threw the paper up into the air and sang out: "No letters, darling!" as I came over to where Beatrice[63] was lying in the long chair.

---

[49] A comma is added after "unprecedented" in the typescript.

[50] In the typescript, the period after "Don't" becomes an exclamation point, and the exclamation point after "good-bye" becomes a period.

[51] The typescript omits "dreadful" but changes the end punctuation from a period to an exclamation point.

[52] The *Collected* changes the exclamation points to question marks.

[53] An ellipsis is added in the *Collected*.

[54] "My wonder! My Queen" becomes "My Wonder! My Joy" in the typescript; the capitalization of the "w" and "j" are noted in ink on the typescript (Pois-TS-NL, leaf 4).

[55] The initial "And" of this sentence is omitted in the typescript, while "lifting her up" is changed to "lifting her in my arms," after which Mansfield adds a period; she then capitalizes the following "and" to begin the new sentence. The *Collected* reinserts "up" to read: "lifting her up in my arms."

[56] On the typescript, Mansfield underlines "are" by hand, to create an emphasis retained in the *Collected*.

[57] The typescript omits "very" in "for the very first time"; a comma is added after "I'd known her," and the comma after "Heaven" becomes a dash.

[58] Beatrice's response remains part of the same paragraph in both of Mansfield's versions, while the *Collected* shifts it to a new paragraph.

[59] A comma is added after "I simply stood there" in the typescript.

[60] The typescript omits "quickly" from this sentence, and it places this sentence at the end of the paragraph just above it.

[61] A second dash is added after "well" in the typescript.

[62] In the typescript, the exclamation point after "lettres" is changed to a period and then to a comma in the *Collected*; "she sang" becomes "said she."

[63] "Beatrice" becomes "the beloved woman" in the typescript.

For a moment she didn't reply. Then she said slowly as she tore off the newspaper wrapping:[64] "The world forgetting <u>by</u> the world forgot."[65]

There are times when a cigarette is just the very one thing that will carry you over the moment. It is more than a confederate even; it is a secret perfect little friend who knows all about it and understands absolutely.[66] While you smoke you look down at it—smile or frown, as the occasion demands; you inhale deeply and expel the smoke in a slow fan. This was one of those moments. I walked over to the magnolia and breathed my fill of it. Then I came back and leaned over her shoulders.[67]

But quickly she tossed the paper away on to the stone.[68]

"There's nothing in it," said she. "Nothing. There's only some poison trial. Either a man did or didn't murder his wife and twenty thousand people have sat in court every day and two million words have been wired all over

[Pois-MS-NL, leaf 6]

the world after each proceedings."[69]

"Silly world!" said I, flinging into another chair. I wanted to forget the paper—to return,[70] but cautiously, of course, to that moment before the postman came. But when she answered I knew from her voice the moment was over for now. Never mind. I was content to wait—five hundred years, if need be—now that I knew.

"Not so very silly!"[71] said Beatrice. After all it isn't only morbid curiosity on the part of the twenty-thousand."

"What is it, darling?"[72]

"Guilt!" she cried. "Guilt! Don't you realise that? They're fascinated like sick people are fascinated by anything—any scrap of news about their own disease.[73] The man in the dock may be innocent enough but the people in court are nearly all of them poisoners.[74] Haven't you ever thought—" she was pale with excitement—["]of the amount of poisoning that goes on?[75] It's the exception to find married people who don't poison each other—married people and lovers. Oh," she cried, "the number of cups of tea, glasses of wine, cups of coffee that are just tainted. The number Ive had myself, and drunk, either knowing or not knowing—and risked it![76] The only reason why so many couples—" she laughed—"survive,[77] is because the one is frightened of giving the other the fatal dose.

---

[64] "Wrapping" is changed to "wrapper" in the typescript.

[65] On the typescript, Mansfield underlines "by" by hand, to ensure the emphasis noted in the manuscript. The *Collected* inserts a comma after "forgetting."

[66] The typescript adds commas after "confederate" and "secret."

[67] "Shoulders" becomes "shoulder" in the typescript.

[68] It is not perfectly clear, but the manuscript seems to suggest a new paragraph where Beatrice tosses the newspaper. The spacing, though, makes this inconclusive.

[69] "Either a man" is changed to "Either some man" in the typescript; the *Collected* adds a comma after "wife." On the typescript, the "s" of "proceedings" is stricken through.

[70] On the typescript, Mansfield has hand-written the exclamation point after "Silly world"; the dash after "paper" becomes a comma.

[71] In the typescript, the exclamation point becomes a period which is then changed to a comma in the *Collected*.

[72] The typescript includes the aside, "Heaven knows I didn't care," after "What is it, darling?" (Pois-TS-NL, leaf 6).

[73] "Their own disease" is changed to "their own case" in the typescript.

[74] The *Collected* includes a comma after "enough."

[75] The question mark becomes a colon in the *Collected*.

[76] The exclamation point is changed to a period in the typescript.

[77] Mansfield underlines "survive" by hand on the typescript, to make sure it is emphasized.

That **does take nerve** . . .[78] But its bound to come sooner or later. There's no going back once the first little does[se] has been given. It's the beginning of the end, really. Dont you agree?[79] Don't you see what I mean?"

[Pois-MS-NL, leaf 7]

She didn't wait for me to answer. She unpinned the lilies-of-the-valley and lay back drawing them across her eyes.

"Both my husbands poisoned me," said Beatrice. "My first husband gave me a huge dose almost immediately but my second was really an artist in his way.[80] Just a tiny pinch, now and again, cleverly disguised—oh, so cleverly!—until one morning I woke up and in every single particle of me, to the ends of my fingers and toes, there was a tiny grain . . . I was just in time—"[81]

I hated to hear her mention her husbands so calmly. It hurt—especially today.[82] I was going to speak but suddenly she cried mournfully:[83]

"Why—why should it have happened to me? What have I done? Why have I been all my life singled out by . . . It's a conspiracy!"[84]

I tried to tell her it was because she was too perfect for this horrible world—too exquisite, too fine. It frightened people. I made a little joke.

"But I—I haven't tried to poison you."

Beatrice gave such a queer, small laugh and bit the end of a lily stem.[85]

"Oh, you!"[86] said she. "You wouldn't hurt a fly."

Strange. That hurt, though—most horribly.[87]

At that moment Annette ran out with our aperitifs.[88] Beatrice leaned forward and took a glass from the tray and handed it to me. I noticed the gleam of the pearl on what I called her pearl finger. How could I

---

[78] While it is possible that Mansfield here intends "that dose takes nerve" as it appears in later drafts, made more likely by the spelling correction from "does" to "dose" just two lines later, it seems equally likely that the typist may have inverted the "es" of "does" to create "dose" in the latter instance. The typescript reads: "That dose take⁚ nerve⸱!" where Mansfield has added the "s" and the exclamation point, signaling that she may have edited (knowingly or not) to accommodate a potential typographical error (Pois-TS-NL, leaf 6). The exclamation point replaces the ellipsis in the typescript.

[79] The typescript reads: "It's the beginning of the end, really—don't you agree?" (Pois-TS-NL, leaf 6).

[80] A comma is added after "immediately" in the typescript.

[81] The ellipsis is changed to a period and the dash changed to an ellipsis in the typescript.

[82] The typescript reads: "I hated to hear her mention her husbands so calmly, especially today. It hurt" (Pois-TS-NL, leaf 6).

[83] The Collected inserts a comma after "speak."

[84] The typescript does not have this statement separated from the previous paragraph, but the new paragraph is retained in the Collected. The exclamation point becomes a period in the typescript.

[85] The typescript omits the word "such" as well as the comma after "queer."

[86] "Oh" is eliminated in the typescript.

[87] The typescript reads: "That hurt, though. Most horribly" ((Pois-TS-NL, leaf 7).

[88] "At that moment" is changed to "Just then" in the typescript, and Mansfield underlines "aperitifs" and adds the accent over the "e" by hand.

[Pois-MS-NL, leaf 8]

be hurt at what she said![89]

"And you," I said, taking the glass, "youve poisoned anybody." That gave me an idea; I tried to explain. "You—you do just the opposite. What would be the name for one who ^like you . . . instead of poisoning people, filled them—not only me—but everybody—the postman, the man who drives us, our boatman, the flower seller—with new life, with something of your own radiance, your beauty, your—"[90]

Dreamily she smiled; dreamily she looked at me.

"What are you thinking of—my lovely darling?"

"I was wondering," she said, "whether, after lunch, you'd go down to the post office and ask for the afternoon letters. Would you mind, dearest? Not that I'm expecting one—but—I just thought, perhaps—its silly not to have the letters if they are there. Silly to wait till tomorrow—Isn't it?"[91]

She twirled the stem of her glass in her fingers. Her beautiful head was bent. But I lifted my glass and drank, sipped, ra~~xx~~^ther—sipped slowly, deliberately, looking at that dark head of [sic] thinking of—the postman and blue beetles and farewells that were not farewells and—[92]Good God! Was it fancy? It was not fancy.[93] The drink tasted chill, bitter, <u>queer.</u>

Katherine Mansfield

---

[89] The exclamation mark becomes a period in the typescript and a question mark in the *Collected*.

[90] The typescript reads: "What is the name for one like you who instead of poisoning people, fills them—everybody, the postman, the man who drives us, our boatman, the flowerseller, me,—with new life, with something of her own radiance, her beauty, her—" (Pois-TS-NL, leaf 7). Note the omission of "not only me" reduced to "me" at the end of the sequence, and the shift to third person, "her." The *Collected* adds a comma after "who" and omits the comma after "me."

[91] The typescript inverts the order of the last two sentences: "Isn't it? Silly to wait till tomorrow" (Pois-TS-NL, leaf 7).

[92] "The postman" becomes "postmen" and the dash becomes an ellipsis in the typescript, and the lines that follow are on a separate line.

[93] The typescript reads: "Was it fancy? no, it wasn't fancy," adding "no" to the sentence (Pois-TS-NL, leaf 8).

A Note on the Manuscript of "The Non-Compounders [Daughters of the Late Colonel]"

Originally titled "The Non-Compounders," a term used at Queen's College for day-students,[1] the story appeared first in the *London Mercury* in May 1921 and then was included in Mansfield's third collection of short stories, *The Garden Party and Other Stories* (1922). While there is a small fragment of the story held at the Alexander Turnbull Library, the only complete manuscript of the story—bearing the original title—is held by the Newberry Library. It is unclear when Mansfield decided to change the title of the story as—unlike "The Stranger," where she strikes through the original title and replaces it with the new one—the manuscript retains "The Non-Compounders" as its title, though there are edits throughout. However, two months after the story was completed in mid-December 1920, Mansfield refers to the story by its published title on February 9, 1921, in a letter to Sydney Waterlow.[2]

While there are some heavy edits on the Newberry manuscript of "The Non-Compounders," the existence of the fragment held by the Turnbull Library, as well as—and perhaps most compelling—the fact that Mansfield includes a dedication at the top of the first page, suggests that this version is a copy from an earlier draft. The Turnbull fragment, a single piece of paper, may have been part of an earlier full draft of the story, or it could be a scrap on which Mansfield simply worked out details she incorporated into the full draft. However, further evidence for an earlier version lies in the fact that some sections of the manuscript, including the first few pages, and another run of pages toward the end, are particularly clean, with few if any edits.

---

[1] See CW2, 283, note 1.
[2] *Letters* 4, 178.

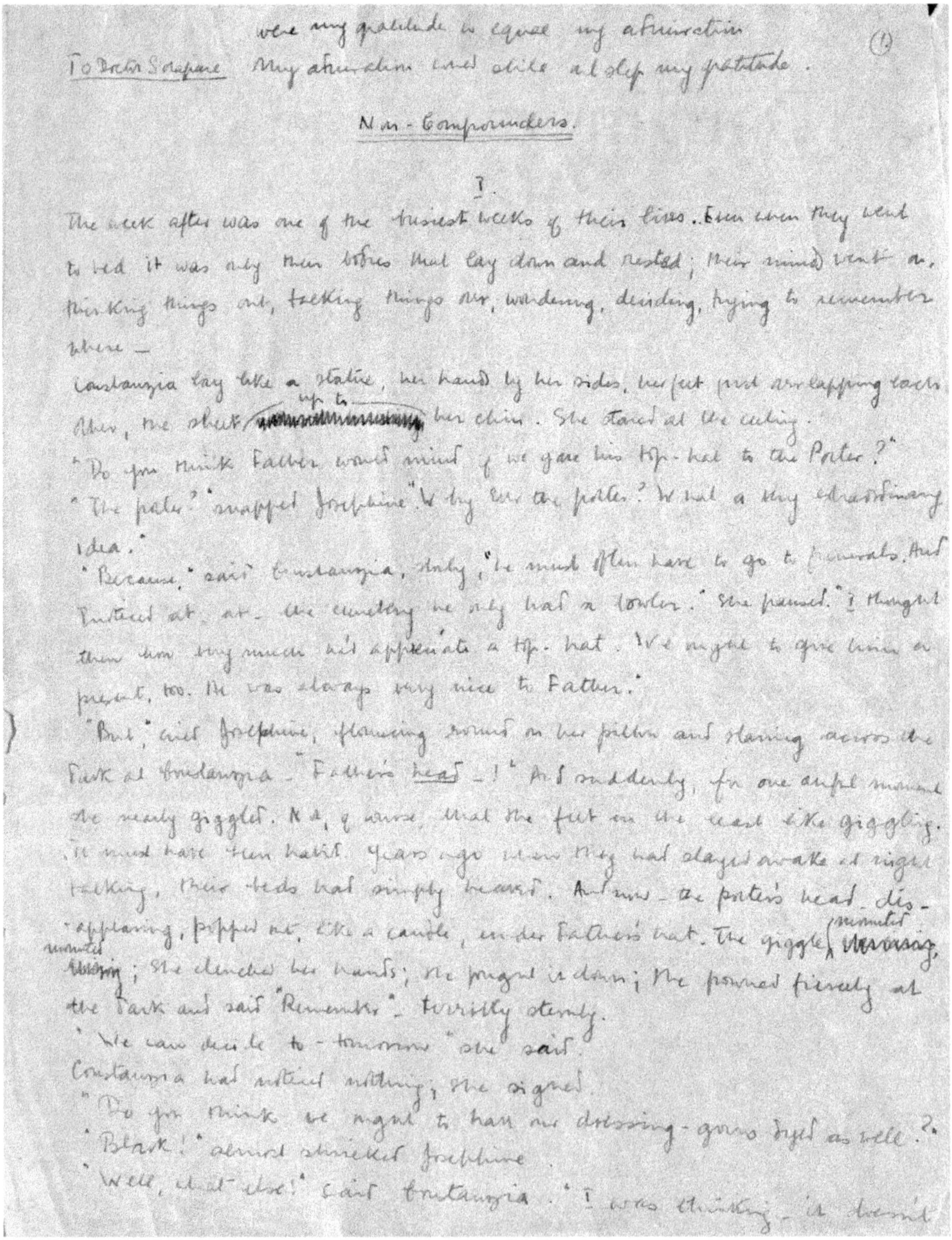

Non-Compounders.

1.

The week after was one of the busiest weeks of their lives. Even when they went to bed it was only their bodies that lay down and rested; their minds went on, thinking things out, talking things over, wondering, deciding, trying to remember where —

Constantia lay like a statue, her hands by her sides, her feet just overlapping each other, the sheet ~~up to~~ her chin. She stared at the ceiling.

"Do you think Father would mind if we gave his top-hat to the Porter?"

"The porter?" snapped Josephine. "Why ever the porter? What a very extraordinary idea."

"Because," said Constantia slowly, "he must often have to go to funerals. And I noticed at - at - the cemetery he only had a bowler." She paused. "I thought then how very much he'd appreciate a top-hat. We ought to give him a present, too. He was always very nice to Father."

"But," cried Josephine, flouncing round on her pillow and staring across the dark at Constantia. "Father's head —!" And suddenly, for one awful moment, she nearly giggled. Not, of course, that she felt in the least like giggling. It must have been habit. Years ago when they had stayed awake at night talking, their beds had simply heaved. And now - the porter's head, dis-appearing, popped out, like a candle, under Father's hat. The giggle mounted mounted; she clenched her hands; she fought it down; she frowned fiercely at the dark and said "Remember"— terribly sternly.

"We can decide to - tomorrow" she said.

Constantia had noticed nothing; she sighed.

"Do you think we ought to have our dressing-gowns dyed as well?"

"Black!" almost shrieked Josephine.

"Well, what else!" said Constantia. "I was thinking - it doesn't

FIGURE 19: Leaf 1, "Non-Compounders [Daughters of the Late Colonel]," Katherine Mansfield Papers, Newberry Library, (box 1, folder 41), 32 leaves. Image courtesy of the Newberry Library.

[DLC-MS-NL, leaf 1]

Were my gratitude to equal my admiration
<u>To Doctor Sorapure</u>[3] My admiration would still outstep my gratitude.

<u>Non-Compounders</u>

I.

The week after was one of the busiest weeks of their lives. Even when they went to bed it was only their bodies that lay down and rested; their minds went on, thinking things out, talking things over, wondering, deciding, trying to remember where —

Constanzia[4] lay like a statue, her hand by her sides, her feet just overlapping each other, the sheet ~~xxx xxx~~^{up to} her chin. She stared at the ceiling.

"Do you think Father[5] would mind if we gave his top-hat to the Porter [*sic*]?"
"The porter?" snapped Josephine. "Why ever the porter? What a very extraordinary idea."

"Because," said Constanzia, slowly, "he must often have to go to funerals. And I noticed that at—at—the cemetery he only had a bowler."[6] She paused. "I thought then how very much he'd appreciate a top-hat. We ought to give him a present, too. He was always very nice to Father."

"But," cried Josephine, flouncing round on her pillow and staring across the dark at Constanzia. "Father's <u>head</u>—!" And suddenly, for one awful moment she nearly giggled. Not, of course, that she felt in the least like giggling. It must have been habit. Years ago when they had stayed awake at night talking, their beds had simply heaved. And now— the porter's head—disappearing, popped out, like a candle, under Father's hat. The giggle ~~was rising, rising~~ ^{mounted, mounted}; she clenched her hands; she fought it down; she frowned fiercely at the dark and said "Remember"—terribly sternly.

"We can decide to - tomorrow" she said.[7]

Constanzia had noticed nothing; she sighed.

"Do you think we ought to have our dressing-gowns dyed as well?"

"Black!" almost shrieked Josephine.

"Well, what else!" said Constanzia. "I was thinking—it doesn't

[DLC-MS-NL, leaf 2]

seem quite sincere, in a way, to wear black out of doors and when we're fully dressed and then, when we're at home –"

---

[3] Dr. Victor Sorapure was one of the doctors Mansfield consulted concerning her tuberculosis in early 1919; more importantly, he pushed her focus beyond the physical symptoms to consider the spiritual implications of the disease (*Letters* 2, xiii). These spiritual explorations eventually led her to George Gurdjieff's Institute for the Harmonious Development of Man.

[4] This spelling is used for the first half of the story, after which it changes to "Constantia," the spelling used in the published version.

[5] "Father" is capitalized throughout the manuscript, though not in the published version.

[6] The published version reads: "'And I noticed at—at the cemetery that he only had a bowler'" (CW2, 266).

[7] The printed version merely has "tomorrow," without the hesitation.

"But nobody sees us," said Josephine. She gave the bedclothes such a twitch that both her feet came uncovered and she had to creep up the pillows to get them ~~under the xxx xxx xxx~~ well under again.

"Kate does," said Constanzia. "And the postman very well might."

Josephine thought of her dark red slippers which matched her dressing-gown and of Constanzia[']s favourite indefinite green ones which went with hers. Black! Two black dressing-gowns and two pairs of black wooly slippers creeping off to the bathroom like black cats!

"I don't think it[']s absolutely necessary," said she.

Silence. Then Constanzia said: ["]We shall have to post the papers with the notice in them tomorrow to catch the Ceylon mail . . . How many letters have we had up till now?"

"~~Thirty~~ ^{Twenty} three."[8]

Josephine had replied to them all, and ~~thirty~~-^{twenty} three times when she came to: "We miss our dear Father ~~very~~ ^{so} much" she had broken down and had to use her handkerchief and on some of them ^{even to} soak up a very ~~faded~~^{light-} blue tear with an edge of blotting paper. Strange. She couldn't have put it on—but ~~thirty~~-^{twenty}-three times! Even now, though, when she said over to herself, sadly: "We miss our dear Father <u>so</u> much,"[9] she could have cried if she wanted to.

"Have you got enough stamps?" came from Constanzia.

"Oh, how can I tell!" said Josephine crossly. "What's the good of asking[10]

[DLC-MS-NL, leaf 3]

me that now."

"I was just wondering," said Constanzia, mildly.

Silence again. There came a little rustle, a skurry [sic], a hop.

"A mouse," said Constanzia.

"It can[']t be a mouse because there aren't any crumbs" said Josephine.

"But it doesn't know there aren't," said Constanzia.

A spasm of pity squeezed her heart. Poor little thing! She wished she'd left a tiny piece of biscuit on the dressing-table. It was awful to think of it not finding anything. What would it do?

"I can't think how they manage to live at all," she said slowly.

"Who?" demanded Josephine.

And Constanzia said more loudly than she meant to: "Mice."

Josephine was furious. "Oh what nonsense, Con," she said. "What <u>have</u> mice got to do with it? You're asleep.

"I don't think I am," said Constanzia. She shut her eyes to make sure. She was.

Josephine arched her spine, pulled up her knees, folded her arms so that her fists[11] came under her ears and pressed her cheek hard against the pillow.

---

[8] Many of the emendations in the manuscript are in a darker ink, suggesting that they were done after the draft was complete. That Mansfield changes "thirty" to "twenty" in three instances on this page reinforces this idea.

[9] While the *London Mercury* retains the emphasis on "so," the *Collected* does not.

[10] The "tail" of an illegible letter is marked out under the "s" of "asking."

[11] Mansfield retraces "fists."

2[12]

Another thing which complicated matters was they had Nurse Andrews staying on with them that week. It was their own fault; they had asked her. It was Josephine's idea. On the morning—well, on the last morning when the doctor had gone Josephine

[DLC-MS-NL, leaf 4]

had said to Constanzia: "Don[']t you think it would be rather nice if we asked Nurse Andrews to stay on ^for a week^ as our guest?

"Very nice," said Constanzia.

"I thought," went on Josephine quickly, "I should just say, this afternoon, after I've paid her[13]: 'My sister and I would be very pleased, after all you've done for us, Nurse Andrews, if you would stay on for a week as our guest.['] I[']d have to put that in about being our guest in case –"

"Oh but she couldn't expect to be paid!["][14] cried Constanzia.

"One never knows," said Josephine, sagely.

Nurse Andrews had of course jumped at the idea. But it was a bother. It meant that they had to have regular, sit-down meals at the proper times, whereas, if they'd been alone, they could just have asked Kate if she wouldn't have minded bringing them a tray wherever they were. And meal times now that the strain was over, were rather a trial.

Nurse Andrews was simply fearful about butter. Really, they couldn't help feeling that about butter, at least, she ~~simply~~ took advantage of their kindness. And she had that maddening habit of asking for just an inch more bread to finish what she had on her plate and then, at the last mouthful—absentmindedly—of course it wasn't absentmindedly—taking another helping. Josephine got very red when this happened and she fastened her

[DLC-MS-NL, leaf 5]

small bead-like eyes on the table cloth as if she saw a minute strange insect creeping through the web of it. But Constanzia's long, pale face lengthened and set, and she gazed away—away—far over the desert to where that line of camels unwound, like a thread of wool.

"When I was with Lady Tukes," said Nurse Andrews, "she had such a deenty little contrayvance for the buttah. It was a silvah Cupid balanced on the—on the bordah of a glass dish holding a tayny fork.[15] And when you wanted some buttah you simply pressed his foot and he bent down and speared you a piece. It was quite a gayme!"

Josephine could hardly bear ~~it~~ ^that^.[16] But: "I think those things are very extravagant" was all she said.

"But whey?" asked Nurse Andrews, beaming through her eyeglasses. "No one, surely, would take more buttah than one wanted—would one!"

---

[12] While the initial section begins with a Roman numeral, the subsequent sections are circled Arabic numbers.

[13] "Her" is retraced.

[14] The *Collected* reads: "Oh, but she [could hardly] expect to be paid!" (CW2, 268).

[15] The manuscript's spelling of "deenty," to convey Nurse Andrews's accent, is changed to "dainty" in the printed versions. *The London Mercury* corresponds to the manuscript's spelling of "contrayvance" while the *Collected* adds a hyphen (i.e. "contray-vance") likely to emphasize the pronunciation (*London Mercury*, 17; CW2, 268).

[16] Mansfield writes "tha" over the "i" of "it."

"Ring, Con!" cried Josephine. She couldn't trust herself to reply. And proud young Kate, the enchanted Princess, came in to see what the old tabbies wanted <u>now</u>. She snatched away their plates of mock—something or other—and slapped down a white terrified blancmange.[17]

"Jam, please, Kate," said Josephine kindly.

Kate ᵏⁿᵉˡᵗ ᵃⁿᵈ burst open the side-board, lifted the lid of the jampot, saw that it was empty, put it on the table and stalked off.

"I[']m afraid," said Nurse Andrews, a moment later, "there isn't any."

[DLC-MS-NL, leaf 6]

"Oh, what a bother!" said ~~Constanzia~~ ᴶᵒˢᵉᵖʰⁱⁿᵉ. She bit her lip. "What had we better do![']"

Constanzia looked dubious.

"We can[']t disturb Kate again," she said softly.[18]

Nurse Andrews, waited, smiling at them both. Her eyes ~~xxx xxx xxx~~ʷᵃⁿᵈᵉʳᵉᵈ ˢᵖʸⁱⁿᵍ ᵃᵗ ᵉᵛᵉʳʸᵗʰⁱⁿᵍ behind her eyeglasses. Constanzia in despair went back to her camels. Josephine frowned heavily—concentrated. If this idiotic **woman*** ~~wasn't~~ ʰᵃᵈⁿ'ᵗ ʰᵃᵛᵉ ᵇᵉᵉⁿ ᵗhere she and Con would, ~~have~~ ᵒᶠ course, have eaten their blanc mange without.[19] Suddenly the idea came.

"I know," she said—"marmalade! There's some marmalade in the side board; get it, Con."

"I hope," laughed Nurse Andrews, and her laugh was like a spoon tinkling against a medicine glass: "I hope it[']s not very bittah marmalayde."

3

But after all it was ~~only a week~~ ᵃ ᶠᵉʷ ᵈᵃʸˢ not long now and then she'd be gone for good. And there was no getting over the fact she had been very good to Father[20]—She had nursed him day and night at the end. Indeed, both Constanzia and Josephine felt privately she had rather over done the not leaving him at the very last. For when they had gone in to say good-bye Nurse Andrews had sat beside his bed the whole time holding his wrist and pretending to look at her watch. It coudn't have

[DLC-MS-NL, leaf 7]

been necessary. **x** It was so tactless, too. Supposing Father had wanted to say something— something private to them. Not that he had. Oh, far from it. He lay there, purple, a dark angry purple in the face, and never even looked at them when they came in. Then as they were standing there, wondering what to do he had suddenly opened one eye. Oh, what a difference it would have made what a difference to their memory of him—how much easier to tell people about it—if he had only opened both. But no—one eye only. It glared at them a moment and then—went out.

---

[17] The *Collected* eliminates the dashes around "something or other" (CW2, 268).

[18] While this is Constanzia speaking, Mansfield begins the dialogue on the following line, as indicated here.

[19] When Mansfield strikes through "wasn't," she also adds a "t" to the original "here," making it "there." This is suggested by the darker ink of the "t." The *Collected* reads: "If it hadn't been for this idiotic woman [. . .]" (CW2, 269).

[20] The *Collected* adds "that," changes "good" to "kind," and makes "Father" lowercase: "And there was no getting over the fact that she had been very kind to father" (CW2, 269).

4

It had made it very awkward for them when Mr Farolles of St John's called the same afternoon.

"The end was quite peaceful, I trust," were the first words he said as he glided towards them through the dark drawing-room.

"Quite," said Josephine faintly. They both hung their heads. Both of them felt certain that eye wasn't at all a peaceful eye.

"Won't you sit down," said Josephine.

"Thank you, Miss Pinner," said Mr. Farolles gratefully. He ~~began~~ folded his coat tails and began to lower himself into Father's armchair, but just as he touched it he almost sprang up and slid into the next chair instead.

He coughed. Josephine clasped her hands; Constanzia looked vague.

[DLC-MS-NL, leaf 8]

"I want you to feel, Miss Pinner," said Mr Farolles, "and you, Miss Constantia,[21] that I[']m trying to be~x~ helpful. I want to be helpful to you both, if you will let me. These are the times," said Mr Farolles, very simply and earnestly, "when God means us to be helpful to one another."

"Thank you very much, Mr Farolles," said Josephine—and Constantia.

"Not at all," said Mr Farolles, gently: He drew his kid gloves through his fingers and leaned forward. "And if either of you would like a little Communion, either—or both of you—here—and now—you have only to tell me. A little Communion is often very help—a great comfort," he added tenderly.

But the idea of a little communion terrified them! What! ~i~In the drawing-room by themselves—with no—no altar or anything![22] The piano would be much too high, thought Constantia + Mr Farolles could not possibly lean over it with the chalice. And Kate would be sure to come bursting in and interrupt them, thought Josephine. And supposing the bell rang in the middle. It might be somebody important—about their mourning. Would they get up reverently and go out or would they have to wait—in torture –

"Perhaps you will send round a note by your good

[DLC-MS-NL, leaf 9]

Kate if you would care for it later," said Mr Farolles.

"Oh, yes, thank you very much," they both said.

Mr Farolles got up + took his ~~soft felt~~ black straw hat from the round table.

"And about the funeral," he said softly. "I may arrange that—as your dear Father's old friend and yours Miss Pinner[23] and Miss Constantia?"

Josephine + Constantia got up too.

"I should like it to be quite simple," said Josephine firmly, "and not too expensive. At the same time I should like –"

---

[21] This is the first instance in the manuscript where Mansfield changes the spelling to "Constantia."
[22] The edits in these two sentences are in another, sharper pen, including the final exclamation point.
[23] The "r" of "Pinner" is retraced.

"A good one that will last," thought dreamy Constantia—as if Josephine were buying a nightgown. But of course Josephine didn't say that—"one suitable to my father's[24] sposition [*sic*]."[25] She was very nervous.

"I[']ll run round now to our ^good^ friend, Mr Knight," said Mr Farolles ~~very~~ soothingly. "I will ask him to come and see you. I am[26] sure you[']ll find him very helpful indeed!"[27]

[DLC-MS-NL, leaf 10]

5

Well, at any rate all that part of it was over though neither of them could possibly believe that Father was never coming back. Josephine had had a moment of absolute terror at the cemetery while the coffin was lowered to think that she and Constantia had done this thing without asking his permission. What would Father say when he found ^out;^ for he was bound to find out sooner or later. He always did.
     "Buried!28 ~~"~~You two girls had me <u>buried</u>!" She heard his stick thumping.29

Oh, what would they say! What possible excuse could they make. It sounded such an appalingly [*sic*] heartless thing to do. Such a wicked advantage to take of a person because ~~they~~ ^he^ happened to be helpless at the moment. The other people ~~were~~ seemed to take it all as a matter of course—they were strangers; they couldn't be expected to understand that Father was the very last person for such a thing to happen to. ^No, the entire blame for it all would rest on her and Constantia.30^ "And the expense!" she thought, stepping into the tight-buttoned cab. When she had to show him the bills. What would he say then!

She heard him absolutely roaring: "And do you expect me to pay for this gimcrack excursion~~!~~ ^of yours."31^

"Oh!" groaned poor Josephine aloud. "We shouldn't have done it, Con."
And Constantia, pale as a lemon in all that blackness said in a frightened whisper[,] "Done what Jug?"

"Let them bu-bury Father like that!" said Josephine, breaking down and crying into her new queer smelling mourning handkerchief.

["]But what else could we have done,["] asked Constantia wonderingly. "We couldn't have kept him Jug—we couldn't have kept him

---

[24] The *Collected* changes "my father's" to "our father's" (CW2, 270).

[25] The misspelling, "sposition," is retained in *The London Mercury* version (19). This suggests that, at least initially, Mansfield considered trying to capture Josephine's nervousness through her speech.

[26] Mansfield retraces the "m" of "am."

[27] In the *Collected* "you'll" becomes "you will" (CW2, 270).

[28] "Buried!" is noticeably smaller and is flush with the left-hand side of the paper, suggesting it was added after what follows was written. Further, the quotation mark just after the addition is stricken through.

[29] This sentence is written with a finer pen and is slightly smaller than what comes before and after, suggesting it may have been added later.

[30] This sentence is squeezed between the one above and below, suggesting it was added after the others were already drafted. "Would rest" is changed to "would fall" in the *Collected*.

[31] The "o" of "of" is written over the initial exclamation mark.

[DLC-MS-NL, leaf 11]

unburied. At tany[32] rate not in a flat that size."

Josephine blew her nose; the cab was dreadfully stuffy.

"I don't know," she said forlornly. "It is all so dreadful. I feel we ought to have tried to, just for a time at least. To make perfectly sure. "[sic] One thing's certain" and her tears sprang out again: "Father will never forgive us for this—never."

6

Father would never forgive them! That was what they felt more than ever when two morning's [sic] later they went into his room to go through his things. They had discussed it quite calmly. It was even down on Josephine's list of things to be done. "<u>Go through Father's things and settle about them</u>." But that was a very different matter to saying; after breakfast:

"Well, are you ready, Con?"

"Yes Jug when you are."

"Then I think we'd better get it over."

It was dark in the hall. It had been a rule for years, never to disturb Father in the morning. Whatever happened.[33] And now they were going to open the door without knocking even. Constantia's eyes were enormous at the idea; Josephine felt weak in the knees.

"You, you go first," she gasped, pushing Constantia. But Constantia said as she always had said on these occasions: "No, Jug that's not fair. You're eldest!"

Josephine was just going to say—what at other times she

[DLC-MS-NL, leaf 12][34]

wouldn't have owned[35] to for the world—what she kept for her very last weapon: "But you're tallest" when they noticed that the kitchen door was open and there stood Kate –

"Very stiff!" said Josephine, grasping the door handle and doing her best to turn it.

As though anything ever ~~took~~ ^{deceived} Kate ~~in~~!^[36]

It couldn't be helped. That girl was—^{Then} ~~But the cold, pale room froze Kate in their xxx~~ The door was shut behind them, but—but they weren't in Father's room at all—They might have suddenly walked through the wall by mistake into a different flat altogether. Was the door just behind them? They were too frightened to look. Josephine knew that if it was it was holding itself tight shut ~~and secretly something xxx~~ ^{against} them;^[37] Constantia felt that, like the doors in dreams it hadn't any handle at all. ~~At any moment from anywhere the little man might appear~~[,] ~~the little murderer something so menacingly—~~

---

[32] "At tany" is also used later in the manuscript in relation to Constantia, suggesting Mansfield was experimenting with speech sounds. See DLC-MS-NL, leaves 14 and 21.

[33] The *Collected* reads: "It had been a rule for years never to disturb father in the morning, whatever happened" (CW2, 271).

[34] Leaves 12 and 13 seem to be in a much more rushed hand than what comes before and after, and there are more edits.

[35] The "d" of "owned" is retraced.

[36] The "ate" of "Kate" is retraced. The *Collected* changes "As though" to "As if."

[37] "Against them" is omitted in the *Collected*.

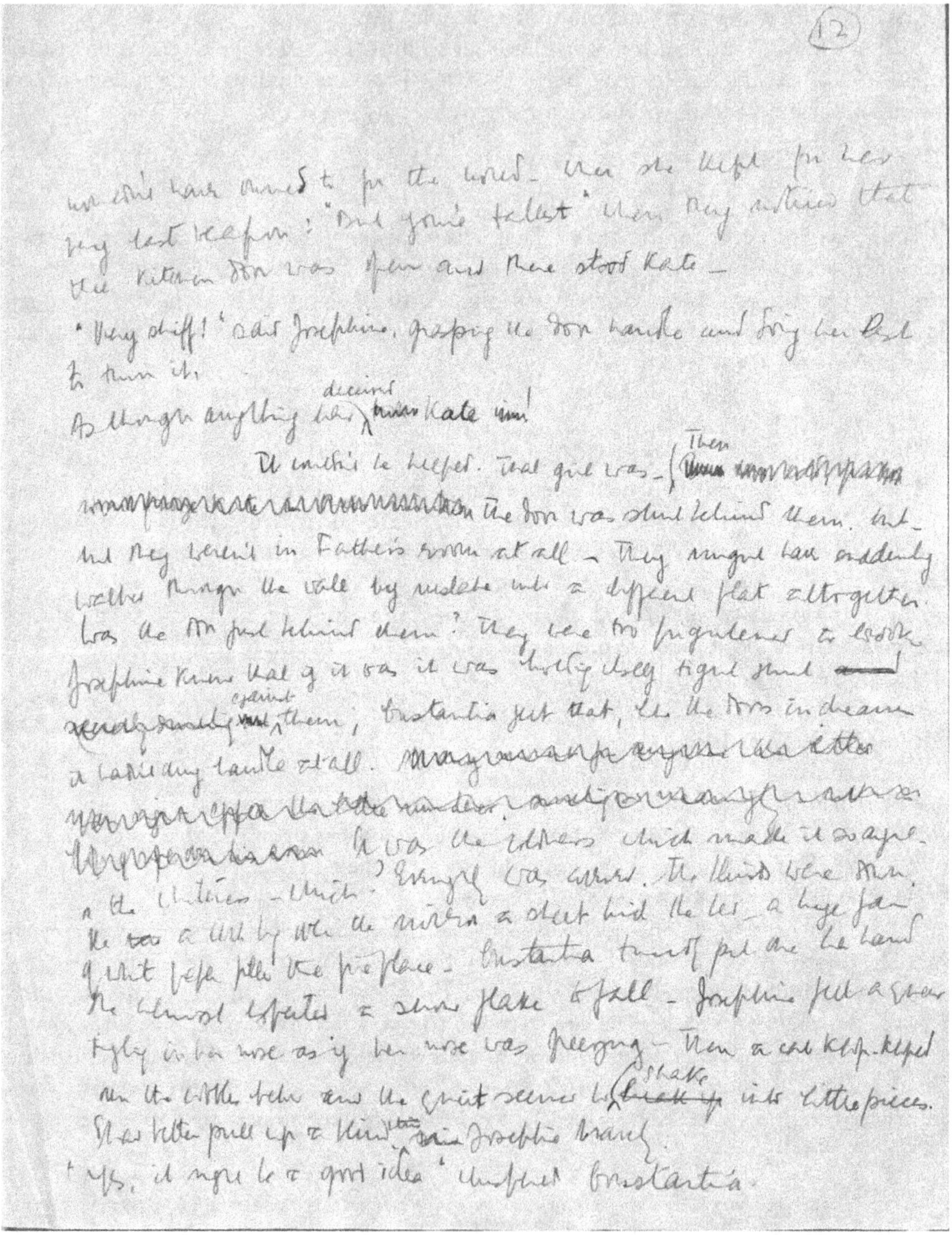

FIGURE 20: Leaf 12, "Non-Compounders [Daughters of the Late Colonel]," Katherine Mansfield Papers, Newberry Library, (box 1, folder 41), 32 leaves. Image courtesy of the Newberry Library.

~~with a loop of rope over his arm.~~ It was the coldness which made it so awful—or the whiteness—which? Everything was covered. The blinds were down. He ~~had~~ a **cloth hung***
over the mirror[,] a sheet hid the bed—a huge fan of white paper filled the fireplace—
Constantia timidly put out her hand[;] she almost expected a snow flake to fall—Josephine
felt a queer tingling in her nose as if her nose was freezing—Then a cab klop-kloped over
the cobbles below and the quiet seemed to ~~break up~~ ^{shake} into little pieces.

I had better pull up a blind ~~said~~ ××× Josephine bravely.[38]

"Yes, it might be a good idea" whispered Constantia.

[DLC-MS-NL, leaf 13]

She[39] only gave the blind a touch but it flew up + the cord flew after rolling round the
blind stick + the little tassel tapped ~~××× ××× ××× were frightened~~ ^{as if trying to ~~escape~~ get free}. That
was too much for Constantia.

["]Don't you think—don't you think we might put it off for another day["] she
whispered.

["]Why,["] snapped Josephine, feeling ^{as usual} much better now that she knew for certain that
Constantia was terrified. ["]Its got to be done—but I do wish you wouldn't whisper Con."

"I didn't know I was whispering,["] whispered Constantia.

["]And why do you keep on **staring*** at the bed,["] said Josephine, raising her voice
almost defiantly. ["]Theres **nothing*** <u>on</u> the bed.["]

"Oh Jug don[']t say so." said poor Connie. ["]At any rate not so loudly."

Josepine felt, herself, she had gone too far. She took a wide **swerve over*** to the chest
of drawers—She put out her hand—but quickly she[40] drew it back again.

"Connie!" she ~~cried~~ ^{gasped}, ~~terrified~~ + then[41] wheeled round + leaned with her back
against the chest of drawers –

"Oh Jug <u>what</u>"

Josephine could only glare. She had the most **extraordinary*** feeling that she'd just
escaped something simply awful—~~If she'd opened that drawer!~~ But how could she explain
to Constantia

[DLC-MS-NL, leaf 14][42]

that Father was in the chest of drawers! He was in the top drawer with his handkerchiefs
and neckties, or the next with his shirts and pyjamas, or in the lowest of all with his suits.
He was watching there, hidden away—just behind the door handle –ready to spring.

She pulled a funny old fashioned face at Constantia just as she used to in the old days
when she was going to cry.

"I can[']t open," she nearly wailed.

---

[38] While the print version retains "said," the manuscript deletes "said" and replaces it with an illegible word.

[39] While the manuscript uses "she" as the subject, the *Collected* begins, "They only gave . . ." (CW2, 272).

[40] The published version omits "she."

[41] "Then" is replaced with "she" in the *Collected*.

[42] The verso of leaf 14 includes this fragment, with a circled 2 in the right-hand corner, suggesting page two of another work:

> We do not see why he has attempted it. If they are devoid of imagination he cannot hope to change their hearts; all he can expect to do is to rouse an involuntary feeling by as perfect an illusion as possible.
> If there is a German officer hammering at a little French girl's bedroom door

"No, don't, Jug," whispered Constantia, earnestly. It[']s much better not to. Don't lets open anything. At tany[43] rate not for a long time."

"But—but it seems so weak," said Josephine, ~~quite~~ breaking down.

"Well,[44] why not be weak for once Jug," argued Constantia, whispering quite fiercely— "if it is weak." And her pale stare flew from the locked writing table—so safe—to the huge glittering wardrobe and she began to breathe in a queer panting way. "Why shouldn't we be weak for once in our lives, Jug—It[']s quite excusable. Let[']s be weak—be weak Jug. It[']s much nicer to be weak than to be strong."

And then she did one of those amazingly ~~brave~~ bold things that she'd done about twice before in their lives; she marched over to the wardrobe, turned the key and took it out of the lock. Took it out of the lock and held it up to Josephine, showing Josephine by her extraordinary smile that she knew what she'd done[45]—she'd risked deliberately,[46] Father being in there among his overcoats.

[DLC-MS-NL, leaf 15]

If the huge wardrobe had lurched forward—had crashed down on Constantia Josephine wouldn't have been surprised. On the contrary.[47] She would have thought it the only suitable thing to happen. But nothing happened. Only the room seemed quieter than ever and bigger flakes of cold air fell ~~from the~~ on Josephine's shoulders and knees. She began to shiver.

"Come Jug," said Constantia, still with that awful callous smile. And Josephine followed just as she had that last time when Constantia had pushed Bennie into the Round Pond.[48]

7[49]

But the strain told on them when they were back in the dining-room. They sat down, very shaky, ~~xxx~~ and looked at each other.

"I don't feel I can settle to anything," said Josephine "unless I[']ve had something. Do you think we could ask Kate for two cups of hot water."[50]

"I really don[']t see why we shouldn't," said Constantia carefully. She was quite normal again. I won't ring. I[']ll go to the kitchen door and ask her."

"Yes, do,["] said Josephine, sinking down into a chair—["]Tell her just two cups, Con, nothing else—on a tray."

"She needn't even put the jug on, need she," said Constantia—as though Kate might very well complain if the jug had been there.

---

[43] See note 32.
[44] The *Collected* opens this passage with "But" rather than "Well."
[45] The *London Mercury* version has a period after "she'd done," while the *Collected* has a comma.
[46] The "de" of "deliberately" is retraced.
[47] While the period after "contrary" is retained in the *London Mercury* version, the *Collected* has a comma.
[48] At this point in the manuscript the spelling is "Bennie" while it later changes to "Benny," which is as it appears in the *Collected*.
[49] The circled "7" is squeezed between the two lines, suggesting it was added later.
[50] "Unless" is changed to "until" in the *Collected*.

"Oh, ~~know~~,[51] certainly not—The jug[']s not at all necessary. She can pour it direct out of the kettle," cried

[DLC-MS-NL, leaf 16]

cried [*sic*] Josephine, feeling that would be a labour saving indeed!

Their cold lips quivered at the greenish brims. Josephine curved her small red hand round the cup; Constantia sat up and blew on the wavy steam. She liked to see it flutter from one side to the other.[52]

"Speaking of Bennie" said Josephine.

And though Bennie hadn't been mentioned Constantia immediately looked as though he had.

"He'll expect us to send him something of Fathers, of course. But it[']s so difficult to know what to send to Ceylon."

"You mean things get unstuck so on the voyage," murmured Constantia.

"No, lost!" said Josephine sharply. "You know there's no post. Only runners."

~~And xxx~~ Both paused to watch a black man in white linen drawers running through the pale fields for dear life with a large brown paper parcel in his hands. Josephine's black man was tiny; he skurried ~~away~~ along, glistening, like an ant; but there was something blind and tireless about Constantias tall thin fellow which made him, she decided, a very unpleasant person indeed! On the verandah, dressed all in white and wearing a cork helmet stood Bennie. His right hand shook up and down as Fathers did when he was impatient. And behind him, not in the least interested, sat Hilda

[DLC-MS-NL, leaf 17]

the unknown sister-in-law ~~who wears xxx xxx~~ She swung in a cane rocker + flicked over the leaves of The Tatler.

"I think his watch would be the most suitable present,["] said Josephine. Constantia looked up; she seemed surprised.

"Oh—would you trust ~~his~~ a gold watch to a native!"

"But of course I'd disguise it!" said Josephine. "No one would know it was a watch." She liked the idea of having to make a parcel such a curious shape that no one would guess what it was. She even thought for a moment of a ~~long~~ hiding the watch in a narrow cardboard corset box that she'd kept by her for a long time waiting for it to come in useful53 for something. It was such beautiful firm cardboard. But no, it wouldn't be appropriate for this occasion. It had lettering on it. Medium Womens 28. Extra firm busks! It would be almost too much of a surprise for Benny[54] to open that and find Father's watch inside.

"And of course it isn't as though it would be going—ticking, I mean," said Constantia, who was still thinking of the native love of jewellery. "At least," she added, "it would be very strange if—after all that time it was."

---

[51] While it is difficult to discern the initial word, the manuscript strikes out the first and last letters of the word, to make "no," which is how it appears in the *Collected*.

[52] The *Collected* reads: "Constantia sat up and blew on the wavy steam, making it flutter from one side to the other" (CW2, 274), omitting "She liked to see it . . . ."

[53] The added word "useful" in the manuscript does not make it into the *Collected*.

[54] Here Mansfield begins using the spelling, "Benny."

8

Josephine made no reply. She had flown off on one of her tangents. She had suddenly thought of Cyril. Wasn't it more usual for the only grandson to have the watch. And then—dear Cyril was

[DLC-MS-NL, leaf 18]

so appreciative, and a gold watch meant so much to a young man. Benny, in all probability, had quite got out of the habit of watches; men so seldom wore waistcoats in those hot climates. Whereas Cyril in London wore them from years end to years end. And it would be so nice for her and Constantia, when he came to tea to know it was there. "I see you've got on grandfather's watch, Cyril." It would be somehow, so satisfactory.

Dear boy! What a blow his sweet sympathetic little note had been. Of course they quite understood; but it was most unfortunate.

"It would have been such a point having him,["] said Josephine.

"And he would have enjoyed it so," said Constantia, not thinking what she was saying.

However, as soon as he got back he was going to tea with his aunties. Cyril to tea was one of their rare treats.

["]Now Cyril, you needn't[55] be frightened of our cakes. Your Auntie Con + I bought them at Buszards this morning. We know what a man's appetite is. So don't be ashamed of making a good tea."

Josephine cut recklessly into the dark rich cake that stood for her winter gloves or the soling and heeling of Josephine's only respectable shoes.[56]

But Cyril was most unmanlike in appetite.

"I say Aunt Josephine I simply can[']t. I[']ve only just had lunch, you know."

[DLC-MS-NL, leaf 19][57]

"Oh, Cyril, that can't be true—It[']s after four" cried Josephine. Constantia sat with her knife lifted poised over over [sic] the chocolate roll.

"It is, all the same," said Cyril. "I had to meet a man at Victoria and he kept me hanging about till—there was only time to get lunch and to come on here. And he gave me—'phew,'["] Cyril put his hand to his forehead, ["]a terrific blow out," he said.

It was disappointing—today of all days. But still, he wouldn't be expected to know –

[DLC-MS-NL, leaf 20]

"But, You'll have a meringue, won[']t you Cyril," said Aunt Josephine. "These meringues were bought specially for you. Your dear father was so fond of them we were sure you are, too."

---

[55] "Needn't" becomes "mustn't" in the *Collected*.

[56] The manuscript inadvertently names Josephine when referring to the shoes, despite the previous reference to her regarding the gloves, an oversight corrected in the *Collected*.

[57] The material on this leaf only takes up the top half of the page, and when the text ends a line is drawn slantwise toward the lower righthand corner. Above the line are two short wavy lines. This page may have been inserted later, but there is no sign that the page numbers have been adjusted—unless Mansfield numbered the pages after the story was complete. The following leaf opens with "But you'll have a meringue, won't you Cyril," which reasonably follows the text from either the end of leaf 18 or this fragment on leaf 19.

"I am," Aunt Josephine ~~lied~~ cried Cyril ardently. "Do you mind if I take half to begin with?"

"Not at all, dear boy. But we mustnt let you off with that."

"Is your dear father still so fond of meringues?" asked Auntie Con, gently; she winced faintly as she broke through the shell of hers.

"Well, I don't quite know, Auntie Con," said Cyril, breezily. At that they both looked up.

"Don't know!" almost snapped Josephine. "Don't know a thing like that about your own father, Cyril?[")]

"Surely!" said Auntie Con, softly.

Cyril tried to laugh it off. "Oh well," he said—"its such a long time, you know since –" He faltered. Their troubled old[58] faces were too much for him.[59]

"Even so!" said Josephine.

And Auntie Con looked.

Cyril put down his tea-cup. "Wait a bit," he cried. "Wait a bit, Aunt Josephine. What am I thinking of." He looked up. They were beginning to brighten, wonderfully. Cyril slapped his knee.[60] "Of course!" he said, "It was

[DLC-MS-NL, leaf 21]

meringues! How could I have forgotten. Yes Aunt Josephine you're quite right![61] Father's most frightfully keen on meringues."

They didn't only beam. Aunt Josephine went scarlet with pleasure; Auntie Con gave a deep, deep sigh.[62]

"And now, Cyril, you must come and see Father," said Josephine. "He knows you were coming to-day."

"Right!" said Cyril ~~a shade too~~ very firmly and heartily. He got up from his chair; suddenly he glanced at the clock.

---

[58] The "b" of "troubled" and "old" are retraced.

[59] The *Collected* reads: "'Oh, well,' he said, 'it's such a long time since –' He faltered. He stopped. Their faces were too much for him" (CW2, 276), omitting "you know" and "troubled old," adding "He stopped" after "He faltered."

[60] "He looked up" is set as a new paragraph in the *Collected*, which also omits "wonderfully."

[61] "Quite right" becomes "perfectly right" in the *Collected*.

[62] The Alexander Turnbull Library contains a fragment of this story. The fragment, written in a rough hand and obviously torn from a notebook, lays out part of this conversation with Cyril—possibly an earlier draft of it. A wavy line from the top left corner to the right lower corner suggests that Mansfield may have intended to discard this material; however, the text of the fragment is mostly intact in this manuscript version, though there are minor changes:

["]Surely![")] said Aunt Con gently.
Cyril tried to laugh it off. ["]Oh well["] he said he said [*sic*] ["]it[']s such a long time ~~after~~ since["]. ~~But~~ he faltered. Their troubled old faces **were*** too much for him.
["]Even so["] said Josephine –
And Aunt Con looked.
Cyril put down his cup. ["]Wait a bit![")] he said ["]wait a bit Aunt Josephine. What am I thinking of.["] She looked up: They were beginning to **brighten*** wonderfully—Cyril slapped his knee. ["]Of course["] he said—["]it was meringues. Always Aunt Josephine you[']re quite right. Father[']s still most **frightfully*** keen on meringues.["]
They didn[']t only beam. Aunt Josephine went **scarlet*** with pleasure. Aunt Con gave a deep deep **smile** (DLC-Frag-ATL).

"I say, Auntie Con, isn't your clock[63] a bit slow? I[']ve got to ~~be at~~ ᵐᵉᵉᵗ ᵃ ᵐᵃⁿ ᵃᵗ at [sic]—Paddington just after five. I'm afraid I shan[']t be able to stay very long with grandfather.

"Oh, he won't expect you to stay <u>very</u> long," said Aunt Josephine.

Constantia was still gazing at the clock. She couldn't make up her mind if it was fast or slow. It was one or the other—She felt almost certain of that. At tany[64] rate—it had been.

Cyril still lingered.

"Aren't you coming along, Auntie Con?"

"Of course!" said Josephine. We shall all go. Come on, Con."

9

They knocked at the door and Cyril followed his aunts into Grandfather's hot, sweetish room.

"Come on," said Grandfather Pinner. "Don't hang about. What is

[DLC-MS-NL, leaf 22]

it? What've you been up to?"

He was sitting in front of a roaring fire, clasping his stick. He had a thick rug over his knees. On his lap there lay a beautiful pale yellow silk handkerchief.

"It's Cyril, Father" said Josephine shłyly. And she took Cyril's hand and led him forward.

"Good afternoon, Grandfather," said Cyril, trying to take his hand out of Aunt Josephine's.[65]

Grandfather Pinner shot his eyes at Cyril in the way he was famous for. Where was Auntie Con? She stood on the other side of Aunt Josephine; her long arms hung down in front of her; her hands were clasped. She never took her eyes off Grandfather.

"Well!" said Grandfather Pinner, beginning to thump. "What have you got to tell me?"

What had he? What had he got to tell him? Cyril felt himself smiling like a perfect imbecile. The room was stifling, too.

But Auntie[66] Josephine came to his rescue. She cried, brightly: "Cyril says his father is still very fond of meringues, Father, dear."

"Eh?" said Grandfather Pinner, curving his hand, like a purple meringue shell, over his ear.

Josephine repeated: "Cyril says his father is still very fond of meringues!"

[DLC-MS-NL, leaf 23]

"Can't hear!" said old Colonel Pinner, and he waved Josephine away with his stick, then pointed with his stick to Cyril. "Tell me what she's trying to say!" he said.

(My God!) "Must I?" said Cyril, blushing brightly and starring at Aunt Josephine.

---

[63] The "loc" of "clock" is retraced.

[64] See note 32.

[65] "Grandfather" is not capitalized in the *Collected*, and the following lines about Constantia are retained within the current paragraph.

[66] In a darker ink, Mansfield retraces the "t" of the initial "Auntie" so that its tail strikes through the "ie" of "Auntie."

"Do, dear," she smiled. "It will please him so much."

"Come on! Out with it!" cried old Colonel Pinner testily, beginning to thump again.[67]

And Cyril leaned forward and yelled:

"Father's still very fond of meringues."

At that Grandfather Pinner jumped as though he'd been shot.

"Don't shout!;" he cried. "What[']s the matter with the boy! <u>Meringues</u>? What about 'em?"

"Oh, Aunt Josephine—must we go on!" groaned Cyril desperately.

"Its quite all right, dear boy," said Aunt Josephine, as though he and she were at the dentist's together. "He'll understand in a minute." And she whispered to Cyril: "He's getting a little bit deaf, you know."[68] Then she leaned forward and really bawled at Grandfather Pinner.

"Cyril only wanted to tell you, Father dear, that his father is still very fond of meringues!"

Colonel Pinner heard that time—heard and brooded—looking Cyril

[DLC-MS-NL, leaf 24]

up and down.

"What an estraordinary[69] [sic] thing," said old Grandfather Pinner—"What an estraordinary thing to come all this way here to tell me!"

And Cyril felt it <u>was</u>!

"Yes, I shall send Cyril the watch," said Josephine.

"That would be very nice," said Constantia. "I seem to remember last time he came there was some little trouble about the time."

10[70]

They were interrupted by Kate bursting through the door in her usual fashion, as though she were breaking through some secret panel in the wall.[71]

"Fried or boiled?" ~~said Kate~~ ^{asked} the bold voice.

Fried or boiled? Josephine and Constantia were quite ~~startled~~ ^{bewildered} for a moment.[72] They could hardly take it in.

"Fried or boiled—what—Kate?" asked Josephine trying to begin to concentrate.

Kate gave a loud sniff. "Fish!"

"Well, why didn't you say so immediately—Josephine repr~~imanded~~^{oached} her gently. "How could you expect us to understand—Kate. There are a great many things in this world, ^{you know,} which are fried or boiled." And after such a display of courage she said quite brightly to Constantia: "Which do you prefer, Con?[']"

"I think it might be nice to have it fried," said Constantia,

---

[67] The *Collected* omits "old."

[68] "Little" of "little bit deaf" is omitted from the *Collected*.

[69] The published version uses two "ss" in both instances of "estraordinary," eg. "esstraordinary."

[70] The ink at this point becomes darker, suggesting perhaps she picked the story back up after a pause.

[71] The *Collected*: "as though she had discovered some secret panel in the wall" (CW2, 278).

[72] The *Collected* reads "for the moment."

[DLC-MS-NL, leaf 25][73]

on the other hand, of course, boiled fish is very nice. I think I prefer both equally well—unless you . . . In that case."

"I shall fry it!" said Kate, and she bounced back, leaving their door open and slamming the door of her kitchen.

Josephine gazed at Constantia; she raised her pale eyebrows until they rippled away in[74] her pale hair. She got up. She said in a very lofty, imposing way: "Do you mind following me into the drawing room, Constantia. I have something of great importance to discuss with you.

For it was always to the drawing room they retired, when they wanted to talk over Kate.

Josephine closed the door meaningly, "Sit down Constantia," she said, still very grand ~~almost as though she were~~ She might have been ~~welcoming~~ receiving Constantia for the first time. And Con looked round vaguely for a chair as though she felt, indeed, quite a stranger.

"Now the question is," said Josephine, bending forward, ["]whether we shall keep her or not."

"That is the question," agreed Contantia.[75]

"And this time," said Josephine firmly "we must come to a decision.[76]["]

Constantia looked for a moment as though she might begin going over all the other times, but she pulled herself together and said: "Yes Jug."

"You see, Con," explained Josephine, "everything is so changed now."

[DLC-MS-NL, leaf 26]

Constantia looked up quickly.

~~Instea~~ went on Josphine[77] "We're[78] not dependent on Kate as we were, ~~went~~ I mean," and she blushed faintly—"theres not Father to cook for."[79]

"That is perfectly true," said Constantia, too heartily. "Father certainly doesn[']t want any cooking whatever else . . ."[80]

Josephine ~~pulled her up~~ broke in sharply: "You[']re not sleepy, are you Con?"

"Sleepy Jug?" Constantia was ~~eye~~ wide eyed ~~at the idea~~.

"Well, concentrate more!" said Josephine crossly,[81] and she returned to the subject—["]what it comes to is, if we did," and this she barely breathed, glancing at the door, "give Kate notice –" she raised her voice again—"we could manage our own food" –

---

[73] The page number in the top right corner was originally "35" but the 3 is written over with a 2.
[74] The *Collected* replaces "in" with "into."
[75] The *Collected* does not include the emphasis on "is."
[76] The *Collected* adds "definite," (e.g. "a definite decision").
[77] The phrase "went on Josephine" is circled and an arrow points to just after "~~went~~," as it appears in the *Collected*.
[78] "We're" is written over another, illegible word.
[79] The *Collected* shows further revision: "'I mean,' went on Josephine, 'we're not dependent on Kate as we were.' And she blushed faintly. 'There's not father to cook for'" (CW2, 278–279).
[80] "Too heartily" is omitted in the *Collected*, and "cooking" is not emphasized.
[81] In the *Collected*, "crossly" is changed to "sharply."

"Why not?" cried Constantia. She couldn't help smiling. The idea was so very exciting—she clasped her hands—"what should we live on—Jug?"[82]

["]Oh—eggs in various forms—said Jug, lofty again. And besides there are all the cooked foods!

"But I[']ve always heard," said Constantia, ["]they are ᶜᵒⁿˢⁱᵈᵉʳᵉᵈ so very expensive –"

"Not if one buys them in moderation," said Josephine. But she tore herself away from this fascinating bye path and dragged Constantia with[83] her.

["]What we've got to decide <u>now</u> ʰᵒʷᵉᵛᵉʳ, Constantia—is whether we feel justified—whether we really do trust Kate or not.["][84]

Constantia leaned back. Her high[85] flat little laugh flew from her lips. ["]Isn't it curious Jug,['] said she ["]that just on this one subject I[']ve never been

[DLC-MS-NL, leaf 27]

able to quite make up my mind![']

She never had.[86] The whole difficulty was to prove anything. How did one prove things—how could one? S̲uppose Kate has stood in front of her + delibriatly [sic] made a face. Mightn't she very well have been in pain. Wasn't it improbable, at any rate t̶o̶ ̶t̶h̶i̶n̶k̶ ᵗᵒ ᵃˢᵏ Kate if she was making a face at her? If Kate c̶r̶i̶e̶d̶ ᵃⁿˢʷᵉʳᵉᵈ "no" + of course she would say "no," what a position. How undignified! A̶n̶d̶ ̶F̶a̶t̶h̶e̶r̶ ̶h̶a̶t̶e̶s̶ ̶x̶x̶x̶ ̶x̶x̶x̶ ̶x̶x̶x̶ ̶x̶x̶x̶ ̶x̶x̶ ̶x̶x̶x̶ ̶x̶x̶x̶ Then again Constantia suspected—she was almost certain that Kate went her [sic] chest of drawers when she and Josephine were out—not to take things but to spy. H̶o̶w̶ m̶Many times she had come back to find her amethyst cross in the most e̶x̶t̶r̶a̶o̶r̶d̶i̶n̶a̶r̶y̶ ᵘⁿˡⁱᵏᵉˡʸ places—o̶n̶ ̶h̶e̶r̶ t̶i̶e̶s̶ ̶l̶o̶o̶k̶i̶n̶g̶ ̶a̶s̶ ̶t̶h̶o̶u̶g̶h̶ ̶t̶h̶e̶y̶ ̶h̶a̶d̶ ̶b̶e̶e̶n̶ ̶x̶x̶x̶ ̶f̶o̶l̶d̶e̶d̶ˣˣˣ ˣˣˣ under her ties or on top of her lace bertha[87] x̶x̶x̶More than once She had m̶a̶d̶e̶ laid a trap for Kate. She had arranged things in a special order* + then called Josephine to witness.

"You see Jug!"

"Quite Con!"

"Now I[88] shall be able to tell"

But oh dear, when she did go to look she was as far off from a proof as ever. If anything was displaced* y̶o̶u̶ it ˣˣˣ might as well have happened as she closed the drawer—m̶i̶g̶h̶t̶n̶'̶t̶ ̶i̶t̶ h̶a̶v̶e̶ ̶b̶e̶e̶n̶ a jolt might have done it so easily.[89]

---

[82] The *Collected* reads: "The idea was so exciting. She clasped her hands. 'What should we live on, Jug?'" (CW2, 279).

[83] "With" becomes "after" in the *Collected*.

[84] "Now" is not emphasized in the published version, and the phrase, "Constantia—is whether we feel justified," is omitted. The *Collected* reads: "'What we've got to decide now, however, is whether we really do trust Kate or not'" (CW2, 279).

[85] "High" is eliminated the *Collected*.

[86] The *Collected* identifies this as section XI; however, the manuscript retains this as part of section X. Thus, the numbering of the sections that follow do not coincide with those in the published version. Further, much of this page appears to have been written with a pen low on ink, so several words and phrases are retraced.

[87] The *Collected* reads: ". . . under her lace ties or on top of her evening Bertha" (CW2, 279).

[88] "I" becomes "we" in the *Collected*.

[89] "Might as well have" becomes "might so very well have" in the *Collected*.

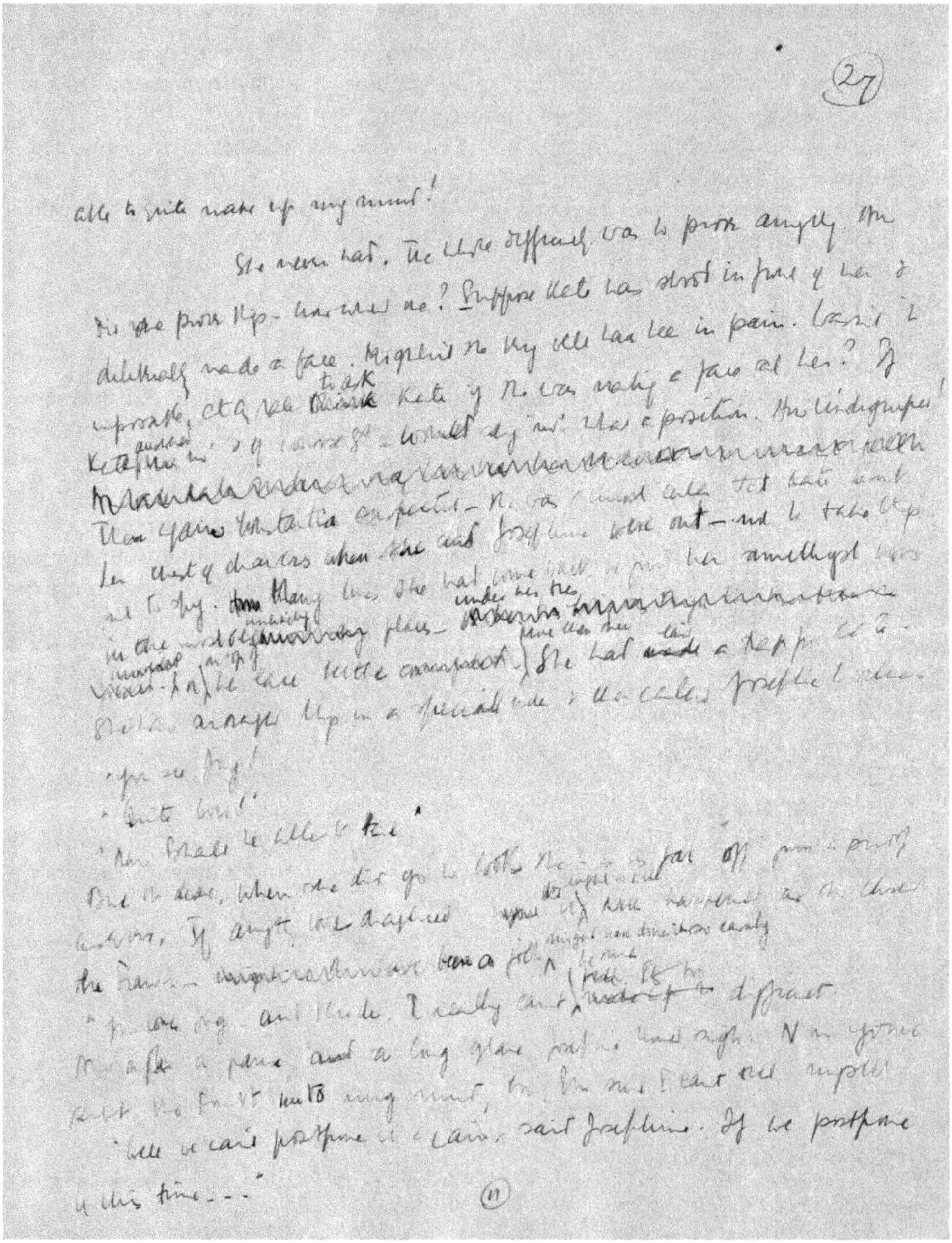

FIGURE 21: Leaf 27, "Non-Compounders [Daughters of the Late Colonel]," Katherine Mansfield Papers, Newberry Library, (box 1, folder 41), 32 leaves. Image courtesy of the Newberry Library.

"You come Jug, and decide. I really can[']t ~~make up my~~ tell be sure. Its too difficult.["]⁹⁰ But after a pause and a long glare Josephine would sigh: ["]Now you[']ve put the doubt into my mind, Con. I[']m sure I can[']t tell, myself.["]

"Well we can't postpone it again,["] said Josephine. ["]If we postpone it this time - - -"

11⁹¹

[DLC-MS-NL, leaf 28]

~~And then,~~ But at that moment, in the street below a barrel organ struck up. Josephine and Constantia sprang ~~up~~ to their feet together.

"Run, Con," said Josephine. Run! Quickly!⁹² There[']s sixpence on the - - -"

~~And then~~ Before she remembered⁹³ . . . it didn't matter—They would never have to stop the organ grinder again. Never again would she and Constantia be told to make that ~~man +~~ ~~his~~ monkey take his noise somewhere else—never would ~~come~~ sound that loud strange bellow of rage⁹⁴ when Father thought they were not hurrying enough—The organ grinder might play there all day and the stick would not thump.

It never will thump again
It never will thump again
Played the barrel organ –

What was Constantia thinking? She had such a strange smile: She looked different—She couldn't be going to cry.

"Jug! Jug!" said Constantia softly pressing her hands together. "Do you know what day it is—Its Saturday—It's a week today—a whole week."

"A week ~~ago~~ since Father died
A week since Father died"

cried the barrel organ. And Josephine somehow forgot to be practical ~~+~~ + sensible; she smiled too, faintly strangely.⁹⁵ On the* Indian carpet there fell a square of ~~xx~~ weak sunlight, pale red—it came + went and came—and stayed, deepened—until it shone almost golden.

"The sun's out" said Josephine, as though it really mattered.

A perfect **fountain*** of bubbling notes shook from the barrel organ—round bright notes—carelessly scattered—

Constantia lifted her big cold hands as if to catch them and

[DLC-MS-NL, leaf 29]

then her hands fell again—She walked over to the mantelpiece—to her favourite Buddha. And the ~~big~~ stone + gilt image whose smile always gave her such a queer feeling—almost a

---

⁹⁰ This becomes "I really can't. It's too difficult" in the *Collected* (CW2, 280).

⁹¹ Leaf 27 ends with a circled 11, which is repeated at the top of leaf 28. This is section XII in the published version.

⁹² This is in a darker ink, suggesting it was added later.

⁹³ A check mark in a darker ink has been made in the margin at the beginning of this line. The *Collected* begins, "Then they remembered . . ." (CW2, 280).

⁹⁴ The *Collected* changes "bellow of rage" to simply "bellow."

⁹⁵ The *Collected* reads: "And Josephine, too, forgot to be practical and sensible; she smiled faintly, strangely" (CW2, 280).

(28)

(27)

pain—and yet a pleasant pain—seemed today to be more than smiling. He knew something; he had a secret. ["]I know something that you don't know["] said her Buddha—Oh what was it. What could it be. And yet she had always ~~known~~ felt there was . . . something.

The sunlight pressed through the windows—thieved its way in—flashed its light over the furniture + the photographs. Josephine watched it. When it came to Mother's photograph—the enlargement over the **piano***—it lingered—as though puzzled to find so little remained of Mother except the ear-rings shaped like tiny pagodas + a black feather boa. Why did the photographs of dead people always fade so? wondered Josephine. As soon as a person was dead their photograph ~~was dead~~ died too. But of course this ~~photograph~~ one of Mother was very old. It was taken 35 years ago.[96] Josephine remembered standing on a chair + pointing out the feather boa to Constantia and telling her it was a snake that had killed their mother in ~~Ind~~Ceylon. Would everything have been different if Mother hadn't died. ~~After that Fathers sister~~ She didn't see why. Aunt Florence had lived with **them*** until ~~Josephine was seventeen~~ they had left school and then Father had retired and they[']d moved three times and had their yearly holiday and—and—there had been changes of servants, of course.[97]

Some little sparrows, young sparrows they sounded

[DLC-MS-NL, leaf 30]

chirped on the window ledge—"Yeep eyeep—yeep –" But Josephine felt they were not sparrows not on the window ledge. It was inside her. That queer little crying noise— "yeep eyeep—yeep!" Ah, what was it crying—so weak + forlorn? ~~But to have children they would have to~~ What If Mother had lived might they have married;[98] ~~And~~ But there had been nobody for them to marry—there had been father[']s ~~xxx Indian~~ Anglo Indian friends—before he quarreled [sic] with them—but after that she + Constantia never met a single man except ~~old~~ clergymen How did one meet men. **How** would they have met ~~men~~ them?[99] Or even if they had met them how could they have got to know them well enough ~~for them~~ to be more than strangers? One read of people having adventures—being followed ~~in~~ + so on. But nobody had ever followed Constantia and her. Oh yes, there had been the year at Eastbourne a mysterious man at their boarding house who had put a note on the jug of hot water outside ~~Constantias~~ their bedroom door. But by the time Connie found it the steam had made the **writing*** too faint to read they could not even make out and he had left next day[100] . . . And that was all. ~~And now she was 43 and Constantia was 38.~~ The rest had been looking after Father—and at the same time keeping out of Father[']s way. But now? But now? The thieving sun touched Josephine— gently—She lifted her face—she was drawn over to the window—by those gentle beams[101] . . . .

Until the barrel organ stopped playing Constantia stayed before the Buddha— wondering—but not as usual—not vaguely.

---

[96] This sentence becomes "It was thirty-five years old" in the *Collected* (CW2, 281).

[97] "And then father had retired" is omitted in the published version.

[98] Before the edits, the sentence originally read: "But to have children they would have to have married."

[99] This sentence is absent in the *Collected*.

[100] The *Collected* reads: "[. . .] they couldn't even make out to which of them it was addressed. And he left next day" (CW2, 281).

[101] "By those gentle beams" becomes simply "by gentle beams" in the *Collected*.

[DLC-MS-NL, leaf 31]

This time her wondering +was a longing.[102] She remembered the time[103] she had come in here, crept out of bed in her nightgown when the moon was full + come in here + lain on the floor with her arms outstretched as though she was crucified—Why? The pale glittering moon had made her do it.[104] The horrible dancing figures on the carved **screen*** had leered at her and she hadn't minded—She remembered too—how when^{ever} they were at the sea side she had gone off by herself + got as near to the sea as close as she could + let down her hair + sang something—something she had made up—while she gazed over all that moving water.[105] There had been all[106] this other life—running out, bringing things home in bags, getting things on approval, discussing them with Jug + taking them back to get more things on approval—+ arranging Father's trays + trying not to annoy Father—But it all seemed to have happened in a kind of tunnel. It wasn't real—It was only when she came out of the tunnel + leaned out of the window perhaps in a thunder storm—she never felt so at rest as in a thunder storm that in the moonlight or by the sea or above all in a thunder storm that she felt <u>herself</u>.[107] But what did it mean? What did it all lead to? What was it she was always wanting?[108] Now? Now?

She turned away from the Buddha with one of her vague gestures. She went over to Constantia where Josephine was standing—She was frightened; she wanted Jug She wanted to say something to Josephine ^{something frightfully important about}—about the future and what ["]Don't you think perhaps,["] she began—But Josephine interrupted her. "I was wondering if now"

[DLC-MS-NL, leaf 32]

> She murmured. They stopped—they waited for each other.
> "Go on Con" said Josephine.
> "No—no Jug a after [*sic*] you said Josephine Constantia –[109]
> ["]No—say what you were going to say—after all you <u>began</u>,["] said Josephine.
> ["]I—I[']d rather hear what you are ^{were} going to say first["] said Constantia –
> "Dont be absurd! Con!"
> "Really, Jug!"
> ["]Connie![["]]
> ["]Oh <u>Jug</u>![["]]

---

[102] The *Collected* reads: "This time her wonder was like longing" (CW2, 281).

[103] The *Collected* has this in the plural, but here it is clearly singular.

[104] "Pale glittering moon" becomes "big, pale moon" in the *Collected*.

[105] The *Collected* reads: "[. . .] she had gone off by herself and got as close to the sea as she could, and sung something, something she had made up, while she gazed all over that restless water" (CW2, 282).

[106] "All" is omitted in the *Collected*.

[107] "Above all" is omitted in the *Collected* which adds "really" (e.g. "really felt herself") while eliminating the emphasis on "herself."

[108] There are arrows indicating the order of the questions should be switched, placing "What was it she was always wanting?" before "What did it all lead to?" which is the order in the *Collected*.

[109] The additional "a" before "after" suggests that Mansfield perhaps intended a stutter in Constantia's response.

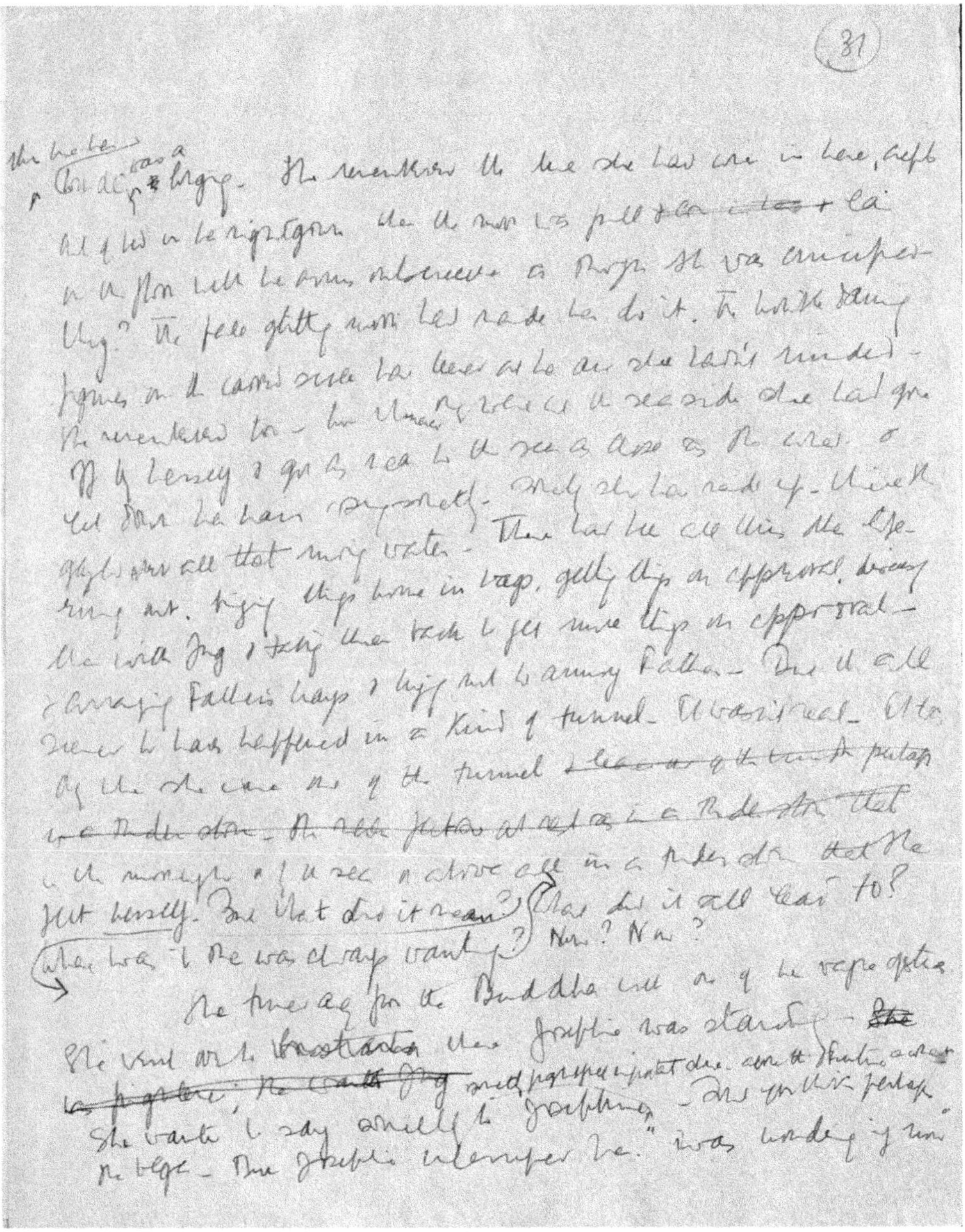

FIGURE 23: Leaf 31, "Non-Compounders [Daughters of the Late Colonel]," Katherine Mansfield Papers, Newberry Library, (box 1, folder 41), 32 leaves. Image courtesy of the Newberry Library.

A pause. Then Constantia said faintly. ["]I can[']t say what I was going to say Jug because Ive forgotten what it was—that I was going to say.["]

Josephine ~~did not reply~~ x was silent for a moment. ~~then she replied shortly so I have~~. She stared at ~~the~~a big cloud where the sun had been—Then she replied shortly: ~~So have I!~~ ["]Ive forgotten, too."

—— ——
—— ——
|
13
xii
1920

A Note on the Manuscript of "Mr and Mrs Dove"

"Mr and Mrs Dove" was originally published in the *Sphere*, a "popular" magazine, in August 1921. Mansfield was not satisfied with the story, writing in her notebooks:

> July. Just finished Mr and Mrs Dove yesterday. I am not altogether pleased with it. It's a little bit made up. It's not inevitable. I mean to imply that those two may not be happy together—that that is the kind of reason for which a young girl marries. But have I done so? I don't think so. Besides it is not strong enough. [. . .] I want to use all my force even when I am tracing a fine line. And I have a sneaking notion that I have, at the end, used the doves unwarrantably. [. . .] Is that quite my game? No, it's not. It's not quite the kind of truth I'm after.[1]

Despite her reservations about the story, she still chose to include it in her collection, *The Garden Party and Other Stories* (1922).

Although many of Mansfield's manuscripts which are not included in her longer notebooks are written on loose-leaf paper, "Mr and Mrs Dove" stands alone in a thin, orange, paper-covered exercise notebook on the cover of which Mansfield has written the title and underlined it twice. There is, however, evidence of a torn page on which something had been written. The writing begins in a clear hand, but it becomes progressively worse as the story progresses; on the fourth page Mansfield changes from a pen to a pencil, but perhaps one she had close at hand as the penmanship remains comparable after the switch. On the seventh page she reverts back to a pen. Many of the edits on the manuscript must have been done during a second reading, for even the section written in pencil is edited in pen.

[1] Notebooks 2, 278.

~~Sunday April 3rd 1921~~[2]

Mr and Mrs Dove
by
Katherine Mansfield

Of course he knew—no man better—that he hadn't the ghost of a chance—he hadn't an earthly! The very idea of such a thing was preposterous. So preposterous that he'd perfectly understand it if her Father—well—whatever her Father chose to do he'd perfectly understand . . . In fact nothing short of desperation—nothing short of the fact that this was positively his last day in England for God knows how long would have screwed him up to it. And even now—He chose a tie out of the ~~xxx~~ chest of drawers, a blue and cream check tie, and sat down on the side of his bed—supposing she replied: "What impertinence!" just that.[3] Would he be surprised? Not in the least, he decided, turning up his soft collar + turning it down again over the tie. He expected her to say something like that. He didn't see—if he looked at the affair dead soberly, what else she could say.

Here he was! And nervously he tied a bow in front of the mirror, jammed his hair down with both hands, pulled out the flaps of his jacket pockets—making between £500 and £600 a year on a fruit farm in—of all places—Rhodesia. No capital. Not a penny coming to him. No chance of his income increasing for at least 4 or five years.[4] As for looks and all that sort of thing he was completely out of the running. He couldn't even boast of top hole health, for the ~~e~~East Africa business had knocked him out so thoroughly that hed had to

take six months leave . . . ~~And~~ he was still fearfully pale ~~even more~~ worse, even than usual this afternoon he thought[5] ~~He bent~~ bending forward and peer~~ed~~ing into the mirror. Good Heavens! What had happened. His hair looked almost bright green. Dash it all. He hadn't green hair, at all events. That was a bit too steep. And then the green lighted [sic] trembled in the ~~mirror~~ glass;[6] it was the shadow from the tree outside. ~~He~~ Reggie turned away, took out his cigarette case, ~~then~~ but remembering how the mater hated him to smoke in his bed—women,[7] put it back again, and drifted over to the chest of drawers. No, he was dashed if he could think of ~~a single~~ one blessed thing in his favour while she . . . Ah! He stopped dead, folded his arms andleaned + ~~squeezed hard~~ hard against the chest of drawers.

---

[2] For some reason, Mansfield has stricken through the date at the top of the page.

[3] The published version reads: "[. . .] and sat on the side of his bed. Supposing she replied, 'What impertinence!' would he be surprised?" (CW2, 300).

[4] The print version merely notes "for at least four years" (CW2, 300).

[5] This addition is written in the left-hand margin, with an arrow from the end of the line after "pale." While the majority of the manuscript is written in ink, "Even more" is stricken out in pencil, and "worse, even" also added in pencil, suggesting this change was made after the initial addition.

[6] The published version reads, "green light trembled" (CW2, 300).

[7] "Bed" becomes "bedroom" in the published version, and "women" is omitted.

And ~~in spite of everything~~ in spite of her position, her father's wealth, the fact she was an ~~old~~[8] only child and by far and away the most popular girl in the neighborhood.[9] In spite of her beauty and her cleverness. Cleverness! It was a great deal more than that! There was nothing she couldn't do;[10] he **fully*** believed ~~xxx~~ had it been necessary—she would have been a genius at anything . . . In spite of the fact that her parents adored her and she them and theyd as soon let her go all that way as . . [*sic*] In spite of **every*** single thing you could think of, so terrific was his love that he couldn't help hoping. Well—was it hop~~ing~~[e]? Or was this queer timid ~~xxx~~ longing to have the chance of looking after her—~~to~~ [of] make[ing] it his job to see[11] that she had everything she wanted ~~to make her life just as perfect~~ and that nothing came near her that wasnt perfect. ~~was it~~ just . . . love?[12] How he loved her! He squeezed

[MMD-MS-NL, page 3][13]

hard against the chest of drawers + **murmured*** ~~to himself~~[14] into it I love her I love her! And just for one moment he was with her on the **next train** on the way to Durban.[15] It was night. She sat in the **corner*** asleep. Her soft chin was tucked into her coat collar,[16] her golden brown lashes lay ~~so lightly~~ on her cheeks. He doted on her ~~fine~~ **delicate*** little nose her perfect lips, her ear like a babys ear[17] the golden brown curl—~~of soft hair~~ that half covered it. They were passing through the jungle—It was warm + dark and [far][18] away ~~from xxx everybody + she slept as he felt xxx xxx sleep with her lips just parted as if xxx xxx~~.[19] Then she woke up + said Have I been asleep? And he answered—yes. Are you alright. Here let me. And he leaned forward to—he bent over her. This was such bliss that he could dream no further. But it gave him the courage to bound downstairs—to[20] **snatch*** his straw hat from the hall + to say as he closed the front door—Well I can only try my luck—that's all. But his luck gave him a jar to say the least almost immediately.[21] **Promenading*** up + down the garden path with Chinny + Biddy, the ancient **Pekes***, on her heels was ~~his~~ the Mater.[22] Of course Reginald was fond of the mater—and all that. She—she meant well. She

---

8   It appears that Mansfield began to write "oldest," but opted for "only."
9   The phrase "by far and away" becomes simply "far and away," and "the fact" is changed to "the fact that" in the print version.
10   The print version adds "really" between "was nothing."
11   Mansfield seems to have retraced this last phrase: "it his job to see."
12   Instead of "[. . .] that nothing came near her that wasn't perfect just . . . love," the published version reads: "[. . .] that nothing came near her that wasn't perfect—just love?" (CW2, 301).
13   The ink on this page is lighter than the previous page.
14   "To himself" and the arrow indicating where it was initially to be inserted are both in pencil.
15   The published version reads: "And just for the moment he was with her on the way to Umtali," changing "one moment" to "the moment" and omitting "on the train" as well as—most significantly—changing Durban to Umtali (CW2, 301). Durban is a coastal city in South Africa; however, as Mansfield identifies Rhodesia (current day Zimbabwe) as Reggie's place of employment, the final, published version changes the city to Umtali (now called Mutare) which, more accurately, was in Rhodesia. "Durban" is retained in the original publication in *The Sphere* (172).
16   What I read as "coat collar" becomes "soft collar" in the published version.
17   The published version omits this second "ear," reading: "her ear like a baby's" (CW2, 301).
18   Mansfield retraces the "ar" of "far."
19   The edits here are in a darker ink than the rest of the page.
20   Mansfield retraces "to" in pencil.
21   The published version adds "nasty" before "jar."
22   "On her heels" is omitted from the published version, and "Mater" is lower-case.

had no end of—of—grit and so on.[23] But there was no denying it she was rather a grim parent. And there had been moments—many of them—in Reggie's life—before Uncle

[MMD-MS-NL, page 4]

Alick died + left him the fruit farm when he was **convinced*** that to be a widows only son was ~~to be~~ about the worst punishment a chap could have. And what made it rougher than ever was that she was positively <u>all</u> that he had. She wasn't only a **combined*** parent, as it were but she had quarreled with all her own + Paters relations before Reggie had won his first trouser pockets.[24] So that, whenever ~~Reggie~~ he was homesick ~~his only~~ out there, **sitting*** on his dark his dark [*sic*] verandah ~~**where**~~ **by starlight*** while the gramophone cried Dear What is Life and Love—~~**positively**~~ his only vision was of the mater, tall + stout ~~on~~ rustling* down the garden path ~~in her black silk dress~~ with Biddy and Chinnie at her heels . . .[25]

~~At this moment~~ ~~The Mater~~[26] with her scissors outspread to snap the head of a dead something or other stopped at the sight xxx Reggie.

~~Are you going out~~ You are not going out Reginald? she asked. ~~He~~ ~~**sounded**~~ ~~astounded~~ seeing that he was mater [*sic*].[27]

Ill be back for tea ~~Mother~~ said Reggie weakly—plunging his hands in his jacket pockets.[28]

Snip. Off came ~~the~~ a[29] head. Reggie almost ~~xxx~~ ~~leaped~~ jumped.

I should have thought you could have spared me[30] your last afternoon said she.

Silence. The Pekes ~~were listening~~ stared. They understood every word.[31] Biddy lay down with her **tongue*** poked out—she was so fat and glossy she looked like a lump of

[MMD-MS-NL, page 5][32]

half melted toffee—But Chinnie's china[33] eyes gloomed at Reginald. ~~xxx~~ And he sniffed faintly ~~as xxx~~ as though the whole world ~~was~~ were[34] one unpleasant smell . . . Snip! went the scissors again ~~as Reginald eyed the roses~~ Poor little beggars they were getting it. And where are you going if ~~may~~ ask [*sic*] your mother may ask!—asked the Mater.[35]

---

[23] The published version reads simply, "she had no end of grit," eliminating the repetition (CW2, 301).

[24] "Paters relations" becomes "the governor's relations" in the published version. The writing in the manuscript after this point is in pencil.

[25] The published version inverts "Biddy and Chinny," perhaps to parallel the order of their first mention. In the manuscript, Mansfield switches from "Chinny" to "Chinnie" on several occasions.

[26] Mansfield has made a check before "The," suggesting she wishes to retain this previously omitted phrase, which is the case in the published version.

[27] It appears that Mansfield originally intended to present Reggie's response using free indirect discourse, which could explain the residual "mater" at the end; however, she revises this last sentence to emphasize the "mater's" perspective.

[28] While "Mother" is omitted here, the published version retains the reference, but uses "mater" instead.

[29] "A" is written over "the."

[30] "Me" becomes "your mother" in the published version.

[31] The published version reads: "They understood every word of the mater's," adding the last phrase (CW2, 302).

[32] The lower half of the left margin has two rough sketches of flowers, one smaller with a stem and leaves, the other just the flower head.

[33] The published version substitutes "porcelain" for "china."

[34] "Were" is superimposed on "was."

[35] The "y" of "may," the "k" of "ask" and the exclamation point of the addition are in a darker ink, suggesting they were retraced later.

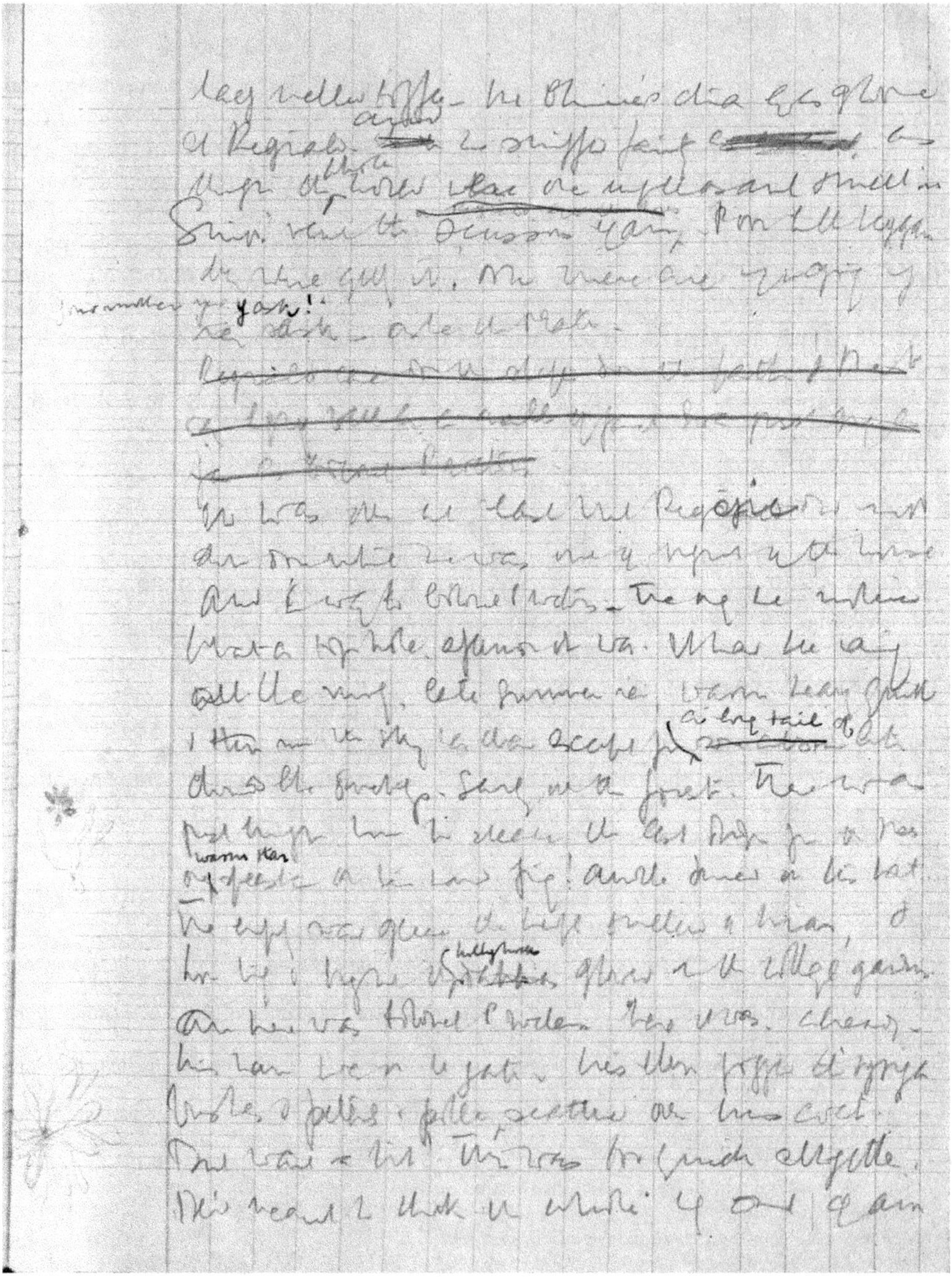

FIGURE 24: Page 5 recto, "Mr and Mrs Dove," Katherine Mansfield Papers, Newberry Library, (box 1, folder 38), 14 pages. Image courtesy of the Newberry Library.

~~Reginald came down the steps~~ **down** ~~the path~~ + xxx ~~to say lightly xxx as a matter of fact I was just going as far as Colonel Proctors~~.

It was over at last but Reginald~~gie~~[36] did not slow down until he was out of sight of the house and ½ way to Colonel Proctors—Then only he noticed what a top hole afternoon it was. It had been raining ~~in~~ all[37] the **morning***, late summer rain, warm heavy quick + ~~then~~ now the sky was clear except for ~~some above~~ a long trail of little clouds like ducklings—Sailing over the forest. There was just enough **wind*** to shake the last drops from[38] the trees one warm star splashed on his hand Ping![39] Another **drummed*** on this hat . . . The empty road gleamed, the hedges smelled of briar, + how big + bright the ~~dahlias~~ hollyhocks glowed in the cottage gardens. And here was Colonel Proctors. Here it was, already—his hand was on the gate—his **elbow*** jogged the syringa bushes + petals + pollen scattered over his coat.[40] But wait a bit. This was too quick altogether. He'd meant to think the whole thing out again.

[MMD-MS-NL, page 6]

Here steady! But he was walking up the path with the huge rose bushes on either side. It cant be done like this ~~+~~ but his ~~hand~~ hand had grasped the bell given it a pull + started it pealing **wildly*** as if hed come to say the house was on fire. The housemaid must have been in the hall too, For [*sic*] the front door flashed open + Reginald[41] was shut in the **empty*** drawing room before that confounded bell had stopped ringing—Strangely enough, when it did, that^e big empty room, shadowy, full of mirrors + flowers with some ones parasol lying on top of the grand piano, **bucked*** him up or rather, excited him.[42] It was so quiet and yet so watchful alert xx + ~~yet~~ in one moment the door would open + his fate would be decided.[43] ~~He was almost reckless~~ The feeling wasn't unlike that of being at the dentists He was almost reckless . . . ~~Now he was here he had to go through with it . . .~~ But at the same time to his immense surprise Reginald heard himself saying "Lord thou knowest thou hast not done much for me." That pulled him up. That made him realise again how dead serious it was—Too late. The door handle turned. Anne came in—crossed the shadowy space between them gave him her hand + said ~~I~~in her small soft voice ~~that sounded always to be xxx on the edge of laughter~~. Im so sorry Father is out

[MMD-MS-NL, page 7]

+ Mothers having a day in town—hat hunting. Theres only me to entertain you **Mr Dawes**.[44]

---

[36] The change is made by superimposing "gie" over "inald."

[37] "All" is superimposed over "in."

[38] "From" becomes "off" in the published version.

[39] "Warm star" is written in a darker ink, suggesting it was added later.

[40] The published version has "coat sleeve."

[41] "Reginald" becomes "Reggie" in the published version.

[42] The published version omits "full of mirrors + flowers."

[43] The published version reverts to the initial version, omitting the addition, reading: "It was so quiet, and yet in one moment the door would open, and his fate be decided" (CW2, 302). The edits here, and those that follow below, are in a darker ink.

[44] While Anne addresses Reggie informally by his given name in the published version, throughout the manuscript she refers to him more formally as Mr. Dawes.

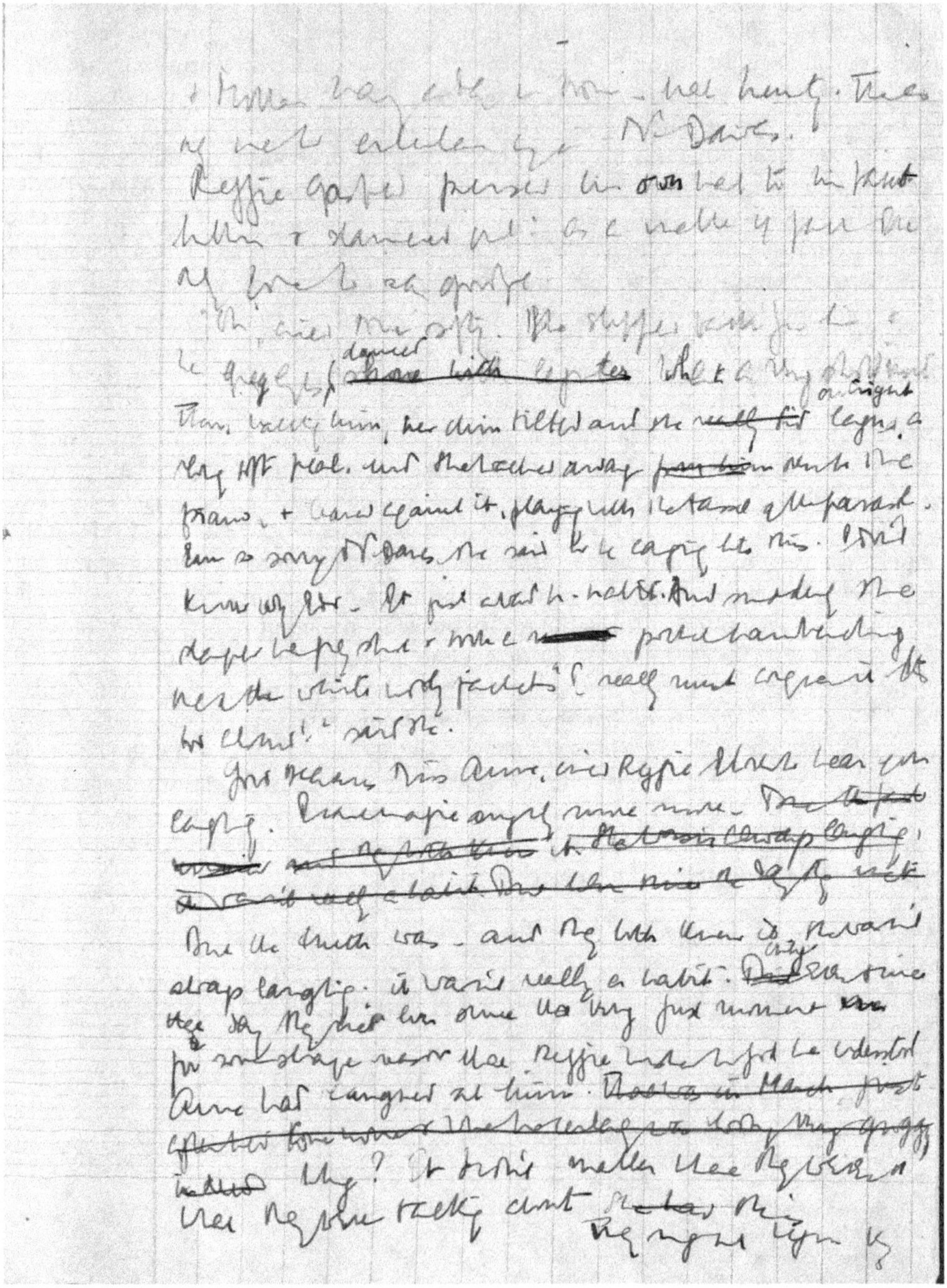

FIGURE 25: Page 7 recto, "Mr and Mrs Dove," Katherine Mansfield Papers, Newberry Library, (box 1, folder 38), 14 pages. Image courtesy of the Newberry Library.

Reggie gasped pressed his own[45] hat to his jacket buttons + stammered out: As a matter of fact I've only come to say goodbye.[46]

"Oh," cried Anne softly. She stepped back from him + her grey eyes ~~shone with laughter~~^{danced}. What a very short visit.[47] Then, watching him her chin tilted and she ~~really did~~ laugh^{outright}, a long soft peal, and she walked away ~~from him~~ over to the piano,[48] + leaned against it, playing with the tassel of the parasol. I am so sorry Mr **Dawes** she said to be laughing like this.[49] I don't know why I do—Its just a bad h—habit. And suddenly she stamped her grey shoe + took a xxx pocket handkerchief out of the white wooly jacket. "I really must conquer it. Its too absurd!" said she.

Good Heavens Miss Anne, cried Reggie I love to hear you laughing. I can't imagine anything more more—~~But the fact remained and they both knew it. She wasn't always laughing, and it wasn't really a habit. But ever since the day they met~~ But the truth was—and they both knew it—she wasn't always laughing. It wasn't really a habit. ~~But~~ ^{Only} ever since the day they met ever since that very first moment ~~she~~ for some strange reason that Reggie wished to God he understood Anne had laughed at him. ~~That was in March, just after hed come home + when he certainly was looking very groggy indeed~~ Why? It didn't matter where they were or what they were talking about ~~she had~~ this [sic][50] They might begin by

[MMD-MS-NL, page 8]

being as serious as possible, dead serious, at any rate as far as he was concerned but she suddenly—in the middle of a sentence Anne would glance at him and a little quiver passed over her face—her lips parted, her eyes danced and— she began laughing.[51] Another queer **thing*** about it was Reggie had an idea she didn't know herself[52] why she laughed. He had seen her **turn away***—frown, suck in her cheeks, press her hands together. But it was no use—~~even xxx xxx her eyes half closed~~ + ~~t~~The long soft peal sounded even while she cried: I don't know why Im laughing . . . It was a mystery . . .

Now she tucked her handkerchief away. Do sit down she said[53] xxx. And smoke wont you. There are cigarettes in that little box beside you. Ill have one, too. He lighted a match for her + ^{as} she bent forward he saw **the tiny flame*** glow in the ~~opal~~ ^{pearl} ring she wore. It is **tomorrow*** that youre going—isn't it said **Anne***.

Yes tomorrow as ever was[54] said Reggie leaning against the arm of a chair + he blew a little fan of smoke.[55] Its so frightfully hard to believe he added. Why on earth was he so nervous—**nervous*** wasn't the word for it.[56]

Yes—isn't it said Anne ^{softly} + she leaned forward

---

[45] "Own" is retraced in a darker ink.

[46] The published version reads: "'I've only come . . . to say good-bye'" (CW2, 303), adding the ellipsis.

[47] The edits here are in a darker ink, as is the whole of the rest of the page, suggesting that Mansfield changed pens and may have left off writing and recommenced later.

[48] The deleted "from him" is retained in the published version.

[49] The published version omits the direct address.

[50] It is likely that Mansfield intended to delete "this" along with the rest of the phrase.

[51] The published version changes "little quiver" to "little quick quiver" and omits the pause indicated by the two dashes in the manuscript.

[52] Mansfield uses an editorial mark to indicate that "known herself" should be inverted.

[53] Mansfield used an editorial mark signaling to transpose "she said."

[54] "Was" becomes "is" in the published version.

[55] The published version omits "leaning against the arm of a chair."

[56] A line indicates Mansfield wanted to move this last sentence to just after "fan of smoke," which is how the published version reads.

[MMD-MS-NL, page 9]

and rolled the point of her cigarette round the green ash tray—How beautiful she looked **like*** that—Simply beautiful + she was so small in that immense chair. Reginalds heart swelled with tenderness, **but it*** was her voice, her soft voice that made him tremble. "I feel you've been here for years" ~~you~~ ˢʰᵉ said." [*sic*]

Reginald took a deep breath of his cigarette. Its ghastly, this idea of going away⁵⁷ he said.

Coo Roo coo coo coo sounded from the quiet.

But youre fond of **being*** out there—aren't you said Anne. ~~Father was only saying.~~ She **hooked her finger*** through her pearl necklace. Father was only saying the other night how **lucky*** he thought you were to have a life of your own. And she looked up athim [*sic*].⁵⁸ Reginald ~~gave her a wan smile~~ ˢᵐⁱˡᵉ ʷᵃˢ ʳᵃᵗʰᵉʳ ʷᵃⁿ. I don't feel fearfully lucky, he said lightly.

Roo coo coo. Coo! came again—And Anne murmured. You mean its lonely.

Oh, it isn't the loneliness I care about said Reg + he **stumped*** his cigarette **savagely*** into on [*sic*] the **green*** ash tray. I could stand any **amount*** of it + I used to like it even⁵⁹—it's the idea of. Suddenly to his **horror*** he felt himself **blushing***.

Roo coo cooo! roo coo coocoo!

Suddenly Anne jumped up.⁶⁰ Come + say goodbye to ~~my~~ ᵗʰᵉ⁶¹

[MMD-MS-NL, page 10]

~~doves~~ ᵍᵃʳᵈᵉⁿ⁶² she said. ~~Theyve been moved to the side verandah~~ and she looked back over her shoulder.⁶³ Do you⁶⁴ like doves, don't you! Mr. Dawes.

Awfully said Reggie. ~~At the moment he couldn't have told a dove from a raven~~ ˢᵒ ᶠᵉʳᵛᵉⁿᵗˡʸ that as he opened the french window for her + stood to one side ~~she~~ ᴬⁿⁿᵉ ~~her light laugh~~ ran forward + laughed at the doves instead.⁶⁵

~~Have I shown them to you before?~~

ʸᵒᵘ ˢᵉᵉ! ~~said Anne, The one in front is Mrs Dove. She's always in front. She gives a little coo + Mr Dove comes bows + bows + follows her.~~

To and fro to and fro over the fine red sand on the floor of the dove house walked the two doves. ~~But o~~One⁶⁶ was always in front of the other. One ran forward **uttering*** a little cry—+ the other followed, solemnly **bowing + bowing***—You see ~~said~~ ᵉˣᵖˡᵃⁱⁿᵉᵈ Anne the one in front—~~is~~ ˢʰᵉ'ˢ Mrs. Dove. ~~Shes always in front~~—She looks at Mr Dove + gives that little laugh + runs forward + he follows her **bowing + bowing***. And that makes her laugh again. + ~~again she~~ away she runs + after her, cried Anne + she sat back on her

---

⁵⁷ "Going away" becomes "going back" in the published version.
⁵⁸ Mansfield seems to have conjoined "at" and "him."
⁵⁹ "+ I used to like it even" becomes simply "used to like it even" in the published version.
⁶⁰ The published version eliminates "Suddenly."
⁶¹ The published version reverts back to "my."
⁶² A check mark after "doves" signals that, while it was originally struck through, it is to be retained.
⁶³ The published version retains "They've been moved to the side veranda" but deletes "and she looked back over her shoulder" (CW2, 304).
⁶⁴ "You" is circled and a line indicates it should be moved before "Do."
⁶⁵ The edits here are in a darker ink.
⁶⁶ The capital "O" is written over the lower case "o."

heels, comes poor Mr Dove bowing + bowing . . . and that's their whole life. They never do anything else, you know. She got up + took some yellow grains **out*** of a bag on the roof of the dovehouse. When you think of them out in Rhodesia Mr Dawes—you can be **sure*** ~~to~~ that that is what they will be doing . . .

But ~~whether Reggie had seen~~ ^{Reggie gave no sign of having seen} the doves or

[MMD-MS-NL, page 11]

~~whether he had heard~~ ^{or of having heard a word} a word [*sic*] that Anne had said.[67] ~~nobody will ever know~~. For the moment he was conscious of only[68] the of the [*sic*] immense effort to [*sic*] took to tear his secret out of himself + to offer it to Anne. ^{Anne} Do you think you could ever care for **me***? It was done. It was over. And in the little pause that followed Reginald saw the garden open to the light the blue quivering sky the flutter of leaves on the verandah poles + Anne ~~with~~ ^{turning*} ^{over} the grains of maize in her palm with a **finger***. Then slowly she shut her hand + the **new world*** faded as she murmured slowly "no never in that way. But[69] he had scarcely time to feel . . . anything before she walked quickly away + he followed down the steps—along the garden path under xxx pink rose **arches***, across the lawn.[70] There with **the gay herbaceous border behind*** her ~~she~~ ^{Anne} faced Reginald. "It isn't that I am not awfully fond of you" ~~said Anne~~. ^{she said.} "I am. But," her eyes widened "not in **that*** way"—a quiver passed over her face. **She** ought to be f - fond[71]—her lips parted—+ she couldn't stop herself—She began laughing. There you see, you see she cried! ^{Its your check tie} Even at this **moment*** when one would think ^{one really would be solemn—even—}--- your tie reminds me so fearfully of the bow tie that cats wear in pictures. Oh please forgive me for being so horrid. Please!

Reggie **caught*** hold of her little warm hand. Theres no question of forgiving he said quickly how could there be? And I do believe I know why I - I make you laugh. Its because youre so far above me in every way that I am—somehow ridiculous. I see that Anne. But if I were to

[MMD-MS-NL, page 12]

No, no. Anne squeezed his hand hard. Its not that—that's all wrong. Im not far above you at all. Youre much better than I am. Youre marvelously unselfish and—and, kind and simple. Im not Im none of those things.[72] You **don't*** know me. Im the **most awful*** character said Anne. Please don't interrupt. ~~But thats why I couldn't don't you see. The man I marry must be~~ And **thats not*** the point.[73] The point is, she xxx her head. I couldn't

---

[67] The published version eliminates "that Anne had said."
[68] "Of only" is inverted in the published version.
[69] "But" is written in darker ink over an illegible word.
[70] The ellipsis is not in the published version.
[71] While the *Sphere* version of the story often substitutes an ellipsis for the dashes that appear in the *Collected*, in this case the placement of the ellipsis affects how one reads the sentence. The *Sphere* version, it reads: "'I am. But . . .' Her eyes widened, 'not in the way'—a quiver passed over her face—'one ought to be fond of . . .'" (173), placing a pause after "But." However, the *Collected* has: "'I am. But'—her eyes widened—'not in the way'—a quiver passed over her face—'one ought to be fond of—'" (CW2, 305), eliminating the apparent hesitation in the dialog. Neither records the stammering of "f - fond."
[72] "Im not" is omitted in the published version.
[73] The published version places "besides" after "And."

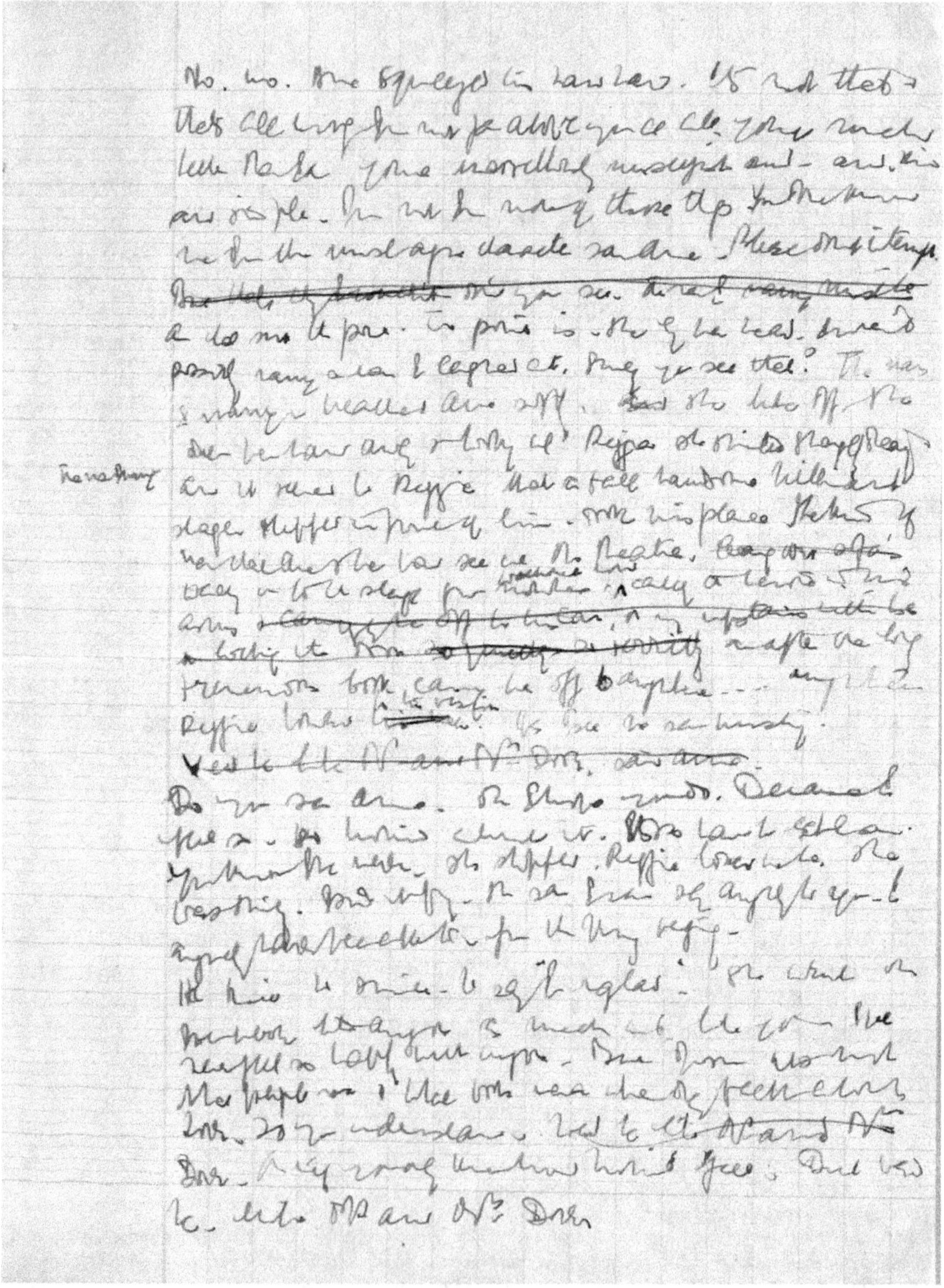

FIGURE 26: Page 12 recto, "Mr and Mrs Dove," Katherine Mansfield Papers, Newberry Library, (box 1, folder 38), 14 pages. Image courtesy of the Newberry Library.

possibly marry a man I laughed at.[74] Surely you see that? The man I marry—breathed Anne softly, ~~and~~ she broke off—she **drew*** her hand away + looking at Reggie she smiled strangely, **dreamily***. ^The man I marry[75]^

And it seemed to Reggie that a tall handsome brilliant stranger stepped in front of him, took his place. The kind of man that Anne + he had seen at the theatre, ~~leaning over sofas~~ walking on to the stage from nowhere ^without a word^ **catching*** the heroine in his arms + ~~carrying her off to his car, or xx upstairs with xxx or locking its door so quietly, so secretly~~ and after one long tremendous look carrying her off to anywhere ---- anywhere.[76]

Reggie bowed ~~his head~~ ^to his vision.^ Yes I see he said **huskily***.

~~Wed be like Mr and Mrs Dove, said Anne.~~

Do you said Anne. O I hope you do. Because I feel so—so horrid about it. Its so hard to explain. You know Ive never—she stopped. Reggie looked at her. She **was smiling***. Isnt **it funny***—she said I can say anything to you—I always have been able to—from the very beginning—

He tried to smile—to say "Im glad –" She went on. I've never liked anyone as much as I like you[77]—Ive never felt so happy with anyone—But **Im sure its*** not what people **mean*** + what books mean when they talk about Love.[78] Do you understand—~~Wed be like Mr and Mrs~~ Dove.[79] Oh if you only knew how horrid I feel. But wed be—like Mr and Mrs Dove.[80]

[MMD-MS-NL, page 13]

That did it. That seemed to Reginald final—+ so **terribly*** true that he ~~winced as though~~ ^could hardly bear^ it. Dont drive it home he said + he **turned*** away from Anne + looked across the lawn. There was the gardeners cottage with its tall ilex tree beside. A blue **thumb*** of transparent **smoke hung*** above its **chimney***.[81] It did not look real. How his throat ached. Could he speak. He had a shot. I must be getting along home ~~said Reginald~~ ^he croaked^ + he began walking across the lawn. But Anne ran after him. No, don't you cant go yet.[82] You cant possibly go ~~yet~~ ^away^ feeling like that. + she **stared*** up at him— **frowning***—**biting*** her lip.

"Oh that's all right" said Reggie, giving himself a shake. Ill, Ill—+ he waved his hand as much as to say "get over it."

But this is awful said Anne. + she clasped her hands + stood in front of him. Surely you do see how fatal it would be for us to marry—dont you—

Oh quite quite said Reginald—looking at her with haggard eyes.

---

[74] As in note 71, the two published versions disagree on the placement of pause. The *Sphere* version reads: "'The point is . . .,' she shook her head, 'I couldn't marry a man I laughed at'" (173), suggesting Anne hesitates after saying "The point is." The *Collected*, however, reads: "'The point is'—she shook her head—'I couldn't possibly marry a man I laughed at'" (CW2, 305).

[75] This addition is written in the left-hand margin.

[76] The published version eliminates the second "anywhere."

[77] The published version is changed slightly: "'I've never known anyone I like as much as I like you'" (CW2, 305).

[78] The sentence is more concise in the published version: "'But I'm sure it's not what people and what books mean when they talk about love'" (CW2, 305).

[79] While Mansfield likely meant to omit the complete sentence here, she fails to strike through "Dove."

[80] The published version reads: "'But we'd be like . . . like Mr and Mrs Dove'" (CW2, 305).

[81] "A blue thumb" becomes "A wet, blue thumb" in the published version.

[82] The published version adds "she said imploringly" to the end of this sentence.

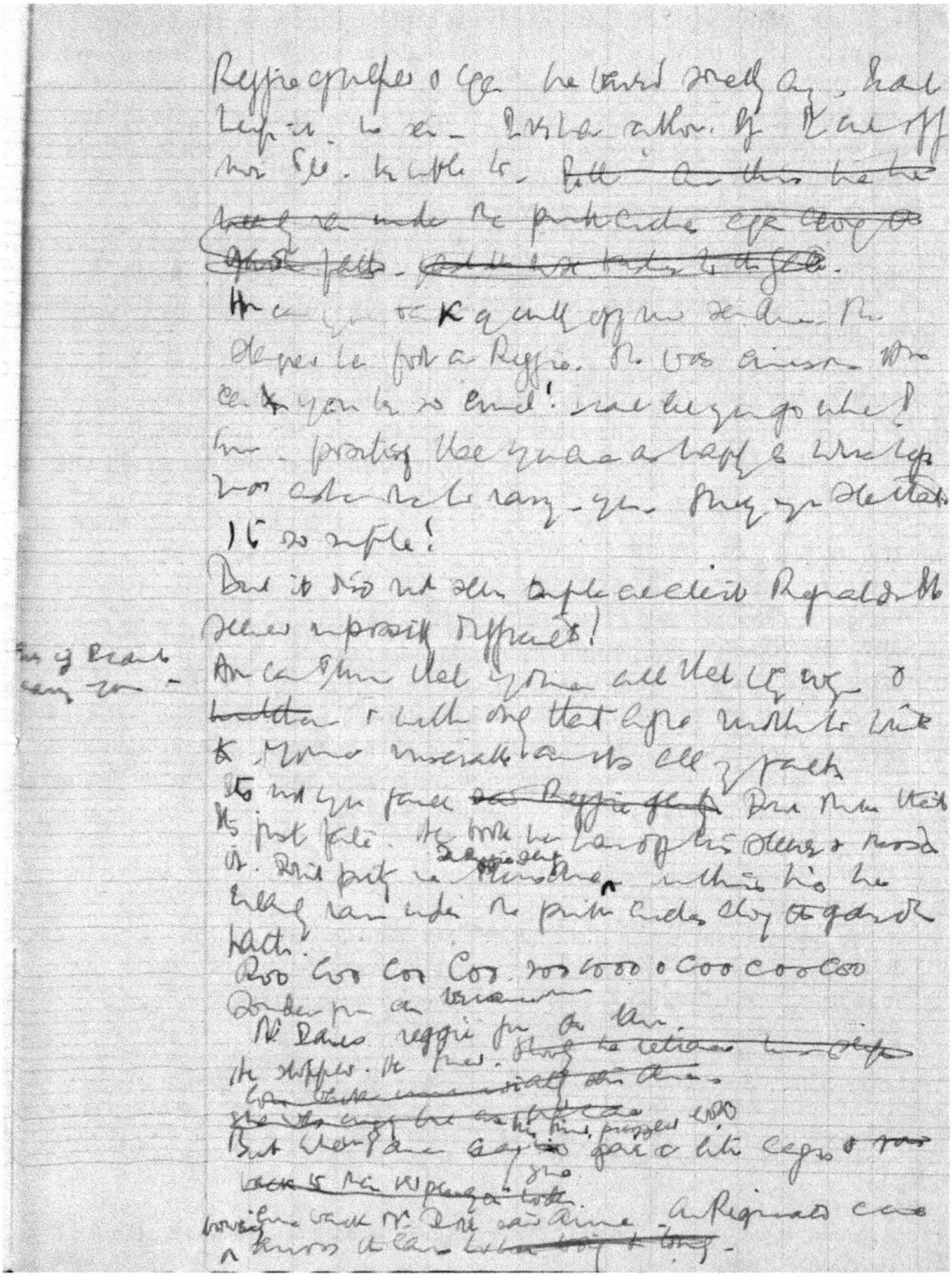

FIGURE 27: Page 14 recto, "Mr and Mrs Dove," Katherine Mansfield Papers, Newberry Library, (box 1, folder 38), 14 pages. Image courtesy of the Newberry Library.

How wrong! Wicked[83]—feeling as I do—I mean—its all very well for Mr + Mrs Dove but **imagine*** that in real life imagine it.

Oh absolutely said Reggie. + he started to walk on—

But again Anne stopped him. She tugged at his sleeve + to his astonishment, this **time*** instead of laughing she looked like a little girl who was going to cry.

Then why—if you ~~do see~~ understand are you so un—unhappy? She whined[84]—Why do you mind so fearfully? Why do you look so Aw—awful?

[MMD-MS-NL, page 14]

Reggie gulped + again he waved something away. I cant help it he said—Ive had a blow. If I cut off now Ill—be able to—~~I'll And this time he nearly ran under the pink arches again along the garden path—past the rose bushes to the gate.~~

How can you talk of cutting off now said Anne.[85] She stamped her foot at Reggie. She was crimson. How can ~~he~~ you be so cruel! I cant let you go until I Im—positive that you are as happy as when **before** you asked me to marry—you—Surely you see that. Its so simple![86]

But it did not seem simple at all to Reginald. It seemed impossibly difficult!

Even if I cant marry you –[87] How can I know that youre all that way away + ~~heartbroken~~ + with only that awful mother to write to—Youre miserable and its all my fault.[88]

Its not your fault ~~said Reggie gently~~ Don't think that. Its just fate. He took her hand off his sleeve + kissed it. Don't pity me dear Anne said Reggie gently.[89] And this time he **nearly*** ran under the pink arches along the garden path.

Roo coo coo Coo roo cooo o coo coocoo sounded from the verandah.

Mr Dawes. Reggie from the lawn.[90]

He stopped. He turned. ~~Slowly he retraced his steps.~~

~~Come back come xxx said Anne.~~

~~She was crying but as he came~~

But when Anne saw ~~him~~ his timid, puzzled look gave a little laugh ~~+ was back to their old xxx xxx~~ She

Come back Mr. Dove said Anne. And Reginald came bowing across the lawn[91]—~~to her bowing + bowing –~~

---

[83] "How" is added in front of "wicked" in the published version: "How wrong, how wicked."

[84] "Whined" becomes "wailed" in the published version.

[85] "Scornfully" is added as an adverb at the end of the sentence in the published version.

[86] The published version reads: "'How can you be so cruel? I can't let you go until I know for certain that you are just as happy as you were before you asked me to marry you. Surely you must see that, it's so simple'" (CW2, 306).

[87] This addition is written in the left-hand margin, before the line that follows.

[88] Rather than a stand-alone sentence, the published version incorporates the initial phrase: "'Even if I can't marry you, how can I know that you're all that way away, with only that awful mother to write to, and that you're miserable, and that it's all my fault?'" (CW2, 306).

[89] The published version interchanges the pronoun, "he," and proper noun, "Reggie"; likewise, it adds a diminutive to his direct address to Anne: "dear Anne" becomes "dear little Anne."

[90] "Mr Dawes" is replaced by a repetition of "Reggie" in the published version.

[91] The published version changes "bowing" to "slowly."

A Note on the Manuscript of "Marriage à la Mode"

Like "Mr and Mrs Dove," "Marriage à la Mode" was written as part of a series Mansfield agreed to write for the *Sphere*. As a whole, Mansfield was not completely pleased with these stories, feeling that they did not represent her best work. She was especially dissatisfied with their presentation in the magazine: "My stories for the Sphere are all done, thank the Lord. I have had copies with ILLUSTRATIONS! Oh Brett! Such fearful horrors. All my dear people looking like—well—Harrods 29/6 crepe de chine blouses and young tailors gents."[1]

As with many of the other manuscripts, it is difficult to say if this is the original draft or a cleaner copy of an earlier version. Despite the fact that the story is fully intact, as are most of the stories in Notebook 5—of which this is a part—there are some heavy edits, including the omission of some fairly lengthy sections. It is possible, then, that just as with "A Cup of Tea," Mansfield may have composed the story in its entirety, making no further edits beyond what we find in this draft. If so, one must believe that Mansfield did much of the composition in her head before putting pen to paper. A potential counter to this theory is that on page twelve of the manuscript, where Mansfield stops writing "Marriage à la Mode" and continues it on the verso pages three through six of the notebook, she includes the date, August 11, 1921. If she started the story the day she dated the first page of the notebook, that would mean she finished the story five days after. Of course, the date on page twelve may signify something completely different.

---

[1] *Letters* 4, 271.

6
viii
1921
Montana

Marriage à la mode.

On his way to the station William remembered with a fresh pang of disappointment that he was taking nothing down to the kiddies. Poor little chaps! It was hard lines on them. Their first words always were as they ran to greet him, ~~always were~~: "What have you got for me Daddie?"[2] And he had nothing. He would have to buy them some sweets at the station. But that was what he had done for the past four Saturdays; their faces had fallen last ~~times~~ when they saw the same old boxes produced again.

And Paddy had said: I had red ribbing on mine be^c-fore![3]

And Jonny had said: Its always pink on mine. I hate pink!

But what was William to do? The affair wasn't so easily settled. In the old days, of course, he would have taken a taxi off to a decent toy shop and chosen them something in five minutes. But nowadays they had Russian toys, French toys, Serbian toys—toys from God knows where. It was over a year since ~~they were~~ Isabel had scrapped the old donkeys and engines and so on because they were so "dreadfully sentimental" and so "appalingly [sic] bad for the babies sense of form."

Its so important the new Isabel had explained, that they should like the right things from the very beginning. It saves so much time later on. Really—if the poor pets have to spend their infant years starring [sic] at these ~~things~~ horrors one can imagine them growing up and ~~being~~ asking to be taken to the Royal Academy. And she spoke~~n~~ as though a visit to the Royal Academy was certain, immediate death to any one . . .

"Well, I don't know," said William, slowly. When I was their

age I used to go to bed hugging an old towel with a knot in it."

The New Isabel looked at him, her eyes narrowed, her lips apart.

"<u>Dear</u> William! Im sure you did!" She laughed in the new way.

Sweets it would have to be, however! thought William gloomily fishing in his pocket for change for the taxi man. And he saw the kiddies handing the boxes round—they were awfully generous little chaps—~~to~~ while Isabel's precious friends ~~who~~ didn't hesitate to help themselves . . .

What about fruit? William hovered before a stall just inside the station. What about a melon each? Would they have to share that, too. Or a pine apple for Pad and a melon for

---

[2] In the published version, "Daddie" becomes "daddy."

[3] Mansfield squeezes the second "e" between "be" and the hyphen.

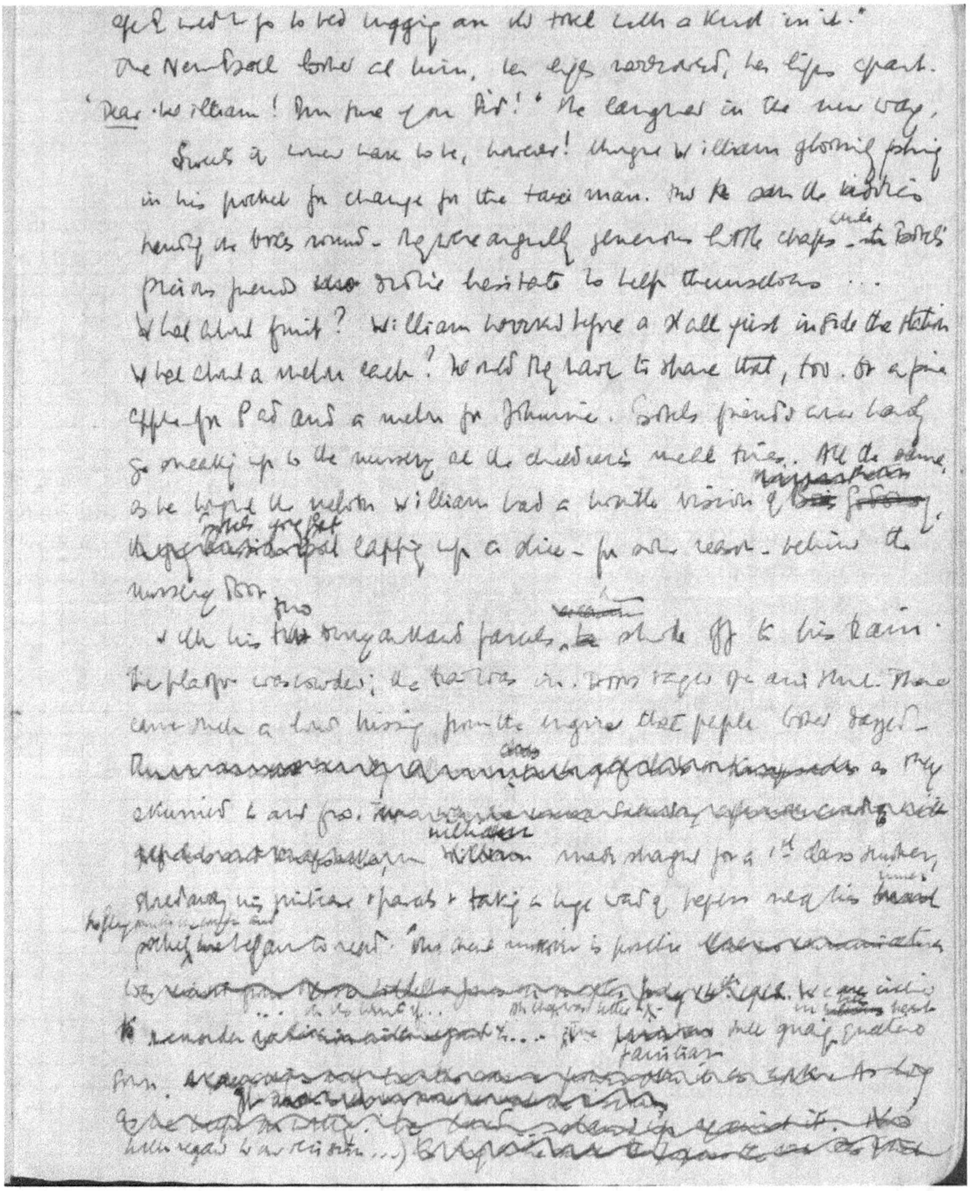

FIGURE 28: Page 3 recto, Notebook 5, "Marriage à la Mode," Katherine Mansfield Papers, Newberry Library (box 2, folder 4), 2–12. Image courtesy of the Newberry Library.

Johnnie.[4] Isabels friends could hardly go sneaking up to the nursery at the children's meal times. All the same, as he bought the melon William had a horrible vision of ~~Boris Godovsy~~ ~~xxx xxx, the young Russian poet~~ ^{Isabels young poet} lapping up a slice—for some reason—behind the nursery door.

With his ~~xxx~~ ^{two} very awkward parcels ~~he~~ ^{~~William~~ he} strode off to his train. The platform was crowded; the train was in. Doors banged open and shut. There came such a loud hissing from the engine that people looked dazed—~~there was the usual Saturday Afternoon crowd with golf clubs and knapsacks~~ as they scurried to and fro. ~~There was the usual Saturday afternoon crowd with golf clubs and knapsacks; William~~ ^{He William5} made straight for a 1st class smoker, stowed away his suitcase + parcels + taking a huge wad of papers out of his ~~breast~~ ^{inner} pocket ^{he flung down in the corner and} ~~he~~ began to read. "Our client moreover is positive ~~that no communication was received from Mssrs Liddell + Jones on or after July 14th 1918~~. We are inclined to reconsider ~~xxx xxx xxx xxx xxx~~ to . . . . ^{Ah that was better -X-6} The ~~persistent~~ familiar dull gnawing ^{in ~~Williams~~ his breast} quieted down. ~~A queer thing—writing had the same power over it as work. As long as he kept on writing he could . . . stand up against it. Now~~ with regard to our decision . . .) ~~As long as he xxx the papers the~~ ~~sad~~ was ~~quiet~~

[MalaM-NB5-NL, 4]

~~When Isabel was away he read himself to sleep every night—he~~ ~~slept under xxx, xxx xxx with the xxx xxx sheets and sheets of stiff xxx paper.~~[7]
~~On at least xxx xxx xxx xx~~. ^{He took} ^{a blue pencil ~~out~~ + scored a paragraph} ^{out} ^{slowly.} Two men came in, stepped across him and ~~sat down in~~ ^{made for} the further corner. A young fellow swung his golf clubs into the rack + sat down ~~beside him~~ ^{opposite}. The train gave a gentle lurch; they were off. ~~William took out is watch, stared at it, glanced up,~~ ~~xxx~~ ~~at the xxx xxx xxx~~ ~~Moyra Morris~~. William glanced up + saw the hot bright station slipping away. A red faced girl raced along ~~the platform~~ ^{by the carriages}; there was something strained and almost desperate in the way she waved and called. Hysterical thought William dully ~~when~~ Then A [sic] greasy ^{black faced} workman at the end of the platform grinned at the ^{passing} train. And William thought ~~xxx~~ ~~xxx~~ ~~William thought~~ ^{~~What a xxx and grey xxx life~~} ~~a filthy life!~~ A filthy life + went[8] back to his papers.

When he looked up again there were fields and beasts ~~standing for~~ shelter^{ing} ~~xxx~~ ^{under9} the ~~spreading~~ ^{dark} trees. A wide[10] river glided into sight ~~+ there was a group of~~ ^{with} naked children splashing in the shallows ^{and was gone again}.[11] The sky shone pale + one bird drifted

---

⁴ While the published version uses "Johnny," Mansfield occasionally spells it "Johnnie" in the manuscript.

⁵ "William" is superimposed over "He."

⁶ The opposing page has a similar mark, an "X" encircled by five dots, placed on the same level as the "-X-" here. Below that, Mansfield has written: "William pressed back his flattened hair + stretched his legs across the carriage floor." Thus, she signals that this sentence should be added here, as it appears in the published version.

⁷ Most of the edits after this point on the page are in a darker ink.

⁸ "Went" is superimposed over another, illegible word.

⁹ "Under" is written over another word; "standing for," although stricken through here, is used in the published version.

¹⁰ Mansfield retraces "wide."

¹¹ An arrow after "shallows" indicates Mansfield wants to move this image of children to the spot following just after "wide river," which is how it appears in the published version: "A wide river, with naked children splashing in the shallows, glided into sight and was gone again" (CW2, 331).

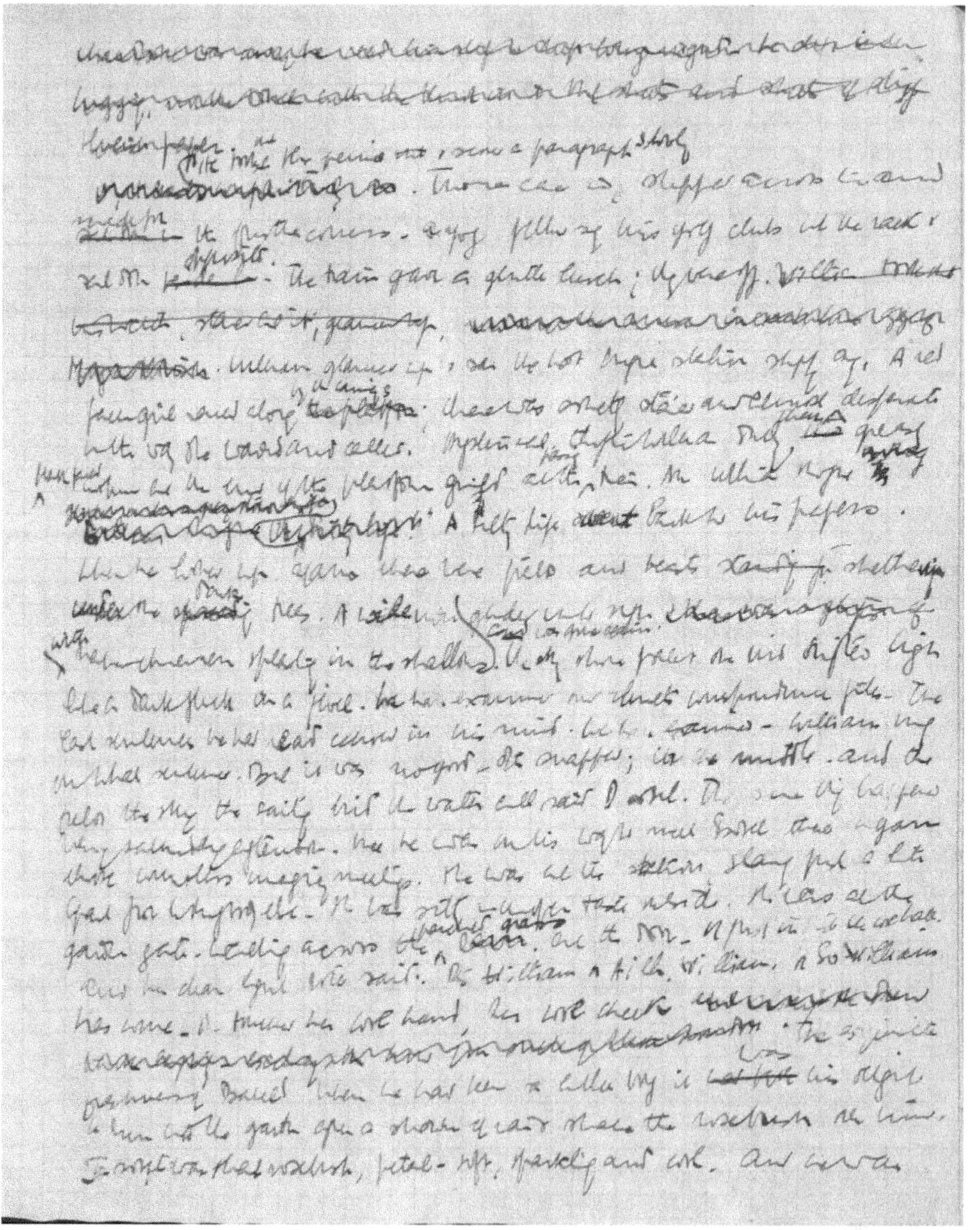

FIGURE 29: Page 4 recto, Notebook 5, "Marriage à la Mode," Katherine Mansfield Papers, Newberry Library (box 2, folder 4), 2–12. Image courtesy of the Newberry Library.

high like a dark fleck in a jewel. We have examined our clients correspondence files. The last sentence he had read echoed in his mind. We have examined—William hung on tohat[12] [*sic*] sentence. But it was no good—**often** snapped, in the middle, and the fields, the sky, the sailing bird, the water, all said Isabel. The same thing happened every saturday [*sic*] afternoon. **When*** he was on his way to meet Isabel there began those countless imaginary meetings. She was at the station standing just a little apart from everybody else—She was sitting in the open taxi outside. She was at the garden gate—walking across the ~~lawn~~ parched grass. At the door—or just inside the xxx hall. And her clear light voice said: "Its William or Hillo, William, or So William has come—He touched her cool hand, her cool cheek ~~and slowly she drew back laughing—exclaiming oh how you smell of xxx~~ ~~smoke~~ the exquisite freshness of Isabel! When he had been a little boy it ~~had been~~ was his delight to run into the garden after a shower of rain + shake the rosebush over him. Isabel was that rosebush, petal-soft, sparkling and cool. And he was

[MalaM-NB5-NL, 5]

still that little boy. But there was no running into the ~~back~~ garden now, no laughing and shaking. The dull persistent thought in his breast* started again.[13] He drew up his legs, ~~and~~ tossed the papers ~~in the seat before him~~ aside, and shut his eyes.

What is it Isabel. What is it, he said tenderly. They were in their bedroom in the new house. Isabel sat on a ~~little~~ painted stool before the dressing table that was strewn with little black + green boxes.

What is what William + she bent forward + her fine light hair fell over her cheeks.

Ah you know. He stood in the middle of the strange room + he felt a stranger.

At that ~~May~~ Isabel wheeled round quickly + faced him.

Oh William she cried imploring + she held up her hair brush. Please! Please don't be so dreadfully stuffy and—and tragic! Youre always saying or hinting or looking as if Ive changed.[14] Just because Ive got to know really congenial people and go about xxx more*15 and am frightfully keen on—on everything you behave as though Id—~~May~~ Isabel tossed back her hair + laughed—killed our innocent love, or something.[16] Its so awfully absurd— she bit her lip—+ its so maddening, William! Even this new house + the servants you grudge me.

~~May~~! Isabel! ~~cried William~~

Yes. Yes—its true in a way—said ~~May~~ Isabel quickly. You think they are another bad sign. Oh I know you do. I feel it she said softly17 every time you come up the stairs! But we couldn't have gone on living in that other poky little hole, William. Be practical at least. Why there wasn't even ~~a proper nursery~~ for the enough room for the ~~children~~ babies even.

No, it was true every evening when he came back from chambers it was to find ~~May~~ ~~with~~ the babies with ~~May~~ Isabel in the little back drawing room.[18] They were ~~going for~~ having

---

[12] Mansfield seems to have spliced together "to that."

[13] "Persistent gnawing" is used in lieu of "persistent thought" in the published version.

[14] The published version reads: "You're always saying or looking or hinting that I've changed" (CW2, 332), inverting the order and changing "as if" to "that."

[15] What appears to be "more" is written over another, illegible word.

[16] While "innocent" is inserted in the manuscript, it is not retained in the published version.

[17] The arrow indicating where the addition should be inserted is after "feel," but grammatically it makes better sense following "it," as reproduced here, which is how it appears in the published version.

[18] The published version omits "little" before "back drawing room."

rides on the le~~a~~opard[19] skin thrown over the sofa back, or they were **playing*** shops with ~~Mays~~ Isabel's desk for the counter or Pad was sitting on the **hearth rug rowing away*** for dear life with a little brass fireshovel [*sic*] while Johnnie shot pirates with the tongs. Every evening they each had a picka back up~~stairs~~ the narrow stairs to their old fat nannie [*sic*].[20]

Yes he supposed it was a poky little house—~~x~~ a little white house with blue curtains and a window box full of petunias. William met their friends at the door with Seen our petunias! Pretty terrific for London—

[MalaM-NB5-NL, 6]

don't you think?

But the imbecile thing the absolutely extraordinary thing was he hadn't the slightest idea that ~~May~~ Isabel wasn't wasn't [*sic*] as happy as he was xxx, God what blindness![21] He hadn't the **remotest*** ~~idea~~ notion in those days that she ~~hated~~ really hated that inconvenient little house, that she was desperately lonely, pining for new people + new music + pictures and **parties** so on, that she thought the old fat **nanny*** was ruining the babies[22] . . . If they hadn't gone to that studio party at Moyra[23] Morrisons. If Moyra Morrison hadn't said as they were **leaving***, "Im going to **rescue*** your ~~Isabel~~ wife, selfish man! She's like an exquisite little Titania." If Isabel hadn't gone with Moyra to Paris—If—If. The train stopped at another station. Bettingford Good Heavens! They'd be there in 10 minutes. William stuffed the papers back into his pocket, the young man opposite had long since disappeared. Now the other two ~~men in the corner~~ got out. ~~Women in cotton~~ frocks~~, little sunburnt barefoot children waited on the station xxx~~. The late afternoon sun shone on women in cotton frocks + little sunburnt barefoot children. It blazed on a silky yellow flower with coarse leaves that sprawled over a bank of rock. The ~~xxx~~ air24 ruffling through the window **smelled*** of the sea—Had Isabel the same crowd with her this weekend—wondered William—+ he remembered the holidays they used to have the four of them—~~with the milk boys sister~~ with a little farm girl—Rose—~~xxx~~ to look after the babies. Isabel wore ~~her hair in a plait~~ a jersey + her hair in a plait. She looked about fourteen. Lord how his nose used to peel! + the amount they ate—the amount they slept in that immense feather bed—with their feet locked together –

~~He~~ William couldn't help a grim smile as he thought of Isabels horror if she knew the full extent of his sentimentality.

[MalaM-NB5-NL, 7]

Hillo, William. She was at the station after all, standing, just as he had imagined apart from the others—and Williams heart leapt she was alone.

---

[19] The "o" is superimposed over "a."

[20] The published version inverts "old fat."

[21] In the margin beside this sentence, Mansfield has written "Kat" and circled it.

[22] This last clause is circled and an arrow indicates it should be placed after "inconvenient little house," which is how it appears in the published version, though "old fat Nanny" becomes simply "fat Nanny": "He hadn't the remotest notion in those days that she really hated that inconvenient little house, that she thought the fat Nanny was ruining the babies, that she was desperately lonely, pining for new people and new music and pictures and so on" (CW2, 332).

[23] While the published version uses "Moira," throughout the manuscript Mansfield uses "Moyra."

[24] "Air" is superimposed over another, illegible word.

"Hullo Isabel" William stared. He thought she looked so beautiful that he had to say something. "You look very cool."

Do I said Isabel. I don't feel very cool. Come along. Your horrid old train is late. The taxis outside. She put her hand **lightly*** on his arm as they passed the ticket collector. Weve all come to meet you she said. But we've left Bobbie Cane[25] at the ~~fruit~~ sweet shop—to be called for.[26]

Oh! said William. It was all he could say for the moment.

Th^ere[27] in the glare, waited the taxi with Bill Hunt + Dennis Green ~~and~~ sprawling on one side, ~~his~~ their[28] hats tilted over their faces ~~their feet in the air~~ while on the other Moyra Morrison, in a ~~hat~~ bonnet* like a huge ~~nasturtium leaf~~ strawberry, jumped up + down.

~~No ice I would~~ No ice! No ice! No ice! she shouted gaily.

And Dennis chimed in from under his hat: Only to be had at the fish mongers.

And Bill Hunt emerg~~ed~^ing[29] added with whole fish in it!

Oh what a bore! wailed Isabel. And she explained to William they have been chasing ~~round the town for ice~~ all around the town* while I waited for you. Simply everything is **running down*** its ~~steep~~ cliffs into the sea beginning with the butter.

~~We shall have to **sift** the butter through a **sieve** said Bill—or~~ We shall have to[30] anoint ourselves with ~~it~~ the butter, said Dennis. May thy head, William, not lack ointment.[31]

Look here said William how are we going to sit. Id better get up by the driver.

No, Bobbie Cane's by the driver, said ~~Isabel~~ Moyra ^Isabel youre to sit between ~~Isabel~~ Moyra and me. The taxi started. What have you got in those ^mysterious parcels—~~William~~.

[MalaM-NB5-NL, 8]

Decapitated heads! said Bill Hunt **shuddering*** beneath his hat.

"Oh fruit!" Isabel sounded very pleased. Wise William. A melon a pineapple. ~~How good it smells.~~ How too nice!

No. Wait a bit said William smiling. But he really was ~~xxx~~ anxious. I brought them down—for the kiddies.

Oh my dear! Isabel laughed + slipped her hand through his arm. Theyd be rolling in agonies if they were to eat them. No, she patted his hand. You must bring them something next time. I refuse to part with my pineapple ^ex tre traordinary[32]

Cruel Isabel. Do let me smell it said Moyra. She flung her arms across William appealingly. "Oh!" the **~~nasturtium hat~~** ^leaf strawberry ~~hat was tilted back~~ the strawberry bonnet fell forward: she sounded quite faint.[33]

---

[25] The published version uses "Bobby," but throughout the manuscript Mansfield changes between "Bobbie" and "Bobby." "Cane" becomes "Kane" in the published version.

[26] This last phrase is crowded in at the end of the line, suggesting it was a later addition.

[27] The "ere" of "There" is written over something illegible.

[28] "Their" is superimposed over what looks like "his."

[29] It appears that Mansfield wrote "ing" over "ed."

[30] This phrase is written in the margin.

[31] Mansfield has made the editorial mark indicating that "not" and "lack" should be inverted.

[32] "Extraordinary" is written more lightly, in a smaller hand, as if Mansfield was trying out spellings. The word is not utilized on this page, though it does occur on pages 6 and 3 verso of the notebook.

[33] Aside from changing "nasturtium hat" to "nasturtium leaf," the remaining edits appear to have been made after the initial writing, as the ink is darker.

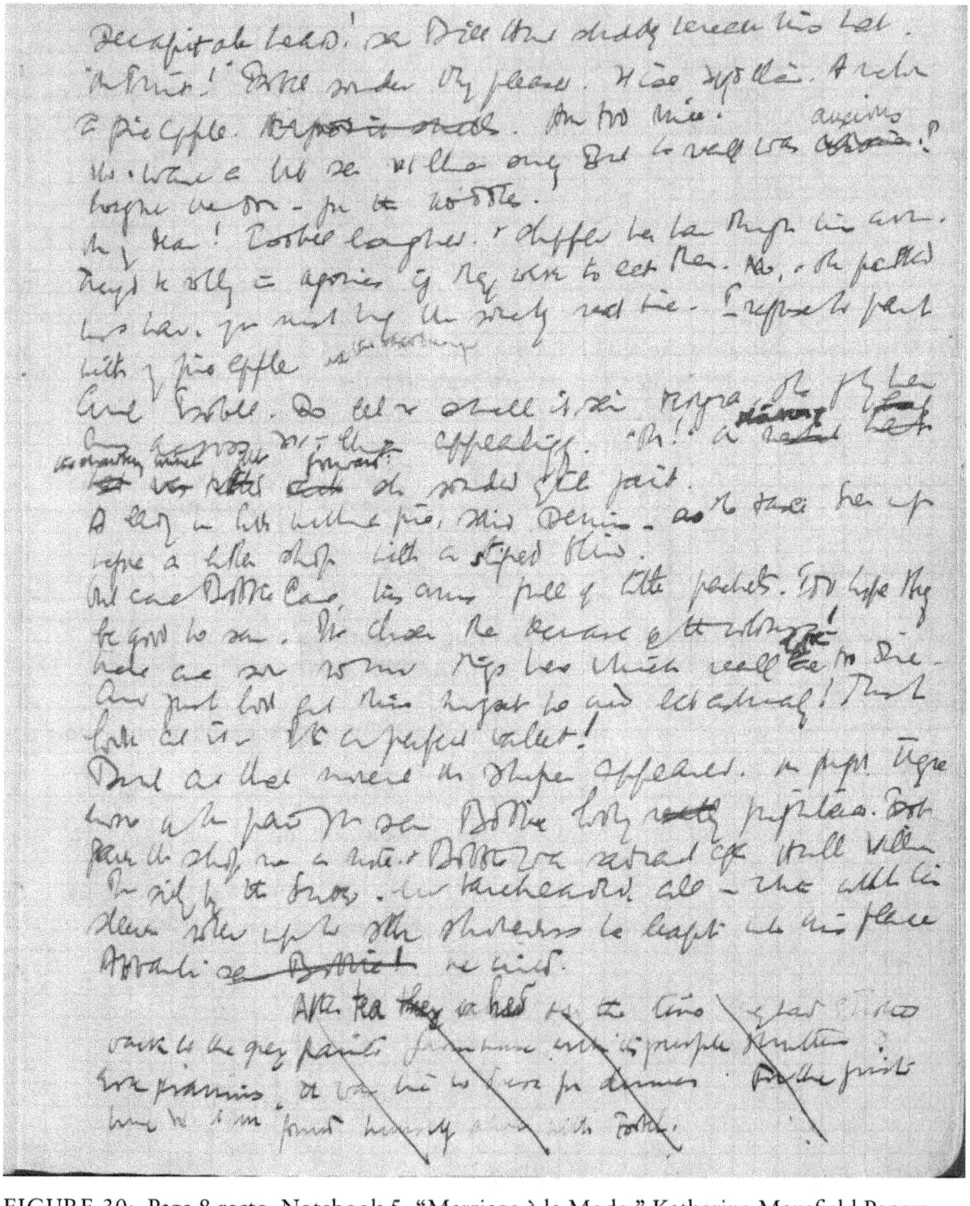

FIGURE 30: Page 8 recto, Notebook 5, "Marriage à la Mode," Katherine Mansfield Papers, Newberry Library (box 2, folder 4), 2–12. Image courtesy of the Newberry Library.

A lady in love with a **fruit**, said Dennis—as the taxi drew up before a little shop with a striped blind.

Out came Bobbie Cane, his arms full of little packets. I do hope they [*sic*] be good he said. I've chosen them because of the colours! There are some round things here which really ~~are~~ ^{look} too divine—And just look at this nougat he cried ecstatically! Just look at it—its a perfect ballet!

But at that moment the shopman appeared. Ive forgot. Theyre none of them paid for said Bobbie looking ~~really~~ frightened. Isabel gave the shop man a note + Bobbie was radiant again. Hullo William. I'm sitting by the driver. And bareheaded, all in white with his sleeves rolled up to **the*** shoulders he leapt into his place Avvanti ~~said Bobbie!~~ he cried.

~~After tea they xxx in the xxx they had~~ ~~strolled~~ ~~back to the grey painted farmhouse with its purple shutters + xxx~~ ~~geraniums~~~~, it was time to dress for dinner. For the first time William found himself alone with Isabel.~~

[MalaM-NB5-NL, 9]

~~How had things gone this week he said awkwardly. Ever since he arrived he had felt~~ ^{been} ~~awkward uneasy + dull; he felt like the man who didnt dance + staring out he xxx to the others xxx and gaily + watched the men make free of Isabel's house . . .~~
~~How have things gone? Isabel~~ **rubbed** ~~her cheeks with a xxx. She sounded vague.~~[34]

After tea they [*sic*] others went off to bathe while William stayed + made his peace with the kiddies. But Johnny + Paddy were asleep. The ~~sky~~ rose-red glow had paled; ~~+~~ bats were flying ~~before the xxx~~ **voices** ~~of the bathers rang through the shadowy air~~ and still the bathers had not returned. As[35] William wandered downstairs, ~~there was a light in the sitting room.~~ the maid crossed the hall carrying a lamp; he followed her into the sitting room. It was a long room ~~painted~~ ^{coloured} yellow. On the wall opposite William someone had painted a young man, over life size with very wobbly legs offering a wide eyed daisy to a young woman who had one very ~~large~~ ^{short} fat arm[36] + one very long thin one. Over the chairs + sofa there **hung*** strips of black material covered with big splashes like broken eggs and everywhere one looked there seemed to be an ash tray full of cigarette ends. William sat down in one of the armchairs. Nowadays when one felt with one hand down the sides it wasn't to come upon a sheep with three legs or a cow that had lost one horn or a very large fat dove[37] out of the noahs [*sic*] ark—one fished up yet another little paper covered book of smudged looking poems——He thought of the wad of papers in his pocket—but he was too hungry + tired to read. The door was opened—Sounds came from the kitchen.

[MalaM-NB5-NL, 10]

The servants were talking as if they were alone in the house. Suddenly there came a loud screech of laughter + an equally loud sh-sh! They had remembered him. William got up

---

[34] There is a noticeable space between this section and the section that follows.

[35] Two short lines are drawn under the "a" of "as," suggesting it is to be capitalized.

[36] The published version reads only "one very short arm," omitting "fat."

[37] "Large" is omitted in the published version, thus reading "a very fat dove."

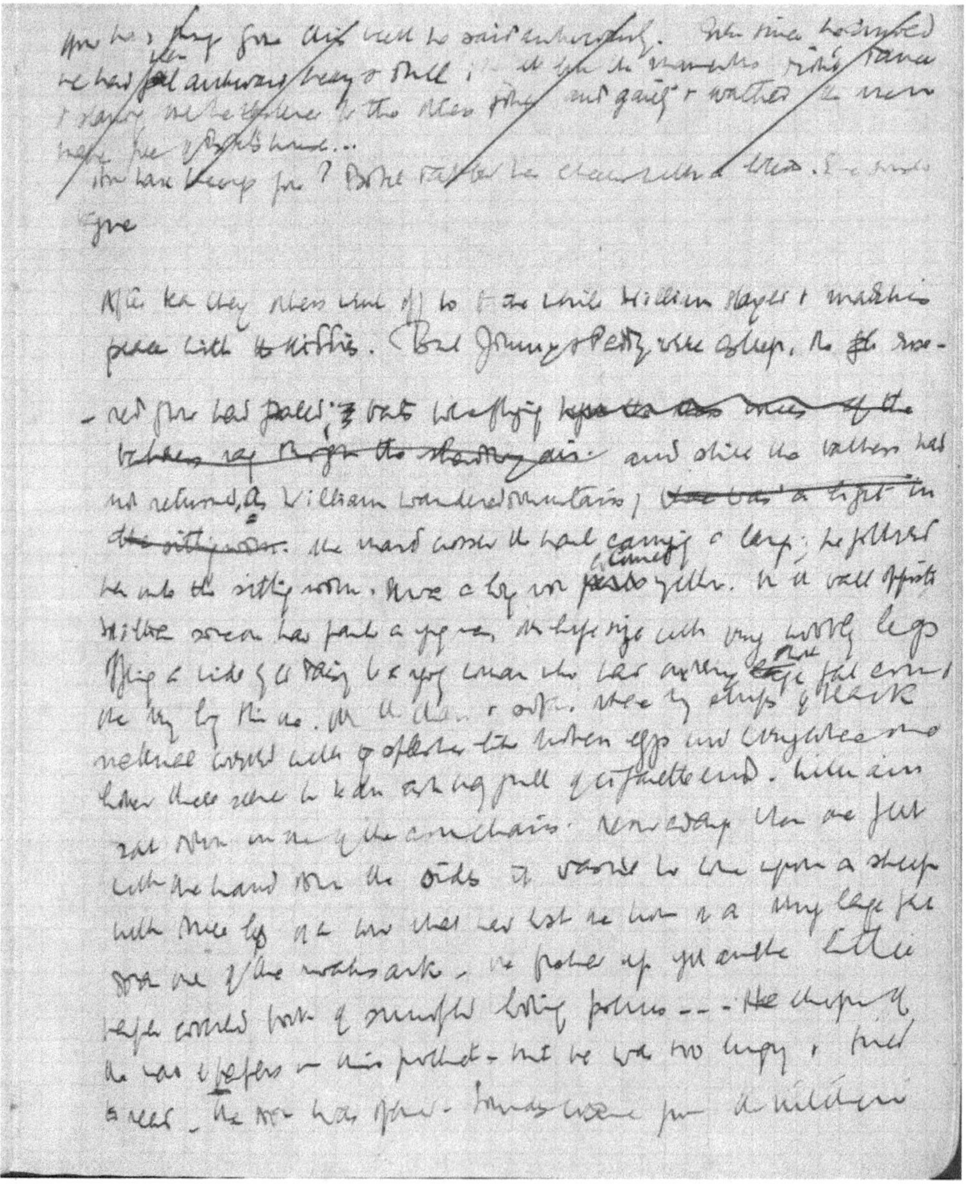

FIGURE 31: Page 9 recto, Notebook 5, "Marriage à la Mode," Katherine Mansfield Papers, Newberry Library (box 2, folder 4), 2–12. Image courtesy of the Newberry Library.

+ went through the french windows into the ~~jardin~~ garden*38 + as he stood there in the shadow he heard the bathers coming up the ~~hard~~ sandy road. Their voices rang through the dusky quiet.

I think its up to Moyra to use her arts and wiles.39

A tragic moan from Moyra.40

We ought to have a gramophone for the week ends, that plays "The Maid of the Mountains!"

Oh no! Oh no! cried Isabels voice. Thats ~~unfair~~ not fair to William. Be nice ~~dearest little ones—leave him to me cried Bobby Cane~~. to him my children! Hes only staying until tomorrow evening.

Leave him to me! Leave him to me!41 cried Bobbie. Im awfully good at looking after people.42

The gate **swung*** open + open [*sic*]. William moved on the terrace they had seen him. Hullo William!43

And Bobbie Kane, flapping his towel, began to leap + dance on the parched lawn.44 Pity you didnt come William. ~~We had a feas~~ The water was divine. And we all went to a little pub afterwards + had sloe gin.

The others had reached the house. I say Isabel—called Bobbie. Would you like me to wear my "**Haute**" costume tonight?45

No said Isabel. Nobodys going to dress we're all starving. Williams starving too. Come along, mes Amis. Lets begin with sardines.

Ive found the sardines said Moyra—She ran into the hall holding a box high in the air +

A Lady with a Box of Sardines—said Dennis—gravely.

[MalaM-NB5-NL, 11]

Well William how's London said Bill Hunt **drawing*** a cork out of a bottle of whisky.

Oh Londons not much changed said William **dryly**.46

Good old London said Bobby Cane very hearty—**spearing*** a sardine.

But a moment later William was forgotten. Moyra Morrioson began wondering what colour legs really were under water.47

Mine are the palest—palest mushroom colour—

Bill + Dennis ate enormously—

And Isabel filled glasses + changed plates + found matches—smiling blissfully. At one moment she said

I do wish—Bill youd paint it.

---

38 "Jardin" is smudged.
39 The published version adds "little," reading: "to use her little arts and wiles."
40 This sentence appears to be squeezed between the two above and below, suggesting it might have been added later.
41 The published version has "Leave him to me" only once.
42 This last sentence is squeezed in at the end of the line and into the right margin, suggesting it was an addition.
43 "Hullo" becomes "Hallo" in the final published version; however, it remains "Hullo" in the *Sphere* version.
44 "Dance" becomes "pirouette" in the published version.
45 While "Haute" is a best guess for the illegible modifier of "costume" here, it is clearly not "Nijinsky dress," as in the published version.
46 "Dryly" is omitted in the published version.
47 The published version adds "one's" before "legs."

Paint what said Bill loudly, stuffing his mouth with french bread.

"Us," said Isabel round the table. It would be so fascinating in 20 years time[48] –

Bill screwed up his eyes + chewed. ~~Too much light~~ Lights wrong he said.[49] Far too much yellow + went on eating—

But that seemed to charm Isabel, too –

And after supper they were all so tired they **could*** do nothing but yawn **until*** it was late enough to go to bed.[50]

It was not until William was waiting for his taxi the next afternoon that he ~~managed~~ found himself to get [sic] ~~xxx be~~ alone with Isabel. When He **brought his*** suitcase down into the hall + Isabel left the others + **went*** over to him—She stooped down + picked up his suitcases. What a weight she said + she gave a little awkward laugh. Let me carry it to the car or to the gate.[51]

No, why should you said William. Of course not give it to me.

[MalaM-NB5-NL, 12]

Oh please do let me said Isabel—I want to. ~~But William~~ Just to the gate. They walked together silently. William felt there was nothing to say now.

There said Isabel triumphantly setting the suit case down + she looked anxiously along the sandy road—I hardly seem to have seen you this time, she said breathlessly. Its so short isn't it. I feel youve only just come. Next time— —

The taxi came into sight. I hope they look after you properly in London said Isabel. Im so sorry the babies have been out all day. But Miss Neil had **arranged*** it. Theyll hate missing you—Poor William. Going back to London. The taxi turned. Goodbye. She gave him a little hurried kiss. ~~The taxi turned [into the] garden—~~she was gone –

Fields, trees, hedges streamed by—They shook through the ~~small ugly~~ empty, blind looking little town—~~climbed the~~ ground up the steep pull to the station. The train was in. William made straight for a first class smoker, put his suit case into the rack—flung back into the corner. But this time he let the papers **alone***. He lay back folded his arms against the dull persistent gnawing. ~~He~~ and began in his mind to write a letter to Isabel.[52]

XI
viii
1921[53]

I don't know how I may write this next story. Its so difficult. But I suppose I shall. The trouble is I am so infernally cold![54]

---

[48] "Time" is placed under "years," suggesting this last part was squeezed in.

[49] The adverb "rudely" is added after "he said" in the published version.

[50] Just below this section, Mansfield has drawn a wavy line, evidently to separate the two sections, a division retained in the published version.

[51] The published version reads: "'Let me carry it! To the gate'" (CW2, 336).

[52] There is a wavy line to indicate a break. The lines that follow are below this break.

[53] If this date marks when Mansfield completed the story, it took her five days to write it from the time she dated the notebook.

[54] Mansfield begins writing "Widoed" [sic] on the following page; however, Margaret Scott suggests the story referred to here is "The Voyage," which begins a page after the abandoned "Widoed" (Notebooks 2, 273, note 224).

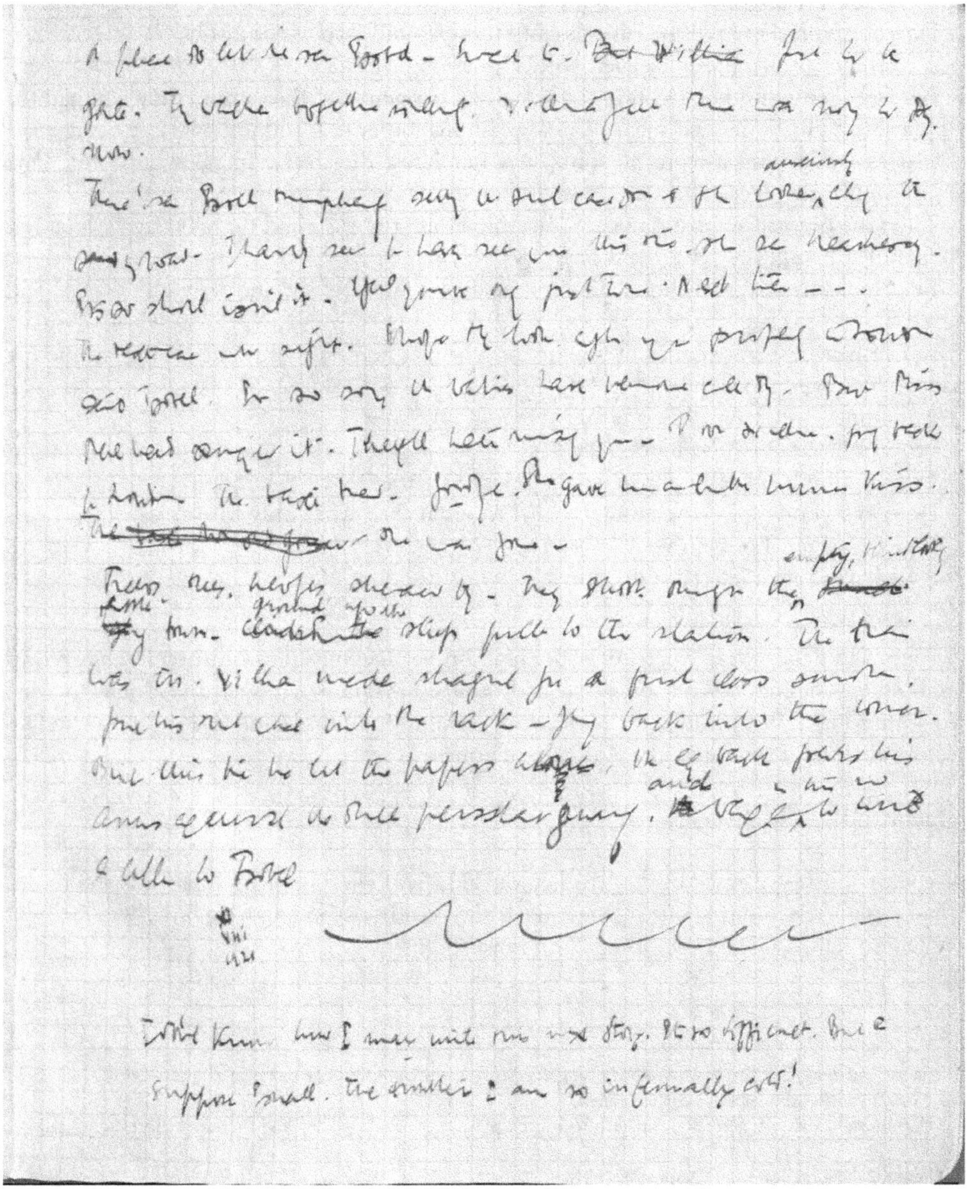

FIGURE 32: Page 12 recto, Notebook 5, "Marriage à la Mode," Katherine Mansfield Papers, Newberry Library (box 2, folder 4), 2–12. Image courtesy of the Newberry Library.

[MalaM-NB5-NL, 3 verso][55]

The post was late as usual ˣˣˣ. They sat outside the house in long chairs under coloured parasols. Only Bobby Cane lay on the turf at Isabel's feet. It was dull, stifling, the day drooped like a flag.

Do you think there will be Monday in Heaven? said Bobby childishly—

And Dennis murmured: Heaven will be one long Monday

But Isabel couldn't help wondering what had happened to the salmon they had had for supper last night.[56] She had meant to have fish mayonnaise for lunch ᵃⁿᵈ ⁿᵒʷ · · ·.

Moyra was ~~sound~~ asleep. Sleeping was her latest discovery. Its so wonderful. One simply shuts ones eyes. Thats all. Its so delicious!

Then the old ruddy postman came beating along the ˢᵃⁿᵈʸ road on his tricycle, one felt the handle ᵇᵃʳˢ ought to have been oars –

Bill Hunt put down his book. Letters! he said complacently, and **they all*** waited and stared.[57]

But ~~of~~ heartless postman. Oh malignant world. There was only one. One fat one for Isabel—Not even a paper.[58]

And mines only from William said Isabel mournfully.

From William. ~~Why so much xxx~~ déjà.[59]

Hes sending you back your marriage lines. As a ~~fragile~~ ᵍᵉⁿᵗˡᵉ reminder.

Does everybody have **such** marriages? I thought they were only for servants.

Pages + pages. Look at her.

A Lady reading a letter! said Dennis.[60]

My darling precious Isabel,

Pages and pages there <u>were</u>. As Isabel read on her feelings of astonishment changed to a still stifled feeling.[61] What on earth had induced William! How extraordinary it was! How ~~amazing~~ What could have made him.[62] She felt confused more + more excited—even frightened. It was just like William, ~~of course~~ Was it? It was

[MalaM-NB5-NL, 4 verso]

absurd of course—it must be ᵃᵇˢᵘʳᵈ· Ridiculous. Ha-Ha! Ha. Oh dear. What was she to do. Isabel flung back in her chair + ~~laughed till~~ she couldn't stop laughing.[63]

"Do do tell us," cried the others. You must tell us.

---

[55] It is unclear why, but rather than continuing the story on the subsequent pages in the notebook, Mansfield chose to finish it on the verso of earlier pages.

[56] The published version, adjusting the verb form, reads: ". . . the salmon they had for supper last night" (CW2, 336).

[57] The published version omits "and stared."

[58] The published version reads: "But, heartless postman—O malignant world! There was only one, a fat one for Isabel. Not even a paper" (CW2, 337).

[59] Rather than "déjà," the published version uses "already."

[60] The line above this is more clearly attributed to Dennis in the published version.

[61] The published version leaves out "still."

[62] The published version adds an ellipsis and changes the exclamation points to question marks.

[63] A check mark is made above "laughed till," suggesting it is to be retained, which is the case in the published version.

^But, ~~But~~ Oh,[64] Im longing to, ^gurgled Isabel—She sat up, gathered the letter waved it ~~xxx~~^at ^them. Gather round—she said. Listen. Its too marvelous. A love letter.

"A Love letter. ~~How so~~ ^But how divine."

~~Đ~~   Darling precious Isabel.

But she had hardly begun reading before they interrupted her with their **laughter***.[65]

Go on. Go on Isabel. It's ~~xx~~ perfect![66]

It's the most marvellous find.

~~I always thought those letters in divorce cases were made up. But they pale before this—~~

Oh <u>Do</u> go on Isabel

God forbid my darling that I should be a drag on your happiness.

Oh! Oh! Oh!

Sh—sh! Sh!

And Isabel went on. When she reached the end they were hysterical. Bobbie rolled on the turf + almost sobbed.

You must let me have it just as it is—Entire for my new book said Bill Hunt firmly.[67] I shall give it a whole chapter.

Ooh Isabel moaned Moyra that wonderful bit about holding you in his arms.

I always thought those letters in divorce cases were made up. But they pale before this.

[MalaM-NB5-NL, 5 verso]

Let me hold it ~~in my own hand~~. Let me read it mine own self, said Bobby Cane.

But to their surprise, Isabel crushed the letter in her hand. She was laughing no longer. She glanced ^quickly at them all; she looked exhausted. No—not just now, not just now, she ~~struggled~~ stammered.

And before they could recover she had run into the house through the hall up the stairs into her bedroom. Down she sat on the side of the bed. How vile—odious—abominable—vulgar! muttered Isabel. Whoever are we?[68] She pressed her eyes with her knuckles + rocked to + fro. And again she saw them—but not four, more like forty, laughing sneering jeering stretching out their hands while she read them Williams letter. Oh what a loathsome thing to have done![69] How could she have done it. God forbid my darling I should be a drag on your happiness. William.

Isabel ^hid ~~buried her head~~ ^pressed her face in the pillow. But she felt that even the ^cool ~~dark~~ ^grave bedroom—~~Even darkness—grave~~ knew her for what she was—a ~~xxx~~ shallow tinkling ~~creature~~—vain.[70]

Presently from the ~~lawn~~ garden ^below there came voices.

Isabel we'er ^all going to bathe. Do come.

---

[64] It seems that "Oh" has been written over "But"; the additional "But" is written in the margin. All of this is omitted in the published version.

[65] The published versions changes "before they interrupted her with their laughter" to "before their laughter interrupted her" (CW2, 337).

[66] The published version does not repeat "go on."

[67] The published version attributes this line to Dennis instead of Bill Hunt.

[68] This question is left out of the published version.

[69] The *Sphere* version retains the exclamation point, while the *Collected* has a period; both published versions change the period of the following sentence to an exclamation point.

[70] The published version deletes "cool."

"Come thou wife of William."
^{Call her once before you go} Call once yet.

Isabel sat up. Now was the moment. Now she must decide. Should[71] she go with them—or stay here + write to William. Which—**which should*** it be. I must make up my mind. Oh, but ~~xxx~~ ^{how could72} there be any question of course she would stay ^{here + write}.

Titania ~~commanded~~ ^{piped} Moyra

Isabel—came from Bill![73]

No it was too difficult.[74]

Ill—Ill go with them + write to William later—some other time. Later. Another time. Not now. But I shall certainly write ^{thought Isabel hurriedly}.

[MalaM-NB5-NL, 6 verso]

^{Coming she cried} ~~And~~ ^{And} Laughing in the ~~new~~ ^{new75} way Isabel ran down the stairs.[76]
"MARRIAGE À LA MODE"   194"MARRIAGE À LA MODE"   194

---

[71] The published version uses "would" in lieu of "should" in this instance.

[72] "How" is written over another word, and "could" is squeezed in alongside it.

[73] The speaker is omitted in the published version.

[74] This line is squeezed in between the lines before and after, suggesting it was added later.

[75] It looks as if Mansfield has stricken through "new" and rewritten "new" more neatly above it; likewise, she has retraced "Laughing" in a bolder hand.

[76] The published version omits "Coming she cried," and changes "Isabel" to "she." Under this final sentence, Mansfield has drawn a jagged line.

A Note on the Manuscript of "The Voyage"

"The Voyage," like "Marriage à la Mode," can be found in Mansfield's Notebook 5 (along with "A Married Man's Story" and some miscellaneous material) and was among the stories written for the *Sphere*. Additionally, as with "Marriage à la Mode," the story is complete and there are no other known drafts, suggesting it was completed more or less in its final form, though there are some heavy edits at various points in the manuscript. Of particular note are the revisions at the end of the story. The original ending appears on page twenty-five of the notebook, which is also the last page of the story manuscript; however, this whole page is marked through with a large "X," and it is reworked on the facing page (twenty-four verso). The prose of the revised version is much tighter, and the final scene takes place in the grandparents bedroom where Fenella sees her grandfather with the framed, *green* text of the aphorism about time above his bed. In the original ending, Fenella finds the *white* text of the aphorism in the sitting room, merely hearing her grandparents talk in the other room. It ends innocuously: "She was in Grandma's house! / Half an hour later she was in bed in grandmas house," which alludes to the stories original title, "Going to Stay with her Grandma." The revised ending and title are both much more effective.

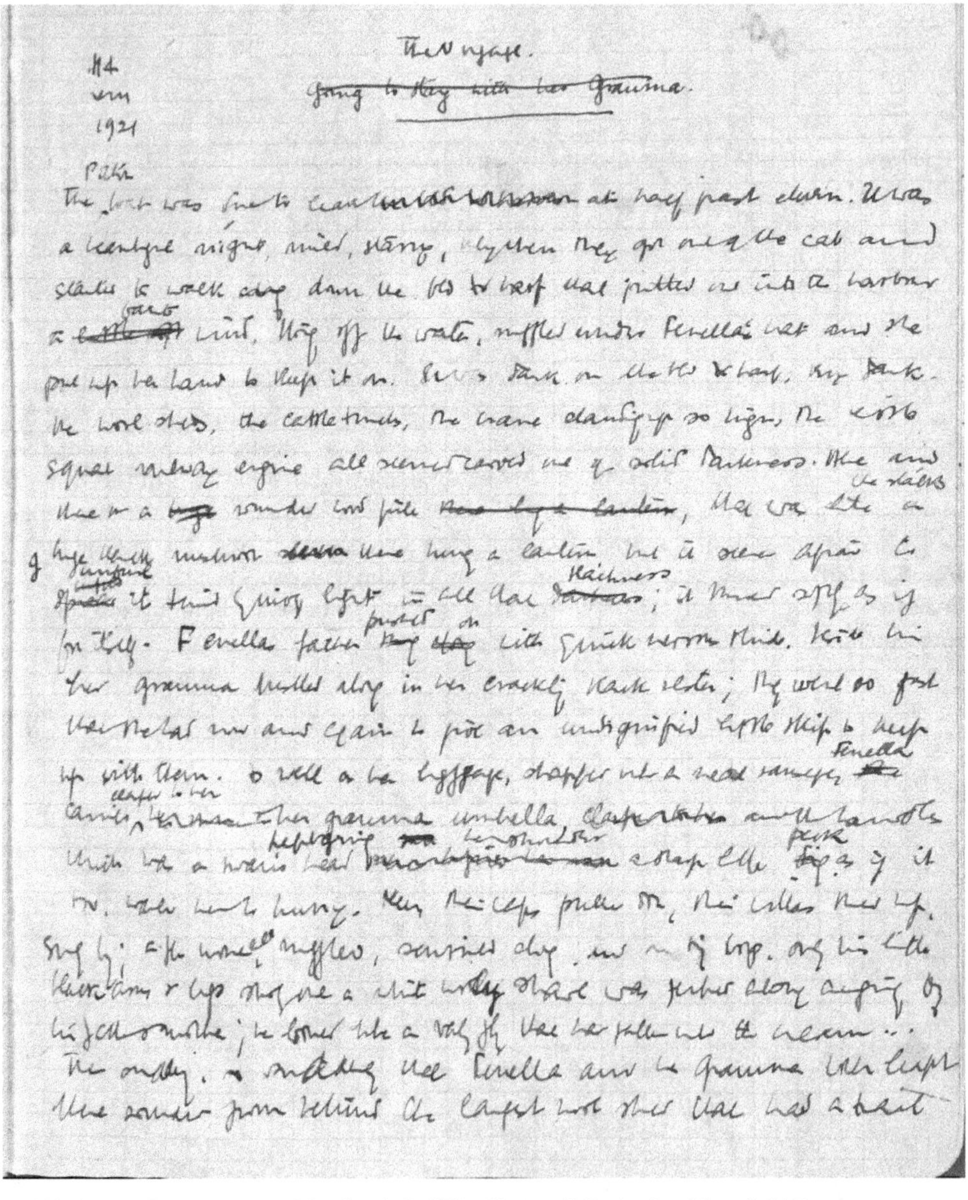

FIGURE 33: Page 14 recto, Notebook 5, "The Voyage," Katherine Mansfield Papers, Newberry Library (box 2, folder 4), 14–25. Image courtesy of the Newberry Library.

[Voy-NB5-NL, 14]

114[1]
viii
1921

The Voyage
~~Going to Stay with her Granma~~

The ^{Picton} boat was due to leave ~~the old harbour~~ at half past eleven. It was a beautiful night, mild, starry, only when they got out of the cab and started to walk ~~along~~ down[2] the old Wharf that jutted out into the harbour a ~~little soft~~ ^{faint} wind, blowing off the water, ruffled under Fenella's hat and she put up her hand to keep it on. It was dark on the old Wharf, very dark. The wool sheds, the cattle trucks, the crane standing up so high, the little squat railway engine all seemed carved out of solid darkness. Here and there on a ~~large~~ rounded wood pile ~~there lay a lantern,~~ that was like a ^{the stalk} of [sic] huge black mushroom[3] ~~stalk~~ there hung a lantern but it seemed afraid to ~~spread~~ ^{unfold unfurl} its timid quivering light in all that ~~darkness~~ ^{blackness}; it burned softly as if for itself. Fenellas father ~~swung along~~ ^{pushed on} with quick nervous strides, beside him her granma bustled along in her crackling black ulster; they went so fast that she had now and again to give an undignified little skip to keep up with them. As well as her luggage, strapped into a neat sausage ~~she~~ ^{Fenella} carried ^{clasped to her} ~~her xxx~~ her granmas umbrella ~~clasped to her~~ and the handle which was a swan's head ~~xxx to give her xxx~~ ^{gave kept giving her shoulder} a sharp little ~~dig~~ ^{peck} as if it too, wanted her to hurry.[4] Men, their caps pulled down, their collars turned up, swung by; a few women ^{all} muffled, scurried along, and one tiny boy, only his little black arms + legs showing over a white wooly shawl was jerked along angrily **between*** his father + mother;[5] he looked like a baby fly that had fallen into the cream . . .

Then suddenly, so suddenly that Fenella and her granma **both*** leapt there sounded from behind the largest wool shed that had a trail

[Voy-NB5-NL, page 15]

of smoke hanging over it Mia-oo-oo-oo-oo![6]

First whistle said her father—~~an~~ briefly **and at*** that moment they came in sight of the ~~ships~~ Picton boat. Lying ~~along~~ ^{beside} the dark wharf all strung all beaded with round golden lights the Picton boat looked as if ~~it~~ ^{she} was ^{more} ready to sail among stars than out into the cold sea. ~~Her granma The~~ people pressed along the gangway. First went her grandma,[7] then her father, then Fenella. There was a high step down on to the deck + a ~~kind faced~~

---

[1] A few pages before this story was begun, Mansfield indicates she completed "Marriage à la Mode" on "XI, viii, 1921," suggesting this is probably "14" August.

[2] In this instance, the correction must have been made immediately as "down" follows on the same line rather than above the omitted word.

[3] The sentence should read "like the stalk of a huge black mushroom"; however, I have recorded the changes as they appear on the manuscript.

[4] Most of the edits here are in a darker ink.

[5] Instead of "showing over," the published version reads: "arms and legs showing out of a white wooly shawl" (CW2, 373).

[6] On the opposing page, Mansfield seems to be toying with the sound of the whistle. At the top left she writes in ink "o-o!" and then several spaces below: "Mia-oo-oo-OO!" The latter is the option which appears in the published version.

[7] This is the first instance where Mansfield uses "grandma" in lieu of "granma," though the published version uses "grandma" throughout.

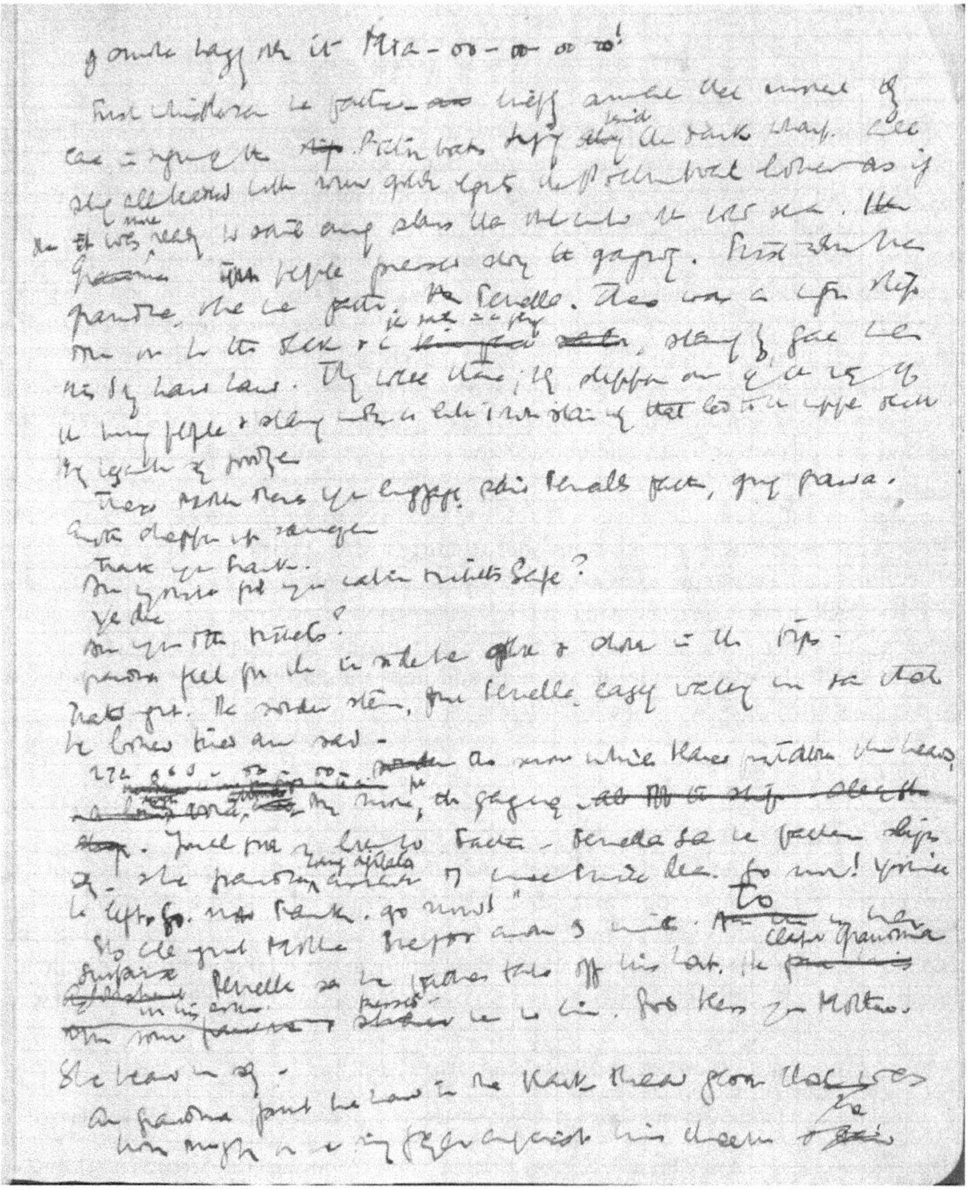

FIGURE 34: Page 15 recto, Notebook 5, "The Voyage," Katherine Mansfield Papers, Newberry Library (box 2, folder 4), 14–25. Image courtesy of the Newberry Library.

~~sailor~~ ^{old sailor in a jersey}, standing by gave her his dry hard hand. They were there; they stepped out of the way of the hurrying people + standing under a little iron stairway that led to the upper deck they began to say goodbye.

There Mother theres your luggage said Fenellas father, giving grandma another strapped up sausage.

Thank you Frank.

And you've got your cabin tickets safe?

Yes dear

And your other tickets?

Grandma felt for it inside her glove and showed him the tips.

Thats right. He sounded stern, but Fenella, **eagerly watching*** him saw that he looked tired and sad—

Mia-ooo-oo-oo- ~~sounded~~ the second whistle blared just above their heads, ~~+ a loud~~ ^{high} ~~voice~~ ^{xxx xxx he were from high in the air} ~~cried~~ ^{xxx} Any more, ^{for} the gangway—~~all over the ship—all of the xxx~~.[8] Youll give my love to Father—Fenella saw her fathers lips say—+ her grandma ^{very agitated} answered "of course I will dear. Go now! You'll be left. Go now Frank, go now!"[9]

Its all **right*** Mother Ive got another 3 minutes. ~~And then~~ ^{To} her ~~astonishment~~ ^{surprise} Fenella saw her father take off his hat. He ~~put his arms round grandma + xxx~~^{clasped grandma in his arms + pressed} her to him. God bless you Mother—she heard him say—

And grandma put her hand in the black thread glove[10] that was worn through on her ring finger against his cheek ~~+ said~~ ^{her}

[Voy-NB5-NL, 16]

~~voice shook~~ ^{and sobbed}. God bless you my ^{own} brave son![11]

This was so awful that Fenella quickly turned her back on them, swallowed, once, twice, + frowned terribly at a little green star on a masthead. But she had to turn around again; her father was going—goodbye Fenella. Be a good girl, his cold, wet mustache **brushed*** her cheek. But Fenella caught hold of the lapels of his coat. "How long am I going to stay." ~~Her f~~ she whispered anxiously—But he wouldn't ~~meet her eyes~~ ^{look at her}.[12] He* shook her off gently ~~saying~~ ^{+ gently said}: We'll see about that. ~~And~~ ^{here! Wheres your hand} he pressed something into her ~~hand~~ ^{palm}—heres a shilling—in case you should need it.

A ~~whole~~ shilling! She must be going away for ever. Father! cried Fenella. But he was gone. He was the last off the ship. The sailors put their shoulders to the gangway—~~Fenella ran to the rail~~. A huge coil of dark rope went flying through the air + fell "thump" on the wharf.[13] A bell rang; a whistle shrilled. ~~Some one called~~ silently the dark wharf began to slip to slide to edge away from them—Now there was a rush of water between.[14] Fenella

---

[8] Aligned with this paragraph on the opposite page, Mansfield has written, "and a voice like a cry shouted," which follows "The second whistle blared just above their heads" in the published version.

[9] The edits here and following are in a darker ink.

[10] The published version revises this slightly, changing "in the black thread glove" to "with the black thread glove."

[11] Following this line, "Leslie Heron Beauchamp" is written neatly, most likely by Mansfield. Leslie was killed during the First World War in 1915, and his presence in her thoughts is evident in several stories from this time period, especially "The Fly" and "Six Years After."

[12] The published version omits "But" at the beginning of this clause.

[13] On the opposing page, Mansfield has written "thump"—incorporated into this sentence—suggesting that she was toying with the word choice.

[14] Mansfield has circled the last bit of the word, perhaps drawing attention to the period, which is otherwise indistinguishable.

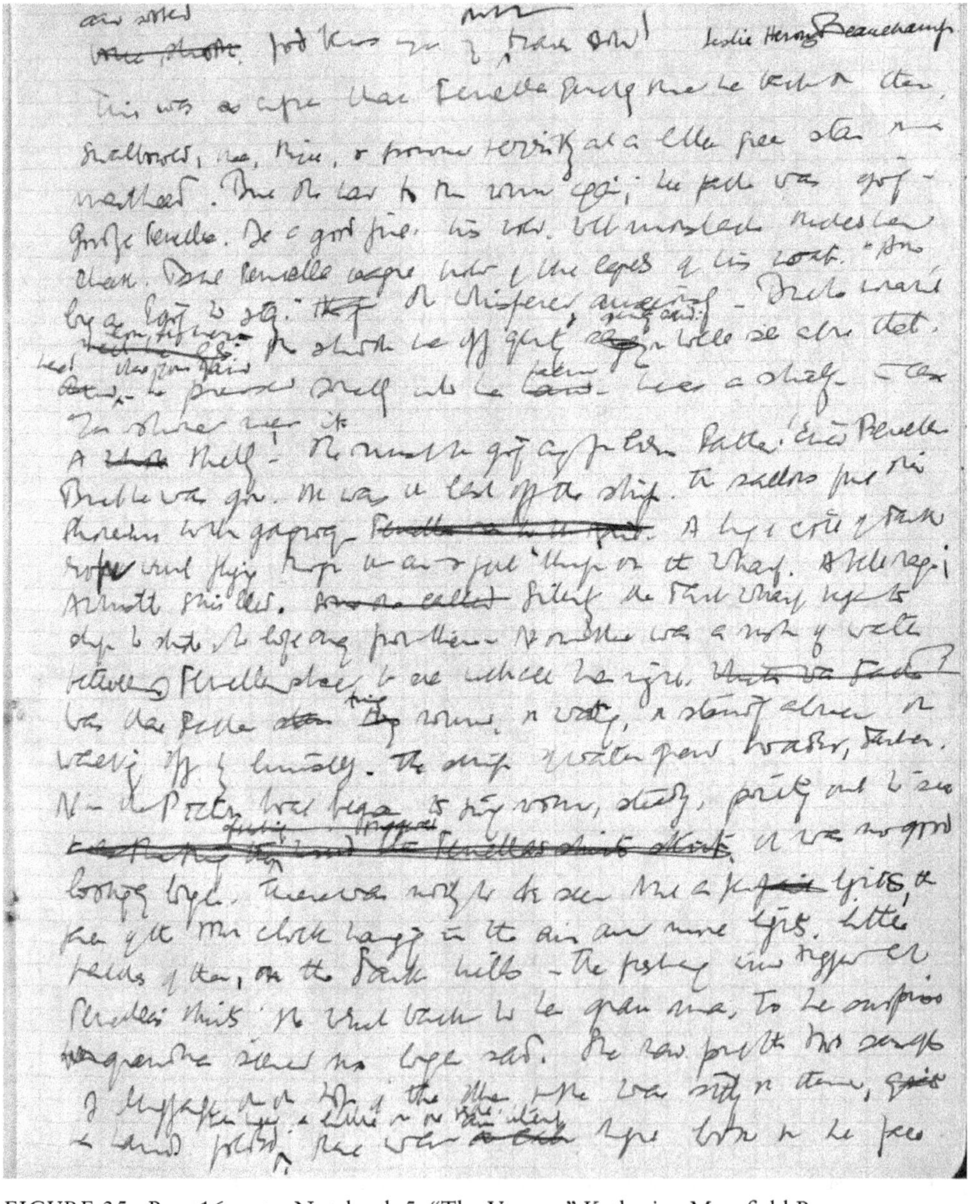

FIGURE 35: Page 16 recto, Notebook 5, "The Voyage," Katherine Mansfield Papers, Newberry Library (box 2, folder 4), 14–25. Image courtesy of the Newberry Library.

strained* to see with all her might, ~~which was father~~ was that Father ~~stan xxx~~ ^turning*^ round, or waving, or standing alone or walking off by himself. The strip of water grew broader, darker. Now the Picton boat began to swing round, steady,[15] pointing out to sea ~~xxx xxx xxx the~~ ^freshening*^ **wind** ^tugged^ ~~at Fenellas shirt skirt~~. It was no good looking longer. There was nothing to be seen but a few ~~faint~~ lights, the face of the town clock hanging in the air and more lights, little patches of them, on the dark hills—the freshening wind tugged at Fenella's skirts; she went back to her granma, to her surprise ~~her~~ grandma seemed no longer sad. She had put the two sausages of luggage one on top of the other + she was sitting on them, ~~quiet~~ her hands folded, ^her head a little on one side.^ There was ~~a calm~~ ^an intent^ bright look on her face.

[Voy-NB5-NL, 17][16]

Then[17] Fenella saw that her lips were moving + guessed that ~~Granma~~ she was praying. But the ~~granma~~ ^old woman^ gave her a light[18] nod as if to say the prayer was nearly over—she **unclasped*** her hands, ^sighed^ clasped them again + bent forward ~~a xxx~~ + ~~then~~ ^at last^ gave herself a ~~little~~ ^soft^ shake.

And now* child; she said, ~~xxx her~~ ^fingering^ the bow of her bonnet strings—I think we ought to see about our cabin—keep close to me + mind you dont slip. ^"Yes granma!"^ And be careful the umbrellas arent caught in the stair rail. I saw a beautiful umbrella broken in half like that on my way over. Yes grandma. Dark figures of men **lounged against*** the rails. In the glow of their pipes a nose shone out, or a ~~peaked~~ cap peak or a pair of ~~bushy~~ ^surprised looking^ eyebrows[19]—Fenella glanced up. High ~~up~~ in the air a ~~dark~~ ^little^ figure, his hands thrust in his short jacket pockets stood staring out to sea.[20] The ship rocked—ever so little—+ she thought the stars rocked, too. And[21] now a pale steward in a linen coat ~~stept~~ holding a tray high in the palm of his hand stepped out of a lighted doorway + skimmed past them—They went through that doorway. Carefully over the high brass **bound*** step, ~~into~~ on to the rubber mat—+ then down such a terribly steep flight of stairs that ~~the~~ grandma ~~p xxx~~ ^had to put^ both feet on each step + Fenella **clutched*** the **clammy*** brass rail + forgot all about the swan necked umbrella. At the bottom ~~the old woman~~ granma stopped + Fenella was rather afraid she was going to pray again. But no! It was only to get out the cabin tickets. They were in the salon.[22] ~~It was xxx in the glare of two hanging lamps. Two more pale stewards were laying the tables in the glare from a hanging lamp.~~ It was glaring bright + stifling ~~the air~~[23] smelled of paint—+ **burnt*** chop bones

---

[15] The *Sphere* version of the story reads, "began to swing round steadily," while the *Collected* reverts back to the initial word form, "steady"; however, the *Collected* does not include the comma before "steady," which does affect the usage.

[16] As on the previous page, at the top of this page Mansfield has neatly written the name of her cousin, Mary Beauchamp, more familiarly known as Elizabeth von Arnim. Mansfield reconnected with her cousin in Switzerland between May 1921 until the beginning of 1922, during which she was writing the stories in Notebook 5, of which "The Voyage" was one.

[17] Mansfield retraces "then."

[18] This is "bright" in the published version.

[19] "Or a cap peak" becomes "or the peak of a cap" in the published version.

[20] Mansfield has circled the period.

[21] "And" is written in bolder ink, over a lighter, illegible word.

[22] The published version has "saloon" instead of "salon." According to the *Oxford English Dictionary*, saloon was derived from salon, and in English they have often been used interchangeably.

[23] There is a small check mark above "air," suggesting Mansfield decided to retain "the air," which is the case in the published version.

[Voy-NB5-NL, 18]

+ india rubber. Fenella wished her granma would go on. But the old woman was not to be hurried. An immense basket of ham sandwiches caught her eye. She went up to them + touched the top one delicately with ~~her~~ ^{her} finger.

How much are the sandwiches she asked.

Tuppence, bawled a rude steward slamming down a knife + fork. Granma could hardly believe it.

Tuppence each! she asked.

Thats right, said the steward + he winked at his companion. ~~The old woman~~ ^{Granma} made a ^{small} astonished face. Then she ~~said~~ ^{whispered} **primly*** to Fenella what wickedness! + they ~~went~~ ^{sailed} out at the further door and along a little passage ~~with~~ ^{that had} cabins on either side.²⁴ Such a very nice stewardess came to meet them + showed them theirs. She was dressed all in blue + her collar + cuffs were fastened with large brass buttons. She seemed to know grandma well. Well Mrs Crane said she ^{unlocking the wash stand}. Weve got you back again. Its not often you give yourself a cabin.

No said grandma. But this time my dear sons thoughtfulness . . .

I hope began the stewardess. Then she **turned round*** + took a long ~~to~~ mournful [*sic*] at grandmas blackness + ^{at} Fenella's black coat and skirt, black blouse + hat with a crepe rose.

Granma nodded. It was Gods will, ~~she~~ said she.

~~And the~~ stewardess ~~taking a deep breath, shut her lips xxx~~ shut her lips + taking a deep breath she seemed to expand.²⁵ What I always say is she said, as though it was her own discovery—sooner or later each of us **has*** to go. And that's a ~~certering~~ ^{certingty}.²⁶ She paused. Now can I bring you anything,

[Voy-NB5-NL, 19]

Mrs Crane. A cup of tea? I know its no good offering you a **little something*** to keep the cold out.

Granma shook her head. Nothing thank you ~~steweardess~~. Weve got **a few*** wine biscuits + Fenella has a ^{very nice} banana.

Then Ill give you a look later on said the stewardess + she went out shutting the door.

What a very small cabin it was! It was like being shut up in a box with granma. The dark round eye above the washstand ~~glared~~ ^{gleamed} at them dully. Fenella felt shy, she stood against the door still clasping her luggage + the umbrella. ~~watching~~ Were they going to get undressed in here. Already her granma had taken off her bonnet + rolling up ~~each~~ ^{the} strings fixed each with a pin to the lining before she hung the bonnet up.²⁷ Her white hair shone like silk; the little bun at the back was covered with a black net. Fenella hardly ever saw her grandma with her head uncovered; she looked strange. I shall put on the woollen fascinator your dear mother crocheted for me, said ~~she~~ ^{grandma} + unstrapping her "sausage" she took it out ~~put~~ + **wound*** it round her head; the fringe of grey bobbles danced at her eyebrows as she smiled tenderly + mournfully at Fenella.

---

²⁴ The published version omits the adjective "little" before "passage."
²⁵ The ink of this line has bled much more than the rest of the page.
²⁶ Mansfield seems to be experimenting with how best to portray the accent here.
²⁷ The published version clarifies the subject of "fixed," reading "she fixed each pin [. . .]."

Then she undid her bodice + something under that + something else underneath that ^after^—then there seemed a short sharp tussle[28] + grandma flushed **faintly***. Snip snap. She had undone her stays. She breathed a sigh of relief + sitting on the ~~velvet~~ plush couch she slowly + carefully pulled off her elastic sided boots + stood them side by side.

By the time Fenella had taken off her coat and skirt

[Voy-NB5-NL, 20]

+ put on her flannel dressing gown grandma was ^quite^ ready.

Must I take off my boots grandma. Theyre <u>lace</u>.

Grandma gave them a moments deep consideration. Youd feel a great deal more comfortable if you did, child, said she. ^She kissed Fenella.^ ~~And~~ dont forget to say your prayers. ~~The Lord is with us even more at sea~~ ^when we are at sea^ ~~than he is on~~ ^than when we are on^ dry land.[29] And because Im an experienced traveller said grandma ~~cheerfully~~ ^briskly^ Ill shall [sic] take the upper berth.

But grandma however will you get up there. Three little spider like steps were all Fenella saw. The old woman gave a small silent laugh before ~~she mounted~~ ^she mounted^ the ~~them~~ them quickly[30]—~~+~~ ^she^ +[31] peered over the high bunk at the astonished Fenella.

You didn't think your granma could do that! did you said she—as she sank back Fenella heard her light laugh again. . . The ~~small~~ hard square of **brown*** soap would not lather + the water in the water bottle[32] was like a kind of blue jelly. ~~xxx~~ How hard it was, too, to turn down those stiff sheets. You simply had to tear your way in. If everything had been different Fenella might have got the giggles. At least she was inside, ~~and all was still excepting from up~~ + while she lay there **panting*** there sounded from above, a long soft whispering—as though someone was gently gently **rustling*** among tissue paper to find something . . . it was grandma saying her prayers.

A long time passed then ~~the door~~ the stewardess came in; she trod softly ~~to~~ + leaned her hand on grandma's bunk.[33]

We're just entering the straits she said.

Oh!

"It's a fine night. But were rather empty. We may pitch a little."

[Voy-NB5-NL, 21]

And indeed at that moment the Picton boat the picton boat [sic] rose + rose + hung in the air just long enough to give a shiver before she swung down again + there was the sound of heavy water slapping against her sides.

Fenella remembered she had left that swan necked umbrella standing up on the little couch—If it fell over would it break?

But granma remembered too, at the same time.

---

[28] The opposing page has "~~And~~ a sharp tussle" written and underlined two thirds down the page, almost even with this passage.

[29] On the opposing page, even with this passage and in a neater hand, Mansfield has written: "Our dear Lord is with us when we are at sea even more than when we are on ^dry^ land." This is how it appears in the published version.

[30] "Nimbly" is substituted for "quickly" in the published version.

[31] The final "+" is written in the margin. The published version includes "and she," which was initially rejected here.

[32] The published version replaces "water bottle" with "bottle."

[33] There is a large "X" beside the next two lines; however, there are no changes in the published version.

I wonder if youd mind stewardess laying down my umbrella she whispered.

Not at all Mrs Crane. + the stewardess coming back to grandma breathed: your little grandaughters in such a beautiful sleep.

God be praised for that! said granma.

Poor little Motherless mite! said the stewardess + granma was still **telling*** the stewardess all about what happened when Fenella fell asleep. But she hadn't been asleep long enough to dream even before she woke up again—to see something waving in the air above her head. What was it? What could it be? It was a ~~little~~ small grey foot.[34] Now another joined it. They seemed to be feeling about for something. There came a sigh.

Im awake grandma said Fenella.

Oh dear, am I near the ladder? said grandma.[35] I thought it was this end.

No grandma it's the other. Ill put your foot on it. Are we there? asked Fenella.

In the harbour, said grandma. We must get up. Child

[Voy-NB5-NL, 22]

You better have a biscuit to steady yourself before you move. But Fenella had hopped out of her bunk. The ~~light~~ lamp was still **burning***; ~~it was still night but~~ ~~but~~ the night was over and it was cold.[36] **Peering*** through that round eye she could see far off some rocks. Now they were scattered over with foam. Now a gull flipped by—+ now there came a long piece of real land –

Its land grandma said Fenella wonderingly as though they had been to sea for weeks together. She hugged herself. She stood on one leg + rubbed it with the toes of the other foot. She was trembling. Oh it had all been so sad lately. Was it going to change? But all her grandma said was: Make haste child. I should leave your nice banana for the stewardess as you haven't eaten it. + Fenella put on her her [sic] black clothes again + a button sprang off one of her gloves to where she couldn't reach it.[37] They went up on deck ~~together.~~

But if it had been cold in the cabin on deck it was like ice. The sun was not up yet and[38] the ~~sky~~ stars were dim ~~in the pale quenched looking sky~~—+ the cold pale ~~sky~~ sky was the same colour as the cold pale sea. On the land a white mist rose + fell. Now they could see quite plainly dark bush—Even the shapes of the umbrella ferns ~~they could see~~ showed—+ those strange silvery withered trees that are like skeletons. Now they could see the landing stage + some

[Voy-NB5-NL, 23]

little houses, pale too, clustered together, like shells on the lid of a box. The other passengers tramped up + down, but more slowly than they had the night before + they looked gloomy.

And now the landing stage came to meet them.[39] Slowly it **swam*** towards the Picton boat, + a **tiny** man **holding*** a coil of rope + a cart with a small drooping horse and another man sitting on the step came too.

---

[34] "Little grey" is written above foot; "small" is written in the margin with an arrow indicating it should replace "little."
[35] "Said" becomes "asked" in the published version.
[36] The published version retains the "but" in "~~but~~ night was over."
[37] The published version adds "and rolled," making it: "[. . .] and a button sprang off one of her gloves and rolled to where she couldn't reach it" (CW2, 378).
[38] "And" becomes "but" in the published version.
[39] The published version reads, "[. . .] came out to meet them" (CW2, 378).

Its Mr **Penreddy***—Fenella come for us—said granma. She sounded ~~very~~ pleased. Her white "waxen cheeks" were blue with cold, her chin trembled + she had to keep wiping her eyes + her little pink nose.[40]

Youve got my—

Yes grandma—Fenella showed it to her.

The rope came flying through the air + smack it fell on to the deck. The gangway was lowered. Again Fenella followed her grandma—on to the wharf over to the ~~little~~ cart,[41] and a moment later they were bowling away—~~the little horses hooves~~ the hooves of the little horse **drummed*** over the wooden piles then sank soft into the sandy road. Not a soul was to be seen—there was not even a feather of smoke. The mist rose + fell + sea [sic] ~~seemed to grate in the sounded~~ still sounded asleep as slowly it ~~fell up the~~ turned on the beach.[42] Their breath was white on the air.[43]

[Voy-NB5-NL, 24]

tiddy[44]

I seen Mr Crane yestiddy said Mr Penreddy. He looked himself, then. Misses ~~sent him over~~ knocked him up a batch of scones last week.

And now the little horse pulled up ~~stopped~~ before one of the shell like houses. They got down. Fenella put her hand on the ~~xxx~~ gate the big trembling dew drops ~~it wet~~ soaked trough her glove tips—~~her grandma it felt~~ her gran went through. + up a little path of round white pebbles they went with drenched sleeping flowers on either side. Grandmas ~~The~~ delicate white picotees were so heavy with dew ~~smelled so sweet~~ that they were ~~were~~ fallen over but their sweet smell ~~rose seemed all part~~ was part of the cold morning.[45] The blinds were down in the little house. They ~~went up~~ mounted the steps—to the verandah. A pair of bluchers ~~were~~ was on one side of the door + a large red watering cane[46] [sic] on the other.[47]

Tut! Tut! Your grand~~father~~pa[48] said grandma, she turned the handle. ~~They entered~~. Not a sound—She called "Walter!" And immediately an ~~old~~ deep voice—that sounded half stifled called back—Is that you Mary?

"Wait, dear," said grandma—go in there.

~~Fenella~~ She pushed Fenella gently into a small dusky sitting room. ~~It The blinds were down but the sun must have just that moment risen—It showed shown through the cracks—on to the table—on to the walls.~~

~~And~~ On on [sic] the table, a large white[49]

---

[40] "Nose" is written directly under "pink," though it is at the end of the line.

[41] "Little" is retained in the published version.

[42] "Turned on the" is written on the line below, but based on the published version, it was intended to be inserted here.

[43] The published version does not reproduce this last sentence.

[44] This is centered at the top of the page, probably a trial for "yestiddy" just below.

[45] The published version changes "fallen over" to "fallen."

[46] This should obviously be "can," as in the published version, but there is a definite "e" at the end.

[47] On the opposing page, Mansfield as jotted "-were," "-was" as if trying to determine which verb form to use after "pair of bluchers." Below this she has also written "picotées."

[48] "Pa" is superimposed over "father."

[49] The published version omits the adjective "large."

[Voy-NB5-NL, 25][50]

cat that had been folded up ~~camelwise in sleep rose~~ like a camel, rose, + stretched, + **yawned***, + stood on ~~its toes~~ the tips of its toes.

    ~~Fenella went over to the cat~~ table ~~The cat stepped~~ It stepped daintily towards her **purring +
blinking**—She ~~put~~ buried* her cold little hand in the white warm fur—~~she~~ She smiled timidly as she
stroked + ~~stroked—while she~~ and listened to grandmas voice + then to the deep rolling
tones of granpa—~~And now the sun a beam of sun fell~~ on the wall + ~~lighted up~~ there was a big
white text in a heavy black frame + Fenella read
    Lost one **silent** gold Hour
    Set with sixty Diamond Minutes
    No reward is offered
    For it is gone for ever—

~~She was in Grandma's house!~~[51]

    ~~Half an hour later she was in bed in grandmas house.~~

~~The blind tapped~~—A far away rooster **called**. The cat sprang off the table. On the wall There
was a big white text in a large black frame Fenella read.
    ~~And she put down the large sausage + the swan necked umbrella. She was in grandma's
house.~~
    Then the door opened + ~~grandma~~[52] came in. She had **got in** her **cap** xxx welcome dear
Fenella she said to your grandmas house!

[Voy-NB5-NL, 24 verso]

cat that had been folded up like a camel rose, stretched itself, yawned, + then sprang on
to the tips of its toes—
    ~~She placing~~ed her Fenella buried* one cold little hand into the white warm fur + smiled timidly
while she stroked—and listened to grandmas gentle voice + the rolling tones of grandpa.
    A door creaked. Come in dear. The old woman beckoned. Fenella followed—+ there
lying to one side of ~~in~~ an immense bed, lay grandpa. Just his head with a white tuft + his rosy face
+ long silver beard showed over the quilt. He was like ~~an ancient~~ very old wide awake bird.
    Well my girl said grandpa. Give us a kiss. Fenella kissed him. Ugh! said grandpa. ~~And he
looked at grandma reprovingly She's frozen said he. Your frozen. Your~~ her little nose is as
cold as a button. Whats that shes holding. Her grandmas umbrella. Fenella smiled again
+ ~~put~~ crooked the swan neck on to the bed rail.[53]
    Above the bed there was a ~~huge~~ big text **green** in a deep black frame.[54]

---

[50] Besides the occasional omission on this page, there are large slash marks in various directions indicating that
the full page should be omitted. One of the lines is an arrow, slanting downward from right to left toward the
opposing page, where Mansfield has revised this section.
[51] The exclamation mark is large and bold.
[52] A check mark is written above "grandma" suggesting the omission is to be retained.
[53] "On to the bed rail" becomes "over the bed-rail" in the published version.
[54] The published version omits "green."

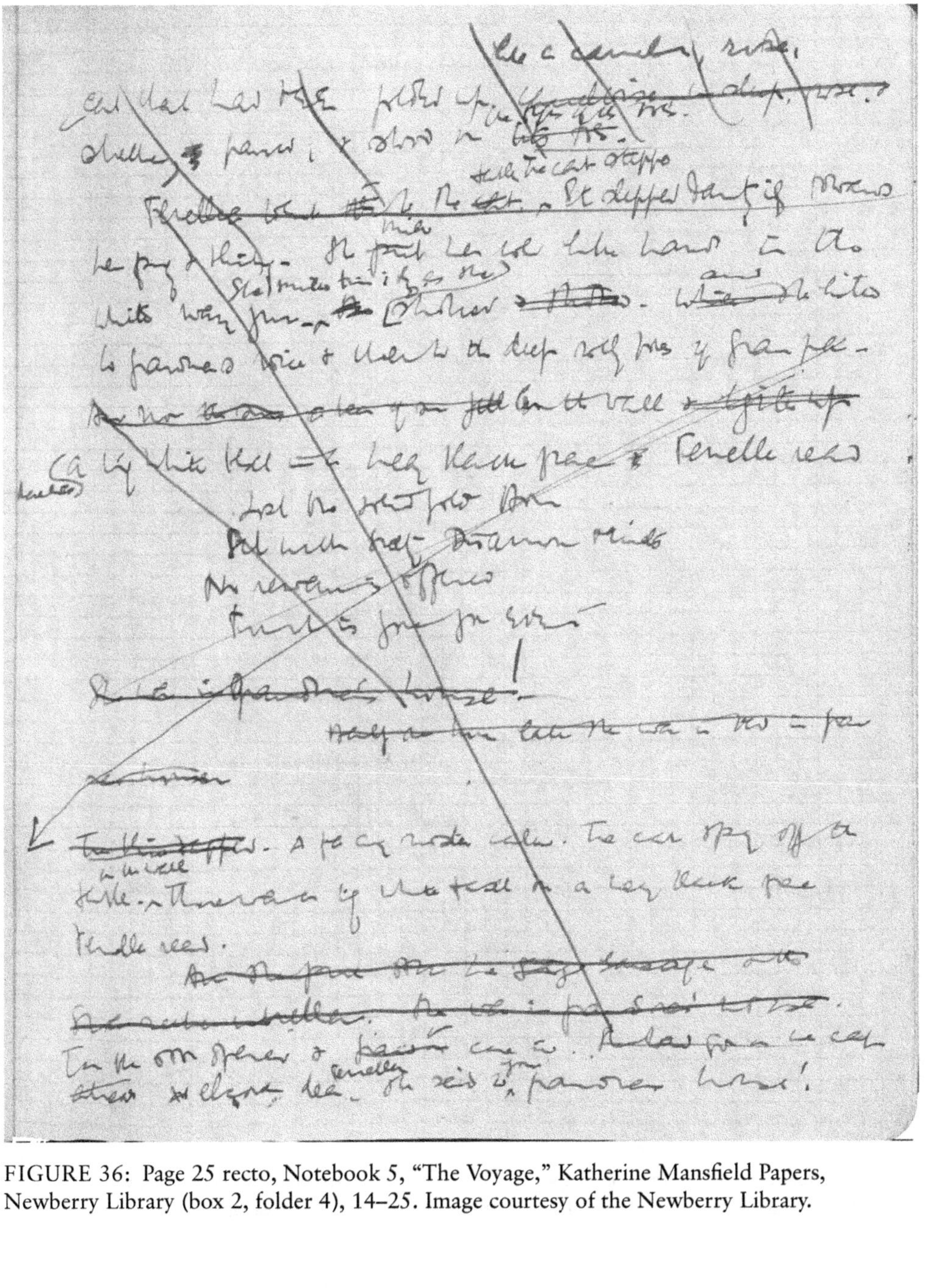

FIGURE 36: Page 25 recto, Notebook 5, "The Voyage," Katherine Mansfield Papers, Newberry Library (box 2, folder 4), 14–25. Image courtesy of the Newberry Library.

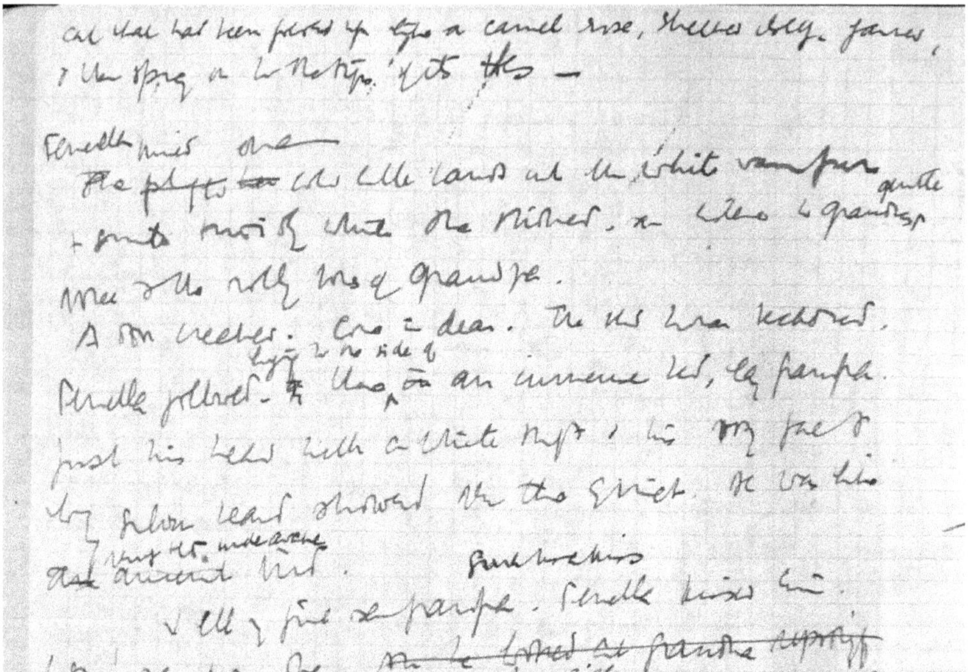

FIGURE 37: Page 24 verso, Notebook 5, "The Voyage," Katherine Mansfield Papers, Newberry Library (box 2, folder 4), 14–25. Image courtesy of the Newberry Library.

> Lost one golden hour
> Set with sixty Diamond Minutes
> NO Reward is offered
> For it is ~~Gone for Ever~~^{GONE FOR EVER}. [55]

Yer Granma painted that said Grandpa + he riffled his white tuft + looked at Fenella so merrily she almost thought he winked at her!

---

[55] "GONE FOR EVER" is boldly superimposed onto what originally seemed to be "Gone for Ever." The version in *The Sphere* only capitalizes the first letter of each word (341) while the *Collected* has it in all caps (CW2, 379).

A Note on the Manuscripts of "Six Years After"

The manuscripts of "Six Years After," which was not published in Mansfield's lifetime, are perhaps the most interesting of all those collected in this volume. For, besides the two almost complete drafts, Mansfield mentions the story twice in Notebook 41, in which one of the drafts is written. These references are part of two different instances where Mansfield has compiled a list of works to include in a new collection of stories. The lists are not identical, but both contain "Six Years After," and both include a brief synopsis of each of the pieces planned for the collection. In the first synopsis, "Six Years After" is described as "The wife and husband in the steamer. The cold buttons" while the second reads, "A wife and husband on board a steamer. They see someone who reminds them."[1] The only reference to "cold buttons" is in the earliest manuscript, the one in Notebook 41. It refers to a memory the mother has of greeting her son after the war and "pressing her head against the cold buttons of his British warm,"[2] a memory omitted in the next draft. Neither story references an individual who reminds them of their son, unless it might be the "delicate looking" steward.

According to the *Collected*, the draft from which John Middleton Murry drew for his posthumous publication of "Six Years After" in *The New Republic* does not survive;[3] however, I believe the draft found in the Newberry Library is the one Murry refers to. The confusion likely arises as B. J. Kirkpatrick, in *A Bibliography of Katherine Mansfield*, incorrectly labels this manuscript "Untitled Story (beginning: Twenty-eight years and it was still an effort) because the manuscript is not titled and the opening paragraphs of the story are missing.[4] It doesn't appear that a page has been removed from the front of the notebook in which the Newberry manuscript is written, suggesting Mansfield may have begun copying a clean draft from Notebook 41 on loose-leaf of paper and then moved to this thin class book. Potentially confirming this, the third page of the notebook is actually labeled as page four and the next as page five. There are significant variations between the two versions.

---

[1] Notebook 2, 297.
[2] See SYA-NB41-ATL, 7, below.
[3] CW2, 425, note.
[4] B. J. Kirkpatrick, *A Bibliography of Katherine Mansfield* (Oxford: Clarendon Press, 1989), 327.

∴ that quick pressure meant, his being said to her being you do understand don't you—+ there was an **answering tremor*** of her fingers I <u>understand</u>.

Six years after.[5]

It was not the afternoon to be on deck, on the contrary. It was exactly the afternoon when there is no snugger place than a warm cabin, a warm bunk. Tucked up with a rug ~~and~~ a hot water bottle, a piping hot cup of tea. She would not have minded the weather in the least. But he—hated cabins, hated to be inside any~~way~~^{where} more than was absolutely necessary. He had a passion for keeping as he called it above board ^{especially} when he was travelling. And it wasn't surprising considering the enormous amount of time he spent cooped up in the office.

So, when he rushed away from her as soon as they got on board and came back five minutes later, to say hed secured two deck chairs on the lee side and the deck steward was undoing their rugs her voice through the high sealskin collar murmured "good," and because he was looking at her she smiled with bright eyes + blinked quickly as if to say "yes perfectly allright [*sic*]—absolutely. ^{and she meant it too} .[6]

Then we'd better said he + he tucked her hand inside his arm and began to rush her off to where their chairs stood. But she just had time to ~~murmur~~ ^{breathe} "not so fast, Daddy please! when he remembered too, and slowed down.

---

[6] The addition is begun in the right margin and continues—squeezed in—in the left margin, so this was evidently added after the main text was already written.

Strange! They had been married 28 years and it still was an effort to him each time to ~~remember that~~ to adapt his pace to hers.

Not cold are you, he asked—glaring sideways at her. Her little nose, geranium pink above the dark fur was answer enough. But she thrust her free hand into the velvet pocket of her jacket + ~~answered only~~ ^{murmured gaily}, I shall be glad of my rug.

He pressed her tighter to his side—a quick, nervous pressure. He knew, of course that she ought to be down in the cabin; he knew that it was no afternoon for her to be sitting on deck in this cold and raw mist, lee side or no lee side, rugs or no rugs, and he realised how she must be hating it. But he had come to believe—that it really was easier for her to make these sacrifices than it was for him—Take their present case for instance. If he had gone down to the cabin with her he would have been miserable the whole time + he couldn't have helped showing it—at any rate she would have found ^{him out} it [sic]—Whereas having made up her mind to fall in with his idea he would have betted anybody she would even go so far as to enjoy the experience. Not because she was without personality of her own—Good Lord! She was absolutely brimming with it[7]—But because—— but here his thoughts always stopped. Here they always felt the need of a cigar as it were, + looking at the cigar tip, his fine blue eyes narrowed: it was a law of marriage, he supposed . . . All the same he always felt guilty when he asked these sacrifices of her. That was what ∴ .[8]

Certainly the steward—good little chap—had done all in his power to make them comfortable. He had put up the chairs in whatever

[SYA-NB41-ATL, 5]

warmth there was **and out*** of the smell. She did hope he would be tipped adequately. It was on occasions like this (and her life seemed full of such occasions) that she wished it was the woman who controlled the purse.[9]

"Thank you steward. That will do beautifully."

Why are stewards so often delicate looking thought she,[10] as ~~he tucked~~ her feet were tucked under. This poor little chap xxx looks as though hes got a ~~xxx~~ ^{chest*} and yet she would have thought—the sea air!

The button of the pigskin purse was undone. ~~In t~~The tray ~~there were xxx~~ ^{was tilted*}. ^{She saw} six pences, shillings, + half crowns.

I should give him five shillings she ~~thought~~ ^{decided} + tell him to buy himself a ~~xxx~~ good nourishing.

---

7 The clean draft in Notebook 3 omits "absolutely"; however, the published version retains it.

8 This signals that the sentence is picked up at the top of the page, where there is a like symbol, which is how it appears in both Notebook 3 and the published version.

9 Notebook 3 reads "the woman who held the purse" instead of "controlled the purse"; however, the published version reverts to "controlled."

10 "Thought she" becomes "she wondered" in Notebook 3 and the published version.

[SYA-NB3-NL, 1]

twenty-eight years and it still was an effort to him each time to adapt his pace to hers.

"Not cold—are you?" He asked, glancing sideways at her.

Her little nose, geranium pink above the dark fur was answer enough. But she thrust her free hand into the velvet pocket of her jacket and murmured gaily "I shall be glad of my rug."

He pressed her tighter to his side, a quick, nervous pressure. He knew, of course, that she ought to be down in the cabin; he knew that it was no afternoon for her to be sitting on deck in this cold and raw mist, lee side or no lee side, rugs or no rugs, and he realised how she must be hating it. But he had come to believe it really was easier for her to make these sacrifices than it was for him.[11] Take their present case, for instance. If he had gone down to the cabin with her he would have been miserable the whole time and he couldn't have helped showing it. At any rate she would have found him out. Whereas, having made up her mind to fall in with his ideas he would have betted anybody she would even go so far as to enjoy the experience. Not because she was without personality of her own. Good Lord! She was brimming with it.[12] But because . . . But here his thoughts always stopped. Here they always . . . felt the need of a cigar,[13] as it were. And looking at the cigar tip his fine eyes narrowed. It was a law of marriage, he supposed.

[SYA-NB3-NL, 2]

All the same he always felt guilty when he asked these sacrifices of her. That was what that quick pressure meant. His being said to her being, "You do understand, dont you?" And there was an answering tremor of her fingers, "I understand."

Certainly the steward, good little chap, had done all in his power to make them comfortable. He had put up their chairs in whatever warmth there was and out of the smell. She did hope he would be tipped adequately. It was on occasions like this (and her life seemed full of such occasions) when she wished it was the woman who held the purse.[14]

"Thank you, steward. That will do beautifully."

Why are stewards so often delicate looking, she wondered, as her feet were tucked under. This poor little chap certainly looked as though he'd got a chest. And yet one would have thought . . . the sea air . . .

The button of the pig-skin purse was undone. The tray was tilted. She saw sixpences, shillings, half crowns.

"I should give him five shillings," she decided, "and tell him to buy himself a good nourishing –"

---

[11] The published version reads, "[. . .] to believe that it really was easier [. . .]" (CW2, 421).

[12] "Absolutely" is added before "brimming" in the published version.

[13] The published version omits the ellipsis.

[14] The published version reads: It was on occasions like this (and her life seemed to be full of such occasions) that she wished it was the woman who controlled the purse" (CW2, 422).

He was given a shilling + he touched his cap + seemed genuinely grateful.

Well ~~she was grateful for small niceties~~ it might have been worse. It might have been sixpence. It might indeed. For at that moment Daddy[15] turned towards her + said half apologetically* stuffing the purse back I gave him a shilling. I think it was worth it don't you?

Oh, quite! Every bit! said she[16] + she gazed over the water –[17]

Grey, unbroken, gently moving water, **veiled*** with slanting-rain. Far out as though idly ~~as though~~ dreaming gulls were flying. Now they settled on the ~~water~~ waves now they beat up into the rainy air, and **they** shone against the pale sky like the lights within a pearl. How big it was out there—how cold and lonely. There will be nothing. Nothing but* the waves + those gulls + rain falling 18

How **lonely*** it will be here ~~xx~~ when we have passed by—and at the thought the xxx steamer, pressing on, **pitching** ghastly seemed to her a **wan living** even precious thing.[19] There were few passengers to be seen. ~~After~~ **Three over from us**—hardened travellers— **stalked** up + down—a little girl in xxx xxx chased after a red cheeked boy.

---

[15] Notebook 3 and the published version replace "Daddy" with "Father."

[16] A line is drawn from this point to a section added at the bottom of the page, beginning "He lay back" (see below). However, while later versions postpone the image of the lonely sea that follows, they retain the passage (though revised) about the hardened men travelers before bringing in the "He lay back" section.

[17] "She gazed over the water" is omitted in later versions.

[18] A line space follows after "a pearl" and the next line. This addition is squeezed into the space between the two.

[19] A version of this sentence and the previous paragraph are inverted and appear several paragraphs after this point in both Notebook 3 and the *Collected*. See SYA-NB3-NL, 4 and CW2, 423.

He was given a shilling, and he touched his hat and seemed genuinely grateful. Well, it might have been worse. It might have been sixpence. It might indeed. For at that moment Father turned

[SYA-NB3-NL, 3][20]

The ship is rolling **leaning**.

rolling + xxx.[21]

towards her and said, half apologetically, stuffing the purse back, "I gave him a shilling. I think it was worth it. Don't you?"

"Oh, quite. Every bit, said she.

It is extraordinary how peaceful it feels on a little steamer once the bustle of leaving port is over. In a quarter of an hour one might have been at see for days. There is something almost touching, childish in the way people submit themselves to the new conditions. They go to bed in the early afternoon, they shut their eyes and its "night" like little children who turn the table upside down and cover themselves with the tablecloth. And those who remain on deck—they seem to be always the same—those few hardened men travellers—pause, light their pipes, stamp softly gaze out to sea and their voices are subdued as they walk up and down. The long legged little girl chases after the red-cheeked boy but soon both are captured, and the old sailor, swinging an unlighted lantern passes and disappears.

He—lay back, the rug up to his chin and she saw he was breathing deeply. Sea air! If any one believed in sea air it was he. He had the strongest faith in its tonic qualities. But the great thing was, according to him, to fill the lungs with it the moment you came on board. Otherwise the sheer strength of it was enough to give you a chill . . .

She slipped down more deeply into her chair.[22]

[SYA-NB3-NL, 4][23]

And the little steamer pressed on, pitching gently, over the grey unbroken gently moving water that was veiled with slanting rain.

Far out, as though idly, listlessly, gulls were flying. Now they settled in the waves, now they beat up into the rainy air, and shone against the pale sky like the lights within a pearl. They looked cold and lonely. How lonely it will be when we have passed by, she thought. There will be nothing but the waves and those birds and rain falling.

---

[20] While this is the third page of the notebook, Mansfield has numbered it as page four with a "4" circled in the top right corner.

[21] The ink of these lines is lighter and feathers more than the rest of the page, and where they fit into the story is not clear. They are omitted in the published version.

[22] There is a section of the printed version in which his linen cap is discussed, but it is missing here (see CW2, 423); it appears in SYA-NB41-ATL, 6.

[23] While this is the fourth page of the notebook, it is labeled as page five. The top center of the page has a wavy line. On the opposing page there is some incidental material. "And" appears even with the sentence beginning "But immediately," while adjacent to "And it seemed to her [. . .]"—where the ink becomes darker—is written: "Can it be true. It seems to have started at last."

and Then an old sailor passed carrying a lantern and that was all.[24] She pressed down more deeply into the chair; she yielded to the rocking to the steady vibration. It was as though she tried to xxx herself with this **tiny spot** that she was now.[25]

He lay back the rug up to his chin, and she saw that he was **breathing*** deeply.[26] If any one had faith believed* in sea air it was he. He had the greatest deepest faith[27] in its tonic qualities. But the **great thing*** was, according to him to fill the lungs with it as soon as you came on board. Otherwise the sheer strength of it was enough to give you a chill. She gave a small chuckle + he **turned*** to her quickly what is it.[28]

[SYA-NB41-ATL, 6]

Its your cap said she. I never can get used to you in a cap. You look such a thorough burglar.

Well—what the deuce am I to wear? He shot up one grey eyebrow + **wrinkled*** his nose. It's a very good cap too—very fine specimen of its kind. Its got a very rich white satin lining. He paused. He **declaimed*** as he had hundreds of times before at this stage. "Rich + rare were the gems she wore."

But she was thinking he really was childishly proud of the white satin lining. He would like to have taken off his cap + make her feel it—feel the quality! How often had she rubbed between finger + thumb his coat his shirt cuff, his tie, sock, linen handkerchief while he said that.

---

[24] An extended version of this scene appears in the later versions of the story. See SYA-NB3-NL, 3, and CW2, 422–423.

[25] These last two sentences become simply, "She slipped down more deeply into her chair," in the revised versions.

[26] There is a space separating this section from what comes before. Mansfield has written "sea air" in the margin; in Notebook 3, "Sea air!" follows just after "breathing deeply." A line is drawn from that point to just after the line reading, "Oh, quite! Every bit!" See note 16.

[27] This becomes "strongest faith" in the revised versions.

[28] Notebook 3 omits her chuckle and the passage about his linen cap below; however, it is reincorporated in the published version. Notebook 3 continues instead with the image of the steamer pressing on. See note 22.

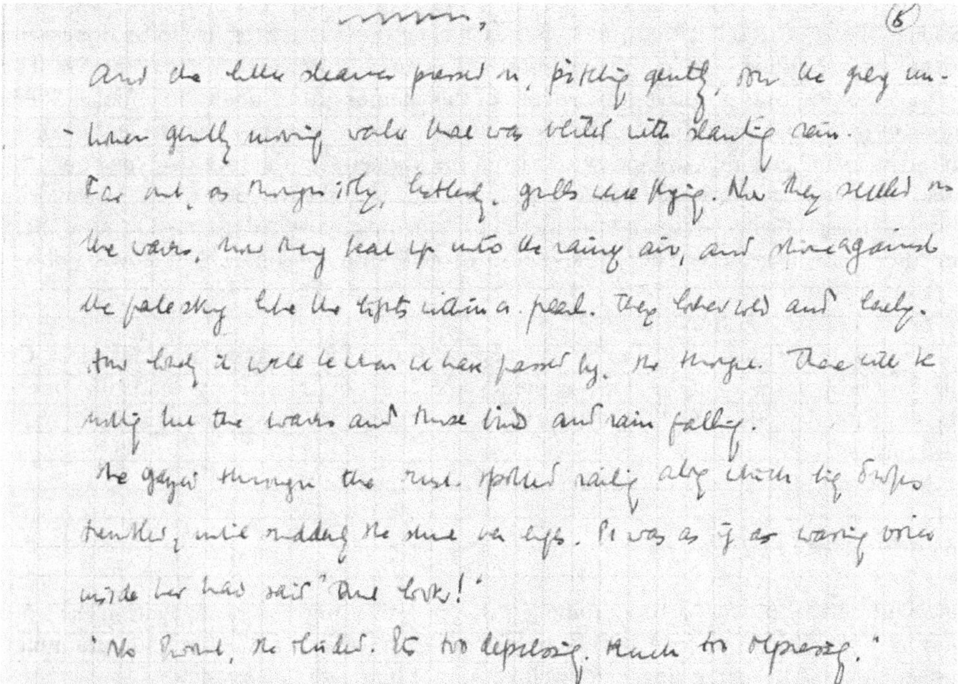

FIGURE 38: Page 4 recto (despite 5 at top of page), Notebook 3, "Six Years After," Katherine Mansfield Papers, Newberry Library (box 2, folder 2), 1–5. Image courtesy of the Newberry Library.

And then finally there is his first leave.[29] She does not go to the station to meet him—Daddy goes alone. As a matter of fact she is frightened to go. The shock may upset her + spoil their joy. So she tries to bear it at home—

Late afternoon. The lights on—gorgeous fires everywhere—in his bedroom too, of course. She goes to see it too often—but each time there is something to be done—the curtains to be drawn—or she makes sure he has enough blankets. ~~or that the xxx~~ For some reason there is no place for the girls in this memory; they might be unborn. She is alone in that warm **breathing bright*** house except for the servants. Each time she comes in the hall she hears that distant twitter from the kitchen—in the race of steps down the area. They are on the look out. And at this point she always remembers his favorite dinner—roast chicken—asparagus—meringes—champagne—And then—Oh God help me to bear this moment—Theres the taxi Its **turned*** into the square. Is it slowing now.

Here it is—'m.

No Nellie—I dont think so.

Yes, yes. It is. Courage. Be brave. Its stopping. Is that fathers glove at the window. Oh the door is open she is on the step—Fathers **voice rings*** out Here he is—and all at one + the same moment the taxi ^stops + bursts^ opens—a young muffled figure bounds up the steps. Mummy—

My precious precious son! But here its no use—here

[SYA-NB41-ATL, 7]

She must break down—just a moment just one—pressing her head against the cold buttons of his British warm. Child he holds her—+ now Father is behind him **grabbing*** his shoulders + his laugh rings out. Well youve got him. Are you satisfied?

The door is shut. He is pulling off his xx xxx—his gloves + scarf and coat + **pressing*** them on to the chest in the hall. The old familiar quick shot back of his head while he looks at her laughing while he describes how he spotted Daddy immediately + Father absolutely refused to recognise him.

---

[29] This section, separated by a space from the previous section, is written in a lighter ink, suggesting it was added later. According to the *Collected*, while this passage was included in a version edited by Antony Alpers, Mansfield did not include it in her revised or published versions; thus, it is published as a fragment (CW2, 425, note). This fragment extends through page seven of Notebook 41.

Instead of the literal homecoming of her son from the war and the mother's reflection on his future, the revised version is more abstract, with the mother hearing the voice of her son coming from the sea and hears the dead son's "dream" of being swallowed up by a blackberry vine in his grave, reminiscent of "The Fly." See SYA-NB3-NL, 4–5.

She gazed through the rust spotted railing along which big drops trembled, until suddenly she shut her lips. It was as if as warning voice inside her had said "Dont look!"[30]

"No I wont, she decided. Its too depressing. Much too depressing."

But immediately she opened her eyes and looked again. Lonely birds, water lifting white, pale sky—how were they changed?

And it seemed to her there was a presence far out there ^between the sky^ on the water;[31] someone very desolate and ~~hungry~~ ^longing^ watched them pass, and cried as if to stop them—but cried to her alone.[32]

"Mother."

"Dont leave me," sounded in the cry. Don't forget me. You are forgetting me! You know you are." And it was as though, from her own breast there came the sound of childish weeping.

"My son—my precious child—it isn't true."

[SYA-NB3-NL, 5]

Sh, how was it possible that she was sitting there on that quiet steamer beside father[33] and at the same time she was hushing and holding a little slender boy—so pale—who had just **woken**[34] out of a dreadful dream.

"I dreamed I was in a wood—somewhere far away from everybody, and I was lying down and a great blackberry vine grew over me. And I called + called to you—and you wouldn't come—you wouldn't come. So I had to lie there for ever."

---

[30] This paragraph and what follows to the end does not appear in the initial draft of Notebook 41. While Notebook 41 has an extended section on the couple's son coming home and his nightmares as a child, Mansfield trades these specific details to the more nightmarish call of the son from the sea and the image of his grave being slowly covered by a blackberry vine.

[31] This becomes "between the sky and the water" in the published version.

[32] Beginning with this section and to the end of the page, the ink is much darker than the rest of the page above it. Aligned with this section, on the opposing page, there is an isolated "And"; under this, a few lines below and in a similar ink as the first half of the page, is written: "Can it **be time**. It seems to have started at last."

[33] The published version capitalizes "Father."

[34] While the published version uses "waked," the word in the manuscript looks more like "woken."

. . . But softly without a sound the dark **curtain*** has rolled down. There is no more to come. That is the end of the play. But it cant end like that—so suddenly. There must be more—No. Its cold its still. There is nothing to be gained by waiting.

But—did he go back again? Or when the war was over did he come home for good— Surely he will marry—later on—not for several years. Surely one day I shall remember his wedding + my first grand~~son~~child a beautiful dark haired boy **born*** in the early morning—a lovely **morning***—spring.

Oh Mother its not fair to me to put these ideas into my head. Stop Mother stop. When I think of all I have missed I cant bear it. And there was a sound of childish weeping from under the xxx **beckoning** me—a heartbreaking **sound** in that foreign wood where the white cross **gleams misty**.

I cant bear it. She sits up breathing the word + tosses ~~away the~~ dark rug away. ^{My son! My son!35} It is colder than ever—and now the dusk is falling—falling **like*** ash upon the pallid water.

Oh, my **heavens**![36]

[SYA-NB41-ATL, 8]

And the little steamer, **quietly determined*** ^{throbbed on} pressed on, as if at the end of the journey there waited[37]

---

[35] This addition is written above the preceding sentence, but there is no clear indication as to where it should be included, and it does not appear in the published version.

[36] Margaret Scott transcribes this as "oh, my hatred!" See Notebooks 2, 295.

[37] There is no end punctuation here; the published version has an ellipsis.

What a terrible dream! He had always had terrible dreams. ^{How often38} Years ago, when he was small, she had made some excuse and escaped from their friends in the dining room or the **drawing room*** to come to the foot of the stairs + listen. "Mother." And when he was asleep she had ~~carried that~~ his dream ^{had journeyed*} with her, back into the circle of lamp light;[39] it had taken its place there, like a ghost. And now—[40] Far more often, at all times—in all places—like now—for instance—she never settled down—she was never off ~~of~~ her guard for a moment but she heard him. He wanted her. I am coming as fast as I can. As fast as I can I come.[41] But the dark stairs have no ending and the worst **dream*** of all—the one that is always the same—goes for ever and for ever uncomforted.[42]

This is anguish. How is it to be bourne? Still, it is not the

[SYA-NB3-NL, 6]

idea of her suffering, which is unbearable—it is his. Can one do nothing for the dead? And for a long time the answer had been—nothing.[43]

---

[38] This addition is written in the margin, with an arrow pointing up to it.
[39] The published version reads: "And when he was asleep, his dream had journeyed with her back into the circle of lamplight" (CW2, 424).
[40] A paragraph break appears in the published version.
[41] The published version omits "I come" at the end of this sentence.
[42] The published version omits "for" in the second "for ever."
[43] As this is a cleaner copy in which Mansfield is consolidating various passages from Notebook 41 into a more unified whole, that the story ends here suggests an alternate ending to that in the *Collected*. The version that John Middleton Murry published after Mansfield's death follows this version except for the reincorporation of the section about the husband's linen cap (see note 26), and then adds fragments from the end of Notebook 41 in an attempt to conclude the story more formally—a precedent followed in the *Collected*. While the ending presented here is rather dark, as a cleanly copied draft it appears to be the one intended by Mansfield.

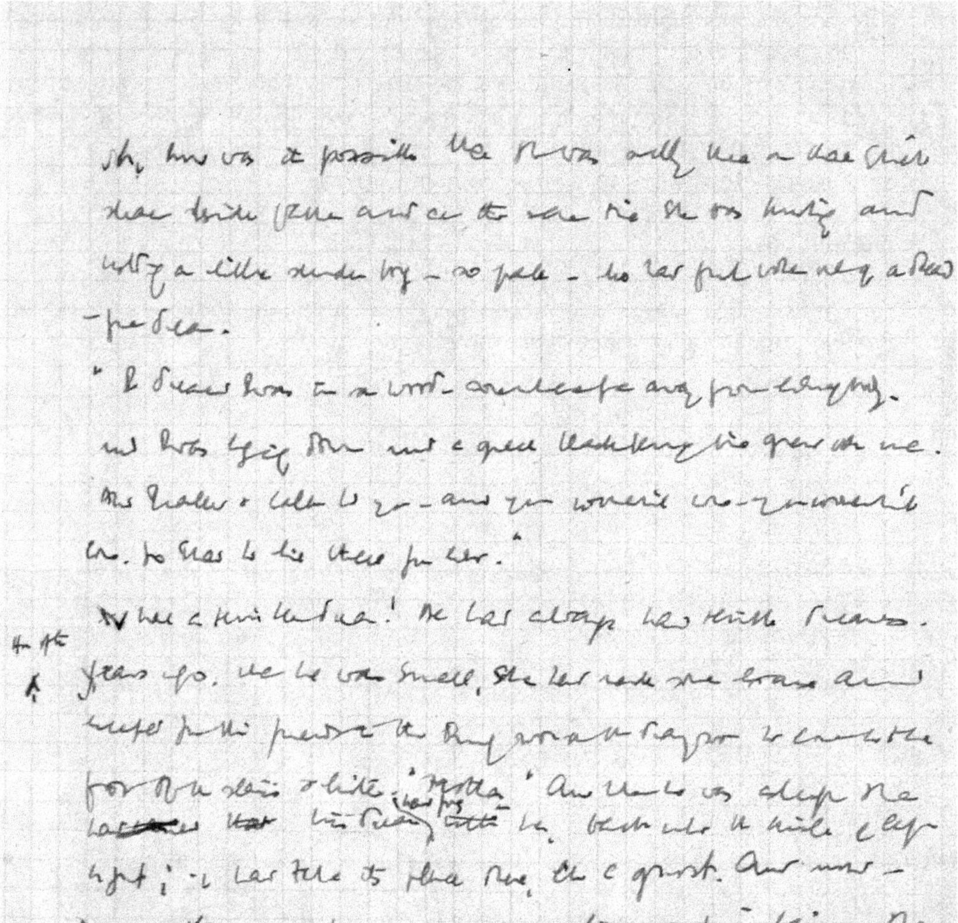

FIGURE 39: Page 5 recto, Notebook 3, "Six Years After," Katherine Mansfield Papers, Newberry Library (box 2, folder 2), 1–5. Image courtesy of the Newberry Library.

A Note on the Manuscript and Typescript of "The Fly"

While "The Fly" was published in *Nation and the Athenaeum* the year before Mansfield died, it was collected in the posthumously published *The Doves' Nest and Other Stories* (1923). As with "Poison," the Newberry Library has two drafts of the story, one a fairly clean manuscript (though there are a few significant revisions on leaves 4 and 6) and the other a typescript on which the published versions of the story are based. Interestingly, in a letter to William Gerhardi, who had praised "The Daughters of the Late Colonel," Mansfield notes: "I'm sorry you did not like The Fly and glad you told me. I *hated* writing it."[1] Why she hated writing it, however, is not evident, though it may have to do with the fact that it deals intimately both with her father and the death of her brother, Leslie Heron Beauchamp. One way that Mansfield may have tried to distance herself from the story was to change the protagonist from a "manager" to the "boss" in the manuscript; her father, Harold Beauchamp, was a bank manager in Wellington. This change is retained in the typescript. Further, Mansfield was becoming weaker due to her tuberculosis and had begun her X-Ray sessions with Manoukhin, which would have weakened her further.

In the case of "The Fly," unlike with "Poison," it is likely that Mansfield typed the typescript herself. She was living in Paris, but in a letter to Dorothy Brett in which she mentions the writing of the story, she mentions that Murry had recently arrived from Switzerland, where the two had been staying together just before,[2] and he would have brought the typewriter with him (if she didn't already have it). Likewise, evidence on the typescript, which includes typed changes not indicated on the manuscript and which a typist would not have taken the liberty to make, suggests Mansfield typed the draft.

---

[1] *Letters* 5, 206. Emphasis in original.
[2] *Letters* 5, 62.

20
II
1922

The Fly.[3]

"Y'are very snug in her," piped old Mr Woodifield, and he peered out of the great green leather armchair by the manager's desk as a baby peers out of its pram.[4] His talk was over with the manager; it was time for him to be off. But he did not want to go. Since he had retired, since his . . . stroke, the wife and the girls kept him boxed up in the house every day of the week except Tuesday. On Tuesdays he was dressed and brushed and allowed to cut back to the city for the day.[5] Though what he did there the wife + the girls couldn't imagine. Made a nuisance of himself to his friend,[6] they supposed . . . Well, perhaps so. All the same,[7] we cling to our last pleasures ~~like~~ as the tree clings to its last leaves. So there sat old Woodifield, smoking a cigar and staring[8] almost greedily at the manager,[9] who rolled in his office chair, stout, rosy, five years older than he, and still going strong. Still at the helm.[10] It did one good to see him.

Wistfully, admiringly, the old voice added "Its snug in here—upon my word!"

"Yes, its comfortable enough" agreed the manager, and he flipped the Financial Times with a paper knife.[11] As a matter of fact he was proud of his room; he liked to have it admired, especially by old Woodifield. It gave him a feeling of deep solid satisfaction to be planted there in the mi^dst of it in full view of that frail old figure in the muffler.[12]

"Ive had it done up lately," he explained, as he had explained for the past—how many?—weeks. "New carpet" and he pointed to the bright red carpet with a pattern of large white rings.[13] "New furniture," and he nodded toward the massive book case and the table with legs like twisted treacle. "Electric heating."[14] He waved almost exultantly towards the five transparent, pearly sausages glowing so softly in the tilted copper pan.

But he did not draw old Woodifields [sic] attention to the photograph over the table of a grave looking boy in uniform standing in one of those spectral photographer's parks with photographer's storm clouds behind him. It was not new. It had been there for over six years.

"There was something I wanted to tell you," said old Woodifield, and his eyes grew dim, remembering.[15] "Now what was it.[16] I had it in my mind when I started out this morning." His hands began to tremble and patches of read showed above his beard.

---

[3] "The Fly," by Katherine Mansfield, copyright © 1923 by Penguin Random House LLC, copyright renewed 1951 by J. Middleton Murry. Used by permission of Alfred A. Knopf, an imprint of the Knopf Doubleday Publishing Group, a division of Random House LLC. All rights reserved.

[4] The typescript replaces "by the manager's desk" with "by his friend, the boss's desk."

[5] "City" is capitalized in the typescript.

[6] "Friend" is made plural in the typescript.

[7] The typescript omits the comma after "same."

[8] The typescript misspells "staring" as "stairing," but it is not corrected.

[9] "Manager" is changed to "boss" throughout the typescript.

[10] The typescript joins "Still at the helm" with the previous sentence.

[11] In the typescript, a comma follows "enough" and "The Financial Times" is underlined.

[12] The typescript adds a comma after "deep."

[13] The typescript adds a comma after "new carpet."

[14] The period is replaced with an exclamation point in the typescript.

[15] The *Collected* omits the comma after "dim," though it is retained in the typescript.

[16] The period becomes a question mark in the typescript.

Poor old chap! He's on his last pins, thought the manager.[17] And feeling kindly

[Fly-MS-NL, leaf 2]

he winked at the old man and said jokingly "I tell you what. Ive got a little drop of something here that will do you good before you go out into the cold again. Its beautiful stuff. It wouldn't hurt a child." He took a key off his watch chain, unlocked a cupboard below his desk and drew forth a dark squat bottle.[18] "Thats the medicine," said he. "And the man from whom I got it told me on the strict Q. T. it came from the cellars at Windsor Cassle."[19]

Old Woodifield [*sic*] mouth fell open at the sight. He couldn't have looked more surprised if the ~~manager~~ had produced a rabbit.[20]

"Its whiskey, ain't it?" he piped feebly.[21]

The ~~manager~~ ᵇᵒˢˢ turned the bottle and lovingly showed him the label.[22] Whiskey it was.

"D'you know," said he, peering up at the manager, wonderingly,[23] "they won't let me touch it at home." And he looked as though he was going to cry.

"Ah, thats where we know a bit more than the ladies!" cried the manager,[24] swooping across for two tumblers that stood on the table with the water bottle and pouring a generous finger into each.[25] "Drink it down. It will do you good. And don't put any water with it. Its sacrilege to tamper with stuff like this. Ah!" He tossed off his, pulled out his handkerchief, hastily wiped his moustaches and cocked an eye at old Woodifield who was rolling his in his chaps.[26]

The old man swallowed, was silent a moment and then said faintly "Its nutty!"[27]

But it warmed him; it crept into his chill old brain. He remembered.[28]

"That was it" he said, heaving himself out of his chair. "I thought you'd like to know. The girls were in Belgium last week having a look at poor Reggies grave and they happened to come across your boys. They're quite near each other it seems."[29]

Woodifield paused but the ~~manager~~ ᵇᵒˢˢ made no reply. Only a ~~change~~ quiver in his eyelids showed that he heard.[30]

"The girls were delighted with the way the place is kept," piped the old voice. ["]Beautifully looked after. Couldn't be better if they were at home. You've not been across—have yer?"[31]

---

[17] The exclamation point after "chap" becomes a comma.

[18] The typescript adds commas after "old man," after "jokingly," and after "below his desk."

[19] "Cassel" is lower case on the typescript, but Mansfield has underlined the "c" twice to indicate it should be capitalized.

[20] On the typescript, Mansfield begins typing "manager" but changes it to "boss": e.g. "if the ~~manag~~ boss."

[21] The *Collected* places a comma after "piped."

[22] This is the first instance on the manuscript where Mansfield changes "manager" to "boss," which she maintains throughout the rest of the manuscript, appearing to change any overlooked instances during a second reading. This change is reflected throughout the typescript.

[23] The comma after "manager" is omitted in the typescript.

[24] The typescript changes the exclamation point after "ladies" to a comma.

[25] The *Collected* adds a comma after "water bottle."

[26] Commas are added after "moustaches" and "Woodifield" in the typescript.

[27] The typescript adds a comma after "moment."

[28] The period after "brain" becomes a colon in the typescript, while the *Collected* has a dash.

[29] The typescript adds commas after "'That was it,'" "Reggie's grave," and "near each other." It also inserts the missing apostrophes.

[30] A comma is added after "paused" in the typescript.

[31] The typescript replaces the dash with a comma.

"No. No!" For various reasons the ~~manager~~ ^{boss} has not been across.[32]
"There's miles of it," quavered old Woodifield, "and its all as neat as a garden.

[Fly-MS-NL, leaf 3]

Flowers growing on all the graves. Nice broad paths." It was plain from his voice how much he liked a nice broad path.

The pause came again. Then the old man brightened wonderfully.

"D'you know what the hotel made the girls pay for a pot of jam?" he piped. "Ten francs. Robbery I call it. It was a little pot, so Gertrude says, no bigger than a half crown and she hadn't taken more than a spoonful than they charged her ten francs.[33] Gertrude brought the pot away with her to teach ~~them~~ ^{em} a lesson. Quite right, too. Its trading our feelings.[34] They think because we're over there having a look ~~at the poor boys grave we'll~~ ^{around were [sic] ready to} pay anything.[35] Thats what it is." And eh turned toward the door.

"Quite right. Quite right," cried the ~~manager~~ ^{boss}. Though what was quite right he hadn't the least idea.[36] He came round by his desk, followed the shuffling footsteps to the door and saw the old fellow out. Woodifield was gone.

For a long moment the ~~manager~~ ^{boss} stayed staring at nothing while the grey haired office messenger, watching him, dodged in and out of his cubby hole like a dog that expects to be taken for a run.[37] Then—"Ill see nobody for half an hour Macey," said the manager.[38] ["]Understand? Nobody at all."[39]

"Very good, sir."

The door shut, the firm, heavy steps recrossed the bright carpet, the fat body plumped down in the spring chair, and leaning forward the manager covered his face with his hand. He wanted, he intended, he had arranged to ~~xxxx~~ weep . . .[40]

It had been a terrible shock to him when old Woodifield sprang the remark upon him about the boy's grave. It was exactly as though the earth had opened and he had seen the boy lying there with Woodifield's girls staring down at him—~~lying there asleep~~. For it was strange. Although over six years had passed away the manager never thought of the boy except as lying, unchanged, unblemished, in his uniform, . . . ~~soundly sleeping~~ ^{asleep forever}.[41] ["]My son! My little man! groaned the manager.[42] But no tears came yet. In the past, in the first months and even years after the boys death he had only to say those words ~~and~~ to be overcome by such grief that nothing short of a

---

[32] The typescript reads: "No, no!" Also, "has" is changed to "had," lessening the immediacy of the present tense.
[33] The typescript replaces the period after "ten francs" with an exclamation point, adds a comma after "robbery," and divides the sentence into two after "half crown."
[34] The typescript omits the comma after "Quite right" and combines the two sentences with a comma after "too"; the *Collected* reinserts the comma and replaces the comma after "too" with a semicolon.
[35] "Around" becomes "round" in the typescript.
[36] The typescript combines these two sentences with a comma and adds an exclamation point after the second "quite right," reading: "'Quite right, quite right!'"
[37] The typescript places commas after "stayed" and "nothing."
[38] The dash is omitted in the typescript, but a colon is added in the *Collected*.
[39] A large "X" is written at the end of this sentence.
[40] The comma after "firm" is omitted and a comma is added after "and."
[41] The typescript adds a comma after "away" and omits the commas after "lying" and "unblemished."
[42] "My little man!" is omitted from the typescript; "manager" is changed to "boss."

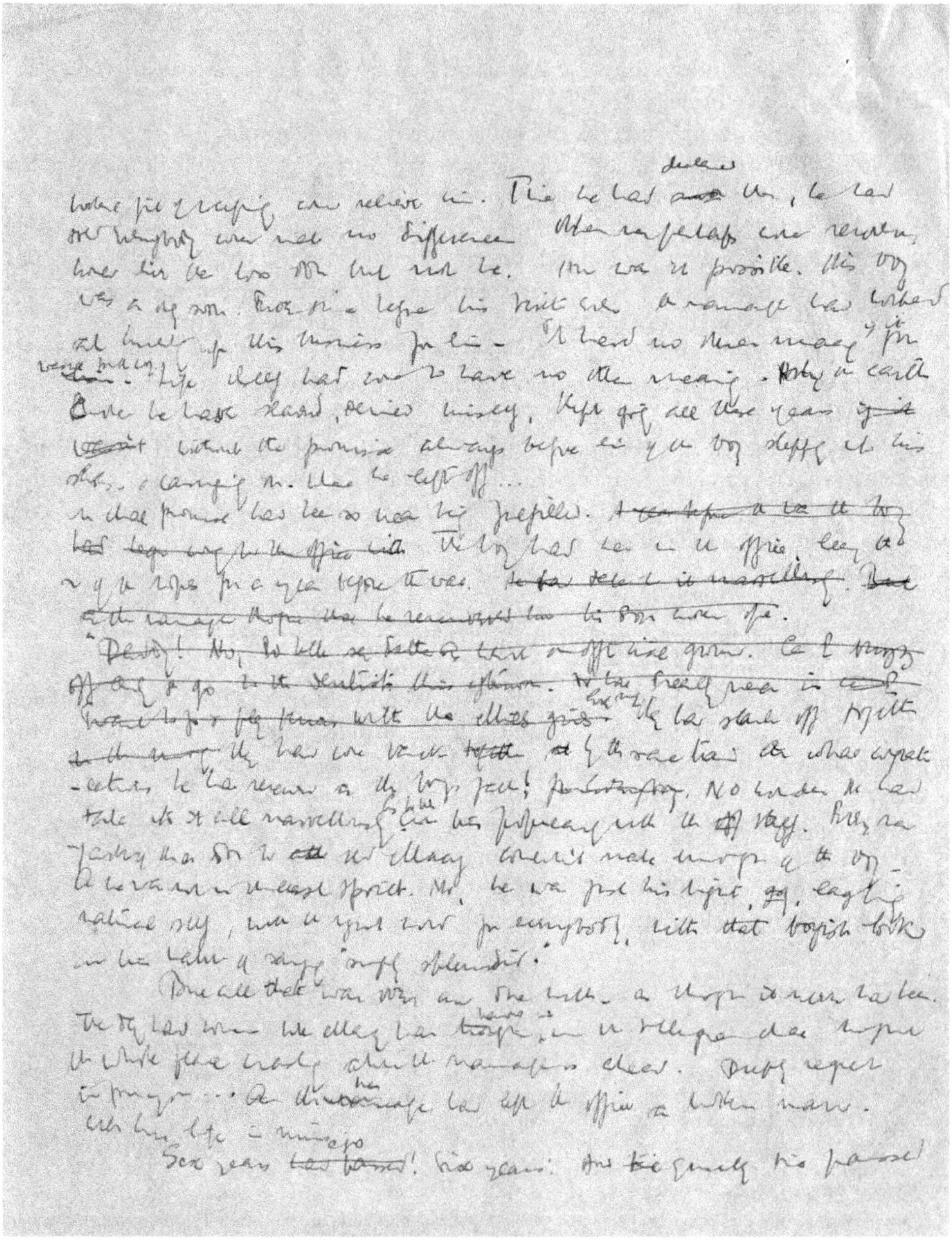

FIGURE 40: Leaf 4, "The Fly [manuscript]," Katherine Mansfield Papers, Newberry Library, (box 1, folder 16), 6 leaves. Image courtesy of the Newberry Library.

[Fly-MS-NL, leaf 4]

violent fit of weeping could relieve him.[43] Time he had ~~said~~ declared then, he had told everybody would make no difference.[44] Other men perhaps could recover, could live their loss down but not he. How was it possible.[45] His boy was an only son. Ever since before his birth even the manager had worked at building up his business for him—It had no other meaning if it for ~~him~~ wasnt for the boy. Life itself had come to have no other meaning.[46] Hxxow on earth xCould he have slaved, denied himself, kept going all these years ~~if it wasn't~~ without the promise always before him of the boy stepping into his shoes—+ carrying on—where he left off . . .[47]

And that promise had been so near being fulfilled. ~~A year before the war the boy had begun coming to the office with~~ The boy had been in the office, learning it—of the ropes for a year before the war.[48] ~~He had taken to it mavellously [sic]. But even the manager thought that he remembered him his son [from] another life.~~

~~"Daddy! No, Id better say father at work on official grounds. Can I buzz off early to go to the dentist this afternoon. What I really need is xxxx. I want to go + play tennis with the xxxxx girls.~~ Every morning* they had started off together ~~in the morning~~ they had come back ~~together at~~ by the same train.[49] And what congratulations he had received as the boys father! ~~for xxxxx boy.~~ No wonder he had taken to it all marellously.[50] Xxx As to his* his [sic] **popularity*** with the ~~off~~ staff. Every man-jack of them down to ~~all~~ old Macy [sic] couldn't make enough of the boy[51]—And he was not in the least spoilt. No, he was just his bright, ~~gay,~~ laughing natural self, with the right word for everybody, with that boyish look and his habit of saying "simply splendid."[52]

But all that was over and done with—as though it never had been. The day had come when Macy had ~~brought~~ him handed him the telegram that brought the whole place crashing about the managers **head***.[53] ["]Deeply regret inform you . . .["] And ~~the manager~~ he had left the office a broken man, with his life in ruins.

Six years ~~had passed~~ago! Six years: How ~~time~~ quickly time passed.[54]

[Fly-MS-NL, leaf 5]

Something seemed to be ~~happening~~ wrong to him. He wasnt he wasnt feeling as he wanted to feel. He decided to get up + have a look at the boys photograph. But it wasnt a favorite

---

[43] A comma is added after "death" in the typescript.

[44] The typescript adds a comma after "time."

[45] "Could" becomes "might" in the typescript; a comma is added after "down" and a question mark inserted after "How was it possible?"

[46] The typescript reads: "Ever since his birth the boss had worked a building up this business for him; it had no other meaning if it was not for the boy" (Fly-TS-NL, leaf 4).

[47] "Promise always" becomes "promise for ever" in the typescript. The end punctuation is a period rather than an ellipsis, and this is changed to a question mark in the *Collected*.

[48] The typescript simply reads: "The boy had been in the office learning the ropes . . ." (Fly-TS-NL, leaf 4).

[49] The typescript adds a comma after "together" while the *Collected* uses a semicolon instead.

[50] A semicolon is added after "No wonder" in the typescript.

[51] The typescript changes the period after "staff" with a comma and makes the "e" of "every" lowercase.

[52] "Laughing" is eliminated in the typescript, and the final part reads: ". . . his habit of saying, 'Simply splendid'" (Fly-TS-NL, leaf 4).

[53] The phrase "about the managers head" becomes "about his head" in the typescript.

[54] The exclamation point after "ago" becomes a comma in the typescript, and the colon an ellipsis. The *Collected* replaces the period with an exclamation point.

photograph of his. The expression wasn't natural. It was cold. Even stern looking + the boy never looked like that.

The manager took his hands from his face. He was puzzled. It might all have happened yesterday. ~~It was so~~[55]

At that moment the manager noticed ^that ~~a fool of~~ a little fly had fallen into his **broad***
mouthed inkpot and was trying feebly but desperately to clamber out again.[56] Help! Help![57] Said those struggling legs. ~~It fell back~~ But the sides of the inkpot were wet and slippery; it fell back ~~again~~ and began to swim. The manager took up a pen ~~and~~ picked the fly out of the ink + shook it on to a piece of blotting paper.[58] For a fraction of a second it lay still on the dark patch that oozed round it. Then the ^front legs waved—took hold, and pulling its small sodden body up it began the immense task of ~~freeing the ink~~ cleaning the ink from its wings.[59] Over and under, over and under went a leg along the wing as the stone goes over and under the scythe. Then there was a pause while the fly ~~attempted to~~ seeming to stand on the tip of its toes, tried to expand just one wing and then the other.[60] It succeeded at last and sitting down it began like a minute cate to clean its face. Now one could imagine that its little front legs rubbed against each other lightly joyfully.[61] ~~It had~~ ~~escaped. It was ready to~~ The horrible danger was over; it had escaped; it was ready for life again. But just then the manager had an idea. He plunged his pen back into the ink, leaned his ~~fat~~ thick wrist on the blotting paper and just as the fly **whirred** its wings—down ^came ~~the dark~~ ^a wet a great ~~blot of ink~~ heavy blot.[62] What would it make of that![63] ~~Xxx xxx~~ What indeed! The little beggar seems absolutely cowed—stunned and ~~as if~~ afraid to move because of what would happen next.[64] But then, as if painfully it dragged itself forward— ~~again~~ the front legs waved, caught hold—and more slowly this time, ~~patiently, persistent~~ the task began ~~again~~ from the beginning ^again.[65] Hes a plucky little devil thought the manager. And he felt a real admiration for ~~the little beggar's~~ ^the fly's **spirit** ^courage.[66] That was the way to tackle things; that was the right spirit. ~~You could get over anything if you make it.~~ ~~xxx was xxx never to say die.~~ ^Never say die. It was only a question of.[67] But ~~at that moment~~ ^xxxxx the fly

---

had again finished its ~~washing~~ labourious ~~progress~~ toilette, and the manager had just time to refill his pen—to shake one more fair and square on the new cleaned body yet another ~~the~~ dark drop ~~of ink~~.[68] A painful moment of suspense followed but behold! the

[Fly-MS-NL, leaf 6]

front legs were again waving. The manager felt ~~such~~ a rush of relief ~~that~~ he **leaned*** over the fly + said to it tenderly—you artful little b—.[69] And he actually had the brilliant ~~idea~~ notion of breathing on ~~the fly~~ it ~~while it cleaned itself~~ to help the drying process. All the same, there was something timid ~~and~~ about its efforts ~~this time~~ now, and the manager decided ~~he would xxxxx~~ this time should be the last ~~time~~ as he dipped the pen deep into the ink pot.[70]

~~But~~ The last blot ~~lay~~ fell on the soaked blotting paper and the ~~ruined~~ draggled fly lay in it and did not stir.[71] The back legs were stuck to the body, the front legs were not to be seen.[72] ~~Minute, draggled~~ Come on said the manager Look sharp! + he stirred it with ~~the~~his pen—~~tried to lift a wing~~ raise ~~its head—to lift a wing~~—in vain. He waited. Nothing happened or was likely* to happen. The fly was dead.[73] The manager siezed the corpse on the end of the paperknife + flung it into the waste paper basket but such a **grinding*** feeling of wretchedness ~~overcame him~~ seized him that he ~~could~~ felt positively frightened—He started forward + pressed the bell for Macy.[74] ~~When the messenger appeared~~

Bring me some fresh blotting paper, ~~said the manager~~ he said sternly—+ look sharp about it! And ~~while the old dog padded away~~ ~~he leaned back waiting for Macy return~~ [sic]—he fell to wondering what it was he had been thinking about before. ~~The business with the fly . . . He couldn't f~~For the life of him he couldn't then remember.

What was it. It was. No—no use. He took out his handkerchief + passed it inside his collar.[75]

---

[68] The typescript changes "toilette" to "task."

[69] The typescript reads: "What about this time? A painful moment of suspense followed. But behold, the front legs were waving; the boss felt a rush of relief. He leaned over the fly and said to it tenderly 'You artful little b—'" (Fly-TS-NL, leaf 6).

[70] The typescript reads: "All the same there was something timid and weak about its efforts now, and the boss decided that this should be the last, as he dipped the pen deep into the inkpot" (Fly-TS-NL, leaf 6).

[71] At the beginning of this paragraph, the typescript adds: "It was." It also adds a comma after "blotting-paper." After "fly" there is an indication that Mansfield planned to insert something, but an arrow before "fly" to where she adds "draggled" seems to reveal her intended positioning; the initial arrow was abandoned due to its placement.

[72] The comma after "body" is changed to a semicolon in the typescript.

[73] The typescript begins a new sentence after "Look sharp!" and omits "He waited."

[74] "The manager seized" becomes "The boss lifted" in the typescript. The typescript also ends the sentence after "waste-paper basket."

[75] Mansfield has drawn a line from after "thinking about before" to these final lines, indicating that they are to be incorporated accordingly. The final paragraph of the typescript reads:

> And while the old dog padded away he fell to wondering what is was he had been thinking about before. What was it? It was . . . He took out his handkerchief and passed it inside his collar. For the life of him he could not remember. (Fly-TS-NL, leaf 6)

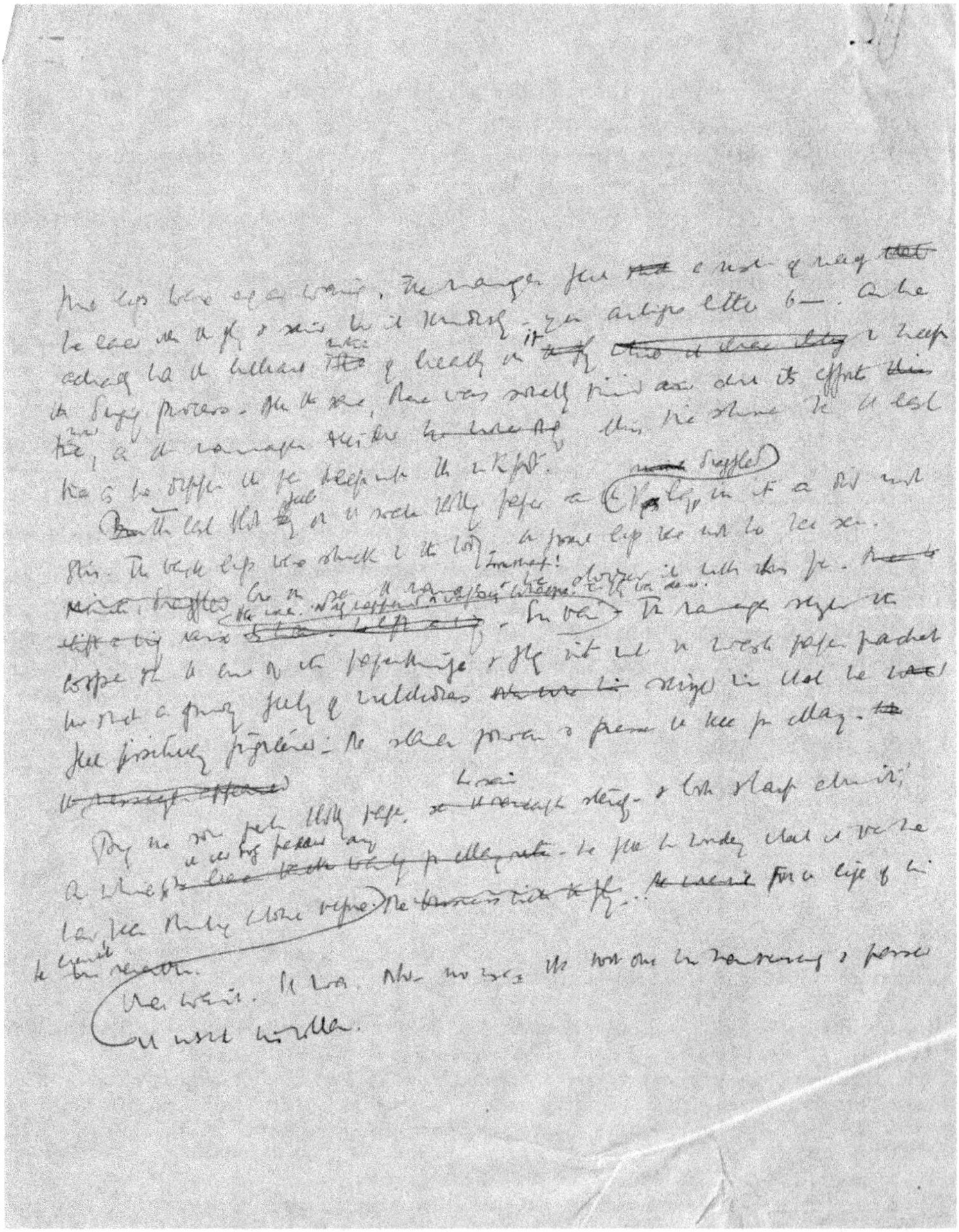

FIGURE 41: Leaf 6, "The Fly [manuscript]," Katherine Mansfield Papers, Newberry Library, (box 1, folder 16), 6 leaves. Image courtesy of the Newberry Library.

Critical Responses

"With a strong accent on the less": Tracing Voices in the Textual Genetics of "Je ne parle pas français"

CLAIRE DAVISON

The blotter, that banal, functional and, today, almost extinct writer's aid, plays a fascinating, often quite highly charged supporting role in a number of key stories by Katherine Mansfield; "Je ne parle pas français" (1919) is a fine case in point.[1] One is conveniently at hand when the self-appointed raconteur and café-haunting poseur Raoul Duquette mechanically reaches for a writing pad on the next table to note down a poetic turn of phrase he rather admires. He finds only a scrap of well used blotting paper, duly adorned with the conventional jottings, hearts, and other scribbles left by distracted former users. Amongst these doodles, a "silly stupid, stale little phrase" in green ink performs the "geste" which transfigures the commonplace, interrupts the flight of fancy, and ushers in the story within the story, at the same time turning the glib, garrulous narrator into a forlorn, forsaken dog.[2] Already quite a highly charged device in narratological terms, however, there's considerably more to be said about this little epiphanic inscription than meets the eye. The would-be writer is brought up short by the traces of a previous writer who had been there before; logic falters, as an unknown "je" speaks a language to claim they do not speak it; physical, human presence dissolves into pure emotion—"agony agony agony"[3]—and in its wake, the speaking subject, erstwhile "mMaster of the Situation,"[4] disintegrates into the most basic two-dimensional traces that make up the caricatural stick-man:

> It was as if all of me, except my head and arms, all of me that was under the table, had simply dissolved, melted, turned into water. Just my head remained and two sticks of arms pressing on the table.[5]

---

[1] "The Fly" is the other story in which blotting paper has a powerful signifying role; see also "Widowed," "Mr and Mrs Williams," "Mr Reginald Peacock's Day," and "The Daughters of the Late Colonel."

[2] See CW2, 114–15.

[3] JNPP-rough-NL, leaf 6 recto.

[4] Ibid., leaf 3 recto.

[5] CW2, 114–15. The two published versions (both 1920) will be referred to in the chapter as CW2 (first "Heron" publication) and *Bliss* (*Bliss and Other Stories*), respectively.

Here in miniature, the finished, published text reads as an essential modernist epiphany. By sheer coincidence, however, the same form of multi-layered textual inscription on the blotter, which both reveals and is revealed by traces of an earlier writerly presence, is prominent in exactly the same extract in its one extant manuscript version. This rough copy, although probably not the earliest draft as will be explained below,[6] proves to be quite heavily reworked compared to the passages just before and after, the successive deletions, rewordings, and additions suggesting the extent to which the author strove to capture the precise sensation of dissolution, at both an affective and a verbal, syntactic level:

> It was as if all of me except for my head + my arms—all of me that was under the table had simply dissolved[,] melted—**turned*** into water. Just my head remained ~~with two round eyes~~ + two of arm ~~sticks*~~ ~~leaning~~ pressing on the table—[7] [see Figures 1 and 2]

In other words, at both a published and a genetic level, and as both an operative trope within the story—triggering a return of the repressed, so to speak—and as a very literal performance of the stages of composition, we find a fascinating textual palimpsest. It's also a fitting demonstration of how, in characteristic Mansfield style, the scriptural becomes oral, the word becomes voice, ink becomes sound, and vice versa.

This is what this chapter sets out to explore: it highlights ways in which the text silences, represses, and flaunts voices as they reverberate back and forth from first scribblings to final typescript, and thence into the fine textual performances of "speakingness" that generations of readers have acknowledged as one of the most distinctive features of Mansfield's work. After briefly evoking the context of composition and evocations of work-in-progress to be found in her letters and notebooks, I address the play of disarmingly foreign French and English voices being inscribed, negotiated, and effaced as part of the textual genesis. I then turn to other forms of voice and "countervoice"[8] which form part of the story's complex soundscape as it wells up through the manuscript. We thus "listen" to the script as one might an orchestral score, picking out theatrical, musical, and other sonic resonances which sometimes linger on into the two published variants[9] we know as a single printed work.

As is quite fitting for a story about "not speaking French," "Je ne parle pas français" was written at the beginning of a particularly complicated stay in France. It was just before Christmas 1917 that Mansfield's doctor advised her not to spend winters in Britain, on account of an unexplained "*loud deafening* creak" in her left lung. A trip to Bandol, where she and Murry had already been so happy (at least in her retrospective vision of the stay)

---

[6] See also editorial notes, 15.

[7] JNPP-rough-NL, leaf 5 recto and leaf 6 recto.

[8] See Paula R. Feldman, "Mansfield's 'Je ne parle pas français'—a comparison of texts," (unpublished manuscript, Criticism and Interpretation, MS-Papers-4318, Alexander Turnbull Library, 1990); and Paula Feldman and Theresa Kelley, eds, *Romantic Women Writers: Voices and Countervoices* (University Press of New England, 1995).

[9] Completed in December 1919, the independent booklet form of *Je ne parle pas français* was published in February 1920 by the Heron Press, the independent home-based company set up by John Middleton Murry and his brother Richard. The story was included in the collection, *Bliss and Other Stories,* published later the same year by Constable & C°, but with certain bowdlerized passages, at the insistence of the director, Michael Sadleir. Mansfield was initially outraged at the conditions imposed, and refused to comply, preferring to withhold the story. The next day, however, the more pressing pragmatics of professional necessity incited her to give in. See below for more details.

seemed guaranteed to make her "burst into leaf and flower again."[10] Within two weeks, and after near heroic action to book her passage and obtain the necessary legal and medical documents for cross-Channel travel in war time, she had reached the port in France, still exhilarated by the promise of peace and quiet, restorative sunshine, and creative inspiration. Her buoyant spirits took a turn for the worse as soon as she left Paris: rudimentary travelling conditions, train carriages packed with uncouth, aggressive troops, bitter cold, makeshift hospitality, and arrogant, negligent officials left her lonely, homesick, and desperately anxious to start work.[11] By the end of the month, however, and after a tumultuous series of ups-and-downs (which included cursing French blotting paper, which "dont blot curse it"[12]), she had begun writing, diffidently announcing to Murry that "It looks to me like the real thing," while raging against certain species of Frenchmen whom she "loathe[d] and abominated."[13] By February 3, she was "fully launched, right out in the deep sea," her little boat "driving along the deep water as though it smelt port,"[14] while suffering acutely from insomnia in her race to complete the work. The next day, a first chapter of this new composition, by which she would "stand or fall," had been copied out and sent to Murry, along with a succinct explanation of what she perceived as its origins; even these clarifications end abruptly, however, thus revealing less than the reader might expect:

> The subject I mean lui qui parle is of course taken from—Carco & Gertler & God knows who. It has been more or less in my mind ever since I first felt strongly about the French [. . .] It's a mystery. Theres so much much less taken from life than anyone would credit. The African laundress I had a bone of—but only a bone—Dick Harmon of course is partly is.[15]

She remained in "a state of work" until February 10, when she completed "Je ne parle pas," telling Murry it was "an achievement of our most blessed love" before duly packing it off for his approval; the same day, she set to work on "Sun & Moon," which had come to her in a dream the night before.[16]

Given the length of "Je ne parle pas français" and the fact that it went through at least two draft stages before reaching the presentable manuscript extract copied out for Murry, the timeline of composition is impressive indeed: less than two weeks in all. Her near frenzied state at times, however, is well reflected in the surviving drafts: one notebook version, hand-written in lead pencil and sometimes all but illegible, which begins about half way into the narrative, at the first meeting of Dick and Raoul at a party, and continues until the end, and another, neater draft of two extended sequences written in black ink on loose, numbered sheets. This latter version comprises the incipit and opening sequences, with, on the reverse side of each page, the central sequences, which were either conceived to intercalate with the rougher notebook variant, or begun as a cleaner copy of which a number of sheets have since been lost. The opening sentences of this copy are very neatly written, suggesting the ideas and even the text had already been drafted in a now lost Ur-text of sorts; the handwriting in this version deteriorates along the way—suggesting

---

[10] *Letters* 1, 356–7. Emphasis in original.
[11] See in particular the letters to Murry dated 11 January and to Ottoline Morrell, dated 18 January 1917 (*Letters* 2, 6–8; 23–4).
[12] *Letters* 2, 42.
[13] Ibid., 51–2.
[14] Ibid., 54.
[15] Ibid., 56.
[16] Ibid., 65.

either exhaustion and an aching wrist, or the incorporation of new inspirations as she worked. Each version, the pencil-written notebook draft and the fountain-pen-written, loose-page draft, has further interlinear amendments; these subsequent modifications are made mostly with the same writing instrument—the pencil or the pen—perhaps indicating they were incorporated during the same sitting; a number of ink-pen changes to the pencil version lends weight to the intuition that the notebook variant predates the loose-page variant. The last pre-text, i.e. the first "chapter" copied out and sent to Murry, has also survived, and only the slightest changes were then made to the first published edition—the complete "Heron" version.

A SUBJECT THAT IS 'MORE OR LESS FRENCH?

So, what story might the textual variants tell? Our close-up perusal of the manuscript starts from the disarmingly foreign words of the title when they first enter the story itself on the café blotting paper and then reverberate in Duquette's abruptly disjointed narrative. In the words of both published variants:

> But then, quite suddenly, at the bottom of the page, written in green ink, I fell on to that stupid, stale little phrase: *Je ne parle pas français*.
> There! it had come—the moment—the *geste*! And although I was so ready, it caught me, it tumbled me over; I was simply overwhelmed [. . .]
> *Je ne parle pas français. Je ne parle pas français.* All the while I wrote that last page my other self has been chasing up and down out in the dark there.[17]

The draft, however, tells a difference story:

> But then quite suddenly at the bottom of the page, written in green ink I ~~read~~ fell on to that silly stupid, stale little phrase "~~I dont spik Engleesh~~." je ne parle pas francais There! It had come the moment—the "geste" + though I was so ready—it caught me—+ ~~bowled~~tumbled me over—I was simply overwhelmed . . .
> [. . .]
> I do not spik English. I do not spik English.
> ~~I mean always you resist seeing anybody little Liar~~.[18] All the while I wrote that last page my other self has been chasing up and down—**out in the*** dark there. It left me just as I began to analyse my grand moment—dashed off distracted like a lost dog who tha^inks at last at last he hears the familiar step again—[19] [see Figures 1 and 3]

The slippage from one speaking "I" and one "self" to another—and from one voice to a "countervoice"[20]—points the way to disconcerting blends of erased and accentuated foreignness that function differently in their pre-textual and textual variants.

---

[17] CW2, 114–15.

[18] Although not backed-up by other allusions in the text, it is worth noting that the erased "Liar" in this passage, which foregrounds the speaker's self-confessed unreliability quite ostentatiously, invites parallels with the paradox of the Cretan Liar, and the classical dialogue and eclogue forms of Theocritus and Aristophanes that Mansfield had been exploring three years earlier.

[19] JNPP-rough-NL, leaf 5 recto; leaf 7 recto.

[20] Picking up on the looser uses of "countervoice" in Feldman and Kelley, cited above, the term is taken specifically here to describe a) forms of voice under erasure, present in the drafts, but written out in the published version; b) voices that resonate or echo in the text as a result of deliberate or unconscious allusion, intertextuality, and rhythmic memory; c) lyric voices bringing a musical supplement to the written text.

For the reader familiar only with the published text, the effect is rather like that recorded by Duquette ("All the while I wrote that last page my other self has been chasing up and down"): two possible but entirely incompatible stories pull us in two opposing directions. Written in French, the words attest the previous presence of another writer / speaker recording their out-of-placeness in a country or its language. But who might the words "I do not spik Engleesh" be spoken by? Clearly not Mouse or Dick, but not by Duquette either if he's in France, unless he's failing to communicate with foreigners in Paris. And yet, if a Frenchman previously *spoke* these words, as the clichéd transcription of accent implies, he would hardly have *transcribed* his own mispronunciation. To accommodate linguistic logic, two alternative narratives would be called for: either the story would have to be set outside France or within a foreign or expat community in France, or the words would have to be written by someone who is not the speaking "I" (or "je"), but who records and mimics the foreign accent of a Frenchman or woman speaking in English. In other words, "I do not spik Engleesh" would imply either that "I" had already been out of place before "the moment—the 'geste,'" or that the "I" who spoke was not the "I" who wrote, but a countervoice.

Mimetic logic was perhaps what quickly prompted Mansfield to delete the foreignized English in favor of foreignizing French; nevertheless, in either case, the transcribed words on the blotter perform a radically alienating role, foregrounding out-of-placeness by troubling the presumed seamless correlation of geographical setting, native language, and self-expression. Thus Duquette's "strong accent on the less"[21] in the opening paragraph proves (entirely fortuitously of course) to be a highly fitting metaphor for the way foreignness and Frenchness are being negotiated, flaunted, or attenuated in the genetic making of the text, as the writer strove to find the right balance of familiar foreignness and—sometimes disconcerting—native ease. "I dont spik Engleesh" is the most arresting example, but there are a number of other such dislocations.

The substitution of "je ne parle pas français," for example, involves a translational shift from foreignized (mispronounced) English to standard French. A series of similar normalizing effects efface foreign traces and thereby favor the clarity of a single language: the mispronounced "Deeck" (with its attendant mockery of Duquette's accent) is twice changed to the neutral "Dick."[22] Similarly, Duquette's Parisian home, the lease of which marks his self-generated coming-into-being ("I date myself from the moment that I became tenant") is referred to as his "appartement" in the earlier draft,[23] but his "flat" in the later draft and published text, thereby effacing accent and voice in favor of non-intrusive standardization. Meanwhile, an intriguingly signposted cultural transposition (an acknowledged process of translation) occurs in Duquette's smug evocation of his seductive powers: the "very serious very distinguished young lady talking Ravel" in the first draft becomes a "very distinguished young lady, discussing *le Kipling.*"[24] The French modernist composer is thus strangely domesticated and displaced, becoming an arch-Victorian writer, but with a foreign touch ("*le* Kipling") which adds accent and a certain social posturing.

---

[21] JNPP-rough-NL, leaf 1 recto. The word "less" is underscored.
[22] JNPP-rough-NL, leaf 14 recto.
[23] Compare JNPP-Notebook14-ATL, 6 recto, with JNPP-rough-NL, leaf 16 recto.
[24] Compare JNPP-rough-NL, leaf 12 recto, with JNPP-clean-NL, leaf 12.

Other "Frenchifying" effects are removed altogether. The French words "Fais Dodo mes petits" ["Go to sleep, my little ones"] are initially added to an intriguing, very visual cameo portrait of "Madame" standing at the café window at lighting-up hour, for example, but then effaced:

> Your white hands hover over your dark shawl—like two birds that have come home to roost. ~~You~~ They are restless, restless. You tuck them finally under your warm little armpits. Fais Dodo mes petits.25 [see Figure 2]

Mansfield's hesitation here, adding and then taking away, is fascinating. The French import would have created an oralizing, tonal disjunct, their infantilizing "babytalk" adding either tenderness or cloying sentimental excess: "Dodo" is a conventional babyism from the verb "dormir" [to sleep] and would conventionally be translated as "bye-byes," "night-night," or "sleepy-byes" in English. In context here, moreover, it recalls the French lullaby "Fais dodo, Colas mon p'tit frère," which would sound strangely out-of-place in Duquette's narrative stance. Other Gallicizing effects likewise get effaced: an advertising slogan, "petit chocolat qualité" on the blotting paper,26 and the "smoking" cited among Duquette's "quantities of good clothes"27—"le smoking" itself being a conventional Anglicism in French to designate a tail-coat, but only if pronounced with a suitable French accent.

A more sexually connoted Gallicism to be played down in the final version is a slightly smug evocation of "Parisians of ~~our~~ classe" who are attracted to Duquette, so he claims, because he is "~~constantly more or less~~ in a state of more or less constant physical excitement."28 Here, even the wavering of the adverbial clauses in the draft—"constantly" / "more or less" / "constant" implies doubts about whether to play up or to play down sexual innuendo, irrespective of whether such hesitations are those of the author or the narrating persona. This vacillation is similarly mirrored by the shifting pronominal forms "appealed to *them*" / "*our* classe" [my emphasis], making Duquette's own status more ambivalent: is he one of "them," or isn't he? The published version, however, opts for "less" rather than "more," avoiding the overplay of national and sexual signifiers which might exacerbate satire at the expense of subtler forms of irony and social critique.

Another type of negotiated Frenchness discernible in the textual genetics is what we might call the lexicalized prompt—French imports left unchanged in English, but which invite the reader to "read with a French accent." Such prompts perform verisimilitude without, presumably, hindering comprehension even for a monolingual Anglophone reader. They include the already cited "geste," "Madame," "sous" [a monetary unit of little value], "soiree," and "comme il faut," and they undergo varying degrees of accentuation whether by the author's choice or at the publisher's level. Mansfield herself sometimes highlights their "Frenchness"—and presumably the accent required to pronounce them—by underlining them or using quotation marks. The editorial convention is to italicize systematically—thereby accentuating linguistic boundaries and clear-cut language shifts where the manuscripts tend to opt for linguistic porosity, allowing numerous crossings from French into English and back to occur imperceptibly.

---

25 JNPP-rough-NL, leaf 6 recto.
26 Ibid., leaf 5 recto [see Figure 1].
27 Ibid., leaf 11 recto.
28 Ibid., leaf 9 recto.

Meanwhile, a number of submerged French resonances sound on in the polished, Anglicized text, many of which might escape the attention of readers who don't speak French. Take Duquette's rakish, leeringly gallant encounter with a coquette and her proprietorial husband on the metro:

> Ah **Pardon Monsieur said the tall charming*** creature in black with the big full bosom + a **great*** bunch of violets dropping from it—As the train swayed ~~my nose~~ [it] thrust the bouquet ~~under my very nose~~ into my eyes—Ah Pardon Monsieur—But I looked up at her **saying** mischievously there is **nothing*** xxx at all Madame, I love more than flowers xxx on ~~a~~ the balcony—
>
> At **the very moment of*** speaking I caught sight of the huge man in the fur coat among whom my **charmer*** was leaning—He poked his head over her shoulder + ~~his nose~~—he went white to the nose—in fact his nose stood out a **sort*** of cheese green—
>
> ~~Monsieur~~ what was that you said to my wife—?!
>
> Well! ~~It appeared we were at a face off~~. N.P. Gare St Lazare saved me but ~~you own~~ you'll [own] that even as the author of False Coins, Wrong Doors + Left Umbrellas (+ 2 in preparation) it wasnt too easy to go on my triumphant way.[29]
>
> [see Figures 9, 10, and 11]

"Pardon," "Monsieur," "Madame," and "Gare St Lazare" are near transparent imports—so long as "Pardon" is understood to signify "I beg your pardon" and not, "could you repeat?" "Charming creature" and "flowers on the balcony," on the other hand, hover midway between the two languages, comprehensible but differently connoted in each. The two images are heavily imbued with the stale clichés of gallantry in French, reaching back to late-eighteenth century social and literary stereotypes. In English, however, "charming creature" may sound oxymoronic to the non-French-speaking reader, while recalling other animalesque associations and forms of metaphoric beastliness disseminated through the text.[30] Likewise, the conventional metaphor of the decorative balcony might be perceived in English as less hackneyed and less gross than it would have sounded in the context of a chance exchange between passengers on the Parisian metro in 1918.

Meanwhile, a moment of burlesque wit gets deleted: Duquette's remark, "It appeared we were at a face off" (a "face-à-face" in French), puns both on Duquette's nose getting thrust into the violets and the husband's grotesque, cheese-green nose. More subtly wavering between the two languages are the absurd titles of Duquette's books: "False Coins" is a word-to-word rendering of the French "faux jeton" which also signifies "hypocrite"; in a later section of Notebook 14, "Left Umbrellas" is rendered "Lost Dogs," creating an interesting tension both in the overall network of animal imagery and in Duquette's very unexpected image of himself as a fox-terrier—which might explain why this detail is erased in the published version.

To complete this overview of Frenchness under erasure, it is worth noting that the post-publication cuts (the cruder or more explicit sexual overtones that Michael Sadleir insisted on removing), are also incisively "France"-inflected, which doubtless contributed to Mansfield's indignant rejection of such editorial intrusiveness. Her forthright objection

---

[29] JNPP-Notebook14-ATL, 27 recto through 29 recto.

[30] While beyond the remit of the present chapter, and only tangentially enriched by textual genetics, it is worth nothing that "Je ne parle pas français" is probably Mansfield's richest "animalesque" story, the connotations of which exceed by far the very obvious fox-terrier and mouse references. The repercussions in philosophical and ethical terms of this textual bestiary would merit an extensive critical study.

to overt innuendo and publicly tolerated expressions of sexuality and sexism in contemporary France are voiced in her letters, but the notebook draft of "Je ne parle pas français" makes the causal link between her feelings of impatient outrage in France and the genesis of the story far more explicit. Notebook 14 is devoted almost exclusively to an early draft of part of the story, starting from the words "Who is he?"[31] The first page of the notebook, however, which is also pencil-written and in a hand so similar to that of the story that they would indeed appear to date from exactly the same time, reads as a diary entry that literally sets the scene for the key themes, motifs, and authorial point-of-view of "Je ne parle pas français," the fictional version merely replacing an (apparently) unrestrained personal outburst with a certain narrative objectivity:

> But Lord! Lord! how I do hate the french. With them it is always rutting time. See them come dancing and sniffing round a woman's skirts.
>
> Mademoiselle complains that she has the pieds glacés. Then why do you wear such pretty stockings & shoes Mademoiselle, leers Monsieur. Eh—oh la—c'est la mode.
>
> And the fool grins well content with the idiot answer—[32]

Relatively rare and uncharacteristic in her personal writings, the irascible impatience correlates resonantly with her initial response to Murry, who had relayed Sadleir's conditions:

> No, I certainly won't agree to those excisions if there were 500000000 copies in existence. They can keep their old £40 & be hanged to them. Shall I pick the eyes out of a story for £40. Im furious with Sadler. No, Ill never agree [. . .] The outline would be all blurred. It must have those sharp lines.[33]

Three passages were specifically targeted by Sadleir: the alarmingly abusive, predatory passion of the laundress for Duquette as a boy; explicit mentions of prostitution; and Duquette's closing speculations. Setting three variants (the manuscript, the Heron edition, and *Bliss and Other Stories*) side-by-side shows up the different levels at which de-sensationalizing processes were introduced: not only is explicit sensuality cut, but restraint is also introduced at the syntactic level. This includes the sudden hiatus and change of a paragraph in the first draft which, as the following quotation shows, invite the reader to imagine the unspeakable excesses taking place between "put me to her—~~to~~" and "When she set me down":

> (JNPP-rough-NL) She took me into a little outhouse at the end of the passage + set down her basket + caught me up in her arms + began kissing me—Oh such kisses—

---

[31] CW2, 119.

[32] CW4, 238. This is the opening entry in Notebook 14, followed by a separate passage, inset below as transcribed in CW4. The draft copy of "Je ne parle pas français" begins on the following page, from the words "Who is he?". The apparent link between Mansfield's exasperated impatience with coarse innuendo and ingratiating sexualized sophistry in France and her pencil drafts of "Je ne parle pas français" is noted by Antony Alpers in *The Life of Katherine Mansfield* (Viking Press, 1980), 272. In the same vein, the following notebook jotting or autoreferential, writerly observation breaks the sequence of the concluding sections of "Je ne parle pas français," and yet remains strikingly concordant in terms of theme and style:

> How immensely easier it is to attack an insect that is running away from you rather than one that is running towards you. The scuttling tribe. Spiders as big as half crowns with long gooseberry hairs (CW4, 238).

[33] *Letters* 3, 273.

especially those kisses inside my ears that nearly deafened me! And then with a soft growl she tore open her ~~lace~~ bodice + put me to her—~~to~~

When she set me down again she took out of her pocket a little round fried cake [. . .].[34]

(Heron) She took me into a little outhouse at the end of the passage, caught me up in her arms and began kissing me. Ah, those kisses! Especially those kisses inside my ears that nearly deafened me.

And then with a soft growl she tore open her bodice and put me to her. When she set me down she took from her pocket a little fried cake.[35]

(*Bliss*) She took me into a little outhouse at the end of the passage, caught me up in her arms and began kissing me. Ah, those kisses! Especially those kisses inside my ears that nearly deafened me.

When she set me down she took from her pocket a little fried cake [. . .].[36]

The "soft growl" creates gendered and inter-species effects which disarm, along with sinister, racialized resonances, all conjuring up a perverse, violent assault. Whether supposedly characteristic of "Parisian" or French "rutting" or not, the significance of such explicit sexuality becomes more apparent when recalled alongside the other heavily censored passage at the end of the story. In the closing sequences of Notebook 14 and the Heron versions, Duquette portrays himself as a panderer, lusciously promoting his latest catch; he then indulges in a few callously idle, prurient speculations about "Madame":

(JNPP-Notebook14-ATL) I have seen two people **suffer*** as I suppose I ever shall again—And ["]goodnight my little cat["] I said impudently to the fattish old prostitute picking her way home through the slush. I didnt give her time to reply.

[. . .]—and so on and so on until some dirty old gallant comes up to my table + sits opposite and begins to grimace and yapp [*sic*]. Until I hear myself say—"But Ive got the little girl for you mon vieux—so little—so little—and a **virgin***.["] I kiss ~~my lips~~ the tips of my fingers—["]a virgin["] and lay them on my **heart***.

I give you the word of honour of a gentleman[,] a writer, serious young + extremely interested in modern english literature.

I must go—I must go—I reach down my hat + coat—Waiter!

Madame knows me—"You havent dined yet" she said.

No, not yet Madame—

I['d] rather like to dine with her—Even to sleep with her afterwards—would she be pale like that all over— —

But no. She[']d have large moles—They go with that kind of skin and I cant bear them. They remind me, somehow, disgustingly of mushrooms.[37]

In the bowdlerized *Bliss* edition, the lurid Parisian "under world"[38] and its sordid, predatory glints are so diaphanized that the scene fades into an almost reassuring, homely glow:

---

[34] JNPP-rough-NL, leaf 9 recto.
[35] CW2, 116.
[36] *Bliss and Other Stories* [1920] (London: Constable, 1924), 9–80.
[37] JNPP-Notebook14-ATL, 37 verso, 31 verso through 27 verso.
[38] JNPP-rough-NL, leaf 10 recto.

(*Bliss*) I have seen two people suffer as I don't suppose I ever shall again
[. . .]—and so on and so on until some dirty old gallant comes up to my table and
sits opposite and begins to grimace and yap. Until I hear myself saying:

"But I've got the little girl for you mon vieux—so little—so tiny." I kiss the tips of
my fingers and lay them on my heart. "I give you my word of honour as a gentleman,
a writer, serious, young and extremely interested in modern English literature."

I must go. I must go. I reach down my hat and coat. Madame knows me. "You
haven't dined yet?" she smiles.

"No, not yet Madame."[39]

Censoring the closing image of mushrooms also effaces the last, more sordid interlingual
echo: "mushroom" in French, as Mansfield would have known—"champignon"—is a
much more generic term signifying fungal growth as well as the familiar vegetable.

Sadler's preemptive editorial censorship is puzzling given that no voice of outrage was
heard when the Heron edition was published, a paradox Mansfield herself underlined.[40]
But his professional wariness about offending codes of decency may also stem from more
intuitive, discomfiting impressions inspired by the text—a certain hypersensitivity to its
"countervoices" for example, especially having been part of Murry and Mansfield's
Parisian world in 1911 and 1912 as an early contributor to *Rhythm*. Might he not have
heard more sinister resonances lurking between the lines and complicating the codes of
fiction or the indices of biographical referentiality (which to this day dominate critical
readings of the text)?[41] After all, given Murry and Carco's admiration for the text,
apparently without recognizing their supposed, very unflattering, alter egos—not to
mention the inappropriateness of Mansfield sending Murry the story as a token of her
love if it reads as a lascivious portrait of her passionate lover three years before[42]—there's
also a very good case to be made for *not* reading "Je ne parle pas français" as a rudimentary
roman à clef "starring" Francis Carco (Duquette), John Middleton Murry (Dick Harmon),
and Mansfield (Mouse) herself.[43] Without providing any firm evidence of sorts, closer
scrutiny of the drafts can shed light on some of the more tenuous voices and milieux

---

[39] *Bliss*, 114–15.
[40] See *Letters* 3, 273–4. The short but perceptive review Mansfield cites was "Two Stories," published in the
Times Literary Supplement, January 29, 1920: p. 7.
[41] See Julie Beth Napolin, *The Fact of Resonance: Modernist Acoustics and Narrative Form* (New York: Fordham
University Press, 2020), 160–8, for a splendid conceptualization of sinister resonance as "the phonic substance
caught between meanings, traditions, lands, and languages" which dislocates, displaces and leaves aside as a result
of trauma or censorship (161). The *Rhythm* world of 1911–12 included not just Sadleir, Mansfield, and Murry
themselves, but also Francis Carco, Frederick Goodyear, and John Fergusson, all of whose shadows may have
been discernible to those concerned in 1918–19. The war years, too, although absent from the surface text of the
story, rumble in more suggestive or sinister fashion, between the lines. See also note 43.
[42] See Mansfield's letter to Murry referring to the story notably as her "love offering" (*Letters* 2, 68).
[43] Too rich to be explored here, there are sinister echoes of Carco's first two novels (*Jésus-la-Caille* and *Les
Innocents*) in terms of character studies, themes, and background evocations of civilian and returnee soldiers'
lives in wartime Paris to be heard between the lines of "Je ne parle pas." Meanwhile, there's a good case to be
made for various other literary forebears (amongst whom Dostoevsky's Underground Man, Chekhov's "Moscow
Hamlet," and T. S. Eliot's "Prufrock" and "Portrait of a Lady") seeping into the text-in-the making. See in
particular David Rampton's "Je ne parle pas français: Reading Mansfield's Underground Man," in *Katherine
Mansfield and Russia*, 11–23, and Colin Norman's "Prufrock, Freud, and the Late Colonel's Daughters," in
English Studies in Canada, 25 (1999), 19–37.

lurking between the lines in the story's sub-text and soundscape,[44] suggesting that her perplexity about textual referents ("It's a mystery. Theres so much much less taken from life than anyone would credit"[45]) might be more reliable than critics tend to admit.

An ideal starting-point for a reader tuning in to the soundscape of "Je ne parle pas français" is to be found within all the drafts of the story—the two loose-page variants and the notebook version. In each case, scenic divisions are very clearly marked not by numbers, random figures, or bold horizontal lines such as Mansfield tends to use, but with a single, centrally placed treble clef:

Admittedly, treble clefs and other musical doodles in her letters and notebooks suggest these were signs she clearly liked, and practiced writing, but the treble clef's careful inclusion in these drafts—actually gaining in frequency in the final extant manuscript variant—favors the hypothesis of a connotative function rather than a mere typographical break. They invite a musical interpretation, as if each scene were divided by a musical interlude of sorts. The effect is most striking in the passages detailing the heightened suspense when Dick withdraws, supposedly to write a letter:

> And still hoping it wouldn't be **inconvenient** to me he went out of the room + shut the door + we heard him cross the passage.

> I scalded myself with mine in my **hurry*** to take my cup back to the table + say as I stood there—
> "You mustnt forgive me if I am impertinent. If Im too frank—But Dick hasn't tried to disguise it—Has he—~~Is~~ There ⁱˢ something the matter. Can I help?
> ~~Ah that's strange. I almost expected we should have heard~~ sSoft music—+ Mouse ~~stood xxx xxx~~ ᵍᵉᵗˢ up ~~walked~~ˢ the stage for a moment or so—before she returns to her chair + pours me out oh such a ~~cup~~ ᵇʳⁱᵐᵐⁱⁿᵍ* ~~so brimming so full~~ ˢᵘᶜʰ ᵃ ᵇᵘʳⁿⁱⁿᵍ* ᶜᵘᵖ then the tears came into the friends eyes while he sipped while he drained it to the bitter dregs.
> I had **time*** to think all that before she replied. First she looked into the tea pot, filled it with hot water + ~~poured me out a second cup~~.
> [. . .]

---

[44] The "milieu" is the term used to refer to the Parisian underworld particularly in the early twentieth century, as well as urban criminal underworlds in general. Etymologically, it proves particularly fitting here, denoting the "half-place" [*mi-lieu*], i.e., a place of dislocation, situated between two worlds, where suppressed voices linger on.
[45] Mansfield to Murry, 4 February 1918, *Letters 2*, 56.

In some ~~mysterious~~ way she saw my hand move to my breast pocket half draw out a cigarette case + put it back again for the **next thing*** she said was ["]matches in the candlestick. I saw them.["] + I heard from her voice she was crying.

Ah thank you yes yes. Ive found them. I lighted my cigarette + walked up + down smoking.[46]

In none of these visual divides do the signs indicate a conventional scene change—they feature within the same scene in the hotel bedroom; they do, however, create a caesura, momentarily interrupting the narrative. They also occur immediately after an evocation of acoustic effect, thereby textualizing sound, and rhythmatizing reading, inciting the reader to perceive in their mind's ear the implied soundtrack: "We heard him cross the passage / 𝄞 "; "I heard from her voice that she was crying / 𝄞." Incorporated thus into the scene, they heighten dramatic suspense, creating the sort of theatrical effect now known as the Pinteresque or Chekhovian pause; they also feature at the precise moment when, in contemporary "silent" films, intense music would be heard from the orchestral pit, or from a piano in the wings, "performing" the emotional tension of the moment. Exactly the same melodramatic effect—one that doesn't mark a change of scene, but which deliberately slows down or interrupts the action to enhance suspense in a moment of silence, following up on sounds heard or imagined—is to be found before eight other treble clefs in the drafts.

Were these symbols the only indicators of textualized performance-effects bringing attention to a sonic background, it might still be over-bold to endow them with too much potential meaning. A close reading of the text, however, in both its draft variants and its final published versions, illuminates the much richer network of cinematographic and theatrical references giving sonic and dramatic depth to the story, and shifting the setting from biographical verisimilitude to stage and performance. The character of Duquette, for instance, is defined from the outset by emphatically designated costumes and disguises: his English overcoat and grey felt hat; the "good clothes," "silk underwear," evening suits, and patent leather boots; the tweed knickerbockers, pipe and ginger whiskers; the "blue kimono embroidered with white birds"; a "black silver-spotted tie."[47] As with all the instances of genetic variability evoked in this chapter, the passages most richly invested with theatrical or cinematographic resonance are also the most heavily annotated or reworked, further bolstering the hypothesis that their symbolic or suggestive import mattered. What's more, each mention of his clothing (whether actually worn or imagined, as in the case of the knickerbockers and whiskers) occurs in combination with an evocation of a mirror or glass in which he observes himself posturing, an effect which further reinforces the themes of staged performance, spectatorship, and role-play which run like leitmotifs throughout the text. All these observed "self-as-other" reverberations are noticeably more tangible in the genetic variants. In the extract below, for instance,

---

[46] JNPP-rough-NL, leaf 4 verso to leaf 2 verso.
[47] CW2, 113; 118–9; 122–3.

Mansfield's own hesitations over whether to use the pronoun "I" or "he" are both tangible and audible:

> Portrait of Madame Butterfly said I on hearing of the arrival of ~~Mr le capitain~~ ce cher Pinkerton.
>
> ~~But~~ According to the books I should have felt tremendously relieved and delighted + ~~but I didn't—I mainly felt a little~~ Going **over to the window he*** drew the curtains + looked out on to the ~~little~~ Paris trees just **breaking*** into green. Dick! Dick! My English friend.
>
> But ~~he~~ I didn't. ~~He~~ I merely felt a little sick—~~After~~ Having* been as it were for my first ride in an aeroplane ~~he~~ I didn't want to go up ~~so high~~ again just now [. . .]
>
> It was impossible **not to believe*** all this of the person who ~~turned round for~~ **surveyed*** himself finally from top to toe **drawing*** on his ~~xxx~~ **soft grey*** gloves—~~the while—Ive~~ he begun looking the part ~~I~~ he was the part, NL that gave me an idea. I took out my notebook and still in full view **jotted down a note or two***. How can one look the part + not be the part. Or be the part + not look the part. Isnt **looking*** being? At any rate who is to say its not.[48]
>
> [see Figures 6–8]

Such waverings between observed other, observed self, and embodied observer in their rudimentary, more ostentatious prototypes play into the more grotesque, ludic interpretations of the text, while also reaching out to some of its more obvious intertextual resonances (already evoked above)—Dostoevsky's Underground Man, and Eliot's "Prufrock," for example, the performance-rich appeal of which Mansfield herself had first demonstrated.[49] They likewise play into impressions of artifice, hyperbole, and farce whereby the speaking character himself insists that he is not to be taken at face value, drawing attention to himself as a caricatural, performing stage type—the camp musical-hall or cabaret compeer flamboyantly weaving a sequence of separate scenes into one for example. Once again, the compeer-type roles and voices have greater sonic and theatrical effect in the drafts:

> But what I wanted to do was to behave in the most extraordinary fashion way like a clown—to start **singing*** with large extravagant gestures to point out [the] window + cry ~~you~~ "We were now passing Ladies + Gentlemen one of the **sights*** for which notre Paris is justly famous—to ~~have suddenly~~ jumped suddenly **out*** of the taxi while it was going—climbed over the roof + dived in by the other door; to ~~lean half~~ hang out of the window + ~~begin looking~~ search for the **hotel*** through the long end of a broken telescope—which was also a peculiarly ear splitting trumpet![50] [see Figure 12]

The explicit theatrical and cinematographic motifs in the text likewise prove to have interesting genetic forebears. The already cited kimono and its *Madame Butterfly* echoes are a case in point. The notebook variant reads, "Portrait of Madame Butterfly said I on hearing of the arrival of ~~Mr le capitain~~ ce cher Pinkerton,"[51] the more ingratiating, ironic

---

[48] JNPP-Notebook14-ATL, 14 recto; 20 recto to 21 recto.
[49] Mansfield tells Woolf she reads "Prufrock" as a short story. See *Letters* 2, 318. A party performance of the poem has become a classic moment in Bloomsbury folklore, but it was only recalled hesitantly many years later. See Clive Bell, *Old Friends* (London: Chatto and Windus, 1956), 121–2.
[50] JNPP-rough-NL, leaf 11 verso.
[51] JNPP-Notebook14-ATL, p. 14 recto.

tones of "ce cher Pinkerton" replacing more formal designations in French or English ("Monsieur le capitaine" or "Mr Pinkerton") being written out in the published text. The American fictional intertext (the novelette by John Luther Long, in which the portrayal of Madame Butterfly is far more condescending) thus vies for visibility with Puccini's more Gallicized, translingual opera adaptation; both variants, however, gain in terms of performance art if we recall that a silent film adaptation had been released in 1915, which Mansfield was more likely to have seen, or seen advertised, in Paris rather than London. Closer focus on this intertext, whether via Puccini's opera or Long's novelette and stage-play, also invites tighter parallels between Mouse, the (fox-terrier) Duquette, and "The Butterfly," not only in relation to the story's bestiary, but also in terms of its denouement.[52] Although both Duquette and Mouse get abandoned by the sea-faring (or at least Channel-crossing) Harmon / Pinkerton character, neither will embrace the tragic destiny of their prototype Cio-Cio-San. Unlike Duquette, however, who ends as a rather sad café-haunt accosting tenants to whom he recounts his tale, Mouse enigmatically vanishes, having quite resolutely chosen to manage alone, married or unmarried.

Beyond the explicit Madame Butterfly references, other cinematographic / theatrical conceits echo more elusively in the drafts, the visually powerful allegorical incarnation of the American film industry for instance, strikingly bolder in pre-publication variants:

(JNPP-rough-NL) And why do I see her as a rag picker on the ^american^ cinema—and her hair in a horsetail shuffling along wrapped up in a **filthy*** shawl with her old claws crooked over a stick. Affection or as xxx say mind. I am perhaps ^NL Answer^ the ^direct^ result of the cinema ^most likely^ acting upon a weak mind—[53]

(Heron) And why do I see her as a rag picker on the American cinema shuffling along, wrapped in a filthy shawl, with her old claws crooked over a stick?

Answer: The direct result of the American cinema acting upon a weak mind.[54]

Another example explicitly reveals the evolution from a music-hall simile in the draft copy to the edgier, more contemporary (but in fact less apt) cinema metaphor in the published text:

(JNPP-rough-NL) If the pale sweaty garcon had __not__ appeared at that moment carrying the tea tray ^high^ xxx xxx high as though ^if^ the cups were cannon balls + he were a heavy weight lifter ^champion^ in **the music halls**—[55]

(Heron) If the pale, sweaty *garcon* had not come in at that moment, carrying the tea-tray high on one hand as if the cups were cannon-balls and he a heavy weight lifter on the cinema. . . .[56]

The figure of the garçon or waiter arriving to serve at the table may also point to a richer function in the musical, theatrical metaphors circulating in both the drafts and, albeit to a lesser degree, the final print versions of the text. He recalls the conventions of the archly Parisian café-theatre of the day, and—given the sleezy setting and sawdust-sprinkled floors—the particularly fashionable "Apache" scenes, the "Apaches" being the

---

[52] For a recent discussion of this intertextual reference, see Wen-Shan Shieh's "Katherine Mansfield's Art of Changing Masks," *Journal of Literature and Art Studies* 6, no. 8, (2016): 869–881 (874–5).
[53] JNPP-rough-NL, leaf 3 recto.
[54] CW2, 113.
[55] JNPP-rough-NL, leaf 6 verso.
[56] CW2, 129.

sleek urban hooligans and street ruffians who set the pace of Parisian lowlife and affrighted (and excited) the bourgeoisie. Part of the appeal of Apache performances was that, at some unexpected point in the evening, customers supposedly sitting quietly at their tables turned out to be actors waiting their turn to act out their roles. These always included staged, stylized quarrels, brawls, and sexualized dances, usually with a musical accompaniment, and although dating back to the late nineteenth century, they had been further popularized in the early years of the century by the film industry (two notable 1915 releases being *Les Apaches de Paris* and *Les Vampires*). The fashion then burgeoned anew in the early Parisian novels of Francis Carco (who would make the capital's pimps, prostitutes, and sleazy cafés his early literary trademark), the first two of which, *Jésus-la-Caille* (1914) and *Les Innocents* (1916), were particularly well known to Mansfield.[57]

"Je ne parle pas français" includes just such an unexpected performance, almost magically conjured up as Duquette sits alone at his café table and takes his first sip of whisky. At this precise moment, a form of narrative montage or splicing occurs, seamlessly shifting the story back in time to the occasion when Duquette and Harmon first met:

> "No Monsieur he answers, ^sadly we don't sell american drinks^ ~~without the least surprise~~, + having smeared a corner of the table he goes back to have another couple of dozen taken by artificial light.
>
> Ugh! the smell of it! and the sickly sensation when ones throat contracts!
>
> "Its bad stuff to get drunk on" says Dick Harmon, **turning*** his little glass in his fingers + smiling his slow dreaming smile, ~~while~~ ^so^ he gets drunk on it slowly + dreamily + at a certain moment begins to sing very low very low [. . .][58] [see Figure 4]

Although it begins in the tradition of Parisian café-theatre performances, the style of the ensuing musical interlude—musically and theatrically speaking—breaks starkly, even comically, with Apache models, even foregrounding the transition from the garish nightlife and racy criminal underworld of Paris to the grey, seedy poverty of London (as fantasied by Duquette). Like the other embedded acoustic effects and theatrical metaphors evoked here, the episode's significance is amplified by contextualizing it within both the textual genesis and Mansfield's own allusions to the story-in-the-making:

> [. . .] **about a man who*** walked up and down trying to find some place where he could get some dinner. Ah! **how*** I loved that song + how I loved the way he sang it slowly slowly, in a dark soft voice.
>
> There was a man
> Walked up + down
> To get a dinner in the town—town—
> It seemed to hold in its gravity + muffled measure all those tall grey **buildings***—those fogs, those endless streets those sharp shadows of policemen that mean England—And then the subject. The ~~poor~~ ^lean^ starved creature walking up + down—with every house

---

57 The rich network of resonances found echoing to-and-fro between Carco's fictional characters, their possible biographical referents, both authors' retrospectively constructed "memories," and Mansfield's "Indiscreet Journey" and "Je ne parle pas français," merits further study. For the richest exploration to date of Carco's complex life and literary world in English, see Gilles Freyssinet's "Francis Carco—the Poet of 'Paname,'" in *Katherine Mansfield's French Lives,* ed. Claire Davison and Gerri Kimber (Leiden: Brill Rodopi, 2016), 58–70. See also Francis Carco, *Jésus-la-Caille* (Paris: Mercure de France, 1914) and *Les Innocents* (Paris: Renaissance du livre, 1916).
58 JNPP-rough-NL, leaf 13 recto.

barred against him because he has <u>no</u> home—how extraordinary english that is! I remember **it ended*** ~~when~~^{where} he did at last find a place—+ ordered a lone cake of fish but when he asked for bread the waiter said contemptuously in a low voice we don't serve bread with one "fish ball." What more do you want! How profound these songs are—there is the whole pysology [*sic*] in a people—+ ~~w~~how unfrench how unfrench!

Once more Deeck! Once more! ~~How~~ I would ~~beg and~~ ^{plead}, **clasping*** my hands + making ~~my~~ a pretty mouth **at him*** . . . He was perfectly content to sing it for ever— —[59] [see Figures 4 and 5]

The song, in fact a late-nineteenth-century students' song from Boston, had been brought to France by American troops and is therefore as spuriously, meretriciously English as Duquette's whisky, whiskers, knickerbockers, and verbal interjections ("old chap," "old man," "I say," etc.). The song's rhythmic patter and upbeat music, meanwhile, in roundelay form with jaunty, sing-along lyrics, would have been more at home in the old music hall or comic operetta than in a tough, sensual Apache bar. Given Mansfield's ear for tone, pulse, melody, and dissonance, it's surely impossible for the stark disjunct between a jolly song about a fish ball, Harmon's performance ("he sang it slowly slowly, in a dark soft voice") and Duquette's lachrymose sentimentality to be anything other than gleefully deliberate.

However superficially frivolous, the American students' song, like so many popular ballads and folksongs, is rooted in harsh social realities—economic vulnerability, hunger, public humiliation (the waiter who shames an impoverished student for expecting bread with his single fish ball), and thus, in Mansfield's reincorporation of the song in between the lines, it still has a number of tales to tell. Sung by American troops as a marching song in France, or taken up around a café table away from the front line, the song expresses both the hunger and the homesickness of troops, not to mention the sheer absurdity of so much of a foot-soldier's daily drudge. A letter of Mansfield's to Murry, meanwhile, suggests it wasn't merely army life, or student life, in general that she had in mind when hesitating over the song Dick Harmon was to sing, but a memory of Frederick Goodyear, who had died at the front the year before:[60]

> Oh God—is it good? I am frightened. For I stand or fall by it. Its as far as I can get at present and I have gone for it, bitten deeper & deeper & deeper than ever I have before. Youll laugh a bit about the song. I could see Goodyear grin as he read that . . . .[61]

---

[59] JNPP-rough-NL, leaves 13 recto to 14 recto.

[60] Although partly indecipherable, the words under erasure in this passage may suggest the song she initially toyed with was not "The Lone Fish Ball," but another jaunty, possibly Scottish, ballad:

> "smiling his slow dreaming smile, ~~while~~ ^{so} he gets drunk on it slowly + dreamily + at a certain moment begins to sing very low very low ~~something about a MacPherson + his friend or every Mac xxx~~ about a man who* walked up and down trying to find some place where he could get some dinner" (JNPP-rough-NL, leaf 13 recto).

[61] Frederick Goodyear, an Oxford contemporary of Murry and Michael Sadleir, had been part of their group living in Paris in 1911–13. Like Murry, he was working on a long autobiographical novel, while contributing to early issues of *Rhythm* and discovering the heady life of Paris's subculture, likewise via the intermediacy of Francis Carco, Tristan Derème, and their circle of upbeat poets. By the time Mansfield began her story, Goodyear was dead, having been appallingly mutilated in 1917 by an explosion in his dug-out less than two months after receiving his first commission. See Leith Ross, ed., *Frederick Goodyear: Letters and Remains 1887–1917* (London: McBride, Nast & C°, 1920), viii–x.

Beloved by his friends for his "scholar-gipsy temperament," but just as renowned for his fits of despondency and overwhelming shyness, Goodyear's "swansong," perhaps, is as much a part of the textual genetics of "Je ne parle pas français" and its disarmingly elusive protagonist Dick Harmon ("Dick Harmon of course is partly is ——") as the other Oxford contemporaries who set off for Paris in 1911.[62] In the silence of the text, in other words, Mansfield has also hollowed out a space in which to record the memory of a lost friend's smile.

Here, then, are some of the sounds of France and the sounds of music possibly resonating from the margins of the text. Admittedly, returning to the draft versions of a work of fiction is always something of a perilous undertaking, constantly confronting us with the impossible task of deciding whether blanks, deletions, revisions, and marginal annotations are significant, signifying voices, deliberately discarded hints, or merely disconnected, even unrelated background noise. The closer one looks at the draft variants, however, and the more attentively one listens, the more resonant even the abandoned or apparently fortuitous coincidental notes become. Mansfield's Notebook 14 is a case in point. Unlike the loose-leaf sheets on which two variants of "Je ne parle pas" are written up, which are concerned exclusively with the on-going version of the story, the notebook contains more potentially extraneous material and is thus even more comparable to a conductor's orchestral score than the annotated loose pages. The notebook's cover page alone bears the title "Mouse," clearly added with hindsight, but still enacting another shift in focus from Duquette's self-centered story, which riffs on "not speaking French"— or "English"—as it emerges from a second-hand sheet of blotting paper, to the enigmatic female character and the stories she may or may not tell. Whenever it was added, even the single-word title "Mouse" invites speculation. Whether Mouse does or doesn't speak French, and whether or not she really does represent or speak for Mansfield herself, it is tempting to read the rare sounds of her voice in the drafts and the finished text as some form of particularly resonant textual alternative, both inviting us in and running away before we have time to listen, just as Madame Butterfly in her kimono is also, tangentially, a portrait of the artist.[63] As Duquette puts it so effectively, when Mouse speaks, "it wasn't her voice any more—it was like **the*** voice you **might imagine coming*** out of a tiny cold sea shell ~~left~~ ˢʷᵉᵖᵗ high + dry at last by the **salty*** tide."[64] And perhaps, even before the story speaks, hers is the voice noting, on the first page of the notebook:

> When I am sitting above the rocks near the edge of the sea I always fancy that I hear above the plash of the water the voice of two people talking somewhere I know not where. And the talking is always broken by something which is neither laughter nor sobbing but a low thrilling sound which might be either and is a part of both.[65]

Or is this Mansfield herself, listening in Bandol to the sounds of the Mediterranean and hearing the lost voices of Goodyear and her brother Leslie? Or the voices of England, or

---

[62] *Letters* 2, 56.

[63] The image is exactly the one found in Mansfield's "Night-Scented Stock" (1917) in which a playfully evasive lady partly screened by a fan appears to be, at least in part, the persona of the poet herself. See Gerri Kimber and Claire Davison, ed., *The Collected Poems of Katherine Mansfield* (Edinburgh: Edinburgh Univeristy Press, 2016), 117.

[64] JNPP-Notebook14-ATL, 36 recto.

[65] CW4, 238.

New Zealand, speaking through a pang of loneliness or homesickness? Or is this Duquette, trying out an idea that never makes it into his story, listening to the background hubbub of a café, comparing it to a seascape, and working the thrilling promise of stories into a tale of his own? It all depends on where the accent falls, and whether we choose to hear "more" or "less," but either way, the invitation is to listen alertly, and to read again.

The Journey from "Non-Compounders" to "The Daughters of the Late Colonel"

GERRI KIMBER

GENESIS AND PUBLICATION

Katherine Mansfield's long, episodic story "The Daughters of the Late Colonel" was begun in the south of France at the Villa Isola Bella in late November 1920 and completed through the course of one exhausting day on December 13, with her companion Ida Baker staying up until 3am to provide a celebratory cup of tea once the story was completed. As Mansfield later explained in a diary entry for January 17, 1922, "The only occasion when I ever felt at leisure was while writing The Daughters of the Late Col. And then at the end I was so terribly unhappy that I wrote as fast as possible for fear of dying before the story was sent."[1]

The first mention of the story comes in a letter from Mansfield to her husband, John Middleton Murry, on November 27, 1920: "I have a long story here—very long which I want to get published serially. Its supremely suitable for such a purpose. And it would bring me in money. Its form is the form of The Prelude BUT written today—not then. The Prelude is a child's story."[2] As she subsequently explains to Murry's brother Richard on January 1, 1921, "Its the outcome of the *Prelude* method—it just unfolds and opens. But I hope its an advance on Prelude. In fact I know its that because the technique is stronger."[3]

In the story Mansfield affectionately immortalizes Ida and her cousin Sylvia Payne, all of whom had attended the same school—Queen's College in Harley Street, London. The protagonists Constantia (Con) and Josephine (Jug) are two middle-aged spinster sisters who have had their wants and desires so subjugated by those of their domineering father (the late Colonel) that, after his death, they find themselves unable to make the simplest decision for themselves. Ida's middle name was Constance and "Jug" was the nickname for Sylvia. The story also preserves something of the Baker family circumstances whilst

---

[1] CW4, 405.
[2] *Letters* 4, 123. Letter to John Middleton Murry, November 27, 1920.
[3] Ibid., 156. Letter to Richard Murry, January 1, 1921.

growing up, when Ida and her sister, May (together with their brother Waldo), lived with their widowed and domineering father, Colonel Baker. The first seven years of Ida's life had been spent in Burma. Her mother died in 1903, and Ida was sent to board at Queen's College, where she met and befriended Mansfield. As Antony Alpers notes: "Since Ida's childhood had been spent in Burma the family home in Welbeck Street was full of oriental carvings, but it was empty of a mother, and the role foreseen for her was that essentially Victorian role that awaits the Colonel's daughters in the story, Con and Jug."[4] The first tentative title of the story was "Non-Compounders," a term used at Queen's College for girls who attended only some of the college's courses, or those who were not boarders but lived at home, such as Sylvia.

Mansfield dedicated the first draft of the story to Victor Sorapure, her much-beloved doctor, and perhaps the only one of the many she consulted who truly understood her: "To Doctor Sorapure Were my gratitude to equal my admiration my admiration would still outstep my gratitude."[5] Sorapure was clearly on her mind during the story's composition. This was a particularly low point in her life, both physically and emotionally, compelling her to write in a notebook under the heading "Suffering":

> Here, for a strange reason, there rises the figure of Doctor Sorapure. He was a good man. He helped me not only to bear pain but he suggested that perhaps bodily ill health is necessary, is a repairing process—and he was always telling me to consider how man plays but a part in the history of the world. My simple kindly doctor was pure of heart as Tchekhov is pure of heart.[6]

In her will, Mansfield requested that Sorapure, alongside a few of her closest friends, be given one of her favorite books. Ida herself noted in her own memoirs that the original dedication of the story to Sorapure was omitted when she copied out the story: "when I parted with it [the manuscript] I did not copy out the dedication and it was not printed with the story. I think this should be known, as it was the expression of the great debt of gratitude she felt and of her very genuine affection."[7]

The story was first published in May 1921, in the *London Mercury*.[8] A month before, Mansfield had written to Sydney Schiff: "My long story 'The Daughters of the Late Colonel'—comes out next month. I hope you will care for it. It means more to me than any other."[9] The *London Mercury*, edited by J. C. Squire (who had edited the *New Statesman* from 1913–1919), was a relatively new literary monthly, the first issue having appeared in November 1919, but with a solid reputation and growing readership. (In January 1922 it would go on to publish Mansfield's "At the Bay," the sequel to "Prelude.") "The Daughters of the Late Colonel" subsequently appeared in the last collection of stories published in Mansfield's lifetime, *The Garden Party and Other Stories*, published on February 23, 1922.

---

[4] Antony Alpers, *The Life of Katherine Mansfield* (London: Viking, 1980), 27.
[5] DLC-MS-NL, leaf 1.
[6] CW4, 336.
[7] Ida Baker, *Katherine Mansfield: The Memories of LM* (London: Michael Joseph, 1971), 129.
[8] Katherine Mansfield, "The Daughters of the Late Colonel," *London Mercury* 4, no. 19, May 1921, 15–30.
[9] *Letters* 4, 206. Letter to Sydney Schiff, April 18, 1921.

THEMES AND COMPOSITION

Death is a constantly recurring theme in Mansfield's stories. As Françoise Defroment asserts, "[w]ritten as they are in an elusive style that relies on impressionistic touches, Katherine Mansfield's short stories radiate an atmosphere of light and lightness. Yet underneath this aerial world the inexorable sweep of the sickle of death can be perceived."[10] We see its mark in "The Garden Party," "Life of Ma Parker," "Six Years After," "At the Bay," "The Child-Who-Was-Tired," "The Fly," "The Canary," and of course "The Daughters of the Late Colonel." Though each death described has already taken place, for Joseph Flora they, "look at death in its living aspect, grief. Wedged between her brother's death and her own, these stories represent an interesting compromise between being awash with grief in life and coming to terms with it, however briefly, in art."[11]

On the surface, "The Daughters of the Late Colonel" tells the outwardly simple story of two timid spinster sisters coming to terms with life in the week following the death of their irascible and intimidating father—the late Colonel. It offers an indictment of the patriarchal society in which Mansfield lived, where the bullying of women—and particularly spinsters, as here—was commonplace. In the utilization of two middle-aged women at the center of her narrative, who have had no life to speak of and done nothing of any importance, Mansfield fashions one of her most powerful yet humorous stories. Constantia and Josephine have had their wants and desires so subjugated by those of their domineering father that after his death they find themselves unable to make the simplest decision for themselves. As Yukiko Kinoshita affirms, "the middle-aged, unmarried, bourgeois women, socially belong to their father; they are 'nobodies.'"[12] As with so many of Mansfield's stories, the reader is presented with "ordinary" domestic events and characters. The sisters evoke for Angela Smith "the sexuality, painful sacrifice, and perhaps masochism that a woman defined as a bourgeois spinster with no sexual experience has suppressed."[13] In the following passage, Josephine, one of the spinster daughters, reflects on her life:

> If mother had lived, might they have married? But there had been nobody for them to marry. There had been father's Anglo-Indian friends before he quarrelled with them. But after that she and Constantia never met a single man except clergymen. How did one meet men? Or even if they'd met them, strangers?[14]

These sisters are not fools. They acknowledge that their life has been one of sacrifice, though they have never had the means to do anything about it—lack of personal money again is stressed here. The word "father" is used as a metaphor, a recurrent image as well as a character who is almost more powerful in death than in life. Time and again in the

---

[10] Françoise Defroment, "Impossible Mourning," in *The Fine Instrument: Essays on Katherine Mansfield*, ed. Paulette Michel and Michel Dupuis (Sydney: Dangaroo Press, 1989), 157–65 (157).

[11] Joseph Flora, *The English Short Story 1880–1945: A Critical History* (Boston: Twayne, 1985), 75.

[12] Yukiko Kinoshita, *Art and Society: A Consideration of the Relations Between Aesthetic Theories and Social Commitment with Reference to Katherine Mansfield and Oscar Wilde* (Chiba: Seiji Shobo, 1999), 101. Kinoshita sees this story as Mansfield's Proustian story of habit: "The sisters' perpetual fear of their menacing father, their social and moral repression (their docile acceptance of conventional values), their closed, narrow social circle (their social isolation or 'voluntary' alienation), and the resultant lack of stimulation—have made their life clogged and boring" (289).

[13] Angela Smith, *Katherine Mansfield and Virginia Woolf: A Public of Two* (Oxford: Clarendon Press, 1999), 223.

[14] CW2, 281.

story we see his ruthlessness and selfishness directed at his daughters, for whom he is a hard taskmaster and oppressor. There are in fact three deaths in this story, since with the death of their father, the spinsters' lives are now apparently pointless. Indeed, Rhoda Nathan believes that the colonel "has left his daughters a legacy of dread and impotence in their bereavement."[15]

One technique which acts as a marker for so many of Mansfield's stories, and which is particularly evident here is the use of *in medias res*—cutting straight through to the action, from the very first line, as if a stage direction is being given, with the use of temporal constructions implying a prior knowledge of the event being described: "The week after was one of the busiest weeks of their lives."[16] Indeed, the theatrical/cinematic tone is enhanced in some of the longer stories by their division into sections or "scenes" as in this case. In its division into twelve parts, this story replicates the format of both "Prelude" and "At the Bay."

"Affected" idiolects are a particular favorite of Mansfield's; there is a mockery in her depiction of grandiose yet ridiculous accents. Nowhere is this better portrayed than Nurse Andrews in this story:

> "When I was with Lady Tukes," said Nurse Andrews, "she had such a dainty little contray-vance for the buttah. It was a silvah Cupid balanced on the—on the bordah of a glass dish, holding a tayny fork. And when you wanted some buttah, you simply pressed his foot and he bent down and speared you a piece. It was quite a gayme."[17]

In a few short sentences, the essence of a character is presented to the reader, and more so than any traditional description could provide with a similar number of words. The reader knows Nurse Andrews is a snob, for she feels the need to name her last, titled employer. We know that she is from the lower classes because she makes such an effort with her speech—in effect she tries to lose her working-class origins but succeeds only in making herself sound ridiculous. Her unbridled admiration for the butter spearer only serves to make her appear more ludicrous.

Nurse Andrews is a memorable comic character in a story which nevertheless addresses serious issues. Mary Burgan writes, "The encounters with these aggressive 'professional' servants are among the most Dickensian comic passages in Mansfield's stories. As in Dickens, however, in Mansfield the comedy is inflected by pathos."[18] Mansfield uses comedy in her stories as a means of entertainment, but which at the same time underlines her serious sociological message. As an experienced public performer, she knew and understood as well as anyone that the complicity engendered by laughter makes an audience more receptive to the performer's point of view. Nathan considers "The Daughters of the Late Colonel" to be "one of the stories that best illustrates Mansfield's comic gifts."[19] She sees this story as a species of black comedy, and indeed all the characters

---

[15] Rhoda B. Nathan, *Katherine Mansfield* (New York: Continuum, 1988), 95.

[16] CW2, 266.

[17] Ibid., 268.

[18] Mary Burgan, *Illness, Gender and Writing: The Case of Katherine Mansfield* (Baltimore: Johns Hopkins University Press, 1994), 164–165. Irene Simon asserts, "Irony is close to sarcasm. In a broader sense it refers to a 'conflict between appearance and reality.' As such it is nearer to Socratic irony and implies disguise or deception, whether as flattery, condemnation, or reserve." See Irene Simon, "Irony in the Short Stories of Katherine Mansfield," in *The Fine Instrument*, 97–106 (98).

[19] Nathan, *Katherine Mansfield*, 96.

are either parodies or eccentrics of one sort or another. Yet rather than ridiculing the pathos of the spinster sisters' lives, the comedy intensifies it—they become real for us, we feel for them, we look kindly upon them. Smith concurs with this notion and states, "Their lives are ordinary tragedies, like those of Mansfield's Miss Moss and Miss Brill [. . .]. The delicate comedy with which they are treated acknowledges the problems of making middle-aged women the centre of a narrative."[20] Kinoshita also notes the use of comedy in the story: "The two sisters' fear of their father and their total powerlessness are pathetically but comically exaggerated in the story."[21] Yet, while noting the comedic aspect of her work, none of the above-mentioned critics dwell on it to any great extent; there is no sense that they find this aspect of her work critical to an understanding of her writing and the principles behind it. I contend that in the same way that every story raises a sociological or moral issue, every mature story, even the bleakest, contains an element of humor that is particularly and peculiarly Mansfield's own, used as a vehicle for transmitting her personal philosophy. It is this eye for the absurd in life, this delight in highlighting the ridiculous and pointing it out for us that encourages us to connect with the author and whatever message she might be concentrating on in any given story.

At the very end of "The Daughters of the Late Colonel," Constantia, one of the middle-aged spinster protagonists reflects:

> She remembered the times she had come in here, crept out of bed in her nightgown when the moon was full, and lain on the floor with her arms outstretched, as though she was crucified. Why? The big pale moon had made her do it. [. . .] She remembered too how, whenever they were at the seaside, she had gone off by herself and got as close to the sea as she could, and sung something, something she had made up, while she gazed all over that restless water. [. . .] It was only when she came out of the tunnel into the moonlight or by the sea or into a thunderstorm that she really felt herself. What did it mean? What was it she was always wanting? What did it all lead to? Now? Now?[22]

The moon is Mansfield's mysterious nature symbol, appearing out of the darkness, its strange, ethereal, silvery light so different from the bright, blazing sun. Associated with the feminine cycles of life, it is seemingly only in moonlight that Constantia "really felt herself." Here we are presented with one of Mansfield's characters arriving at an epiphanic moment of self-discovery, the irony being in this case that it simply does not happen; Constantia is unable to understand her feelings, unable to make that leap into self-discovery. But it is nature and its force which has brought her thus far, and this use of nature as a revelatory force permeates Mansfield's narrative text with the same symbols constantly recurring. In her later stories, Mansfield's use of moon and sun imagery has a more esoteric undertone; it is as if she is assuming a subconscious understanding of the workings of the universe through her use of recurring symbols, sometimes anthropomorphized to emphasize their importance. For Hanson, this is a particularly feminine approach:

> Revelation through "the slightest gesture" was, she wrote, her aim [. . .]. This indirection and obliquity might be viewed as particularly feminine, and I think it is

---

[20] Smith, *A Public of Two*, 223.
[21] Kinoshita, *Art and Society*, 187.
[22] CW2, 282.

feminine in the sense that there is a real distinction to be made between Mansfield's symbolist method and that of T. S. Eliot or James Joyce.[23]

The moon for Mansfield is always allied to the feminine, to the mysterious in life.

The sun is completely different. For Mansfield, it overpowers the sea and the moon and subjugates them to its own needs. The sun for Mansfield represents, as in "Sun and Moon," the male. There are frequent references to the sun throughout "The Daughters of the Late Colonel":

> On the Indian carpet there fell a square of sunlight, pale red; it came and went and came—and stayed, deepened—until it shone almost golden.
> "The sun's out," said Josephine, as though it really mattered.
> [. . .]
> The sunlight pressed through the windows, thieved its way in, flashed its light over the furniture and the photographs. Josephine watched it. When it came to mother's photograph, the enlargement over the piano, it lingered as though puzzled to find so little remained of mother, except the ear-rings shaped like tiny pagodas and a black feather boa.[24]

The carpet on which the sunlight falls, is "Indian"; this brings into play the image of the absent father, since it was because of him that the family had moved to Ceylon. The sunlight is not strong to begin with; its color is pale red, with almost something of the feminine in it. This is a chance for the sisters to assert themselves if only they could see it. But the moment to act passes, and gradually the sun's masculine force asserts itself until it shines "golden"—that superficial, metallic, male color. Only then does Josephine notice its presence, when its power is too strong, its force too pronounced to be altered, "'The sun's out,' said Josephine." Now the sunlight has a grip on the room, on their lives, it has "thieved its way in"—they have been taken unawares, with the sense of something having been stolen from them. By now, Josephine is a passive observer to the power of the sunlight; she "watched it." It lingers over the picture of the dead mother, "puzzled." Here, Mansfield shows us how the male and the female never truly understand each other; the mother as a personality is now a distant memory held in a dusty, light-faded photograph. Even in death the sunlight attacks the mother, as it did in life; if the "sun," the male, had not made her go to Ceylon, then she would never have been bitten by a snake and killed. The presentiment of her death was there in life, symbolized by the black feather "boa," wrapped round her in the photograph, for "Josephine remembered standing on a chair and pointing out that feather boa to Constantia and telling her that it was a snake that had killed their mother in Ceylon."[25]

In the final lines of the story it is the oppressive father figure who is symbolized by the sun, yet the power of the sun since his death has become uncertain, ephemeral, and in this final, potentially epiphanic moment, it is initially covered by a cloud: "Josephine was silent for a moment. She stared at a big cloud where the sun had been. Then she replied shortly, 'I've forgotten too.'"[26] The father is now dead, the sun is no more; yet instead of

---

[23] Clare Hanson, "Katherine Mansfield (1888–1923)," in *The Gender of Modernism: A Critical Anthology*, ed. Bonnie Kime Scott (Bloomington: Indiana University Press, 1990), 298–315 (301).
[24] CW2, 280–1.
[25] Ibid., 281.
[26] Ibid., 282.

being able to replace the sun's energy which has for so long dominated her life, Josephine is unable to make that giant leap towards freedom and agency, tragically encapsulated in the sentence which finally closes the story: "Then she replied shortly, 'I've forgotten too.'" As Cherry Hankin affirms, the two daughters

> have spent their lives immersed in the claustrophobic worlds of their father's house and their own confused imaginings. Their Father's death gives them the chance to emerge from their shell, to exchange the misty realm of dream for a life in the real world. There is a tinge of regret in their final unspoken choice of a continuing half-life; yet we, as well as they, know that they have opted for the comparative safety afforded by fantasy, rather than the potential dangers of reality.[27]

PERSONAL AND CRITICAL RESPONSE

Mansfield rarely expressed anything like true satisfaction with her work; "The Daughters of the Late Colonel" was one of the exceptions. In a letter to her brother-in-law, Richard Murry, she writes:

> By the way—Look here. I don't agree with you about women knocking off works of art at thirty or round about and men not until fifty. Or rather I don't agree personally. I'm 33; I feel I am only just beginning to see now what it is I want to do. It will take years of work to really bring it off. Ive done one or two things, like the Daughters of the Colonel which were the right kind. But <u>one</u> or <u>two</u>![28]

Another letter to William Gerhardi expresses similar feelings, in addition to dismay at the critics' misunderstanding of what she was trying to achieve:

> I cannot tell you how happy I am to know that The Daughters of the Late Colonel has given you pleasure. While I was writing that story I lived for it but when it was finished, I confess I hoped very much that my readers would understand what I was trying to express. But very few did. They thought it was "cruel"; they thought I was "sneering" at Jug and Constantia; they thought it was "drab." And in the last paragraph I was "poking fun at the poor old things."
>
> Its almost terrifying to be so misunderstood. There was a moment when I first had "the idea" when I saw the two sisters as amusing, but the moment I looked deeper (let me be quite frank) I bowed down to the beauty that was hidden in their lives and to discover that was all my desire . . . All was meant, of course, to lead up to that last paragraph, when my two flowerless ones turned with that timid gesture, to the sun. "Perhaps *now*." And after that, it seemed to me, they died as truly as Father was dead.[29]

Gerhardi had spontaneously contacted Mansfield after hearing Murry lecture in Oxford and evoke the writings of his wife. Gerhardi's letter, dated June 17, 1921, begins, "I hope you won't mind if I write to tell you how extremely beautiful I think your story is. [. . .] I have only just read it, and I have never read anything of yours before. I think it is, and in

---

[27] Cherry Hankin, "Fantasy and the Sense of an Ending in the Work of Katherine Mansfield," in *The Critical Response to Katherine Mansfield*, ed. Jan Pilditch (Westport, CT: Greenwood Press, 1996), 183–90 (190).

[28] *Letters 5*, 111–12. Letter to Richard Murry, March 16, 1922.

[29] *Letters 4*, 248–9. Letter to William Gerhardi, June 23, 1921.

particular the last long paragraph towards the end, of a quite amazing beauty."[30] Referring to exactly the same sentences that reviewers and readers had, according to Mansfield, misconstrued, Gerhardi insists, "The restraint of that particular paragraph is such that the climax leaves one breathless. I hope you won't think it presumptious [*sic*] on my part to point out to you these qualities in your own work."[31] A few months later, Mansfield is still asserting to him her feeling that the story is one of her best: "The only story that satisfies me to any extent is the one you understand so well 'The Daughters of the Late Col.' & parts of Je ne parle pas. But Heavens! what a journey there is before one!"[32]

Writing to her sister Chaddie, Mansfield explained in greater detail her inspiration for the characters of the two sisters:

> You see the Daughters of the Late C. were a mixture of Miss Edith & Miss Emily, Ida, Sylvia Payne, Lizzie Fleg, and "Cyril" was based on Chummie. To write stories one has to go back into the past. And its as though one took a flower from all kinds of gardens to make a <u>new</u> bouquet. But this is a thing which no amount of talking can change. One either feels it, or doesn't feel it . . .[33]

The story garnered a postbag of mail, including a letter from Thomas Hardy, sent via his wife, with many people, however, misreading her intentions with the story, as she explained to Dorothy Brett: "For I put my all into that story & hardly anyone saw what I was getting at. Even dear old Hardy told me to write more about those sisters. As if there was any more to say!"[34] As Alpers notes:

> Those last astonished words [about Hardy's response to the story] express in the end her total confidence in the *form* which she had made her own, but which in English was not yet sufficiently familiar. The problem [. . .] was the loneliness [. . .] of the form [. . .]—indeed, of the very idea that form could have equal status with the content, in a "story." That idea, being essentially poetic, seemed foreign to what so visibly was "prose." In the hands of other practitioners it later became so familiar that the boldness and originality of her innovation began to be forgotten.[35]

Renowned twentieth-century literary critic David Daiches views this story as

> a landmark in the history of the short story [. . . where] everything has reference to the mood of the story, everything is organised so as to bring "the deepest truth out of the idea." That so much should be achieved by such an economy of means is the greatest tribute to Katherine Mansfield's technique.[36]

Indeed, Mansfield's technique, he believes, is unique to her:

> It is not the most obvious way of telling a story, nor is it the easiest. To make the content so dependent on the form, as it were, by relying on the method of presenting

---

[30] William Gerhardi to Katherine Mansfield, June 17, 1921. Letters to and from Katherine Mansfield and friends / collected and annotated by John Middleton Murry, MS Papers 4003–37–1, Alexander Turnbull Library.

[31] Ibid., MS Papers 4003–37–1–2.

[32] *Letters 5*, 55. Letter to William Gerhardi, February 8, 1922.

[33] Ibid., 146–7. Letter to Charlotte (Beauchamp) Perkins (known to family and friends as "Chaddie"), April 8, 1922. "Chummie" was the Beauchamp family's nickname for Leslie, Mansfield's beloved younger brother, who had been tragically killed in Belgium in 1915.

[34] *Letters 4*, 316. Letter to Dorothy Brett, November 11, 1921.

[35] Alpers, *Life of Katherine Mansfield*, 330.

[36] David Daiches, *New Literary Values: Studies in Modern Literature* (Edinburgh: Oliver and Boyd, 1936), 105.

the situation in order to make it a situation worth presenting, without distorting the facts to meet the idea and without any comment, is to risk complete failure. There can be no half measures with this method; the critic cannot say, "A thoroughly well-told story, though a little pointless," because the point is so bound up with the telling that if it cannot be brought home the telling has no purpose—indeed, no separate existence—at all.[37]

In "The Daughters of the Late Colonel," Mansfield achieves a synthesis of technique and confidence in her craft, resulting in one of her most memorable and career-defining stories.

MANUSCRIPT

The manuscript of "The Daughters of the Late Colonel," now in the Newberry Library in Chicago, was apparently rescued from Mansfield's wastepaper bin by Ida Baker, with its dedication to Dr Victor Sorapure, and its original title of "Non-Compounders." As noted above, it was begun at the Villa Isola Bella in Menton in late November 1920 and completed on December 13. Mansfield's handwriting is quite legible throughout, but there is a clear sense of the writing being rushed in the last few pages, as she hurried to complete the story in the early hours of the morning.

The manuscript is remarkably clean, and the published version, aside from punctuation errors, is little changed from Mansfield's handwritten version. Nevertheless, some of the corrections Mansfield made attest to the honing of her modernist technique, where suggestion replaces more detailed description. This is a technique clearly visible in the polishing of her long story "The Aloe" into "Prelude." Together with its companion "At the Bay," both stories, together with "The Daughters of the Late Colonel," present us with the minutiae of quotidian life, where almost nothing happens of any consequence. In addition, as C. K. Stead notes, one of the major achievements of the story, also seen in the earlier masterpiece "Je parle pas pas français," "is that it establishes a central point of reference and then moves in circles about it, going backward and forward in time. The result is a further thickening of texture."[38]

All three stories have an identical narrative style, reflecting their modernist origins: an omniscient point of view combined with multiple limited points of view represented as free indirect discourse; together with a plotless form, the result is an intimate method of storytelling, where, for certain moments, we become intimate with the character on the page. This use of free indirect discourse would become a hallmark of Mansfield's narrative technique, together with the episodic nature of certain stories and their theatrical quality; as Mansfield remarked in a letter, discussing "Prelude": "What form is it you ask? [. . .] As far as I know it's more or less my own invention."[39] As noted earlier, some years later she referred to "the *Prelude* method—it just unfolds and opens."[40] Andrew Gurr takes these ideas one stage further, claiming a link with Eliot: "'Prelude' was in all sorts of ways an innovation. Its form, twelve episodes or scenes [. . .] was original in fiction, its closest kin perhaps being the associative form Eliot developed at the same time for *The Waste*

---

[37] Ibid., 84.

[38] C. K. Stead, "Katherine Mansfield and the Art of Fiction," in *Critical Response*, 155–72 (166).

[39] *Letters* 1, 331. Letter to Dorothy Brett, October 11, 1917.

[40] *Letters* 4, 156. Letter to Richard Murry, January 1, 1921.

Land."[41] Mansfield, ever the innovator and seeker after new experiences, was also fascinated with the new medium of the cinema. Her narrative art reflects this interest in the deliberate cinematic impression of so many of the stories; it is as if the narrator has a moving camera, panning across, then focusing in, which affords all three stories a unique "pictorial" characteristic.

"The Aloe" would become the draft for the more polished "Prelude." As Vincent O'Sullivan notes, "If critics can now say that 'a good case could be made for the short story being the most flexible of all forms and, as such, the key to "modernism,"' and refer to its range as 'analytical or lyrical, dramatic or rhapsodic,' that is partly because of what Mansfield did, and did for the first time in [these] two versions."[42] A comparison of the equivalent passages from "The Aloe" and "Prelude" reveals how the former was condensed, its verbosity tightened, the images made more direct, fashioned into polished, lyrical, *modernist* prose. At sixty-nine pages, "The Aloe" easily fits into the definition of a novella. Its condensed counterpart, "Prelude" at half the length does too, but "The Aloe" has far more items introduced—people, animals, images—and much more lengthy descriptions. Here is the same passage in both texts:

> "The Aloe": Dawn came sharp and chill. The sleeping people turned over and hunched the blankets higher—They sighed and stirred, but the brooding house all hung about with shadows held the quiet in its lap a little longer.

> "Prelude": Dawn came sharp and chill with red clouds on a faint green sky and drops of water on every leaf and blade.[43]

Almost three lines in the first instance are condensed to just over one line in the second. In "Prelude" a scene is presented, and the reader must visualize the image, subjectively, for him- or herself.

In "The Daughters of the Late Colonel," we can catch glimpses of a similar technique being refined, even though by now, Mansfield's pen is much more assured and so the differences are slight. On the first leaf, for example, "The giggle was rising, rising" is replaced with "The giggle mounted, mounted,"[44] the imperfect tense substituted for a more finite past tense, implying a specific moment in time during which Josephine struggles to contain her irreverent giggle. On leaf 2 of the manuscript, Mansfield makes the decision to change thirty-three to twenty-three, referring to the number of condolence letters the two sisters have received.[45] Thirty-three has a significant religious as well as numerous other connotations. The number twenty-three appears more "random," and Mansfield clearly thought it a better choice for the number of letters received.

Later in the manuscript, Mansfield makes a slight adjustment to her published version of the comical idiolect of Nurse Andrews, whose affected way of speaking is one of the comic highlights of the story. Her original word "deenty" eventually becomes "dainty."[46] It is clear that Mansfield is trying to underpin Nurse Andrew's affected speech by mis-

---

[41] Andrew Gurr, "Katherine Mansfield: The Question of Perspectives in Commonwealth Literature," in *Critical Response*, 197–206 (201).
[42] Katherine Mansfield, *"The Aloe" with "Prelude,"* ed. Vincent O'Sullivan (Manchester: Carcanet, 1983), 8.
[43] O'Sullivan, *"The Aloe,"* 58–9.
[44] DLC-MS-NL, leaf 1 [see Figure 19].
[45] DLC-MS-NL, leaf 2.
[46] DLC-MS-NL, leaf 5.

pronouncing this word, but "deenty" does not work with the rest of her pronunciation (for example "contrayvance" which, if she kept "deenty," would have to be written as "contreevance").

However, during the story's composition, Mansfield also gives the two sisters echoes of their own idiolects. Josephine, for example, says "sposition" for position.[47] This is retained in the *London Mercury* version, but removed by Mansfield in *The Garden Party* collection. This suggests that Mansfield initially considered capturing Josephine's peculiar idiolect, but then thought better of it, and removed the idiosyncratic pronunciation. The same applies to Constance, where Mansfield has her say "At tany rate," on leaves 11, 14 and 21 of the manuscript, but in the *London Mercury* she changes it to the normal "At any rate," which is how it remains in *The Garden Party* collection.[48] Creating two different idiolects for both Josephine and Constance encumbers the modernist prose with unnecessary complications and adds nothing to our understanding of their characters, unlike Nurse Andrews, where her mode of speaking reveals *everything* we need to know about her.

Another instance of Mansfield's eagle eye for physical detail occurs later on in the manuscript, where she adds "folded his coat tails" before the visitor, the local vicar Mr. Farolles, sits down. The coat tails provide additional evidence of his employment, together with his kid gloves and hat; the latter item Mansfield changes from "soft felt" to "black straw" in the manuscript, which adds to the overall clerical description of this comical priest.[49]

The scene in Section VI of the story, where the two sisters enter their father's bedroom to make a start on clearing his things, clearly created some difficulties for Mansfield, as the number of crossings out in the manuscript attests. Leaves 12 and 13 also show evidence of having been written in a hurry. Most of the crossings out underpin Mansfield's "less is more" technique of modernist writing, where suggestion replaces detailed description. For example, five lines of text, describing the sisters' reaction to having shut the door behind them as they enter the room, include: "**At any moment from anywhere the little man might appear[,] the little murderer something so menacingly—with a loop of rope over his arm**"[50] [see Figure 20]. This sentence is crossed out in the manuscript and completely removed in the final version, which reads thus: "Was the door just behind them? They were too frightened to look. Josephine knew that if it was it was holding itself tight shut; Constantia felt that, like the doors in dreams, it hadn't any handle at all."[51] The removal of the sinister and rather gothic reference to a murderer and his rope once more confirms Mansfield's wholly modernist technique of "suggestion" rather than "description." The sisters' fears are more than clear enough from the sparse prose which remains, and there is no need for the almost childish fear of a hidden murderer to emphasize their anxieties.

The manuscript is then remarkably clean, with barely a crossing out, until leaf 27, and the beginning of Section XI. Once more, most of the deletions are to do with conciseness and the omission of superfluous description, as can be seen in the transcription. A mostly illegible sentence beginning "And Father hates . . ." is completely removed, and a long,

---

[47] DLC-MS-NL, leaf 9.
[48] DLC-MS-NL, leaves 11, 14, 21.
[49] DLC-MS-NL, leaf 7.
[50] DLC-MS-NL, leaf 12.
[51] CW2, 272.

descriptive, only semi-legible phrase about Constantia's undergarment lace ties is replaced with the more concise "under her ties"[52] [see Figure 21].

The final section sees a number of corrections to the manuscript in the most symbolic passage of the entire story, where the oppressive father figure is symbolized by the sun, as noted earlier. Any changes in this final section reflect Mansfield's ongoing technique of conciseness, together with the removal of any extraneous description. Nowhere is this better emphasized than on leaf 30 of the manuscript, where Mansfield has crossed out "And now she was 43 and Constantia was 38."[53] Knowing the ages of the two spinster sisters is unnecessary. The information defines them—and indeed corrals them—into a constricting straitjacket, where imagination is replaced by facts. The fluidity of *not* telling the reader how old the sisters are allows them to occupy a fluid place on the page—and in the mind of the reader.

CONCLUSION

The hand-written manuscript of Mansfield's story "The Daughters of the Late Colonel" is remarkably clean on the whole, revealing a writer at the height of her craft, sure about the direction in which she wanted to take her writing and the techniques needed to accomplish it. Without overtly labelling herself a modernist, Mansfield's prose exemplifies this literary genre to perfection. Indeed, Mansfield was, in the words of Peter Childs, "the most important Modernist author who wrote only short stories."[54]

Indeed, in her discussion of Mansfield's masterful short story technique, Cherry Hankin illuminates the differences between the novel and the short story thus:

> While the novel, with its expansive treatment of character, can afford to imitate the open-endedness of life in its conclusion, the linguistic economy of the short story imposes a more rigorous pattern. The closure or ending of the narrative is integral, not only to our sense of the work's completeness but to our perception of the design as a whole.[55]

Added to this, H. E. Bates reflects how, "as in a great drawing, so in a great short story: it is the lines that are left out that are of paramount importance. Not that this is all; it is knowing what lines to leave out that is of the greatest importance, too."[56] Lorna Sage comments that for Mansfield, this editing out of superfluous subject matter made "short stories into intensely crafted and evocative objects-on-the-page, sometimes with nearly no plot at all in the conventional sense."[57] Concurring with this notion, Kathleen Wheeler further elucidates how this rejection of a conventional plot structure and ensuing dramatic action yields to, "impressionistic evocations of epiphanic moments."[58] Wheeler encapsulates all the definitions of the modernist short story which have evolved over the years and sets Mansfield's work into this body of evidence:

---

[52] DLC-MS-NL, leaf 27.

[53] DLC-MS-NL, leaf 30.

[54] Peter Childs, *Modernism* (London: Routledge, 2002), 95.

[55] Cherry Hankin, "Fantasy and the Sense of an Ending in the Work of Katherine Mansfield," in *Critical Response*, 183–90 (183).

[56] H. E. Bates, *The Modern Short Story from 1809 to 1953* (London: Robert Hale, 1988), 8.

[57] Lorna Sage, ed., "Introduction," *The Garden Party and Other Stories* (London: Penguin, 2000), vii–xxi (vii).

[58] Kathleen Wheeler, *Modernist Women Writers and Narrative Art* (Basingstoke: Macmillan, 1994), 124.

Modernist fiction largely dispensed with (or even de-emphasised) plot, action, drama, structure, shape, development, and so on [. . .]. These conventions are used in the service of the greater expression of the interior life, though not at the expense of social relations and externalised dramatics which provide a social-realist context. Mansfield's stories and many other modernist fictions, then, are not quite accurately described as rejecting such conventions, so much as for wrenching them away from traditional emphasis on the realistic representation of external, social, public relations, which relegate interiority to the sidelines or even into virtual non-existence. One could argue that Mansfield artfully hid the "mechanics" of her stories, as artists need to do.[59]

Mansfield's fiction—and literary modernism as a whole—is associated with a rejection of conventional plot structure and dramatic action in favor of the presentation of character through narrative voice. Mansfield is present at the beginning of this movement as one of its most exciting and cutting-edge protagonists, according her a prominent place in literary modernism, with modernist tendencies present throughout her fiction, perfectly exemplified by the process evident in this story.

---

[59] Wheeler, *Modernist Women Writers*, 125.

"All at Sea": Sea Journeys in "The Stranger," "The Voyage," and "Six Years After"

JANET M. WILSON

Sea journeys and their atmospheric, climacteric changes, whether on boats, ships, or steamers, provided Mansfield with a rich array of impressionistic images for narratives which demarcate transitions in states of being. She turned to these settings in three late stories that tell of family crises caused by bereavement that involve perceptions of irrevocable loss. The transitional environment of the sea journey—with its distinctive seascapes and weather patterns; on-board apparatus and requirements; departures, arrivals, and encounters with passengers and stewards—represents a radically altered world that nevertheless remains entangled with the everyday one. Mansfield often alludes to the changes incurred by sea journeys for irony and distance: For example, for Mr Hammond in "The Stranger," his wife's return leads him to believe "The danger was over [. . .]. They were on dry land again"; in "Six Years After" the narrator writes, "There is something almost touching, childish in the way people submit to new conditions."[1] In other words, through narratives of sea voyages she creates metaphoric states of being "all at sea" by representing subjective impressions of disorientation or dissociation, perceptions of psychological change, revelations of memory, and dream. At sea ordinary reality becomes distorted, expectations undercut, assumptions and feelings overturned.

This chapter will discuss "The Stranger" (1921), "The Voyage" (1921), and "Six Years After" (published posthumously, 1923), with reference to Mansfield's processes of writing and revision and the pressures of memory, testimony, and identity that shaped her narrative art. It will examine the revisions of existing drafts and compare the changes between the rough draft, which Pierre-Marc de Biasi defines as "instrumental in the composition and elaboration of a text" and the "clean" or final draft that supersedes it, prior to publication.[2] Observations of Mansfield's compositional practice will be contextualized by her comments in notebooks and letters and biographical and editorial interpretations. This approach is informed by the arguments of genetic criticism, that the

---

[1] CW2, 244, 422.
[2] Pierre-Marc di Biasi, "What is a Literary Draft? Toward a Functional Typology of Genetic Documentation," trans. Ingrid Wassenaar, *Yale French Studies* 8 (1996): 28. Both a rough and final draft survive of "The Stranger" and "Six Years After"; "The Voyage" is a single draft, heavily revised.

archive enables reconstruction of intentionality and understanding of the "material manifestations" of the author at work: i.e. by showing the "temporal development of the text" through draft versions.[3] It will note, for example, Mansfield's "purposive" changes that consist of revised titles of stories and names of characters or appellations alongside extraneous comments on drafts that are outside the world of the story and constitute her thoughts while writing. Examining Mansfield's creative role in this process—that is, her artistic decisions as shown by manuscript drafts—will enable inferences to be made concerning her modernist practice, composition, and aesthetics.

The three stories examined here show strong thematic connections in their exploration of the impact of death and bereavement within a family. "The Stranger" concerns an incident that occurred at sea: a stranger's sudden death in the arms of a married woman and its effect on her husband, registered in his horrified perception of lost marital intimacy. By contrast, in "The Voyage" and "Six Years After," allusions and emendations on the manuscripts suggest they are Mansfield's artistic and aesthetic responses to the tragic death of her brother, Leslie Heron Beauchamp, in a hand grenade accident in Ploegsteert Wood in Flanders in October 1915. Studying her revisions and comparing the different drafts of the stories also reveal her preoccupation with the crisis of the *pater familias*, a figure based on her father, Harold Beauchamp, as she examines masculinity under siege due to unexpected psychological pressure. Whereas Mansfield was writing about her parents in "The Stranger," the other two stories, written a year later, that in different ways memorialize her brother Leslie, are marked by responses to mortality, death in the family, and the futility and waste of the Great War. Her choice of imagery and the development of symbolism in representing character, as revealed by her processes of composition, suggest that in all three Mansfield was also moving towards her famous story, "The Fly" (1922), seen as her ultimate protest against early twentieth-century patriarchy and British post-war attitudes towards the wholescale loss of life.[4]

"THE STRANGER" AND MARITAL ESTRANGEMENT

Written sometime in October 1920 and completed by November 3rd, "The Stranger" marks a time when Mansfield's tuberculosis was entering a new and difficult phase. The sense of time running out made her respond to her writing as if under an overwhelming compulsion, and she wrote to Murry in October 1920 of "a queer kind of *pressure*— which is work to be done. *I am writing*." Of "The Stranger" in particular she wrote: "It seizes me—swallows me completely [. . .] Im lost—gone—possessed."[5] This urgency of her task led her to see the sea voyage as an image for the journey of life: Aware of what lay ahead, she wrote to Murry in the same month that as "[t]he little boat enters the dark fearful gulf," the "greatest failing of all is *to be frightened*" (italics in original).[6] The same

[3] Todd Martin, "'What was It?' The *avante-texte* and the 'Grinding Feeling of Wretchedness' in Katherine Mansfield's 'The Fly,'" *Papers on Language and Literature* 55, no. 1 (Winter 2019): 19, 29–30, and "Resurrecting Katherine Mansfield: the 'Death of the Author' and the Possibilities of Genetic Criticism," *Turnbull Library Record* 50 (2018): 43–54.

[4] Summarized by Janka Kascakova, "The Symbolism of the Ink in 'The Fly,'" in *Re-forming World Literature: Katherine Mansfield and the Modernist Short Story,* ed. Gerri Kimber and Janet Wilson (Stuttgart: Ibidem Verlag, 2018), 288–90.

[5] *Letters* 4, 97.

[6] Ibid., 75.

imagery, however, also encompasses her experience of safe haven through her art as she speculates about having a book ready by Christmas, commenting: "Its just as though the ship had sailed into harbour . . . I can manage rocks and shoals and storms—anything."[7]

The same intensified sense of time passing appears in "The Stranger," in the hero's growing awareness of the ticking away of minutes; after eagerly greeting his wife upon her return from Europe, he discovers that a passenger on the boat died in her arms. Plunged into crisis he realizes their relationship is irrevocably changed. Among the best of her later stories according to Antony Alpers,[8] "The Stranger" is based on an incident in 1909 involving Mansfield's parents: Her mother Annie had returned from a journey to England on the *Tongariro* and met with her father, Harold Beauchamp, in Hobart, Tasmania. During the voyage, an ailing passenger who "touched her heart" had died in her arms just before the ship berthed, a revelation that greatly shocked Beauchamp.[9]

Mansfield drafted the story when staying in the Villa Isola Bella, in Menton, France, and sent her "much corrected" cleaner copy consisting of in-text changes and later revisions to Murry on November 3rd.[10] Both the initial draft and its "accompanying handwritten fair copy" are housed in the Newberry Library.[11] The revision process visible on the rough and fair drafts confirms Ruth Mantz's account of Mansfield's revision of her early pieces.

> It was her custom [. . .] to write the first draft quickly under the impulse of her original idea; then to experiment with it—crossing out words and lines, revising the first text; later to rewrite completely, retaining only certain sentences and phrases from the first draft—really giving the idea a new chance to form itself.[12]

This method, as the draft indicates, shows Mansfield as most concerned with revising and refining the volatile reactions of the protagonist, John Hammond, from his keen anticipation of a passionate reunion with his wife, Janey, wanting her all to himself after months apart, to his shocked reactions to the sudden revelation of the ship-board incident. In her revisions, Mansfield stresses Hammond's emotional insecurity by contrast to his impeccable appearance and air of authority on the wharf, where he "marched up and down twirling his folded umbrella" and "seemed to be the leader of the little crew"[13]; his mounting anxiety after Janey disembarks; and his refusal to believe that she has changed in any way because she is wearing black. Adding to the tension, Mansfield magnifies the mystery of the event on board. New phrases are added to the rough manuscript: For example, when Hammond asks whether Janey had been ill on the voyage, she replies (on both drafts): "Do I look ill?"[14] In the clean manuscript, Hammond asserts, "You have!"[15]

---

[7] Ibid., 97. One of Mansfield's best-known reflections on the process of writing refers specifically to this story: "Ive *been* this man *been* this woman. Ive stood for hours on the Auckland Wharf. Ive been out in the stream waiting to be berthed. Ive been a seagull hovering at the stern and a hotel porter whistling through his teeth" (*Letters* 4, 97).

[8] Antony Alpers, *The Life of Katherine Mansfield* (London: Jonathan Cape, 1980), 321, 327.

[9] Ibid., 94–95 and note. The passenger's name was D. M. Niven and he was buried at sea.

[10] *Letters* 4, 97–98. The story was published in the *London Mercury* in January 1921.

[11] Antony Alpers, *The Stories of Katherine Mansfield* (Auckland: Oxford University Press, 1984), 564.

[12] Ruth Elvish Mantz and John Middleton Murry, *The Life of Katherine Mansfield* (London: Constable, 1933), 261.

[13] CW2, 240.

[14] Stran-rough-NL, leaf 7, and Stran-clean-NL, leaf 9.

[15] Stran-clean-NL, leaf 9.

Mansfield signifies his solipsistic wish for reassurance by adding in a lighter ink on the initial draft that he does not really see her: "He only felt she was looking at him + that there was no need to worry about anything. She was here to look after things. No it was all right. Everything was."16 This is retained in the clean copy, and Hammond's greater uncertainty about the episode on the boat is created by excising the statement in the rough draft about his suspicions ("she was keeping something from him") as well as his jumpy self-assurance ("she was speaking the truth"); it is revised in the clean version to stress his growing insecurity and jealousy: "He was going off to find that fellow (i.e. the doctor) and to wring the truth out of him at all costs," to stress his growing insecurity and jealousy.17

In the clean manuscript, Mansfield also shortens two passages that provide extraneous information. In the final section of the original draft is Hammond's hysterical, incoherent reaction after Janey reveals a stranger has died in her arms—"She who'd never once never in all these years"18—and his incredulity that she would experience such intimacy with a complete stranger is intensified in the revision. The imprecation in the original, "Ah my God," is repeated, but Mansfield crosses out one utterance in the earlier draft and in the revision eliminates the second, replacing it with "never," to create a rhetorical crescendo that recalls King Lear's agony at Cordelia's death: "never [. . .] never [. . .] never," to which she adds the alliterative phrase "single solitary occasion":19 "And yet he died in Janey's arms. She—who'd never—never once in all these years—never in on one single, solitary occasion. . . ."20 A substantial section of this interior lament is crossed out on the rough draft:

> What had she done. Janey had taken him—held him—clasped him—Ah, my God he couldn't think about it – he couldn't face it – he couldn't stand it. She who'd never even Janey had taken that other. No, no he must never think of it again madness lay in thinking about it. His whole life would be ruined. Everything changed.21 [see Figure 18]

It is reduced in the final manuscript to one stark, brief paragraph: "No, he mustn't think of it. Madness lay in thinking of it. No, he wouldn't face it. He couldn't stand it. It was too much to bear!"22 Mansfield's revisions can be read as dramatizing Hammond's panic, which W. H. New attributes to blindness about how his possessiveness masks insecurity: this lack of self-knowledge makes the psychological blow of Janey's revelation more insidious and overwhelming, "unmanning" him and rendering his future uncertain.23

The most significant revisions, I suggest, are in modernist narrative techniques used to convey the onset of Hammond's dark despair in the conclusion in ways that are comparable to the protagonists' "buried misery" in the endings of "The Fly" and "The Canary."24 Mansfield excises the melodramatic statement—"At that Hammond [. . .] felt as though his heart stopped beating"25—in

---

16 Stran-rough-NL, leaf 7.
17 Compare Stran-rough-NL, leaves 7–8 with Stran-clean-NL, leaf 9.
18 Stran-rough-NL, leaf 15.
19 *The Tragedy of King Lear,* ed. Barbara A. Mowat and Paul Werstine, The Folger Shakespeare Library, 5.3.372. https://shakespeare.folger.edu.
20 Compare Stran-clean-NL, leaf 18, with Stran-rough-NL, leaves 14–15.
21 Stran-rough-NL, leaf 15.
22 Stran-clean-NL, leaf 18.
23 W. H. New, *Reading Mansfield and Metaphors of Form* (Montreal and Kingston: McGill-Queen's University Press, 1999), 135.
24 Martin, "'What was It?'" 18.
25 See Stran-rough-NL, leaf 14, where this phrase is actually an amendment.

the final version and rewrites the incomplete, partially crossed-out sentence of the first draft ("Janey ceased speaking ^{but her xx words seemed to float to hover—to ~~settle slowly—fall~~ settle in his heart covering his [sic]"}[26]) to express his dawning recognition affectively, using imagery of rain and snow: "Janey was silent. But her words—so light—so soft—so chill seemed to hover in the air to rain into his breast—like snow."[27] The comparison of Janey's words to falling snow gives a decidedly modernist cast to the ending, especially when read with reference to Enda Duffy's analysis of snow and its connotations of blankness and nothingness in her story "Je ne parle pas français" with its echo of Joyce's "The Dead." Duffy's claim that, unlike Joyce, Mansfield's snow revelation is about "the memory of a dead or discarded friendship" can equally be applied to Hammond's numbed response: The snow imagery in "The Stranger" is "a sign of a fear of death in life [. . .] a fading-out, a *petit mort*, a life-limit."[28] As with the voice of Raoul Duquette in "Je ne parle pas français," it marks Hammond's psychological collapse, the death of affect and the crisis realization of the "limit epiphany," that he is unable to "fully live [. . .] or profoundly feel."[29]

These metaphoric implications are reinforced in the final sentences, which were revised three times to define the change in consciousness. Hammond echoes his wife's words—"It hasn't spoilt our evening—our being ^{alone} together"—but Mansfield revises the first person voice to third person to emphasise his psychological distance from the marriage: "Spoilt ~~our~~ ^{their} evening—spoilt ~~our~~ ^{their} being together—~~They would~~ ^{Didnt she know} never be alone together again [*sic*]. The clean manuscript incorporates the superscript "alone" of Janey's statement to give "being alone together," and it cuts the superscript revision "Didn't she know" to rhetorically underline Hammond's realization: "Spoilt their evening! Spoilt their being alone together! They would never be alone together again"[30] [see Figure 18]. The repetition in this negative epiphany underlines that henceforth they will be strangers to each other. It rebounds against the story's title, "The Stranger" (replacing the draft's original title, "The Interloper"),[31] ostensibly referring to the stranger who dies on the boat but now extended to include their irresolvable marital estrangement and hence Hammond's alienation from the person he thought he was.

Hammond's epiphany anticipates the conclusion of "The Fly" where the boss, also modeled on Harold Beauchamp, unable to grieve for his son's death six years later, finds himself emotionally distracted and disconnected from his train of thought, but also his memory and some part of himself, asking: "What was It?"[32] As a study of besieged masculinity, "The Stranger" is arguably a forerunner of this trenchant representation of psychological impasse. Wary of how her father would react to the story, Mansfield changed the New Zealand place names to Crawford and Salisbury for its publication in *The Garden Party*, so he would not recognize himself.[33]

---

[26] Ibid.

[27] Stran-clean-NL, leaf 17.

[28] Enda Duffy, "Dirty Snow: Mansfield, Joyce and the modernist snow globe," *Katherine Mansfield: New Directions*, ed. Aimée Gasston, Gerri Kimber, and Janet Wilson (London: Bloomsbury, 2020), 47.

[29] Ibid., 48, 49. See Alpers, *Life*, 329 on "The Stranger" and "The Dead."

[30] Stran-rough-NL, leaf 15; Stran-clean-NL, leaf 18 verso.

[31] Stran-rough-NL, leaf 1.

[32] CW2, 480.

[33] Alpers explains that Mansfield was anxious not to offend her father on whom she depended for her allowance (*Stories*, 564; *Life*, 360–61). Recent editors, Alpers and Kimber and O'Sullivan, have restored the original names in their published versions, confirming Mansfield's comment, "It's a 'New Zealand' story'" (*Letters* 4, 97). See Alpers, "The Stranger," *Stories*, 364 ("Auckland"), 370 (Napier); CW2 240, 246.

"THE VOYAGE" AND AN AESTHETICS OF MOURNING

Told through the focalizing gaze of the child, Fenella Crane, "The Voyage" is about her overnight boat journey with her grandmother from Wellington across Cook Strait to Picton in Queen Charlotte Sounds, to her grandparents' house.[34] That a death in the family is the reason for the journey emerges from what Fenella observes of the adult world: her father who sees them off sounds "stern" but looks "tired and sad," and later she overhears the stewardess's comment: "Poor little Motherless mite!"[35] The story recounts the Picton boat's night-time departure from the "dark wharf" in Wellington, the overnight journey and sleeping arrangements, their early morning arrival at Picton, and Fenella's first meeting with Grandpa at journey's end.[36]

Mansfield revised the original manuscript of "The Voyage" (in Notebook 5, dated 14 August 1921) by writing corrections and emendations onto the text as superscripts or alongside particular words or phrases, and occasionally on the page opposite. Mourning and bereavement are implied in Frank's farewell to his mother on the wharf, notably the Christian blessing:[37] "God bless you Mother—she heard him say—" followed by her reply "God bless you my ᵒʷⁿ brave son!"[38] Mansfield emended the parental relationship at this moment of departure to emphasize Frank's efforts to appease Fenella—substituting "meet her eyes" with "look at her" ("But he wouldn't meet her eyes ˡᵒᵒᵏ ᵃᵗ ʰᵉʳ")[39] and animating his dialogue by adding, "And ʰᵉʳᵉ! Wʰᵉʳᵉˢ ʸᵒᵘʳ ʰᵃⁿᵈ he pressed something into her hand ᵖᵃˡᵐ" so he can give her a shilling before disappearing.[40] In this gesture he recalls John Hammond of "The Stranger," who also relies on the discourse of commercial exchange, obligation, and indebtedness for conveying intimacy, further implying his emotional limitation in his inability to meet the eye of the other.[41] This brief portrait of a father burdened with sorrow and unable to reassure his child also recalls the husband of "Six Years After" who is oblivious to his wife's grief, and the boss who is unable to grieve in "The Fly." Mansfield links the family bereavement to her own loss through the "process of memorialisation" that Lisa Stead describes as embedded in the materials of the archive, "enacted through spatial imagery and mapping."[42] The name "Leslie Heron Beauchamp" follows the line, "God bless you my ᵒʷⁿ brave son!"[43] and Todd Martin infers that her brother was in her thoughts

---

[34] This may refer to a journey Mansfield made sometime between 1895–97, as "the Picton boat" in the story has been identified as the *SS Penguin* which inaugurated the interisland ferry service in 1895. Her first (now lost) story, "A Sea Voyage," is about a journey to Queen Charlotte Sounds made about this time. See Redmer Yska, *A Strange Beautiful Excitement: Katherine Mansfield's Wellington 1888–1903* (Dunedin: Otago University Press, 2017), 128; Gerri Kimber, *Katherine Mansfield: The Early Years* (Edinburgh: Edinburgh University Press, 2016), 49.

[35] CW2, 377.

[36] On Mansfield's paternal grandparents Mary and Arthur Beauchamp, and great-uncle Cradock Beauchamp who lived near Picton in Anakiwa, see Yska, *A Strange Beautiful Excitement*, 91–99, and Kimber, *The Early Years*, 9, 49.

[37] The portrait of the grandmother is based on Mansfield's grandmother, Mary Stanley Beauchamp, described as "stoical, saintly"; she was idolized by Harold, and Mansfield also loved her. She is called Mary in the story although her husband, based on Arthur Beauchamp, is given the name of Walter. See Yska, *A Strange Beautiful Excitement*, 92–93, 187; Kimber, *The Early Years*, 17.

[38] Voy-NB5-NL, 15, 16.

[39] Ibid., 16.

[40] Ibid.

[41] New, *Reading Mansfield*, 135.

[42] Lisa Stead, "Introduction," *The Boundaries of the Literary Archive: Reclamation and Representation*, ed. Carrie Smith and Lisa Stead (London: Ashgate, 2013), 3.

[43] Voy-NB5-NL, 15, 16.

when writing this story[44] [see Figures 34 and 35]. Her revisions suggest the shaping of an aesthetics of mourning, that allows "The Voyage" to be aligned with "Six Years After" and "The Fly," her two stories that most explicitly commemorate Leslie's death.

Mansfield's changes also introduce distancing tropes. The original title, "Going to Stay with her Granma," suggesting a child's voice, is replaced with the more impersonal "The Voyage."[45] There is some variability in tone as the narrative voice oscillates between impersonation of Fenella's consciousness and that of the older, distanced narrator; for example, moving between the appellation "granma" and the more orthodox "Grandma" (the standard term in all published versions) and "the old woman," used of her saying her prayers.[46] Furthermore, in recounting the journey, Mansfield correlates the impressionistic descriptions of the night-time departure and early morning arrival to Fenella's subjective observations and nascent feelings. Other small lexical changes include repositioning or replacing some nouns and adjectives for greater visual impact, contributing to a contrastive black and white color symbolism and aesthetic patterning evocative of night and day, darkness and light, death and life. This symbolic dimension delicately encompasses in a metaphysic of spiritual renewal the religiosity of the grandmother's piety, expressed in the blessings exchanged with her son and her prayers. The dark shapes of the wharf at the night-time departure are congruous with her Victorian funeral attire and Fenella's perceptions of separation and mourning, while the early morning frost that greets their arrival at Picton, and then thaws, evokes rebirth and renewal. In demarcating Fenella's transition from the state of mourning to recovery, "The Voyage" is comparable to another travel story by Mansfield, "An Indiscreet Journey," that also resembles a rite de passage.[47]

In the opening paragraphs the word "darkness" is repeatedly associated with the "old Wharf" alongside the blackness of the wood pile (like a "huge black mushroom"), while the description of the lantern is revised from "in all that darkness" to "in all that blackness" to emphasize blackness as penetrated by "its timid, quivering light,"[48] a patterning that recurs in the iconic image of the Picton boat as if about to depart on an unearthly journey: "Lying along beside the dark wharf all strung all beaded with round golden lights the Picton boat looked as if it she was more ready to sail among stars than out into the cold sea."[49] It also introduces associations between black, mourning, and death: the grandmother's "crackling black ulster," Fenella's "black coat and skirt, black blouse + hat with a crepe rose,"[50] and the chiaroscuro description of the "one tiny boy" whose "little black arms + legs" show over "a white wooly shawl," looking "like a baby fly that had fallen into the cream"[51] [see Figures 33 and 34]. This image of pernicious fate—recalling Mansfield's fondness for Shakespeare's axiom in *King Lear*: "As flies to wanton boys are we to th'

---

[44] See Voy-NB5-NL, note 11. Mansfield also included the name of her cousin Mary Beauchamp (i.e. the writer, Elizabeth von Arnim) at the top of two pages of this story (see Voy-NB5-NL, note 16).

[45] Voy-NB5-NL, 14. In changing the title, Mansfield may have been thinking of her original story, "A Sea Voyage"; this may also account for the variation of tone and voice in "The Voyage."

[46] See Voy-NB5-NL. Similarly, in "Six Years After" the wife calls her husband "Daddy" in the original, suggesting conflation of her identity with that of their deceased son; this is replaced by "father" in the revision.

[47] Janet M. Wilson, "'Such rich unlawful gold': Mansfield's Semiotic Manoeuvres in 'An Indiscreet Journey,'" in *Katherine Mansfield and Bliss and Other Stories*, ed. Enda Duffy, Gerri Kimber, and Todd Martin (Edinburgh: Edinburgh University Press, 2020), 189.

[48] Voy-NB5-NL, 14.

[49] Ibid., 15.

[50] Ibid., 14, 18.

[51] Ibid., 14.

gods; / They kill us for their sport"[52]—parallels the perspective of distanced couples in "The Stranger" resembling "little flies walking up and down," barely separate from a "tiny black spider [that] raced up the ladder to the bridge,"[53] and in "The Fly," the fly's representation as a multi-layered symbol of death, incomplete grieving, and psychological stasis.

Mansfield's artistic practices are also illuminated by the anthropomorphism of the swan-necked umbrella that has to be "taken unbroken to the end of the voyage," and so symbolizes Fenella's safe passage.[54] She substitutes the verb "dig," used of its swan's head handle, with "peck," as in "a sharp little ~~dig~~ peck, as if it too wanted her to hurry."[55] This is reinforced by the symbolism of the grandmother's name, "Mrs Crane," and the avian superscript on the draft: "her hands folded, her head a little on one side," as she settles to pray[56] [see Figures 33 and 35]. With these additions and substitutions, Mansfield combines color symbolism, metaphor, and personification to animate her narrative and to suggest a child's perception of intersubjective animal and human worlds, as she forges "her own imaginary land," "untouched by death."[57]

The binary patterning of black and white is completed in the last section of the story devoted to the boat's arrival and culminating in Fenella's meeting with her grandfather. There are few changes in Mansfield's assured description of a motionless and soundless wintry landscape: the adjective "cold" appears in the parallel phrases—"The cold pale sky" and "cold pale sea"—then is reinforced in the comment that on deck "it was like ice."[58] The lack of sun and the silvery outlines of trees complete the impression of a bleak, uninhabited world, matching the mood of Fenella's reflection about being in limbo due to prolonged sorrow. The voyage is evoked as a state of suspended animation: "as though they had been to sea for weeks together," and Fenella's comments—"it had all been so sad lately" and "Was it going to change"—imply the interminability of mourning for the child.[59] But this is overturned by the grandfather's appearance, echoing the avian imagery associated with her grandmother, being depicted as "like a very old wide awake bird," a phrase which replaces "~~an ancient~~ bird" and implies that Fenella's arrival is like a dawning.[60]

In recounting the journey's continuation from the boat by horse and cart, Mansfield introduces different collocations of the adjective white: coldness, moving into light, thaw, and purity: this occurs in phrases such as "a white mist" on the land, "Their breath was white on the air" (in the manuscript, but not included in published versions), followed by visual details that invoke different textures of whiteness, the houses that look "like shells on the lid of a box," the "path of round white pebbles," and "white picotees."[61] These shift to connotations of body heat in the "white warm fur" of the "large white cat" in which Fenella warms her "cold little hand" and culminate in the white tuft and silver

---

[52] *King Lear,* 4.1.41-42.

[53] CW2, 240.

[54] Françoise Defroment, "Impossible Mourning," in *The Fine Instrument: Essays on Katherine Mansfield*, ed. Paulette Michel and Michel Dupuis (Sydney: Dangaroo Press, 1989), 158.

[55] Voy-NB5-NL, 14.

[56] Ibid., 16.

[57] Defromont, "Impossible Mourning," 160.

[58] Voy-NB5-NL, 22.

[59] Ibid.

[60] Ibid., 24 verso.

[61] Ibid., 24, 25.

beard of her grandfather in bed, waiting to greet her[62] and the reinforcement of the opening chiaroscuro with the "white text in a heavy black frame,"[63] as situated in the sitting room. The wording of the text given at this point (but later deleted) reads:

Lost one **silent** gold Hour
Set with sixty Diamond Minutes
No reward is offered
For it is gone for ever—[64]

Mansfield repeats the aphorism at the end of the manuscript, apparently revising the ending, adding and then deleting the adjective "green," describing the text as "green in a deep black frame"—perhaps to symbolically evoke the new, spring season or aesthetically to recall the "little green star" on the boat's masthead.[65] In her revision, this first citation of the framed text is deleted, so that only the second iteration, at the end of the story, remains. Similarly, she reinforces the cat's slow awakening by adding "yawned" to "stretched," but deletes in the print version its "purring + blinking" that accompany Fenella's grandparents' voices.[66] Complementing this visual patterning are phrasal additions to the manuscript to indicate thawing and melting: "big trembling dew drops" on the gate, while Fenella's glove tips are "soaked through."[67] These changes stress nature's coming to life as an image of her relief at arrival, and they are complemented by Grandpa's evocative statement, "her little nose is as cold as a button," which replaces his original words: "She's frozen, said he. Your frozen.'"[68] Mansfield in her revision also excised references to the sun rising, throwing a beam on the walls and lighting up the framed text;[69] it is the white cat and her grandfather, not nature alone, that are the sources of Fenella's warm welcome.

In this conclusion, the anxieties associated with the departure from Wellington and the reasons for the journey are laid to rest as Fenella's journey is completed with an image of grand-paternal benevolence that contrasts to the terse, grief-stricken father with his "cold, wet mustache."[70] The affection emanating from her merrily winking grandfather, whose cheerful words address her state of physical chill, it is implied, soothes her earlier fears at family separation. These contrasts are reinforced by different concepts of time (her father cannot put a time limit on her visit, while the framed text hanging above Grandpa's bed defines the value of an hour), and the black (her grandmother's black gloved finger on her father's cheek) and white (her grandfather's white tuft and silver beard) color symbolism that dominates the narrative. Finally symbolizing this safe arrival and Fenella's emotional reassurance is the newly introduced term to describe Grandma's swan neck umbrella, now safely "crooked" (replacing "put") over the bed rail[71] [see Figures 36 and 37].

---

[62] See the photo of the Beauchamp family outside the house in Anakiwa, including Arthur Beauchamp, in Kimber, *The Early Years*, 11, and Yska, *A Strange Beautiful Excitement*, 90.
[63] Voy-NB5-NL, 25, 24 verso. Mansfield revises the ending three times. In the first two, the framed text is in the sitting room and is white (see Voy-NB5-NL, 25, see Figure 36); in the third, the framed text is above the bed and is green (see Voy-NB5-NL, 24 verso, see Figure 37).
[64] Ibid., 25.
[65] Ibid., 16, 24 verso.
[66] Ibid., 25; CW, 379.
[67] Ibid., 24.
[68] Ibid., 24 verso.
[69] Ibid, 25.
[70] Ibid., 16.
[71] Ibid, 24 verso.

Mansfield's changes in delineating a freeze followed by a thaw enable nature to be read as an objective correlative to the release from psychological entrapment in the rites of mourning and the settling of Fenella's emotions; no doubt for reasons of economy the printed version omits the sentence in the manuscript: "Their breath was white on the air."[72] By contrast, Mansfield revises the typography of the aphorism from lower case into the all-caps of "NO" (in "NO reward") and "GONE FOR EVER" in the manuscript, although not followed in *The Sphere* publication in 1921 (which she no doubt checked); full capitalization is preserved in the authoritative editions.[73] This phrase summarizes the story's literal message of mortality, transience, and loss, but the axiom that what has gone nevertheless leaves a trace is counterpointed and counteracted by Mansfield's memorializing art and this iconic image of the child's instinctive exploration in coming to understand death in her own way.[74]

"SIX YEARS AFTER": THE SEA AND THE SPECTRAL

The couple travelling on a steamer in "Six Years After" are imagined as the parents of a young man killed in the war, dealing with their grief six years later, and this suggests the story is another memorialization of Mansfield's deceased brother, Leslie Beauchamp. The story was written into Notebook 41 in October 1921 and Mansfield copied a shorter, "clean" version into a "thin class book"—i.e., Notebook 3—beginning in early November 1921, six years after Leslie's death in October 1915: "The dates confirm the story was written to mark her feelings after this passage of time."[75] Murry made his own composition of the story based on the most recent version in Notebook 3 (in the Newberry Library), but added fragments from the end of Notebook 41 (in the Alexander Turnbull Library); this posthumous version has provided the basis for all subsequent editions.[76]

Mansfield's process of composition deserves new scrutiny and her revisions further analysis following Todd Martin's recent discovery in the Newberry Library of her revised draft in Notebook 3—long believed lost—that Murry used.[77] Antony Alpers's influential assessment that the story is "incomplete"[78] and speculation that "Six Years After" can be read alongside "The Fly" as "late period Mansfield stories concerned with the aftermath of the First World War" can also be reconsidered in light of Martin's claim that the ending of the later version "appears to be the one intended by Mansfield."[79] The original ending (reinstated by Murry and all editors subsequently) concludes with an ellipsis and anthropomorphizing of the boat's movement: "And the little steamer, quietly determined, throbbed on, pressed on, as if at the end of the journey there waited. . . ."[80] It is the

---

[72] Ibid., 23.

[73] The version of this story published in *The Sphere* only capitalizes the first letter of each word, a typography followed in popular editions.

[74] Defromont points out that this inscription "ironically seems to play with death and deny it" ("Impossible Mourning," 161).

[75] Alpers, *Stories*, 573–74; "Note on the 'Six Years After' Manuscripts."

[76] SYA-NB3-NL, note 43.

[77] Martin points out that it was not labelled by B. J. Kirkpatrick in *A Bibliography of Katherine Mansfield* (1989) because the first page of the story is missing and it is not titled. See "Note on the 'Six Years After' Manuscripts."

[78] Alpers, *Stories,* 571.

[79] Ibid., 574; SYA-NB3-NL, note 43.

[80] CW2, 425. Martin notes that an ellipsis occurs in the published version; the original has no end punctuation (SYA-NB41-ATL, note 43).

culmination of a lengthy denouement in the draft version: notably the theatrical lowering of the curtain as if at play's end, the mother's refusal to accept death's finality, her fantasy of the boy's return after the war, his marriage and child, interrupted by the dead boy's plea, "'Stop, Mother, stop,'" provoking her outburst, "'I can't bear it.'"[81] The much reduced clean version of Notebook 3 focuses on the mother's reverie and fervent wish to be reunited with her son, culminating in her *cri de coeur*: "Can one do nothing for the dead?" and the realization: "And for a long time the answer had been—nothing!"[82]

As Mansfield evidently thought "Six Years After" to be a publishable story, it is worth considering whether the revised manuscript ending can be convincingly identified as the final one, as Martin claims, and hence more representative of her intentions.[83] I draw on Bushell's argument that intentionality can be reconstructed "as a sequence of mental states and acts—which is fundamental to the process of composition."[84] The impact of Mansfield's mental state on the story-telling of the draft (Notebook 41) can be inferred from the narrator's interruption of the ending, using free indirect discourse to convey Mansfield's/the mother's frustration: "That is the end of the play. But it cant end like that—so suddenly. There must be more—."[85] The urgent desire to reach out to the dead through her art, I argue, underlies Mansfield's revision. In the revised version (Notebook 3), she added material that refocuses the narrative on imagining Leslie's death, which follows her mythologizing of it in 1915 in her notebooks. The mother sees a mirage of the boy who foretells his death—"I dreamed I was in a wood"—and his relationship with she who grieves is now the conduit of this vision.[86]

The transition to the shorter version with the revised ending begins with the mother's reflection, following a conversation with her husband, and expansion of the original:

(Notebook 41) Grey, unbroken, gently moving water, **veiled*** with slanting-rain.[87] Far out as though idly ~~as though~~ dreaming gulls were flying. Now they settled on the ~~water~~ ^waves^ now they beat up into the rainy air, and **they** shone against the pale sky like the lights within a pearl. _{How big it was out there—how cold and lonely. There will be nothing. **Nothing but*** the waves + those gulls + rain falling.}

How **lonely*** it will be here ~~xx~~ when we have passed by—[88]

(Notebook 3) And the little steamer pressed on, pitching gently, over the grey unbroken gently moving water that was veiled with slanting rain.

Far out, as though idly, listlessly, gulls were flying. Now they settled in the waves, now they beat up into the rainy air, and shone against the pale sky like the lights within a pearl. They looked cold and lonely. How lonely it will be when we have passed by, she thought. There will be nothing but the waves and those birds and rain falling[89] [see Figure 38].

---

[81] SYA-NB41-ATL, 7.
[82] SYA-NB3-NL, 6.
[83] In her notebook it is listed on 27 October 1921 among "stories for my new book," and again on 16 November. See CW4, 385–86, 390.
[84] Sally Bushell, "Intention Revisited: Towards an Anglo-American 'Genetic Criticism,'" *Text* 17 (2005): 57, cited in Martin, "'What was It?'" 19.
[85] SYA-NB41-ATL, 7.
[86] SYA-NB3-NL, 5.
[87] Martin points out that this sentence has been moved from a point later in the story, in Mansfield's revision (SYA-NB41-ATL, note 19).
[88] SYA-NB41-ATL, 5.
[89] SYA-NB3-NL, 4.

The revised version in Notebook 3 incorporates the incomplete final sentence of the original about the "little steamer's" movement into the mother's cognitive transitions towards a semi- mystical reverie. Her loneliness and billowing grief are expanded with a sudden shift of perception: "She gazed through the rust spotted railing along which big drops trembled, until suddenly she shut her lips. It was as if a warning voice inside her had said 'Dont look!'"[90] This added description, culminating in the boy's ghostly appearance, his plea that she not leave him, and the dream he recounts of being buried and surrounded by a blackberry vine exists only in the revised version but is reproduced in all editions.

Martin comments that in the cleaner copy Mansfield "is consolidating various passages from Notebook 41 into a more unified whole."[91] I suggest the source of this unity comes from dramatic additions: the young boy's spectral appearance and his dialogue with his mother. Bushell's comment on writing "as a repetitive process in which the 'now' is built upon and exists, only as a result of repeated 'nows'" enables amplification of Martin's claim that the revised conclusion is the one that Mansfield intended.[92] Mansfield's crossings out and comments that destabilize the fictional contents of the first draft suggest a wish to synthesize and deepen the mother-child, death-life dichotomies, to bring her brother back from the dead by reconstructing the beloved's mourning as a form of shared distress. This is signposted in the prolonged, poignant ending of Notebook 41 in a short paragraph (mostly excised in the Notebook 3 version), when the son begs "Stop mother stop";[93] the phrase that follows, "a sound of childish weeping," is transferred to Notebook 3. Now the mother's/Mansfield's grief is conflated with the son's/brother's suffering as he entreats her:

> "Don't forget me. You are forgetting me! You know you are." And it was as though, from her own breast there came the sound of childish weeping.
> "My son—my precious child—it isn't true."[94] [see Figure 38]

This intersubjective sorrow can be read as Mansfield's substitution for the unsatisfactory "scene" of the original ending, because the son tells his "terrible dream." It continues with the mother's/Mansfield's vow to never let his voice escape her: "she never settled down—she was never off of her guard for a moment but she heard him," although she recognizes (in anticipation of the ending) that his worst dream is "for ever and for ever uncomforted"[95] [see Figure 39].

Editors have accommodated both endings. Alpers, and recently Kimber and O'Sullivan include another sequence from the draft version, as Martin notes. It begins with the woman's observation of other passengers as "hardened travellers," her admiration of her husband's cap with its "rich white satin lining,"[96] and imagining of her son's return home on his first leave. Although this sequence was excised by Mansfield in the revised version, it is published in all editions, usually demarcated as a fragment, and set apart from the

---

[90] Ibid.
[91] SYA-NB-NL, note 43.
[92] Sally Bushell, "Textual Process and the Denial of Origins," *Textual Cultures: Texts, Contexts, Interpretations* 2, no. 2 (2007): 107.
[93] SYA-NB41-ATL, 7.
[94] SYA-NB3-NL, 4. Compare this to SYA-NB41-ATL, 7: "Stop Mother stop. When I think of all I have missed I cant bear it. And there was a sound of childish weeping from under the xxx **beckoning** me—a heartbreaking **sound** in that foreign wood where the white cross **gleams misty**."
[95] SYA-NB3-NL, 5.
[96] SYA-NB41-ATL, notes 28 and 19. The addition is on CW2, 423.

narrative proper.[97] Conversely, editors also include a section from the revision that is not in the original draft of Notebook 41: an expansion of the mother's reflections on being at sea, after the father has tipped the "delicate looking" steward which begins: "It is extraordinary how peaceful it feels on a little steamer once the bustle of leaving port is over."[98] As the revised version of Notebook 3 is incomplete in other ways, being untitled and beginning later in the story, editors follow the initial draft version for the missing beginning and the title.[99]

Despite the different endings, all published editions of the story follow Murry's influential version in being a pastiche of sections taken from both versions, and they all conclude with the original ending. The belief that Mansfield's revision was lost precluded consideration of the alternative ending as evidence of her changed intent;[100] the editorial decision to combine the two versions from fragments aimed to accommodate Mansfield's negotiations with the material given the loss of the revised version.

Through tracing the mother's changing subjectivity in her revision, it can be seen that Mansfield deepened her exploration into memory, suffering, and mortality triggered six years earlier by Leslie's death. She used the impressionistic atmosphere, contributing to what Alpers calls the story's "numinous quality," by describing the seascapes and climacteric shifts through the mother's observations in order to project her movement into introspective reflection.[101] In the revised version of Notebook 3, the mother intuits her son's spiritual visitation as though emanating from the elements: "And it seemed to her there was a presence far out there between the sky on the water."[102] This catalyzes the story's most "transformative" sequence: her agonized dialogue with her son. His premonitory dream about his death in a wood by being suffocated by a blackberry vine growing over his grave, intensified by his desperate desire to retain contact with her, can be read as a dramatic representation of Mansfield's yearning to reconstruct her real life bond with Leslie. In fact, this story can be read as Mansfield's renewal of her vow for reunion with her brother, originally made in October 1915 upon hearing of his death, "I believe in immortality because [. . .] he is no longer here and I long to join him [. . .] I will come as quickly as I can to you."[103] This is echoed in the story with "I am coming as fast as I can. As fast as I can I come."[104] Other images and phrases recall her earlier responses: the blackberry vine invokes "the tall berry bushes, white and red" of her celebrated poem, "To L.H.B.," and "a wood" is an echo of a diary entry: "he is lying in the middle of a little wood"[105] [see Figures 38 and 39].

---

[97] Murry's amended version (which includes this ending taken from Notebook 41) has been accepted subsequently. Alpers refers to Mansfield's notes for the story—"A wife and husband on board a steamer. The cold buttons. They see someone who reminds them." He includes this section of the mother's reference to her son's British uniform with "cold buttons," using asterisks to signal its parenthetical status (*Stories*, 209); Kimber and O'Sullivan add this section after the story's conclusion with the subtitle, "Fragment of earlier draft" (CW2, 424, 425), although other editors ignore it.

[98] CW2, 422–23.

[99] Martin speculates that Mansfield began copying on a separate sheet of paper. At the point where the revised version begins, "twenty-eight years," she copied the rest into Notebook 3. See "Note on the 'Six Years After' Manuscripts."

[100] Alpers, *Stories*, 574: CW2, 425.

[101] Alpers, *Stories*, 574.

[102] SYA-NB3-NL, 4.

[103] CW4, 171; Leslie's "return" to her after death became inextricable with the renewed spiritual purpose of her art, often defined as "mysterious," as in her vow to write about her country as a "sacred debt" and "told with a sense of mystery" (CW4, 191).

[104] SYA-NB3-NL, 5.

[105] For "To L.H.B," see CW3, 96; on "a little wood," see CW4, 171.

Given the story's reorientation away from the imagined return of the son from war to the more abstract, dream-like representation of the mother's troubled reflection that the suffering of the dead cannot be accounted for, as well as the question of the revised ending, it seems that, as Martin claims, this conclusion is compatible with these alterations and, therefore, is closer to what Mansfield likely intended. Certainly it can be more convincingly aligned with those of two later stories, "The Fly" and "The Canary," than the original ending of Notebook 41. Both ask a seemingly unanswerable question, "What was It," leaving the reader, as Martin points out, with an "unsettled feeling." [106] In this story, however, Mansfield ameliorates the raw realization with: "And *for a long time* the answer *had been*—nothing" (my italics).[107] If this demand to consider the present moment [i.e. until now] is read (with reference to Bushell's comment on writing emerging from repeated "nows") as her comment on the processing of grief, this performative element of the ending demands recognition of the story's memorial function and of her art's affective dimension as counters to the nihilism of what *"had been*—nothing."

CONCLUSION: MEMORIALIZATION, GENDER, REDEMPTION

"Six Years After" and "The Fly" can be read in ways that Alpers found tantalisingly out of reach because he believed "Six Years After" was incomplete:[108] as parallel, post-war gendered responses to death and grief. As memorializations, they are linked by the six-year time-frame, references to the son's uniform, and images of bodily perfection in death.[109]All three stories examined here subvert the authority of the father figure which embodied "Victorian and Edwardian ideals of masculinity" such as the "strong and silent man": the husband in "The Stranger" is undermined in his virility, the father of "The Fly" cannot grieve, while the father of "The Voyage" cannot comfort his daughter, and they all contrast to the mother's intense spiritual reunion with the boy in "Six Years After" and the empathetic daughters of "old Woodifield" in "The Fly."[110] Distinct psychological patterns confirm these gender differences: in "The Fly" the boss's assumptions about masculine power and its legacies (his hope his son would inherit the family business) have immunized him from experiencing a deeper grief over his son's death; the collapse of the authority figure's masculinized expectations has a genealogy in "The Stranger." By contrast the female figures in "The Voyage," "The Fly," and "Six Years After" draw on memory, subjective processes of association, and religious, psychic connections in their more affective responses to tragedy. All three sea stories suggest that representing the devastating impact of death led to Mansfield's preoccupation with her endings, even in

---

[106] Martin, "'What was It?'" 16.

[107] SYA-NB3-NL, 6.

[108] Alpers, *Stories*, 574.

[109] The photograph of the son in "The Fly" had been "over the table [. . .] for over six years," for "six years had passed away" and the boss can never think of his son than as euphemistically "lying unchanged, unblemished in his uniform, asleep for ever" (CW2, 476, 478).

[110] Avishek Parui, "'For the life of him he could not remember': Post-war Memory, Mourning and Masculinity Crisis in Katherine Mansfield's 'The Fly,'" in *Katherine Mansfield and Psychology*, ed. Clare Hanson, Gerri Kimber and Todd Martin (Edinburgh: Edinburgh University Press, 2016), 113–124 (116). Parui also argues that Mansfield depicts women in "The Fly," the daughters of Old Woodifield who visit the grave of their brother in Belgium, as concerned with remembrance and mourning, while "the men inhabit an entanglement of denial and forgetfulness" (116).

"The Voyage," where Fenella's welcome at journey's end represents a redemptive recovery from the mourning with which the story begins. Certainly Mansfield's revisions, especially of "The Voyage" and "Six Years After," suggest she was working creatively through the overwhelming shock of her brother's tragic death, which catalyzed her hostility to the war as having destroyed a generation of young men.[111] More specifically, along with "The Fly" they constitute a protest against powerful male figures whom she held responsible for the war and whom she represents as unable to answer for its consequences, including their own losses.[112] In these ways she indirectly reconfigured her relationship with both her father and brother, and by implication began to find artistic ways to approach and come to terms with her own mortality.

---

[111] It is evident in her comment: "think [. . .] of all that beautiful youth feeding the fields of France" (*Letters* 2, 339).

[112] This can be inferred from her comment: "I cant imagine how after the war these men can pick up the old threads as tho' it had never been" (*Letters* 3, 97).

"A Wholesale Hanging": Katherine Mansfield's *Sphere* Stories

JENNY MCDONNELL

In February 1923, the *Sphere* commemorated Katherine Mansfield in a short obituary, the greater part of which reprinted a tribute by H. M. Tomlinson that had recently appeared in the *Nation and the Athenaeum*. The Tomlinson extract was embedded within an unsigned article that noted the *Sphere*'s "good fortune" in publishing a number of Mansfield's "stories of great merit"—stories that revealed "a personality of rare, almost tenuous texture." Two were singled out for particular praise: "Sixpence" (which was "full to the brim of humour and sympathy") and "Marriage à la Mode" (which "pierced the heart through and through"). The obituary concluded with a list of six of Mansfield's *Sphere* stories, misspelling the title of one in a typographical error ("Mr and Mrs Don") and omitting a seventh, "Her First Ball" (which appeared in a special Christmas number in November 1921).[1] In its inclusion of Tomlinson's lengthy paragraph and some seemingly inadvertent errors, this obituary was characterized by a series of textual disruptions, elisions, and variants. A similar set of qualities permeated the open-ended short stories that Mansfield produced throughout her writing life, both in their manuscript and published forms, and this chapter will explore the significance of these features in two *Sphere* stories in particular: "Mr and Mrs Dove" and "Marriage à la Mode." In doing so, it further develops recent critical reappraisals of Mansfield's "magazine modernism" and positions her writing at the intersection of modernist, "middlebrow," and popular forms in ways that reveal an ongoing destabilization of these categories—a process that is reinforced by considering the stories' textual instabilities as works-in-progress across their manuscript and published versions.[2]

Established in 1900 by Clement King Shorter, the *Sphere* was a popular "Illustrated Newspaper for the Home" (as its masthead read), and published a total of seven of Mansfield's stories between April and December 1921: "The Singing Lesson," "Sixpence," "Mr and Mrs Dove," "An Ideal Family," "Her First Ball," "The Voyage," and "Marriage à la Mode." These contributions appeared alongside coverage of recent news items and articles on such topics as: society weddings and sporting events; profiles of places of

[1] "In Memoriam—Katherine Mansfield" (unsigned), *Sphere*, February 10, 1923, 131. British Newspaper Archive, https://www.britishnewspaperarchive.co.uk.
[2] See Faith Binckes, "Modernist Magazines," in *The Bloomsbury Companion to Modernist Literature*, ed. Ulrika Maude and Mark Nixon (London: Bloomsbury, 2018); Chris Mourant, *Katherine Mansfield and Periodical Culture* (Edinburgh: Edinburgh University Press, 2019).

interest around Britain (from English spa towns to lighthouses on the Scottish coast); illustrated reports on the progress of the 1921 Everest expedition; and Shorter's weekly "Literary Letter" column. With the exception of "The Voyage" (described by Antony Alpers as a "flawless little New Zealand story"), Mansfield's contributions to the *Sphere* have often been dismissed as inferior and lucrative fare.[3] For example, in his 1984 edition of the stories, Alpers identified "Mr and Mrs Dove" and "Marriage à la Mode" as prime examples of her "shallower stories," and effectively categorized the majority of her contributions to the *Sphere* as hastily written money-spinners aimed at an "unperceptive audience," the sole purpose of which was to fund her growing medical expenses.[4] More recently, the editors of the authoritative Edinburgh *Collected Fiction* have offered a more comprehensive and even-handed volume that positions Mansfield's published works alongside multiple unfinished fragments and juvenilia in order "to trace out a writer always in transition"—a writer whose work is itself characterized by an associated sense of flux at both a formal and a thematic level.[5] At the same time, Kimber and O'Sullivan implicitly repeat Alpers' value judgment in a suggestion that "[a] story is process as much as content, a matter of perspective" as distinct from "the 'plotty' narratives she so disliked [. . .] but was partly driven back to when obliged to make money quickly, in her last two years, to cover expensive medical treatment."[6] Mansfield's modernist innovations with form and perspective have frequently been privileged over her "popular," plotted stories in this way, but these categories need not be seen as mutually exclusive. In fact, her stories for the *Sphere* often demonstrate a playful disruption of these closed categories.

By her own admission, Mansfield profited from her association with the *Sphere* at a time when she was increasingly ill and badly in need of money, even if she expressed some reservations about the published products to Dorothy Brett, in particular the "fearful horrors" of drawings by W. Smithson Broadhead that were used to illustrate them.[7] The stories earned her ten guineas apiece, and she observed frankly in a letter to Ottoline Morrell that the *Sphere* "pays better than any other paper I know," though she did worry that the stories were "[t]oo simple" once she finished writing them.[8] Likewise, her notebooks and journals reveal some doubts about them, as in her self-admonishment that "Mr and Mrs Dove" seemed "a little bit made up," "not strong enough," and "not quite the kind of truth I'm after."[9] Mansfield was often her own harshest critic, though, and was constantly refining her craft in the belief that "the next story [. . .] is going to contain everything."[10] Despite any misgivings that she expressed about her contributions to the *Sphere*, she opted to include all but one in *The Garden Party and Other Stories* in 1922 after a last-minute request to her publisher Michael Sadleir (at Constable & Co) to remove "Sixpence" from the planned collection just before it went to press.[11] Moreover, she intended to continue her association with the paper throughout 1922 after Shorter commissioned her to write a long serial, though to Elizabeth von Arnim she queried if she

---

[3] Antony Alpers, *The Stories of Katherine Mansfield* (Auckland: Oxford University Press, 1984), 571.
[4] Alpers, *Stories*, xxiv; xxv.
[5] CW1, xx.
[6] Ibid., xxii.
[7] *Letters* 4, 271.
[8] Ibid., 252.
[9] CW4, 375.
[10] *Letters* 4, 252.
[11] Ibid., 327.

would manage to see this "wholesale *hanging* through," and died before the "thirteen 'curtains' and an adventure note" could be completed.[12]

The editors of the Edinburgh Edition of Mansfield's letters draw attention to her allusion to the theatrical convention of the curtain here, noting its associations with formal stability and order in its allusion to either a "dramatic finale preceding the final falling of the curtain, or (shortened from 'curtain-raiser') a dramatic opening scene."[13] Coupled with her comment about the "adventure note," Mansfield's observations seem to give the impression that Shorter's brief for the *Sphere* serial would require her to adhere to formulaic and established generic conventions in her commissioned work. Indeed, this is one of the grounds on which Alpers critiques the earlier *Sphere* stories in his emphasis on their enforced "'happy endings.'"[14] However, many of the stories that Mansfield published in the *Sphere* fail to offer any such stable resolution at either a narrative or a generic level. Both "Mr and Mrs Dove" and "Marriage à la Mode," for example, feature the romantic trials and tribulations of two couples but refuse the stable (and conservative) fulfilment that might be expected of a romance narrative or a marriage plot. Instead, both stories end in profoundly uncertain territory. Of the two, "Mr and Mrs Dove" was written and published first and depicts an encounter between Anne and Reggie in which she initially rejects his awkward proposal of marriage before seemingly having an abrupt change of heart. At the same time, it establishes a narrative parallel with the titular doves to indicate that the lovers remain caught in an ongoing cycle that may never reach the absolute closure of either a definitive parting or a happy marriage. The resultant uncertainty also suggests that any ensuing marriage would prove to be an ill-fated one for both parties, as Mansfield hoped to convey; she noted in her diaries that "I mean to imply that those two may not be happy together—that that is the kind of reason for which a young girl marries."[15] Mansfield may have had the implications of precisely this kind of inopportune marriage in mind when she began writing "Marriage à la Mode" on August 6, 1921. The later story offers a very overt representation of an unhappy marriage and entirely refuses to resolve the marital difficulties between William and Isabel following his weekend visit to the coastal home in which his wife and two sons currently reside, along with Isabel's coterie of voguish and affected new friends. Instead, "Marriage à la Mode" concludes after William has sent a passionate letter to his wife, to which she responds with a series of rapidly changing emotions and a deferred promise to herself that she will respond to him even as she resumes her dalliance with the circle of insincere friends and her corresponding social performance as the "new Isabel."[16]

Neither "Marriage à la Mode" nor "Mr and Mrs Dove" offers a particularly happy ending, then, and each story disrupts any definitive textual closure, instead working suggestively and obliquely to allow the reader to infer potential future outcomes for each couple. At a structural and narrative level, these uncertain endings may be seen as evidence that each story reflects "[t]he fragmented, elliptical language of the anti-epiphany" that is often found in modernist short fiction more broadly. In Mansfield's stories, her characters often either deny or defer their realization of a "blazing moment" (for example, Bertha

---

[12] *Letters* 4, 301.
[13] Claire Davison and Gerri Kimber, ed., *The Edinburgh Edition of the Collected Letters of Katherine Mansfield: Volume 1* (Edinburgh: Edinburgh University Press, 2020), 35, n19.
[14] Alpers, *Stories*, 568.
[15] CW4, 375.
[16] CW2, 330.

Young in "Bliss" or Beryl Fairfield in "Prelude"), refuting the "unity of effect" that Edgar Allan Poe once insisted that short stories by their very nature produced.[17] Instead, the endings of Mansfield's stories seem to be consistently suspended, revealing the ways in which her characters' lives are themselves in a state of flux. As Teresa Prudente has suggested, Mansfield's writing was "persistently structured [. . .] on disembodied points of view with never-ending [. . .] processes," a form of narrative impersonality that "bears intrinsic connections with writing conceived as an open-ended process."[18] Pierre-Marc de Biasi detects a similarly disruptive principle at work in the concept of a manuscript's rough draft as "one moment" of a text-as-process: "a central moment, to be sure, that forms the very heart of its genetics, but an intermediary and provisional moment" within a process that does not necessarily end with the publication of a finished text.[19] The deferred closure of Mansfield's stories are likewise mere moments within a larger set of textual possibilities, and the negation of stable textual resolution in both "Mr and Mrs Dove" and "Marriage à la Mode" is mirrored in a series of instabilities within the manuscripts that Mansfield first produced.

Mansfield wrote both stories between July and August 1921 at a time when she was living in Montana-sur-Sierre in the Swiss Alps and, at first glance, the frequent critical assumption that the stories were written at speed purely for profit would seem to be borne out. Both drafts seem to betray signs of having been written quickly. They begin as relatively neat fair copies with very few amendments on the opening pages, but untidier handwriting, deletions, and revisions soon become evident throughout. Initially, these tend to look like relatively minor amendments, with very few substantial deletions or refinement of the plot or structure. However, as W. H. New insists, romantic myths that "envisage [Mansfield as] a writer who wrote at white heat, producing creative masterpieces while scarcely blotting a word" can be countered by close examination of her journals and manuscripts, which provide subtle indications of the ways in which she paused in the process of writing and rewriting them.[20] This is apparent in the manuscripts of both stories under discussion. For example, some doodles of flowers in the margins of one manuscript page of "Mr and Mrs Dove" suggest a moment of distraction as Mansfield wrote the story, but also produce a rudimentary illustration of two scenes—the first, in which Reggie makes his escape from his mother as she ruthlessly applies her pruning shears to "the head of a dead something or other," and the second in which he begins his subsequent walk to Colonel Proctor's house along roads and paths that are bordered by hollyhocks and syringa bushes.[21] The same manuscript sees Mansfield switch between writing implements, alternating between pen and pencil throughout the writing process. In turn, these provide evidence of the ways in which "a writer is also [their] first reader" in their interactions with the manuscripts out of which published texts evolve, as is

---

[17] Claire Drewery, "The Modernist Short Story: Fractured Perspectives," in *The Cambridge History of the English Short Story*, ed. Dominic Head (Cambridge: Cambridge University Press, 2016), 149; CW3, 467; Edgar Allan Poe, "Review of Nathaniel Hawthorne's *Twice-Told Tales*," *Graham's Magazine*, May 1842, in *Edgar Allan Poe: Literary Theory and Criticism*, ed. Leonard Cassuto (Mineola, NY: Dover Publications, 2012). <https://www.perlego.com/book/111491/literary-theory-and-criticism-pdf> [accessed 10 June 2022].

[18] Teresa Prudente, "From 'The Aloe' to 'Prelude' and from *The Moths* to *The Waves*: Drafts, Revisions and the Process of 'Becoming-Imperceptible' in Virginia Woolf and Katherine Mansfield," *Textus* 3 (2015): 97.

[19] Pierre-Marc de Biasi, "What is a Literary Draft? Toward a Functional Typology of Genetic Documentation," trans. Ingrid Wassenaar, *Yale French Studies* 89 (1996): 29.

[20] W. H. New, *Reading Mansfield and Metaphors of Form* (Montreal: McGill-Queens University Press, 1999), 55.

[21] MMD-MS-NL, 4; 5.

especially apparent in the varying shades of lighter or darker ink that often reveal later changes to phrasing and syntax throughout the manuscript of "Mr and Mrs Dove."[22]

Similar changes in ink can be identified in the manuscript version of "Marriage à la Mode," a draft text in which Alpers detects "tension rather than pleasurable excitement [. . .] with a good deal of scratching out to obliterate intrusive details, as though the story had been more difficult to manage."[23] The first eleven pages of the story are written on the recto pages of Mansfield's Notebook 5 and focus on William's perspective during his trip to join his wife and children for the weekend, culminating in his eventual departure and resolution to write his love letter to Isabel. At this point, the manuscript records a very pronounced textual break in the form of a jagged line, and the story changes focus to recount Isabel's receipt of the letter and her subsequent response. For reasons that are not immediately apparent, this final section of the story is written on verso pages that had previously been left blank, embedding the story's resolution within the middle of the manuscript itself. Rather than mere evidence of the perceived difficulties of writing the story, however, this material disruption within the text may actually be indicative of the story's unstable narrative structure and uncertain resolution in the depiction of William and Isabel's fraught marriage.

The manuscript of the story in Notebook 5 is seemingly framed by two dates, "6 viii 1921" and "xi viii 1921," suggesting that the timeframe within which Mansfield wrote the story was between August 6–11, 1921. Significantly, the second of these dates does not appear at the very end of the manuscript but rather beside the textual break that occurs just after William resolves to write to his wife. The story's final sentence—in which Isabel elects to delay responding to her husband as she prepares to re-join her friends—stands starkly on its own at the top of a single page in the notebook, underlined by another (shorter) jagged line to signal that the narrative has reached an end, but not necessarily a resolution as the future implications of Isabel's actions remain uncertain. What's more, at the bottom of the page immediately after the textual break, Mansfield provides some insight into the conditions in which she was writing by noting, "I don't know how I may write this next story. Its so difficult. But I suppose I shall. The trouble is I am so infernally cold!"[24] [see Figure 32]. The "next story," to which Mansfield refers here, may be either the unfinished "Widowed" or "The Voyage," both of which she began in the pages that followed immediately in the notebook. However, it is tempting to speculate that she could conceivably be referring to the closing section of "Marriage à la Mode" as the "next story," given the abrupt end to William's narrative at this point in the manuscript and the subsequent doubling-back to document Isabel's reaction to his emotional declaration. At the very least, these manuscript disruptions draw attention to a pronounced change in narrative focalization from William's to Isabel's perspective in ways that reveal the extent to which the pair live their lives at a remove from one another, and there is clear evidence that Mansfield made a series of edits and revisions that serve to reinforce this distance between the two main characters.

The majority of these changes are smaller and subtler than the abrupt textual break noted above, but nevertheless, they prove significant in depicting the schism between William and his wife. As the story begins, William sets out to catch a train in order to join

---

[22] Dirk Van Hulle, *Modern Manuscripts: The Extended Mind and Creative Undoing from Darwin to Beckett and Beyond* (London: Bloomsbury, 2014): 11.

[23] Alpers, *Stories*, 570.

[24] MalaM-NB5-NL, 12.

Isabel at their seaside retreat and finds himself reminiscing about their life together, in particular an earlier family holiday that he remembers as being characterized by a sense of unity, "their feet locked together" in the immense bed that they shared.[25] This image is in marked contrast to his memories of more recent encounters, in which he "stood in the middle of the strange room and [. . .] felt himself a stranger," and in their near-absolute separation throughout the duration of his visit.[26] Aside from two brief moments when William arrives at the train station and as he awaits a taxi the following day, the two characters never spend significant time alone with one another. In the *avant-texte*, Mansfield initially included a section in which "~~[f]or the first time William found himself alone with Isabel~~" as they dress for dinner and make uncomfortable small talk while he contemplates how "~~awkward uneasy + dull~~" he has felt since his arrival.[27] However, she removed this interaction; in the process the encounter in a shared bedroom was elided from the finished draft and published versions of the story. Instead, this scene was replaced with a sequence that more subtly showed the extent of the estrangement between the two. As Isabel and her friends are away bathing, William stays behind to spend time with his children who are already asleep, and so finds himself wandering through a house in which he simply does not fit. This is especially suggested in the story's description of a wall on which "someone had painted a young man, over life size with very wobbly legs offering a wide eyed daisy to a young woman who had one very ~~large~~ short fat arm + one very long thin one," a grotesquely mismatched couple that seemingly share the space as uncomfortably as William and Isabel do[28] [see Figures 30 and 31]. The following day, William finally gets Isabel to himself for a brief moment in a scene that features an example of Mansfield's subtle revisions to phrasing within the story: "It was not until William was waiting for his taxi the next afternoon that he ~~managed~~ found himself to get [*sic*] [. . .] alone with Isabel."[29] Here, she clearly intended to revise the sentence to indicate that William "found himself" alone with his wife (as it is phrased in the published version), the passive phrasing undercutting any clear agency or intent on his part and framing the encounter as another uncomfortable one, before William finally departs to catch his train and begins to draft his fateful letter.

William's act of letter-writing ultimately goes unnarrated in the story, an elision that is given additional significance if read in conjunction with an earlier section that Mansfield opted to delete and revise significantly. On his train journey to join Isabel for the weekend, William aims to distract himself in his usual fashion in an attempt to suppress the persistent "dull gnawing in [. . .] his breast" and his feelings of loneliness when faced with his wife's absence by burying himself in work. More specifically, he prioritizes the acts of both writing and reading, observing that "~~As long as he kept on writing he could . . . stand up against it~~," and describing how "~~When Isabel was away he read himself to sleep every night~~."[30] Here, Mansfield initially offered a rather obvious articulation of the ways in which William sublimates the anxieties he associates with his separation from his wife but ultimately amended this to allow these associations to be inferred instead from his reactions as he "began to read. 'Our client moreover is positive that ~~no communication~~

---

[25] CW2, 333.
[26] Ibid., 332.
[27] MalaM-NB5-NL, 8–9.
[28] Ibid., 9.
[29] Ibid., 11.
[30] Ibid., 3, 4.

~~was received from Mssrs~~ **~~Liddell~~** ~~+ Jones on or after July 14th 1918~~. [. . .] . . . . ^{Ah that was}
^{better}—The **~~persistent~~** familiar dull gnawing [. . .] quieted down."[31] As William endeavors to
read his documents as a ritualistic distraction technique, Mansfield introduces a series of
ellipses between the scraps of sentences on which he can never fully concentrate: "We
have examined our clients correspondence files. The last sentence he had read echoed in
his mind. We have examined—William hung on tohat [sic] sentence. But it was no good"[32]
[see Figures 28 and 29]. These ellipses and unfinished sentences are retained in the
published version of the story, as William's thoughts inevitably come to be invaded by
memories of time spent with Isabel, visions of potential future meetings, and disbelief at
his previous obliviousness to her unhappiness with their life in London. Thus, his
distraction technique fails to sustain him on his train journey to join Isabel, and on the
return trip he rejects the practice entirely: "this time," Mansfield writes, "he let the papers
alone*. He lay back folded his arms against the dull persistent gnawing [. . .] ^{and} began ^{in his}
^{mind} to write a letter to Isabel"[33] [see Figure 32]. His letter remains unwritten at this point
in the story, and the insertion of the phrase "in his mind" in superscript (and its subsequent
inclusion in the published story) raises the possibility that it could end up as merely
another imagined conversation of the kind that preoccupied him on his earlier train
journey. On this occasion, though, William succeeds in expressing his thoughts on paper,
even if the letter itself is never fully articulated within the story, reduced instead to a set
of elliptical, fragmented phrases and subjected to ridicule by Isabel's vogueish friends.

A different kind of elliptical phrase forms the basis of Todd Martin's argument that
Isabel ultimately makes a "definitive choice" of her friends over her husband at the end of
the story, based on an analysis of a suggestive allusion to Matthew Arnold's "The Forsaken
Merman."[34] As Mansfield drafted the story, this intertextual line was inserted as a revision
in superscript, squeezed in between the sentences on either side of it. The quotation was
also included in published versions of the story and offers further evidence of her indirect
narrative style by inviting the informed reader to infer the significance of the reference.
As Isabel sits alone and contemplates her options—respond to William's letter immediately
or defer doing so in favor of resuming her afternoon's entertainment with her new
companions—she hears her friends calling to her with the phrase "Call her once before
you go," and elects to join them.[35] While it is certainly possible to suggest that Isabel has
implicitly made her choice as the story comes to an end, and may never actually respond
to William's letter, the implications of this choice remain unclear and the text can only
ever generate the *sense* of an ending (as the title of Martin's essay suggests), without
offering absolute closure.

In "The Forsaken Merman," a human woman rejects her life with a merman husband
and their children in favor of a conventional life back on land. Martin argues that
Mansfield's story inverts this image ironically to suggest that Isabel rejects a conventional
marriage to William only to embrace a different kind of domesticated conformity in her
performance as surrogate mother to the pretentious and insincere friends that she refers

---

[31] Ibid., 3.
[32] Ibid., 4.
[33] Ibid., 12.
[34] Todd Martin, "The Sense of an Ending in Katherine Mansfield's 'Marriage à la Mode,'" *Explicator* 69, no. 4
(2011): 159.
[35] CW2, 338.

to as her "children" (a rephrasing from "dearest little ones" in the original manuscript).[36] In light of this, the "still stifled feeling" that Isabel experiences as she reads William's letter may actually be suggestive of a sense of claustrophobia that she faces regardless of which choice she ultimately makes—an entrapment that is neatly mirrored by the manner in which the final pages of the story were embedded within the manuscript.[37]

"Mr and Mrs Dove" also produces a form of textual entrapment, but this time at a narrative level, in its depiction of the parallels between the central romantic relationship and the actions of the titular caged birds in their dove-house. Anne describes the birds' dynamic to Reggie as one in which Mr Dove is hopelessly committed to his pursuit of Mrs Dove: "She looks at Mr Dove and gives that little laugh and runs forward, and he follows her, bowing and bowing."[38] In turn, Reggie's pursuit of Anne is presented in similarly cyclical and repetitive terms in the closing stages of the story. After Anne has rejected Reggie, she suddenly calls him back, addressing him as Mr Dove as an apparent term of endearment; in response, he comes "slowly across the lawn" towards her in an echo of the bird's movement.[39] On a superficial level, this allows the reader to assume that Anne has had a genuine change of heart that would satisfy the anticipated romance or marriage plot. At the same time, though, it defers this closure and strongly implies that the relationship will never achieve any kind of satisfactory resolution; it will instead repeat the same patterns as those in which the doves are trapped. By both meeting *and* disrupting these narrative and generic conventions, "Mr and Mrs Dove" shares a subversive potential with the kind of middlebrow writing that Christoph Ehland and Cornelia Wächter discuss as "be[ing] conducive to escapist consumption *and* includ[ing] challenges to the established order."[40] The story ultimately implies that Anne and Reggie's relationship will be characterized by the seemingly unending repetitions enacted by their avian counterparts, a parallel that manages to fulfil both of the impulses that Ehland and Wächter describe, depending on the reader's perspective.

The closing lines of "Mr and Mrs Dove" were subject to some of the most telling syntactical and semantic revisions within the manuscript, as Mansfield tried out different phrasing in order to produce the appropriate textual effects before settling on the lines with which the published text ends:

> He stopped, he turned. But when she saw his timid, puzzled look, she gave a little laugh.
>
> "Come back, Mr Dove," said Anne. And Reginald came slowly across the lawn.[41]

Earlier versions of these final lines had included more detail before being pared back for the more succinct and suggestive phrasing of the *Sphere* and subsequent editions. For example, after Anne calls Reggie back, initially Mansfield wrote that "He stopped. He turned. ~~Slowly he retraced his steps~~," but scored through the final sentence to delay his

---

[36] MalaM-NB5-NL, 10.

[37] Ibid., 3 verso.

[38] CW2, 304.

[39] Ibid., 306.

[40] Christoph Ehland and Cornelia Wächter, "Introduction," in *Middlebrow and Gender, 1890–1945* (Leiden: Brill, 2016): 3. For a discussion of the ways in which "Mr and Mrs Dove" adheres to and disrupts generic convention, see my *Katherine Mansfield and the Modernist Marketplace: At the Mercy of the Public* (Basingstoke: Palgrave, 2010): 153–57.

[41] CW2, 306.

response and to generate some brief tension about how he might react. The manuscript also reveals that Mansfield revised the description of Anne's emotions by replacing a portrayal of her "crying" with a return to her usual state of laughing at Reggie, specifically at ^{"his timid, puzzled look}," a phrase inserted in superscript to replace the more generalized "~~him~~" that Mansfield crossed out. She also drew a line through an overt statement that the couple reverted "~~back to their old~~" behaviors, opting instead to let their actions convey this in the final lines: "Come back Mr. Dove said Anne. And Reginald came ^{bowing} across the lawn ~~– to her bowing + bowing –~~"[42] [see Figure 27]. The description of Reggie's "bowing" is a direct echo of the bird's behavior, but Mansfield's indecision about where best to place this word is indicative of her concerns that she had "used the doves unwarrantably [. . .] to round something off" in a heavy-handed narrative conceit.[43] Significantly, the word "bowing" was omitted from the final description of Reggie in the published story in both the *Sphere* and *The Garden Party and Other Stories*, signaling an attempt to suggest this parallel between Reggie and Mr Dove in slightly more understated terms.

There is further evidence in the manuscript that Mansfield refined references to the doves in an attempt to avoid too blunt a comparison with the central couple of Reggie and Anne, not least in the excision of Reggie's surname (the avian-sounding "Dawes") in the published text. In his edition of the *Stories*, Alpers singled out "the far too obvious play on doves and daws" as evidence of a perceived lack of subtlety in Mansfield's writing for the *Sphere*.[44] The textual parallels between the birds and the central couple are certainly not in any doubt in the published version, but they were even more explicitly stated at the drafting stage. Mansfield repeatedly revised Anne's speech in which she describes their dynamic, with Mrs Dove always in front and Mr Dove following and bowing, rewriting it slightly while she updated the draft text. These revisions evidently sought to establish the most appropriate placement for the speech, crossing it out twice and moving it to the very end of the section in which Anne outlines that her affection for Reggie is "not what people **mean*** + what books mean when **they talk*** about Love"[45] [see Figure 26]. As a result, she builds up to making the comparison rather than directly stating it at the beginning of her justification for rejecting Reggie, as had been the case in the original manuscript version. In the final manuscript revisions and the published text, then, Anne's observation about the doves follows the third-person narrator's seemingly neutral observation of the birds walking "[t]o and fro to and fro over the fine red sand on the floor of the dove house," one "always in front of the other" who follows "**bowing + bowing**."[46] This indicates that the heavy-handed nature of the comparison may in fact be attributable to the character of Anne herself. Ultimately, it is Anne who interprets the significance of this dynamic and imposes this meaning upon their movement before making the direct comparison between the two "couples" after she rejects Reggie's proposal by telling him that "we'd be like . . . like Mr and Mrs Dove."[47] In doing so, the text offers an insight into how she perceives her relationship with Reggie and the power that she seems to hold over him.

---

[42] MMD-MS-NL, 14.
[43] CW4, 375.
[44] Alpers, *Stories*, 569.
[45] MMD-MS-NL, 12.
[46] Ibid., 10. The published version inserts a comma after the first "To and fro."
[47] CW2, 305.

The majority of the revisions to the manuscript of "Mr and Mrs Dove" are similarly subtle, and they generally comprise small textual amendments to syntax and phrasing that produce nuanced developments of characterization, context, and perspective throughout. For example, Mansfield deleted a passing reference to Reggie and Anne's first meeting "~~in March, just after hed come~~ **home** + ~~when he certainly was looking very groggy indeed~~," opting instead to keep the timeframe of their acquaintance more ambiguous.[48] Another temporal elision is produced in a scene in which Reggie's mother interrogates him as to where he is going just before he sets out on his walk to Anne's house. Mansfield deleted a description of him coming down the steps to speak with his mother and to tell her "lightly" that he "~~was just going as far as Colonel Proctors~~," and instead skips straight to Reggie's feelings of relief as soon as he escapes: "It was over at last but Reginald^gic did not slow down until he was out of sight of the house and ½ way to Colonel Proctors"[49] [see Figures 25 and 24]. Similar revisions to Reggie's name recur throughout the manuscript and in the published text, with the more formal "Reginald" often being used by his mother in ways that suggest the reserved, distant nature of their relationship. This formality is further evident in the fact that he calls his mother "the Mater"; in references to the character in the draft story, Mansfield overtly replaced the more personal "his Mater" with "the Mater," and preserved the use of the definite article throughout the remainder of the story in both manuscript and published forms.[50] This serves to emphasize Reggie's perception of her as an authoritative and commanding maternal figure who dominates him—a role that is confirmed through a series of small textual amendments throughout the draft of the story, and which is also seemingly replicated in his relationship with Anne.

Reggie's acquiescence to his mother's imperious manner is evident even before his encounter with her as he attempts to make his escape to Anne's house undetected; for example, he puts away his cigarette case when he remembers that "the mater hated him to smoke in his bedroom" and makes it clear that he regards her as "rather a grim parent."[51] This would seem to be confirmed in the short scene that they share together, both in her ruthless approach to pruning some flowers and in the tone in which she addresses her son. While drafting the story, Mansfield made some small revisions to the Mater's dialogue in ways that reiterate her over-bearing manner, as for example in her passive-aggressive identification of herself as "your mother" when she questions Reggie: "where are you going if ~~may~~ ask [sic] ^your mother may ask!—asked the Mater" (the word "I" is clearly missing in Mansfield's draft here, but she opted to replace "I may ask" with "your mother may ask" for the published text as it appeared in both the *Sphere* and the Constable editions)[52] [see Figure 24]. Earlier in this exchange there is an even more pronounced example of these personality traits when she rephrases a seemingly straightforward question ("~~Are you going out~~") to ^"You are not going out Reginald?" which reads more like an instruction that merely masquerades as a question.[53]

Initially, it seems that Anne will be a polar opposite to Reggie's mother, reversing the Mater's prohibition on smoking, for example, both by encouraging him to take a cigarette

[48] MMD-MS-NL, 7.
[49] Ibid., 5.
[50] Ibid., 3.
[51] CW2, 300–301.
[52] MMD-MS-NL, 5.
[53] Ibid., 4.

and even joining him in smoking a cigarette of her own. In this invitation, however, there is a suggestion that Anne shares some syntactical traits with the older woman, as it is presented as an imperative statement with an added question tag ("And smoke, won't you?").[54] Anne frequently uses this construction throughout her conversation with Reggie, and there are indications in the *avant-texte* that Mansfield refined her dialogue in ways that subtly echo the Mater's sentence construction. In particular, Mansfield indicated that she intended to rephrase "Do you like doves, don't you!" to "You do like doves, don't you!" by circling the word "you" and drawing a line to suggest that it should be placed before the word "do" (as it ultimately reads in the published versions), effectively transforming the sentence from a question to a statement.[55] These subtle resonances between Anne's syntax and that of the Mater reinforce her status as the dominant player in her relationship with Reggie, which is further underlined by the narrative's reintroduction of formal nomenclature in the story's final sentence: "And *Reginald* came slowly across the lawn."[56] By contrast, Reggie himself remains coded as a passive character throughout the draft and published texts, far removed from the kind of romantic hero "that Anne + he had seen at the theatre, [. . .] walking on to the stage from nowhere without a word **catching*** the heroine in his arms [. . .] and after one long tremendous look carrying her off to anywhere — — — —anywhere"[57] [see Figure 26]. Thus, he is positioned as a passive, submissive figure in relation to both his Mater and his prospective wife in ways that once again call into question the possibility for a happy marriage.

There is a further parallel between Anne and the Mater in the original draft of the story in their use of formal naming conventions when addressing Reggie—just as the Mater uses his full name of "Reginald," Anne addresses him as "Mr Dawes" throughout the manuscript. However, the published version of the story largely replaces Anne's use of formal modes of address with the more familiar, abbreviated "Reggie." This is one of a number of variants that can be detected between the draft of the story and its publication in the *Sphere* and *The Garden Party and Other Stories*. Likewise, "Marriage à la Mode" went through some additional revisions between the draft and publication stage. Several of these variants revised phrasing and syntax, as outlined in the transcript notes in the present volume. Others served to correct clear errors; for example, in "Mr and Mrs Dove" a reference to the location of Reggie's Rhodesian farm is corrected from Durban in the manuscript and *Sphere* texts to Umtali in the collection published by Constable in 1922. As "the last printing which she corrected or approved," the Constable edition might with some confidence be invoked as an authoritative text on which subsequent reprints of "Mr and Mrs Dove" can draw, but this is not the case with "Marriage à la Mode," as new errors crept into the 1922 text that were not evident in the *Sphere*.[58] For example, William's memory of returning home from chambers "every evening" inexplicably becomes "every morning" in the Constable text, only to be re-corrected in later republications of the stories, including the recent Edinburgh Edition of the *Collected Fiction*. These textual instabilities recurred across the multiple versions of both stories that were produced within Mansfield's lifetime—from manuscript, to magazine, to book

[54] CW2, 305.
[55] MMD-MS-NL, 10. The published version of the story amended the exclamation mark to a question mark, and therefore changed it further into another imperative statement with accompanying question tag.
[56] CW2, 306. Emphasis added.
[57] MMD-MS-NL, 12.
[58] CW1, xii.

collection. This ultimately suggests the difficulties of establishing an absolute "authoritative" version of each, and even the smallest of amendments to a word or a phrase has the capacity to invite new narrative and interpretive possibilities.

Ali Smith detects similar forms of linguistic "slippage" between Mansfield's published letters and their manuscripts and typescripts in her essay "SIGNES OF SPRING," identifying variants that range from "whole words" to the inevitable changes to punctuation that Mansfield generated as "an unsteady slippery punctuator."[59] The manuscripts for "Mr and Mrs Dove" and "Marriage à la Mode" both display Mansfield's trademark punctuation inconsistencies, in particular in her liberal use of a dash that is variously translated into ellipses, commas, and full stops in the published texts. Different publishing conventions have possibly dictated whether a dash was maintained or amended to ellipses in the printed text, but these instances of "silent editing" can at times produce subtle changes in the overall effect of the text. For example, in the manuscript draft of "Mr and Mrs Dove," Reggie tries to compose himself after Anne's initial rejection and attempts to extricate himself by beginning a sentence with the words: "If I cut off now Ill—be able to—"[60] [see Figure 27]. In the *Sphere*, the first dash is omitted and the second is revised to ellipses, creating the impression that Reggie has trailed off as he searches for the correct words with which to complete his thought. By contrast, in the Constable version, the second dash is maintained, implying that Anne actively interrupts him and cuts him off before he can finish. In both versions, Reggie fails to complete his sentence, but in the *Sphere* it seems that he is unable to do so while in the collection it seems that he is not permitted to.

Even in her lifetime, then, the stories that Mansfield originally wrote for the *Sphere* in Montana-sur-Sierre in 1921 took multiple forms and produced multivalent meanings. Their "epigenetic" afterlives continue to be informed by the instabilities that are recorded in the manuscript drafts with all of their revisions, gaps, and (at times) illegibility.[61] The textual processes displayed in the manuscripts are ultimately mirrored in the formal and narrative open-endedness of the published stories, which consistently refuse absolute closure. These ambiguities and disruptions are re-inscribed and reinstated in the stories' publishing histories, from their original appearance in a magazine to their inclusion in the current volume, so that they can be seen as "protean, existing in multiple and equally authorized forms" simultaneously, in ways that mirror George Bornstein's materialist reading of modernism.[62] In this, Mansfield's stories continue to enact "a wholesale hang*ing*" (with an emphasis on the present participle) as texts that remain in process, producing new interpretive possibilities and inviting new readings with each new iteration.

---

[59] Ali Smith, "SIGNES OF SPRING: A letter from Katherine Mansfield," in *Katherine Mansfield: New Directions*, ed. Aimee Gasston, Gerri Kimber, and Janet Wilson (London: Bloomsbury, 2020), 22.
[60] MMD-MS-NL, 14.
[61] Van Hulle, *Modern Manuscripts*, 14.
[62] George Bornstein, *Material Modernism: The Politics of the Page* (Cambridge: Cambridge University Press, 2001), 34.

"What was it?": The *avant-texte* and the "grinding feeling of wretchedness" in Katherine Mansfield's "The Fly"*

TODD MARTIN

The endings of Katherine Mansfield's stories are often ambiguous, leaving the reader with an unsettled feeling coinciding with the protagonist's revelation or epiphany. Anne Mounic, for example, draws attention to the fact that both Mansfield's "The Canary" and "The Fly" (written only a few months apart) end with a similar question: "What was it?" The first person protagonist of "The Canary," wanting to convince herself that everything will be alright after the death of her canary, verges on a stark realization:

> . . . All the same, without being morbid, or giving way to—to memories and so on, I must confess that there does seem to me something sad in life. It is hard to say what it is. I don't mean the sorrow that we all know, like illness and poverty and death. No, it is something different. It is there, deep down, deep down, part of one, like one's breathing. However hard I work and tire myself I have only to stop to know it is there, waiting. I often wonder if everybody feels the same. One can never know. But isn't it extraordinary that under his sweet, joyful little singing it was just this—sadness?—Ah, what is it?—that I heard.[1]

Mounic ties this to the same question posed at the end of "The Fly": "[The boss] fell to wondering what it was he had been thinking about before. What was it? It was. . . ."[2] But while Mounic posits that "[t]he individual goes beyond the limits of knowledge and opens the infinite. There is no empty centre, therefore, but profusion, abundance, a fountain of

---

* A version of this essay appeared in *Papers on Language and Literature* 55, no. 1 (2019): 16–32. It is republished with permission.

   Research for this project was completed through the funding of the Lester J. Cappon Fellowship for Documentary Editing, awarded by the Newberry Library, and through release time provided by Huntington University as part of the endowed Edwina Patton Chair. I would like to thank both organizations for their support.

[1] CW2, 514.
[2] CW2, 480.

being in the breath of life,"[3] I find in both endings something more sinister. Both seem to suggest a buried misery just below the surface of the illusion each protagonist tries to maintain. What was it, indeed?

Written in February 1922, "The Fly" was originally published in *Nation and the Athenaeum* in March of the same year and is described by Mansfield in a letter to Dorothy Brett as "a queer story [. . .] about a fly that fell into the ink pot and a Bank Manager."[4] In fact, "The Fly" explores the grief of the "boss"—likely based on Mansfield's father, Harold Beauchamp—whose son was killed during the First World War six years prior, a wound inadvertently reopened when a former employee, Woodifield, drops in to visit and mentions that his wife and daughters had seen the gravesite of the boss's son during a recent trip to Belgium.[5] Dazed by the reminder, the boss appears to divert his grief by drowning a fly with drops of ink from his pen. However, when he flings the corpse of the fly into the trash bin, "such a grinding feeling of wretchedness seized him that he felt positively frightened." Faced with the finality of death of his son (reenacted with the fly), the boss again attempts to divert his feelings by throwing himself into his work, "wondering what it was he had been thinking about before. What was it?"[6] But as in "The Canary," there lingers a "deep down" sadness—a "grinding feeling of wretchedness"—that he can no longer escape.

To this end, Thomas Assad asks the right question: What caused the boss to feel wretched, what frightened him so terribly at the end of the story?[7] But what Assad and other critics emphasize is the torture and death of the fly, exploring its potential symbolic significance: the death of the son, the boss's loss of grief, the facing of death itself. However, the fly is significant in itself, suggesting the corruption of the flesh and signaling to the boss the finality of his son's death; it marks the boss's final disillusionment that his son will somehow inherit the business, the only thing that gives his life meaning. Turning to the archive, I will draw on Mansfield's drafts of the story to reinforce this reading of the story.

The study of literary manuscripts poses a challenge: While one might read too much into a manuscript—desiring to enter into the mind of the author—the fact is that there is a materiality evident in the revisions, crossing-outs, etc. which, according to Finn Fordham, reveals the "conflict between a writer and the material of language."[8] While access to this conflict may stop short of revealing what an author was thinking, it does reveal the agency of the author, her manipulation of language and structure to create what ultimately becomes the final document. Thus, in the same way that the historian breathes life into the sterile facts of the archive, not by recreating the past but by

---

[3] Anne Mounic, "'Ah, What is it?—that I Heard': The Sense of Wonder in Katherine Mansfield's Stories and Poems," in *Celebrating Katherine Mansfield: A Centenary Volume of Essays*, ed. Gerri Kimber and Janet Wilson (Houndmills, Basingstoke, Hampshire: Palgrave Macmillan, 2011), 144–157 (156).

[4] *Letters 5*, 76.

[5] Mansfield's father, Harold Beauchamp, was a bank manager who served on the board of the Bank of New Zealand and who, also like the boss of "The Fly," lost his only son, Leslie, during the First World War. The boss's son was killed six years prior to the events of the story, even as Leslie, who was killed in October 1915, died just over six years prior to Mansfield's completion of the story. Like the boss's son, Leslie Beauchamp was also buried in Belgium.

[6] CW2, 480.

[7] Thomas J. Assad, "Mansfield's 'The Fly,'" *The Explicator* 14, no. 2 (1955): 23–25 (23).

[8] Finn Fordham, "The Modernist Archive," in *The Oxford Handbook of Modernisms*, ed. Peter Brooker et. al. (Oxford: Oxford University Press, 2010), 45–60 (51).

representing it,[9] the genetic critic tries to reconstruct and understand the material manifestations of the author at work.

It is precisely this moment of indeterminacy, according to Fordham in his discussion of the "archival turn," that makes modernist scholars comfortable in the archive. Already familiar with work that engages with a "subject's all but lost subjectivity" and that "reflects, sometimes skeptically, on its power to imagine what it cannot know," the modernist in the archive can "refer to the archive without always having to refer back to a fear of the archive's relation to a power which only ever *claims* to know without finally knowing."[10] This "proper spirit—skeptical, fearless, rational, imaginative" in approaching the archive, Fordham posits, "can provide narratives about the making of a work, tell us things about the meaning of process, a writer's sources, contribute to the destabilization of a text, and also contribute to our sense of life."[11]

In using Mansfield's manuscripts as a means of approaching a reading of "The Fly," my goal is not to establish an authoritative reading of the text, but to draw on these materials as evidence of work in progress to reveal "a more sophisticated model of authorially-distanced intention—intention as a sequence of mental states and acts—which is fundamental to the process of composition."[12] The archive, as Fordham implies, allows for the reconstruction of intentionality that belies Roland Barthes' "death of the author." Responding to Barthes, Sally Bushell argues that assuming the death of the author

> elides process by refusing to allow that the creative act has any human "origin." It thus also involves a denial of will and agency, (agency is now located in language rather than in the user of it) and a denial of duration for meaning-production. It does not allow for the conception of writing as a highly repetitive process in which the "now" is built upon, and exists, only as a result of repeated "nows."[13]

According to Bushell, studying the process of creation "is not concerned with the need to somehow 'revisit' or 'reconstruct' the originary moment but [. . .] is equally not able to participate fully in the deconstructive denial of process present in the claim that 'the voice loses its origin, the author enters into his own death, writing begins.'"[14]

The tension between reconstructing meaning and deconstructing intent is replicated in the archive itself, for as both Fordham and Lisa Stead point out, the archive is inevitably incomplete.[15] The literary scholar in the archive, then, must attempt to reconstruct the genetic order of the manuscripts prior to analyzing the texts, an often interpretive task. In many cases, this can prove challenging, for one must pore over the manuscripts attempting not only to divine the chronology of the notes and drafts but also to understand the process of revision. Fortunately, this is a relatively easy task in the case of "The Fly," for the authoritative text in Gerri Kimber's and Vincent O'Sullivan's *Collected Fiction of*

---

[9] Carolyn Steedman, *Dust: The Archive and Cultural History* (New Brunswick, NJ: Rutgers University Press, 2002), 69–70.

[10] Fordham, "Modernist Archive," 59.

[11] Ibid., 59, 50.

[12] Sally Bushell, "Intention Revisited: Towards an Anglo-American 'Genetic Criticism,'" *Text* 17 (2005): 55–91 (57).

[13] Sally Bushell, "Textual Process and the Denial of Origins," *Textual Cultures: Texts, Contexts, Interpretation* 2, no. 2 (Autumn 2007): 100–117 (107).

[14] Bushell, "Intention Revisited," 57.

[15] See Lisa Stead, Introduction, in *The Boundaries of the Literary Archive: Reclamation and Representation*, ed. Carrie Smith and Lisa Stead (Surrey: Ashgate, 2013), 1–13.

Katherine Mansfield is based on that published in 1922 in *Nation and the Athenaeum*, where the story first appeared. The only other extant versions of the story are a manuscript and a typescript of the story held at the Newberry Library in Chicago.[16] Reconstructing the *avant-texte*, then, is pretty straight-forward: the manuscript precedes the typescript which, aside from few minor editorial changes, is reproduced with its handwritten corrections in the final, published version. Further, the typescript was likely typed by Mansfield, herself, for her husband, John Middleton Murry, purchased a portable Corona typewriter for her in early 1920.[17] Mansfield did occasionally hire typists, so one cannot say definitively; however, evidence on the typescript, which includes typed changes not indicated on the manuscript, suggests Mansfield typed the draft. Compare:

(Fly-MS-NL, leaf 3) "My son! My little man!" groaned the manager.

(Fly-TS-NL, leaf 4) "My son!" groaned the boss.

It seems unlikely, for example, that a hired typist would take the liberty of omitting an entire phrase, "My little Man!" from the original. What is certain, though, is that the handwritten corrections on the typescript are in Mansfield's hand.

Once reconstructed, the objective of studying manuscripts with regard to the final work, according to Pierre-Marc de Biasi, is not so much to determine a definitive reading of a text, but, as much as one can,

> to set up the critical relationship on a sure basis, and geneticists are not disappointed if their manuscript study allows them to confirm the results or hunches of textual analysis. It is seldom the case, however, that the rough drafts do not provide a rich crop of discoveries; at the very least they show by what process, with what strategy, and around which elements the structure located by textual criticism has been developed, not to mention all that the text does not manifest directly and which nevertheless constitutes an important, sometimes essential part of its value.[18]

An early draft of a work, then, "offers criticism an essential field in which to validate interpretations that the text often leaves in a hypothetical state, and sometimes in a state of simple conjecture."[19]

To demonstrate the value of drafts, as described by de Biasi, one need look no further than Mansfield's choice to identify the protagonist of "The Fly" as the "boss." The use of "boss" and its repetition throughout the final version of the story suggests the significance of its use without any recourse to the genesis of the text. In fact, early critics like F. W. Bateson and B. Shahevitch draw attention to the etymology of the term, emphasizing the role of the protagonist as one who is in charge.[20] Similarly, Paulette Michel-Michot builds on this etymological emphasis of a boss being a "master" by highlighting that, without a name, the boss becomes tied to his function. She stresses the boss's desire

---

[16] The Alexander Turnbull Library possesses microfilm copies of both documents (Micro MS 251 Reel 1).

[17] The typewriter is part of the Alexander Turnbull Library as part of its Katherine Mansfield collection (Curios-018-1-010).

[18] Pierre-Marc de Biasi, "What is a Literary Draft? Toward a Functional Typology of Genetic Documentation," trans. Ingrid Wassenaar, *Yale French Studies* 89 (1996): 26–58 (57).

[19] Ibid., 29.

[20] F. W. Bateson and B. Shahevitch, "Katherine Mansfield's 'The Fly': A Critical Exercise," *Essays in Criticism* 12, no. 1 (1962): 39–53 (47).

for power, particularly his desire to impose his will on others, regardless of the cost to them.[21]

However, while one may *assume* that an author's word choice is purposeful, a study of Mansfield's manuscripts *confirms* her purposefulness. Throughout the manuscript of the story, as noted in W. H. New's *Reading Mansfield and Metaphors of Form*, Mansfield used "manager" to refer to the protagonist. Revising the manuscript, however, Mansfield makes a conscious choice to use "boss" instead of "manager."[22] On leaf two of the manuscript, for example, where the "manager" offers Woodifield some whiskey, Mansfield strikes out "manager" and writes "boss" above it.[23] Further, while Mansfield uses "manager" rather consistently throughout the rest of the manuscript, there are other instances where she again changes it to "boss." In the typescript, though, she privileges the use of "boss," using it throughout. In at least one instance, where she began to type "manager," she strikes it out with x's (though the "manag" is still partially visible) and types "boss" just afterward.[24] Whether Mansfield made this change in order to emphasize the etymological implications or simply to minimize the biographical connection to her father, opting for a more generic term, the *avant-texte*, by revealing instances of where she omitted the word "manager" in favor of "boss," eliminates any conjecture and validates any critics' privileging of her use of "boss," as de Biasi contends.

What these readings overlook, however, is why Mansfield would want to suppress the word "manager." As implied above, it could be to subdue the biographical ties to her father, who was a bank manager in New Zealand; however, it is equally plausible that it is tied to the implications of the word itself, for while the protagonist's job is to manage, he ultimately fails to manage his grief, the reason for the ambiguous ending of the story. Mansfield's manuscript reveals that the boss's equivocal questioning "What was it?" was added as part of a revision:

> Bring me some fresh blotting paper, ~~said the manager~~ ^he said^ sternly— + look sharp about it! And ^while the old dog padded away^ ~~he leaned back waiting for Macy return~~ [*sic*]—he fell to wondering what it was he had been thinking about before. ~~The business with the fly . . . He couldn't~~ fFor the life of him he ^couldn't^ **then** remember.
>
> What was it. It was. No—no use. He took out his handkerchief + passed it inside his collar.[25] [see Figure 41]

One sees here Mansfield excising the word "manager," as noted above, and one finds her artistic choices coming to the fore—opting to tie Macey back to the dog image of a few pages previously when, after Woodifield leaves, Macey is described as "dodg[ing] in and out of his cubby hole like a dog that expects to be taken for a run."[26] Further, the image

---

[21] See Paulette Michel-Michot, "Katherine Mansfield's 'The Fly': An Attempt to Capture the Boss," *Studies in Short Fiction* 11 (1974): 85–92.

[22] W. H. New, *Reading Mansfield and Metaphors of Form* (Montreal and Kingston: McGill-Queens University Press, 1999), 59–60.

[23] Fly-MS-NL, leaf 2.

[24] Ibid.

[25] Ibid., leaf 6. Mansfield has drawn a line from after "thinking about before" to these final lines, indicating that they are to be incorporated accordingly. The final paragraph of the typescript reads:

> "And while the old dog padded away he fell to wondering what is was he had been thinking about before. What was it? It was . . . He took out his handkerchief and passed it inside his collar. For the life of him he could not remember." (Fly-TS-NL, leaf 6)

[26] CW2, 478.

of the boss wiping his neck under his collar provides a visual that suggests either his shame at what he has done to the fly or his having come face-to-face with a reality he has worked so hard to suppress.

To my purpose, the revisions demonstrate how Mansfield constructs the ending of the story. Her use of free indirect discourse in which "the voices of the narrator and of the character appear to mingle"—a device Mansfield used similarly in her revisions of "Prelude"[27]—creates a degree of ambiguity. Compounding this, Mansfield reinforces the boss's own bewilderment by adding to the manuscript his questioning: "What was it. It was. No. no use" (the "No. no use" being expunged in the typescript). Rather than drawing attention back to the fly, as she does initially in the draft, Mansfield reinforces the notion that the boss has forgotten something, making the reader likewise wonder what it was that the boss has (willfully?) forgotten.

What the boss forgets—or at least tries to forget—is the finality of his son's death exposed earlier in the story:

> It had been a terrible shock to him when old Woodifield sprang that remark upon him about the boy's grave. It was exactly as though the earth had opened and he had seen the boy lying there with Woodifield's girls staring down at him. For it was strange. Although over six years had passed away, the boss never thought of the boy except as lying unchanged, unblemished in his uniform, asleep for ever.[28]

The "shock" of the revelation, here, is contrasted with the boss's own view of his son's being asleep, but while one might ascertain this from the final text, the manuscript helps to limit the conjecture.[29] The evolution of this passage, for example, reveals the extent to which Mansfield wanted to emphasize that the boss never fully wanted to accept the death of his son, for she initially referred to the boy as asleep twice, but opted for a less heavy-handed emphasis on this fact:

> It was exactly as though the earth had opened and he had seen the boy lying there with Woodifield's girls staring down at him—lying there asleep. For it was strange. Although over six years had passed away the manager never thought of the boy except as lying, unchanged, unblemished, in his uniform, . . soundly sleeping asleep forever.[30]

Further, because "the flow of the writing, the vigour of the pen, the boldness of cancellations, the positioning of the writing on the page all inform us about . . . the circumstances in which the writing took place,"[31] it is important to note that the ink for both changes appears to be darker. This seemingly inconsequential detail in fact suggests that the changes came during a second reading rather than occurring in the process of creation; thus, they are not only purposeful, but carefully considered. Further, in the second instance, Mansfield's choice of the more euphemistic and less visual "asleep for

---

[27] Teresa Prudente, "From 'The Aloe' to 'Prelude' and from *The Moths* to *The Waves*: Drafts, Revisions, and the Process of 'Becoming-Imperceptible' in Virginia Woolf and Katherine Mansfield," *Textus* 28, no. 3 (2015): 95–118 (108).
[28] CW2, 478.
[29] de Biasi, "What is a Literary Draft?" 29.
[30] Fly-MS-NL, leaf 3.
[31] Wim Van Mierlo, "The Archaeology of the Manuscript: Towards Modern Palaeography," in *The Boundaries of the Literary Archive: Reclamation and Representation*, ed. Carrie Smith and Lisa Stead (Surrey: Ashgate, 2013), 15–29 (17).

ever" over "soundly sleeping" allows for a more nuanced reading. Likewise, omitting the first instance, "lying there asleep," Mansfield delays the fact that the boss sees his son as simply asleep, but she also insinuates something more significant: When he envisions the open grave into which the Woodifield girls stare, he does not see him simply sleeping, but he sees with their eyes, presumably staring at a decaying corpse. This is why he finds it "strange"; until then, as the next line suggests, he had seen the boy only as "lying, unchanged, unblemished." Now, though, that illusion has been broken.

As in "The Fly," "Miss Brill" follows the protagonist through the aftermath of an epiphany, presenting her attempt to disassociate herself from the revelation. In this story, the protagonist, with her cherished fox stole, imagines herself playing a role in the pageant of the park she visits every Sunday. But when a young couple sits beside her on the bench, mocking her stole and wishing her gone, her illusion of being a part of something beyond her otherwise lonely life is destroyed. The story quickly concludes with Miss Brill returning home to her "little dark room—her room like a cupboard": "She sat there for a long time. The box that the fur came out of was on the bed. She unclasped the necklet quickly; quickly, without looking, laid it inside. But when she put the lid on she thought she heard something crying."[32]

Despite the fact that Miss Brill dissociates herself from the crying, in essence attributing it to the stole, which Clare Hanson notes is "both pet and projection of the self,"[33] one cannot imagine her life ever being the same now that her lonely isolation has been fully exposed. I believe the same is true for the boss in "The Fly." Hanson, however, who explores Mansfield's stories through the lens of Freud's "uncanny," suggests that the boss "re-enacts his son's death," "[d]isplac[ing] his feelings about his son on to the fly," concluding: "Repression and disavowal are complete."[34] Such a view, though, implies that the boss returns to the status quo, that he will continue in the illusion that his son is merely asleep, enabling him to continue his work as if it had purpose.

Jacques Sohier, on the other hand, suggests that the boss has replaced the process of mourning with his own investment in his work, noting that in order to cope with his grief, the boss is "keeping alive the ghost of his son" by continuing to invest in his work, his son's legacy.[35] While I agree that the boss's work is intimately tied to his grief, I believe that, conversely, it is his denial of this son's death—which Avishek Parui ties to the boss's resisting the trauma of loss—that allows the boss to imbue his work with meaning. I think Parui's most cogent point is that the boss relives his grief—by weeping—to retain a proximity to the event and thus to stave off the implications of his son's death.[36] However, when the illusion is broken—when Woodifield brings to mind the image of his son in his grave—the boss loses the immediacy of his grief. Thus, just as Miss Brill's detachment

---

[32] CW2, 254.

[33] Clare Hanson, "Katherine Mansfield's Uncanniness," in *Celebrating Katherine Mansfield: A Centenary Volume of Essays*, ed. Gerri Kimber and Janet Wilson (Houndmills, Basingstoke, Hampshire: Palgrave Macmillan, 2011), 115–130 (120).

[34] Ibid., 126. Clinton W. Oleson also reads the ending as the boss's return to the status quo: "He has [. . .] succeeded in evading once more a full recognition of the terrible reality of death and meaninglessness of his own existence." See "'The Fly' Rescued," *College English* 22, no. 8 (May 1961): 585–586 (586).

[35] Jacques Sohier, "Spectrality in the Short Story 'The Fly' by Katherine Mansfield," *Études britanniques contemporaines* 42 (2012): 139–152 (par. 18, par. 16). https://doi.org/10.4000/ebc.1360.

[36] Avishek Parui, "'For the life of him he could not remember': Post-war Memory, Mourning and Masculinity Crisis in Katherine Mansfield's 'The Fly,'" in *Katherine Mansfield and Psychology*, ed. Clare Hanson, Gerri Kimber and Todd Martin (Edinburgh: Edinburgh University Press, 2016), 113–124 (114, 121).

from the self who is crying belies a reality she wants to ignore but appears unable to, the boss's attempt to reassert his position of power fails. He can no longer imagine his son in such a static state which means his work—like Miss Brill's fox stole—will no longer provide the comfort that it once had.

W. H. New, in discussing many of Mansfield's rhetorical maneuvers, explains how she uses fragmentation as a resistance to closure in many of her stories. Often, "consequences . . . lie outside the story, within range of implication but beyond the reach of closure"; thus, "conclusions of recognition can . . . be resisted," but "the characters, by repressing what they have seen, do not necessarily free themselves from the ongoing pressure of memory."[37] Such is the case of Miss Brill and the boss. Unlike the structure of "Miss Brill," though, "The Fly" offers a lengthier intermediary stage between the revelation and the story's conclusion. This evokes another device New identifies, that of "deliberate narrative delay":

> The delay—or the "deferral" of the characters' or readers' recognition—can variously heighten suspense, complicate the circumstances that affect interpretation, extend the fact of pressure or the illusion of freedom from pressure, prolong a measure of happiness, ignorance, or insensitivity, or perform other narrative functions.[38]

The boss enacts a similar deferral in "The Fly," for rather than fully rejecting the reality of his son's death when it is initially exposed, the boss begins to reflect on the implications and then is distracted by the fly. The effect—unlike in "Miss Brill"—is to allow the consequences of the boss's revelation to build both in his own and in readers' minds, escalating the tension of the story. And, while the fly itself is a key factor in the story, the delay allows Mansfield to reveal how this disillusionment affects the boss through his own reflections. Once the boss has ushered Woodifield from his office and instructed Macey that he is not to be disturbed, he returns to his desk and "covered his face with his hands. He wanted, he intended, he had arranged to weep. . . ." After reflecting on the potential of his son and his dream that his son would eventually take his place, the boss takes his hands from his face, realizing that something is wrong, that something is different.[39] Something has changed that prevents him from crying, and it is singular to this day.

That this is a new experience for the boss, this inability to cry, is emphasized in the manuscript's lexical and syntactical maneuvering. But, while Van Mierlo warns against "privileging mechanics over invention" in genetic readings,[40] New suggests that such changes in Mansfield's drafts "go beyond aural or kinesthetic association"; he notes: "Diction directs interpretation, and grammar directs relationship."[41] Thus, when Mansfield writes of the boss that "**Something** seemed to be ~~happening~~ ᵂʳᵒⁿᵍ to him,"[42] one cannot ignore the implications. The immediacy of the impact he feels from the revelation of his son's death is evident in that something is "happening." But while Mansfield changes "happening" to "wrong," the verb form—"seemed to be"—still implies that the effect is concurrent with this particular moment following the realization that his son is irrevocably gone. The use of "wrong," however, shifts the emphasis from something

---

[37] New, *Reading Mansfield*, 78, 77.
[38] Ibid., 121.
[39] CW2, 478, 479.
[40] Van Mierlo, "The Archaeology of the Manuscript," 23.
[41] New, *Reading Mansfield*, 58.
[42] Fly-MS-NL, leaf 5.

extrinsic working upon the boss to something intrinsic to his sense of self, suggesting a more vital change in his psyche: "Something seemed to be wrong *with* him."[43] The effect of this is that "He wasn't feeling as he wanted to feel."[44] Forced to face reality, the boss will never be the same again, despite his attempt to bury himself back into his work.

Shortly after the boss notes that he is unable to cry, he begins reflecting on what has given his life meaning:

> Ever since his birth the boss had worked at building up this business for him; it had no other meaning if it was not for the boy. Life itself had come to have no other meaning. How on earth could he have slaved, denied himself, kept going all of those years without the promise for ever before him of the boy's stepping into his shoes and carrying on where he left off?[45]

The first two sentences note that that the boss's purpose for building up the business has been since the boy's birth; it was to be his legacy. And developing the business for his son encompasses the entirety of his life's meaning. The manuscript, though, reads, "Ever since before his birth even [. . .],"[46] which Mansfield seems to have revised to avoid redundancy; however, the importance that leaving his son the business is amplified in the original, suggesting that the boss anticipated the birth of a son before his conception, and the implication that "even" then his life had no other meaning suggests a comparative moment, drawing a link between then and now. This initial version, then, implies that the boss has been living and working for the last six years with the same anticipation—that his son, although dead, would inherit the business. Mansfield's revision minimizes such an implication, but the following sentence, whose ambiguity lends itself to two different meanings, may reinforce such a reading: "How on earth could he have slaved, denied himself, kept going all those years" could refer to those years before the death of his son, but it could just as easily refer to the last six years that he has worked since his son's death, reflected in the recent renovations to his office. Further, comparing the manuscript and typescript, one sees that while Mansfield originally has the boss wonder how he could have slaved "without the promise always before him of the boy stepping into his shoes and carrying on,"[47] in the typescript it is "without the promise for ever before him"[48] [see Figure 40]. The change from "always" to "for ever" echoes the wording of when he imagines the Woodifield girls standing over his son's grave earlier in the same paragraph in which he previously "never thought of the boy except as lying unchanged, unblemished in his uniform, asleep for ever,"[49] connecting both to the boss's illusory hope for his son. The appearance of the fly at this point, however—whatever else it may symbolize—reinforces the corruption of the son's body.

The purpose of pointing out such nuance is to emphasize that the boss cannot continue a meaningful existence without imagining his son, somehow, "asleep for ever," inheriting his business; without this promise "for ever," the boss's life loses all import. The change which renders him unable to cry—that which he finds "wrong" with himself—stems from

[43] Fly-TS-NL, leaf 5. Emphasis added to identify the textual change.
[44] CW2, 478.
[45] Ibid.
[46] Fly-MS-NL, leaf 4.
[47] Ibid.
[48] Fly-TS-NL, leaf 4.
[49] CW2, 478.

his present inability to see his son in an uncorrupted form and contributes to his "feeling of wretchedness." His purpose in his work is only valid as long as he believes in the potential of his son's succession. What happens at the end of the story, then, is the final realization that his life has been pointless, that his work has been built on a lie, and so he can no longer take pride in what he has built, for it no longer has any significance—no matter how much he tries to assert otherwise at the end. Therefore, any attempt to throw himself back into his work will ultimately prove empty and unfulfilling; at best, his only recourse is a mechanical existence.

Mansfield concludes her story, "For the life of him he could not remember," suggesting that the boss may have repressed the memory that made him feel wretched, calling into question my notion that the boss will never recover from his disillusionment. But Mansfield's working through the conclusion in the manuscript suggests something more ambiguous. After the boss wonders what it was that he had been thinking of, the manuscript reads: ~~The business with the fly . . . He couldn't~~ fFor the life of him he couldn't then remember[50] [see Figure 41]. The boss's thinking leads him back to the business with the fly, anticipating what it was that the fly had distracted him from. But, taken together, the excised portion—"The business with the fly . . . He couldn't"—suggests that Mansfield may have intended to write, "He couldn't *remember*" or something similar. If failure to remember was all that Mansfield was after, such a phrasing would have sufficed. But purposefully choosing "for the life of him" suggests that this final line of the story is more than a simple idiom. It suggests more poignantly that to remember his son's decaying body would shatter the illusion he created, for to do so would be to lose the sense of life that he had created: To remember would be to lose his life, metaphorically speaking.

Here, I realize, I approach the crux of Derrida's concern in *Archive Fever* about the degree of truth one can derive from the materials of the archive. Derrida acknowledges that the "phantom continues to speak" through archival documents, but he insists that it "will never again *respond*" to queries;[51] instead, the archive provides an illusion of truth, and Derrida warns against accepting archival documents as complete or authoritative.[52] Thus, the place one hopes to find truth, according to Derrida, is precisely where it begins to slip away. We desire to relive the other, but ultimately cannot.[53] Thus, despite the materiality provided by Mansfield's crossing-outs, corrections, and additions, in this last instance especially I begin to rely on conjecture. But such is the value and danger of the *avant-texte*: In revealing the artist at work, it complicates a text, revealing purposeful and identifiable markings the author has left behind which expose authorial agency, but it also tempts the critic toward an intentionality that must ultimately remain speculation. But even as Fordham notes that a turn toward the archive adds to indeterminacy by destabilizing the final text, he suggests that we should respond to it "by imagining, finding out, and testing different ways of making use of it."[54] After all, while the archive (and manuscripts) reveals the fragmentation of our knowledge, they conversely increase our knowledge.

---

[50] Fly-MS-NL, leaf 6.
[51] Jacques Derrida, *Archive Fever*, trans. Eric Prenowitz (Chicago and London: University of Chicago Press: 1995), 62. My emphasis.
[52] Ibid., 12, 27.
[53] Ibid., 91, 98.
[54] Fordham, "Modernist Archive," 50, 48.

Likewise, for Carolyn Steedman, it is precisely at the moment where Derrida sees truth receding that one can step in to "make ink on parchment *speak*" and to "write the People into being."[55] One can achieve this, according to Steedman, by attaching one's sense of self onto the other through a "process of identification,"[56] of imagining oneself alongside the author in the process of discovery and revision; however, one must also limit oneself to what is there, evident in the objective manifestation of revision. When the right balance is achieved, the potential of the *avant-texte* lies in not only confirming textual analysis, but also in "provid[ing] a rich crop of discoveries" and "show[ing] by what process, with what strategy, and around which elements the structure located by textual criticism has been developed."[57] Such has been my attempt in exploring the *avant-texte* of Mansfield's "The Fly." Her manuscript shows revisions that demonstrate evidence of purposeful choices which confirm—even as John T. Hagopian posits[58]—that the boss, who has worked solely for his son, will now find his work hollow and meaningless. Unable to reassert the status quo, the boss must contend with his "grinding feeling of wretchedness."

---

[55] Carolyn Steedman, *Dust*, 70. Emphasis in original.
[56] Ibid., 77.
[57] de Biasi, "What is a Literary Draft?" 57.
[58] John T. Hagopian, "Capturing Mansfield's 'Fly,'" *Modern Fiction Studies* 9, no. 4 (1963–1964): 385–90 (390).

NOTES ON CONTRIBUTORS

Claire Davison is Professor of Modernist Studies at the Université Sorbonne Nouvelle, Paris, and specializes in the intermedial borders and the boundaries of modernism: these include the translation and reception of Russian literature in the 1910s-20s, literary and musical modernism, and modernist soundscapes and broadcasting. Currently writing a monograph on trans-European cultural diplomacy on air in the 1930s, she is also working with co-editor Gerri Kimber on a new four-volume, critical edition of the complete correspondence of Katherine Mansfield for Edinburgh University Press. She and Gerri previously co-edited *The Collected Poems of Katherine Mansfield* (Edinburgh, 2016).

Dr Gerri Kimber is a Visiting Professor in the Department of English at the University of Northampton. She is co-editor of *Katherine Mansfield Studies*, the peer-reviewed annual yearbook of the Katherine Mansfield Society, published by Edinburgh University Press. She is the author of *Katherine Mansfield: The Early Years* (2016), *Katherine Mansfield and the Art of the Short Story* (2015), and *Katherine Mansfield: The View from France* (2008). She is the Series Editor of the 4-volume *Edinburgh Edition of the Collected Works of Katherine Mansfield* (2012–16). Together with Claire Davison, she is currently editing a new 4-volume edition of Katherine Mansfield's complete letters for EUP. Gerri is co-editor of a further thirty books, and has contributed chapters to many other volumes, in addition to numerous journal articles and reviews, notably for the *Times Literary Supplement* (TLS) and *the Los Angeles Review of Books*. She was President of the Katherine Mansfield Society for ten years (2010–2020).

Todd Martin is Professor of English at Huntington University where he teaches twentieth-century British and American literature. He has published articles on such varied authors as John Barth, E. E. Cummings, Clyde Edgerton, Julia Alvarez, Edwidge Danticat, and Sherwood Anderson. He has also published numerous articles on Katherine Mansfield and has served as co-editor of Katherine Mansfield Studies for eight years. He is also the editor of *Katherine Mansfield and the Bloomsbury Group* (2017) and *The Bloomsbury Handbook to Katherine Mansfield* (2021).

Jenny McDonnell lectures in English Literature and Critical Theory in IADT (Institute of Art, Design & Technology), Dún Laoghaire. She has published widely on Katherine Mansfield's work, including the monograph *Katherine Mansfield and the Modernist Marketplace* (Palgrave, 2010), as well as essays on Robert Louis Stevenson, Samuel Butler, and Walter de la Mare. She has also worked on a number of collaborative projects in IADT, including "Memory, Space and New Technologies" (2015) and "The City as Artscape" (2022).

Janet M. Wilson is Professor Emerita of English and Postcolonial Studies at the University of Northampton and Visiting Professor at Birmingham City University. Her research focuses on the diaspora and postcolonial writing of the settler colonies of Australasia, as well as refugee writing, the global novel, transnationalism, and transculturalism. Katherine Mansfield is a special area of interest. She was vice-chair of the Katherine Mansfield Society (2010–2020) and recently coedited with Aimee Gasston and Gerri Kimber *Katherine Mansfield: New Directions* (2020), and "Katherine Mansfield: The Gift of Breath" (2020). Her article on Mansfield's "An Indiscreet Journey" was published in *Katherine Mansfield and* Bliss and Other Stories (2020).

INDEX